THE BRITISH LABOUR PARTY
AND THE WIDER WORLD

THE BRITISH LABOUR PARTY AND THE WIDER WORLD

Domestic Politics, Internationalism and Foreign Policy

Edited by

PAUL CORTHORN

and

JONATHAN DAVIS

Tauris Academic Studies
LONDON • NEW YORK

Published in 2008 by Tauris Academic Studies, an imprint of I.B.Tauris & Co Ltd
6 Salem Road, London W2 4BU
175 Fifth Avenue, New York NY 10010
www.ibtauris.com

In the United States of America and Canada distributed by Palgrave Macmillan
a division of St. Martin's Press, 175 Fifth Avenue, New York NY 10010

Copyright © 2008 Paul Corthorn and Jonathan Davis

The right of Paul Corthorn and Jonathan Davis to be identified as the editors of this work has
been asserted by the editors in accordance with the Copyright, Designs and Patent Act 1988.

International Library of Political Studies 20

ISBN: 978 1 84511 401 5

A full CIP record for this book is available from the British Library
A full CIP record is available from the Library of Congress

Library of Congress Catalog Card Number: available

Printed and bound by Thomson Press India Limited
From camera-ready copy edited and supplied by the authors

CONTENTS

     international student revolts of the 1960s
     David Fowler   167

9.   Humanitarian Intervention, the Labour Party and the Press:
     the break-up of Yugoslavia in the 1990s
     Ann Schreiner   190

10. From Clinton to Bush: New Labour, the USA and the Iraq War
     Mark Phythian   209

     Notes   227
     Index   273

LIST OF CONTRIBUTORS

John Callaghan is Professor of Politics at the University of Wolverhampton and author of *British Labour and Foreign Policy: A History* (Routledge, 2007)

Paul Corthorn is Lecturer in Modern British History at Queen's University Belfast. He is the author of *In the Shadow of the Dictators: The British Left in the 1930s* (I.B.Tauris, 2006). He has published in *Twentieth Century British History* and the *Historical Journal*. He is now working on British politics and the Cold War.

Robert Crowcroft is a research student at the University of Leeds. He is also the author of 'The "High Politics" of Labour Party factionalism, 1950–5' (*Historical Research*, 2008) and 'Maurice Cowling and the writing of British political history' (*Contemporary British History*, forthcoming), and is currently completing a doctorate on Labour's internal politics during the Second World War.

Jonathan Davis is Lecturer in Russian and Modern European History at Anglia Ruskin University, Cambridge. He has written about Labour's visits to Soviet Russia in *Revolutionary Russia* and on various aspects of Soviet history for *20ᵗʰ Century History Review*. He is the author of *Stalin: From Grey Blur to Great Terror* (Hodder Education, 2007).

David Fowler teaches at the University of Cambridge and is a Senior Member of Clare Hall, Cambridge. He is preparing a full-scale biography of Rolf Gardiner, an interwar youth culture enthusiast and supposed British fascist. He is the author of *Youth Culture in the Twentieth Century* (Macmillan, forthcoming, 2007) and *The First Teenagers: The Lifestyle of Young Wage-Earners in Interwar Britain* (Frank Cass, London, 1995), along with several academic articles on modern British youth culture and British social history.

Nicholas Lawton studied History at Clare College, Cambridge. Following the completion of his M.Phil. in 2005, he trained as a History teacher at the

University of Oxford. Originally from Dewsbury, West Yorkshire, he now works in Oxfordshire teaching 11 to 18 year olds.

Mark Phythian is Professor of International Security and Director of the History and Governance Research Institute at the University of Wolverhampton. He has written widely on foreign policy and security and intelligence issues, including *Arming Iraq* (1997); *The Politics of British Arms Sales Since 1964* (2000); *Intelligence in an Insecure World* (with Peter Gill, 2006); and *The Labour Party, War and International Relations* (2007).

Ann Schreiner is Associate Lecturer in History and a Ph.D. research student at the University of Chichester. Her dissertation focuses on the Labour Party and its responses to the break-up of Yugoslavia during the 1990s.

John Shepherd is Visiting Professor of Modern History at Anglia Ruskin University, Cambridge, and is a Fellow of the Royal Historical Society. He teaches nineteenth- and twentieth-century British history and is currently writing a social history of Arsenal Football Club (with Emma Shepherd). His recent publications include *George Lansbury: At the Heart of Old Labour* (Oxford University Press, 2002) and *Britain's First Labour Government* (Palgrave Macmillan, 2006) (jointly written with Professor Keith Laybourn).

Casper Sylvest is a temporary lecturer in International Relations at the University of Southern Denmark. His research interests include British foreign policy 1850–1950, liberal international thought in Britain from the mid-nineteenth century, the international ideas of the British Labour Party, and the historiography of International Relations. His publications include articles in *International Studies Quarterly*, *Review of International Studies* and *The British Yearbook of International Law*.

Andrew Thorpe is Professor of Modern British History at the University of Exeter. His publications include *The British General Election of 1931* (Clarendon Press, 1991), *Britain in the 1930s* (Blackwell, 1992), *A History of the British Labour Party* (1997; 2nd edn., Palgrave, 2001), and *The British Communist Party and Moscow, 1920–1943* (Manchester University Press, 2000). He is currently completing a monograph on party organisation in Second World War Britain for Oxford University Press.

Richard Toye is Senior Lecturer in History at the University of Exeter. He is the author of *The Labour Party and the Planned Economy, 1931–1951* (2003) and *Lloyd George and Churchill: Rivals for Greatness* (2007).

ACKNOWLEDGEMENTS

This collection of essays grew out of a conference held at Anglia Ruskin University in July 2004. We thank all those who attended and made the day both enjoyable and thought-provoking. We are extremely grateful to the History Department at Anglia for generously funding the event and to ProQuest for providing additional sponsorship. In addition to the contributors to this book, Tom Buchanan and Mark Wickham-Jones gave stimulating papers. Eugenio Biagini, Paul McHugh and Andy Flint chaired sessions, while Katherine Borthwick, Liz Hankey and Kim Hall ensured that everything ran smoothly.

Clarissa Campbell-Orr and Rohan McWilliam have offered invaluable support and guidance throughout the different stages of this project. Rohan McWilliam and Tom Buchanan gave us constructive criticism of an earlier draft of the essays. Their comments have greatly strengthened the final version.

At I.B.Tauris we are grateful to Lester Crook for warmly commissioning the collection and for initial guidance. More recently, Elizabeth Munns has patiently directed us through the production process.

On a personal note, we thank Katherine Borthwick, and Sharon and Nina Davis, for encouragement along the way.

Paul Corthorn
Jonathan Davis

INTRODUCTION

Andrew Thorpe

The Labour Party originated as the Labour Representation Committee (LRC), which was formed in February 1900. The new body was not particularly concerned with foreign policy as such; the wider world was not, according to its early pronouncements, of great significance to it. Over the years, indeed, British Labour would gain something of a reputation for insularity. Continental socialists often derided it as hopelessly introspective and parochial. The party itself was often firmly focused on domestic issues. Employment and unemployment, social security, health, and housing have often been seen as the key elements of the Labour Party's appeal. The first majority Labour government played a leading role in creating the North Atlantic Treaty Organisation (NATO) as well as setting up the National Health Service (NHS), but it is the latter that is remembered far more than the former. Labour's radical plans for economic autarchy in the 1970s and early 1980s, sometimes represented as the desire to establish a socialist siege economy, merely confirmed, for some people, the fact that the party was hopelessly unprepared to face the realities of the wider world.

But in fact Labour was formed in the midst of one war (the South African War of 1899–1902); it grew to major party status during and immediately after, and at least in part as a result of, another (the First World War); and it formed its first majority government in the immediate aftermath of a third (the Second World War). The Cold War between the later 1940s and the early 1990s was a significant factor in the party's development. A much more minor conflict – the Falklands War of 1982 – was credited at the time by some commentators as having finally scuppered its chances of defeating Margaret Thatcher after her first term of office. And the premiership of Tony Blair, which began in 1997 with a firmly domestic-policy focus, was in fact characterised by a series of military interventions, the most serious and controversial of which – the March 2003 invasion of Iraq – will almost certainly overshadow his achievements in other areas of policy for many years to come. Therefore even if Labour had wanted to ignore the wider world, it would have found that the wider world would not necessarily ignore it. But most Labourites, most of the time, did not want to ignore the wider world. For them, Labour's values and ideals were not ones that stopped at the English Channel; they were, instead, ones that were, and indeed had to be, transferable to the whole world. Politics were not about Britain alone, but the whole of humanity.

This volume of essays represents an attempt to analyse various aspects of Labour's relationship with the wider world. It makes no claim to be comprehensive, but it does raise themes that, taken in the round, offer a great deal of insight into that relationship and its development over time. This introductory chapter offers a brief outline of Britain's position in relation to the wider world in the period since 1900, before giving an overview of Labour's developing relationship with that world. Finally, it offers a very brief outline of the essays that form the substantive part of the volume.

I

As stated above, Britain could not ignore the wider world. This might be counted a truism, insofar as very few states can exist in isolation. But it was especially true in the British case. Its island status sometimes convinced people that isolationism in one form or another was a real possibility, but they were usually brought back to reality sooner or later. Britain's geographical position made a nonsense of any idea that it could sit back from wider concerns. At the junction of the English Channel, the North Sea, and the Atlantic Ocean, it sat at the centre of trade routes, international disputes, and the like. It looked, not just over the Channel to France, but across the North Sea to the Low Countries, Germany, and Scandinavia, and over the Atlantic to North America, while the Mediterranean was only a hop away through the Bay of Biscay. Far from being some isolated outlier, Britain was in fact a busy junction in the world's shipping and trade. Massive proportions of the world's goods originated from, or passed through, Britain.[1] The Industrial Revolution had been founded to an extent on the export trade. Although by 1900 Britain's status as the only industrial nation was long gone, and although it was increasingly being rivalled by the United States and Germany, Britain still relied on international trade for much of its prosperity. This, in turn, meant that it could not be indifferent to the wider world that was supplying it with raw materials and buying its finished goods.

All this had always made a truly isolationist stance most unlikely. After all, even 'the imperialism of free trade' involved close concern with the outside world, and in any case by 1900 that argument had been very largely lost.[2] The last two decades of the nineteenth century had seen a further shift towards imperialism of a less sophisticated kind with the extension of formal empire in large parts of Africa, in particular. As other powers, most notably France and Germany, extended their holdings in Africa, the British could not afford to be left out. Rival imperialisms became mutually reinforcing. Between 1880 and 1900, therefore, the British Empire expanded dramatically. By the latter date, Cobdenite ideas of 'little England' were heard less and less often, and indeed leading members of the Liberal Party were happy to be styled 'Liberal Imperialists' or 'Lib Imps'.[3] When these holdings were added to territories already controlled in Africa and especially Asia – with India regarded as 'the jewel in the crown' – then any notion of British lack of interest in the wider world became inconceivable. The existence of an empire covering about a quarter of the earth's surface left Britain liable to clashes with other great powers and lesser states in practically every continent: indeed, it was for this reason that Britain would sign ententes clearing up various imperial disputes with France in 1904 and Russia in 1907. Empire certainly had its critics, such as the radical Liberal J. A. Hobson, whose penetrating *Imperialism: A Study* was first published in 1902. But empire was an ongoing political reality, and any serious political party had to take a position on it. It would not be until some years after the Second World War that there would be any serious contemplation in governing circles of wholesale decolonisation.

One result of all this was that Britain had to balance its external interests and policies carefully. As Winston Churchill was to remark, it had to acknowledge the three circles of interest that it had when dealing with the world. First, there was the empire, second, the United States, and, finally, continental Europe. These three spheres vied with each other for primacy for much of the period under discussion in this volume. Imperialists who longed for a united empire were frustrated by the proximity of Canada to the United States. Europeanists who ached for continental unity were frustrated by the need to rely on American firepower in the Cold War. Yet Atlanticists who wanted some kind of English-speaking union that would allow Britain to ignore their foreign-speaking (and often Roman Catholic) continental neighbours came up against the geographical reality that markets in Europe were so much closer, and against American indifference or hostility towards closer ties. Balancing the three circles was never easy, added a further layer of complication to British policymaking, and also added considerable scope for disagreement not just between, but also within, British political parties.

A further problem was the extent to which foreign policy was, is, and has to be reactive. Although it would not do to understate the extent to which this also applies to domestic policy, it would be true to say that external policy is less easy to pre-plan, and is far less within the control of individual national governments. By 1900 there was something in the way of a framework of international law; and the superstructure has developed considerably since then. But there are still, even now, serious shortcomings, grey areas, problems of jurisdiction, and the like. It is because of all this uncertainty that states spy on each other, yet it is still the case that much external policy has to be made up quickly, in reaction to events not wholly expected, and occasionally wholly unexpected. Furthermore, neither principle nor 'common sense' is necessarily an infallible guide to politicians in framing their responses.

Two final background considerations remain. One was the state of the economy. Notions of twentieth-century British 'economic decline' are now very much out of vogue, and 'declinism' has been shown to have been, in part at least, more of a cultural construct than an economic reality.[4] But it would be true to say that in a context where there has been a considerable extension in the role of the state, expenditure on defence, in particular, has come in for close critical scrutiny, and has served to limit at least some of the possibilities available to British governments in their policies towards the wider world. At times of economic difficulty, such as the interwar period and especially the early 1930s, such considerations became paramount. Following on from this, secondly, significant extensions of the franchise in 1884, 1918, and 1928 meant each generation of politicians had new concerns about untried voters and how they would react to the complexities of international policy. Although it is fairly clear that the specifics of foreign policy and the empire rarely gave voters much pause for thought, nonetheless governments that were perceived to have 'failed' internationally could expect something of a backlash; in particular, it is not coincidental that the Liberals who took Britain to war in 1914 were trounced at the general election that followed that conflict, or that the same happened in 1945 to the Conservative Party that had taken Britain into the Second World War just under six years earlier.

II

The formation of the LRC in February 1900 was not attended by any great disquisitions on the state of the wider world, even though the South African War was by then well under way. The committee's initially declared aims were essentially limited, as befitted a body whose existence was rather be-grudged even by some of those involved in forming it. It was in no sense a developed political party with a full-scale programme. Its main immediate concern was to entrench the legal position of trade unions against the perceived iniquities of 'judge-made law'. It therefore had nothing much to say about the wider world. On the face of it, it was as parochial as possible.[5]

But to leave it there would be unfair. Bodies affiliated to the LRC, such as the Independent Labour Party (ILP), did have more to say on imperialism in the context of the South African War.[6] To some extent the 1880s 'socialist revival' that had preceded the LRC's formation had been inspired by foreign thinkers – the Germans, Karl Marx and Friedrich Engels, and the American land reformer, Henry George. Marx's English populariser – indeed plagiariser – H. M. Hyndman, leading light of the Marxist Social Democratic Federation (SDF), saw Marx's ideas in part, at least, as a way of revivifying Britain and its colonial possessions in the face of rivalry from other great powers.[7] The first secretary of the LRC, Ramsay MacDonald, did, it is true, spend most of his time in the early years of the new body building up the organisation, sweet-talking trade unionists into affiliating, and arranging electoral pacts with the Liberals. But he also took the time to read up on continental social democracy, not least the ideas of the German Revisionists, whose most famous figure was Eduard Bernstein. Indeed, the influence of Bernstein's ideas can clearly be seen in much of MacDonald's ideological writing at this time, and MacDonald also wrote on the Empire.[8] Labour affiliated to the Second International in 1908, although its contribution was often seen as limited by continental social democrats who were often distrustful of what they saw as Labour's lack of Marxian rigour and apparent reluctance to make a formal break with Liberalism.[9]

It would be true to say that trade unions, by and large, remained more focused on domestic concerns of central interest to their members in the years prior to 1914. But even here the wider world could intervene. Even at this stage, for example, there were serious attempts to promote co-operation with unions in the colonies of white settlement, like Australia and New Zealand.[10] Unions were concerned with the threat of foreign or empire workers being brought in to do their jobs for lower wages. The 1906 general election controversy over Chinese indentured labour in South Africa, for example, owed its salience, not just to Liberal objections to 'methods of barbarism', but also to labour movement concerns about the setting of a precedent for the importation of cheap labour.[11] Indeed, much of the contemporary union comment on such matters would strike modern readers as clearly racist.[12] At a more individual level, some trade unionists were interested in emigrating to other parts of the world, while others would go abroad to work for short periods while trade was slack at home.

For all that, however, it is difficult to establish that the whole of the Labour movement was deeply concerned with the wider world in the years prior to 1914. Its intrusions on Labour thinking were, for the most part, piecemeal and episodic, as with the celebrations that marked the outbreak of the (ultimately abortive) revolution in Russia in 1905. But this was to change with the Great War.

Even before 1914, Labour had had to consider what it would do in the event of the outbreak of a general European war. As a member of the Second International, it was formally committed to that body's policy, first adumbrated at its 1907 Stuttgart Conference, in favour of a general strike to prevent war.[13] When, in July 1914, it became apparent that war was a real possibility, plans were laid for a major anti-war demonstration in Trafalgar Square, and this was held on Sunday 2 August, the day of the big German offensive in the west. However, the invasion of Belgium and the reality of the British declaration of war on 4 August changed matters. Labour leaders now had to choose between, on the one hand, a principled objection to war, and the hope that this would bring over Liberal critics of the pre-war Liberal government's secret diplomacy; and, on the other, a policy of broad co-operation with the war effort so as to try and gain benefits for the working class, and also to avoid being seen as unpatriotic at a post-war election (this in the context of a war that was not expected to last very long).[14] Ultimately, Labour split, with a minority following the erstwhile chairman of the parliamentary party, MacDonald, in criticising entry into the war, but the majority following his successor, Arthur Henderson, first into offering general support for the war effort, and then into participating in Coalition governments under first H. H. Asquith (May 1915) and then David Lloyd George (December 1916).[15]

The First World War marked a significant change in Labour attitudes towards the wider world. Put simply, the war proved that the latter was a potentially dangerous place that could not be ignored. Opting out was not an option. This was borne in on Labourites at all levels. Henderson, for example, lost his eldest son on the Somme in 1916.[16] He was far from being alone. Modern warfare placed trade unionists in uniform and, all too often, killed them. At home, it threatened huge, and adverse, changes to working conditions, as witness the strong campaigns mounted against 'industrial conscription' during the war.[17] Increasingly, therefore, trade unionists saw that securing peace was the first pre-requisite to the defence of working-class interests. In a sense, foreign policy was as much their business as factory legislation or workmen's compensation. Therefore they became increasingly interested in the post-war settlement, and it was no coincidence that Lloyd George's January 1918 statement on war aims – which anticipated many of US President Woodrow Wilson's 'Fourteen Points' – was made to a trade union audience.[18]

Secondly, the war brought new recruits into the party. In a sense, both Henderson and MacDonald were vindicated for their respective stances in 1914: Henderson's position established Labour's patriotic bona fides, but MacDonald's approach – critical of the majority party line, but remaining within the party – meant that he was able to work with Liberal critics of the pre-war government's diplomatic methods, most notably through the Union of Democratic Control (UDC). The result was the bringing over to Labour of significant radical Liberals like E. D. Morel, C. P. Trevelyan, and Arthur Ponsonby, who would all work to ensure that the party did not slide into parochialism in the years that followed. They were not always very successful in imposing their views on the party – neither Morel in 1924 nor Ponsonby in 1929 was to get the Foreign Secretaryship he craved – but what might be called 'advanced Liberal' views on foreign policy did progress within the party.[19]

Thirdly, and following on from this, the war brought improved political opportunities. By 1917, it was clear that the Liberals would face considerable difficulties once peace returned, and that, if the war was won, Labour might have the chance to break through to major party status. At the most basic level, a party that was seeking power in its own right, rather than mere influence over a larger party, had to have something coherent to say about the wider world, and so the incentive was there. The 1918 election manifesto would be a quantum leap beyond its December 1910 predecessor in its concern for such issues.

The other important development of 1917 was, of course, renewed revolution in Russia. The February Revolution was generally welcomed as a triumph for democratisation, with the overthrow of the Tsar seen as good in itself, but also as being likely to increase the commitment of the Russian people to the war effort against the Central Powers. However, there was a good deal less unanimity about the Bolshevik October Revolution. Bolshevism claimed some common language with Labour's socialism, but was in reality a very different beast, and Labour leaders like Henderson hurried to differentiate Labour from it.[20] However, it was, for a time at least, a struggle to cauterise Labour – especially elements of the rank-and-file – against Communist influence, and relations with the far left would continue to exercise party managers for many years to come. One aspect of dealing with the Bolshevik/Communist threat was a realisation that, to counter Soviet plans to create a new revolutionary international (the Communist International, or Comintern, launched in March 1919), Labour would have to play a leading role in the re-creation of the socialist international that had collapsed on the outbreak of war. Labour would, indeed, have a centrality in the post-1918 international socialist movement that it had never come close to approaching prior to 1914, for that very reason.[21]

Finally, the nature of the peace settlement with Germany helped Labour to mature in the field of international policy. At the end of the war Labour left the Coalition, so it did not share responsibility for the peace settlement with the 1918–22 Lloyd George Coalition. The Treaty of Versailles was arguably less draconian than it has usually been painted (certainly, terms of the treaties imposed on Germany's allies were far sterner).[22] Yet there was widespread agreement across the progressive left in Britain that it was too harsh, and this perception helped further to place Labour at the head of that progressive opinion, and helped it to bond more closely with its recent recruits and also to bring further ones over.

Labour therefore entered the interwar period with a moral force based, in part at least, on its critique of Lloyd George's international policies. During the 1920s it worked hard to develop its own policies in a number of areas. Much thought was given to applying what were seen to be good trade union principles of conciliation and arbitration to international disputes. It was no coincidence that MacDonald considered seriously the possibility of giving the Foreign Office to the wily union negotiator J. H. Thomas in both 1924 and 1929, or that it was Henderson, another man from the union side of the party, who eventually emerged as the party's leading figure in the field, serving as Foreign Secretary in 1929–31. The first two Labour governments (1924 and 1929–31) both claimed some success in the area of foreign affairs, and although in the longer term their achievements can seem ephemeral, they were important at the time. Both governments oversaw renegotiation of German reparations payments, for example, in the shape of the Dawes and Young plans. The 1924 government fell before it could consider seriously the question of whether to ratify the Geneva Protocol, which would have imposed compulsory arbitration in international disputes, failure to accept which would invite military action on behalf of the League of Nations. It may well be that the Labour Cabinet would have rejected it, but the fact that Labour ministers had negotiated it – and that it fell to the subsequent Conservative government to reject it – gave Labour some moral authority.[23] The 1929–31 administration, for its part, moved some way towards increasing the scope of international law in inter-state disputes. It was, in addition, no mean feat for Henderson (Foreign Secretary 1929–31) not merely to get an agreed date for the convening of the League of Nations' world disarmament conference, but also to get himself elected as its president. It was far from self-evident at the time that these efforts would come to naught.[24]

However, the world economic downturn that manifested itself spectacularly in October 1929 can be seen, in retrospect, as having marked the start of a new, tougher era. In place of optimism – which had perhaps peaked in 1924, but which had nonetheless just about been sustained through the Locarno era – came gloom, the rise of political extremism abroad, and, eventually, war. Economic nationalism replaced economic internationalism in Britain as elsewhere, although Labour was initially reluctant to move far in that direction.[25] It continued to believe, as it had throughout the 1920s, that international pacification was the key to the restoration of the international economy to health. This was understandable in one sense – Britain's staple industries (like coal, heavy engineering, and textiles) remained heavily dependent on world markets, and so were heavily depressed, yet they were also the industries where the party's electoral support was strongest. Therefore the 1929–31 government remained just about committed to free trade, and, indeed, the party clung to it all the more desperately in the aftermath of MacDonald's defection to the National government in 1931, in a vain attempt to shore up its electoral position.[26] But the party's catastrophic defeat in the October 1931 general election left MacDonald's new Conservative-dominated government with a huge majority.

The downturn of capitalism, and the collapse of Labour's fortunes, had two effects. One was a sharp increase in apocalyptic rhetoric within the party. This apocalyptic feeling perhaps had its widest expression in the 1930s pacifist movement within the party, and the October 1933 party conference did pass unanimously a resolution demanding the calling of a general strike in the event of the outbreak of a general European war.[27] Two months later, the party leader, George Lansbury, fell down the steps of Gainsborough Town Hall, and appears to have spent the next nine months in bed convincing himself that he had a messianic mission to prevent war by the conversion of Labour to thoroughgoing pacifism.[28] However, by the time he returned to active politics in 1934 any pacifist mood within the party as a whole had already passed. In reality, the 1933 pacifist motion had been allowed to pass without a vote for largely procedural reasons – the NEC wanted to avoid a messy debate immediately before Henderson, as disarmament conference president, was due to give a major set-piece speech to the conference.[29] The extent to which pacifism was off the agenda of the party as a whole – though not of many individual Labourites – was to be graphically illustrated by Lansbury's crushing defeat at the October 1935 party conference.[30]

The wider world also impacted on Labour in other ways, however. First, although Lansbury fantasised about the internationalisation of raw materials, Labour's economic policies were moving decisively from the free trade internationalism of the 1920s towards economic nationalism based on planning and import quotas. In the development of these ideas, the wider world was of considerable importance, with foreign examples feeding significantly into discussions about planning, public works, and the like. In 1932, a group of Labour intellectuals travelled to the Soviet Union, and returned to publish an eclectic, but broadly positive, collection of essays.[31] The USSR was, after all, industrialising rapidly and had no unemployment at just the time when the western world was in the economic doldrums. Two years later, the socialist economist Barbara Wootton was expressing her admiration for aspects of Soviet planning, while also demanding that any British imitation must have a far stronger concern for individual rights.[32] Although some Labour analysts continued to take a more positive view of the Soviet experiment,[33] others became more outspoken in their criticisms.[34] This meant that, by the mid-1930s, attention was moving elsewhere: to Sweden, where a socialist government elected in 1932 was moving ahead with major public works schemes; to the United States, where the New Deal was in full swing from 1933 onwards; and to New Zealand, where Michael Savage's Labour government, elected in November 1935, enacted a series of major progressive reforms.[35] Secondly, the 1930s experience of fascism and Communism gave an incentive to Labour thinkers to reconsider their own commitment to individual liberty, and to think in more detail about the potential tensions between socialism and democracy.[36] Finally, Labour's responses to international events had to be conditioned, to a certain extent, by perceptions of what was most likely to serve the party's best interests. For example, its unwillingness to come out too strongly for the Republican side in the Spanish Civil War (1936–9) was undoubtedly conditioned by uneasiness about the reaction to such a stance of its large number of Catholic supporters at a time when the Vatican was backing the Nationalists under Franco.[37]

In reality, it was fascism, and still more Nazism, that most exercised Labourites as the 1930s progressed. On coming to power in 1933, the Nazis had soon banned rival political parties. That October, Germany left the disarmament conference. Most Labourites saw Nazism as a repulsive doctrine from a very early stage, although a few people did take a more positive view, in some cases right up to 1939.[38] But most saw socialists and trade unionists like themselves being persecuted and imprisoned, racial hatred being deliberately fomented, and so on. The party went through a series of stances which tried to deal with the danger. One key problem, of course, was that there was deep Labour distrust of the National government, based in large part on the way it had been formed and the nature of its election campaigns against Labour.[39] Once it was clear (by 1934) that the disarmament conference had failed, the catch-cry became collective security under the League of Nations. The rejection of Lansbury's pacifism in 1935 was an important moment, although a minority within the party continued to share his views, and indeed a number went on to oppose entry to war in 1939.[40]

The landmarks on the way to Labour's willing participation in the Second World War are well known – the key moments were rethinking of the party's support for non-intervention in the Spanish Civil War in 1936; the decision to abstain, rather than oppose the government, in the parliamentary vote on the defence estimates in 1937; the talk of a 'National Opposition' around the time of Munich in 1938; the refusal to support conscription in early 1939; and the advocacy of an alliance with the Soviet Union in the summer of that year. Ironically, of course, it was the acting Labour leader, Arthur Greenwood, who was famously encouraged by a Conservative back-bencher to 'speak for England' on 2 September 1939, when Chamberlain was still havering about whether or not to declare war following the German invasion of Poland the previous day.[41]

Labour was more united in 1939 than it had been in 1914, and the Labour movement as a whole was to prove less fractious than it had been then. However, there were problems. As already mentioned, there were critics of the decision to enter war. There was adverse comment on the leadership's failure to make an immediate declaration of Labour's peace aims, while the fact that Labour leaders, although rejecting entry into a Chamberlain-led coalition, appeared to be co-operating with ministers raised alarm lower down the party.[42] When the Communist Party changed its stance in October 1939 from one of supporting the British war effort to one of declaring that the conflict was a clash of rival imperialisms in which the working class had no stake, a potential alternative source of leadership suddenly came into existence. Many of the Labourites who now declared for the Communist line might well have been infiltrators, 'sleepers' who were 'turned' at this point; but the Communist line did strike a chord with a minority of 'real' Labourites as well, and it is noteworthy that CPGB membership increased to a then-record high during the so-called 'Phoney War' (September 1939-May 1940).[43] However, most Labourites were behind the leadership, at least once Clement Attlee had published his peace aims in December 1939; and the party's most prominent pro-Communist, the MP and NEC member D. N. Pritt, was expelled from the party in April 1940 for his support of the Soviet invasion of Finland.

Nonetheless, by May 1940 the Labour leadership was coming in for renewed criticism, and it might have had a rough ride at that month's annual party conference but for the fall of the Chamberlain government. The latter's demise, and the formation of the Churchill Coalition, were warmly welcomed in Labour circles. Attlee and Greenwood took two of the five seats in the new War Cabinet, and the country's leading trade unionist, Ernest

Bevin, was appointed Minister of Labour and National Service, and thus placed in effective control of manpower planning for the whole war effort – a hugely significant appointment, intended to utilise Bevin's considerable abilities but also to calm Labour and trade union fears about the direction of labour. Any Labour qualms were soon largely stemmed by the reality of the Nazi threat following the collapse of France in June 1940 and the start of air raids on Britain that September.

At one level, the degree of unity that pertained within the Coalition during the five years of its existence was remarkable. However, there were disputes over post-war reconstruction, and these included disagreements over the conduct of the war and planning for the post-war world. There were some strong disagreements within the Labour Party over the treatment of Germany, for example. Some Labourites were highly critical of the blanket-bombing of German cities.[44] There was considerable debate about the nature of Germany and the Germans themselves. Some prominent Labourites took up the virulent racist views propagated by the former diplomat Sir Robert Vansittart, who argued that the Germans were an essentially warlike people who would need to be kept under close control after the war.[45] But other party members regarded such 'socialist Vansittartism' with horror, and believed that Nazis and Germans were two very different categories.[46] As the end of the war approached there was increasing tension among Labourites as to what the post-war world would portend. They had come increasingly to believe that the war was one to end fascism and reaction, and to promote progressive, if not socialist, politics across Europe. But by the autumn of 1944 they were becoming increasingly concerned that Churchill – and, by extension, his Labour colleagues in government – were concerned only to restore the status quo ante without the radically disruptive forces of fascism and Nazism. It was for this reason that the crisis over Greece in December 1944 and January 1945 was of such importance for Labour in the final winter of the war.[47]

Overall, the war was hugely significant for Labour. In all kinds of ways, it helped transform the struggling party of the 1930s into one capable of winning a landslide in 1945. But it was also important in the specific area of attitudes towards the wider world. It was, first of all, a 'good war'. Few indeed were the Labourites who, by 1945, would admit to having had qualms about fighting it. Many of the people who would lead the Labour Party for the next generation and more had been closely involved in the war effort, either as servicemen (James Callaghan, Denis Healey) or as wartime civil servants (Hugh Gaitskell, Harold Wilson). Further ahead, the war seemed to vindicate the view that it could be legitimate to use force to overthrow a regime that was deemed morally and politically repulsive.

The war also had an impact on the 'three circles'. Labour's interwar attitudes towards the United States had often been hostile. Many had seen it as the archetype of a rapacious kind of capitalism, where trade unionism was frowned on, at best, and where socialism was notable only by its absence.[48] There had been some softening with Roosevelt's New Deal, but American isolationism in the face of the increasing Nazi threat had kept enthusiasm lukewarm. Now, however, the Americans had been allies in a great struggle, and this had increased the respect of some Labourites for the USA. Conversely, the failure of most of continental Europe to stand up to Nazi aggression left at least some Labourites with a rather patronising view of it. Attitudes towards the Soviet Union varied considerably during the war, from great hostility in 1939–40 to huge enthusiasm and respect in 1941–3; thereafter, increasing numbers of Labourites appear to have become a little more wary as the reality of the huge extension of Soviet power that was likely to attend the Red Army's advance towards Germany began to sink in.[49] Finally, there was some realisation that the Empire (or Commonwealth, as it was coming to be known) would need attention, not least in those areas that had been subjected to Japanese occupation during the war.

Experience of office in wartime also taught, or in some cases reminded, Labour's leaders the ways in which the need to make policy, often at short notice and with inadequate information, was a reality of life in government. The position of foreign policy critics who liked to argue from first principles, or make up their minds after periods of sober reflection, was very remote from this perspective. It was all very well, for example, for party members to call for a 'socialist foreign policy', but what that meant in practice would be very slippery and difficult to define. But if their critics could not define it, then Labour ministers were hardly to blame for taking more pragmatic approaches when they needed to respond urgently to the challenges of the post-war world.

Those challenges were immense. The Labour government elected under Attlee in 1945 – the first to have an overall parliamentary majority – faced the prospect, not just of interacting with the wider world, but of remaking it. Hardly surprisingly, the government's record excited controversy at the time, and has continued to do so since.

Underlying all else, however, was a firm commitment to the idea that Britain should – indeed had to – remain a great power. It is true that in 1946 Attlee and his Chancellor of the Exchequer, Hugh Dalton, suggested an extensive withdrawal from east of Suez as a way of cutting the crippling defence bill in a context of economic stringency, when the government had other spending priorities. But the significant point is less that the idea was proposed than that it was decisively rejected by the Cabinet, and not revisited thereafter.[50]

Nor should Attlee and Dalton's line be taken as advocacy of wholesale decolonisation. In the contemporary Labour Party's whiggish view of its own past, it was this government that consciously began to wind up the British Empire.[51] It is understandable that modern-day Labour likes this version of its past – it sits well with a modern multicultural agenda, especially in a context where it relies on the votes of many electors whose origins lie in the former colonies. The evidence usually cited would be the granting of independence to India in 1947, and the withdrawal from Palestine the following year. In reality, however, these withdrawals owed most to expediency and pragmatism. Both were in danger of becoming ungovernable. Withdrawal in each case was carried through without the securing of final settlements that were perceived at the time to be in British interests.[52] This is not to say that the withdrawals were wrong; just that they were not part of any serious planning for the end of the Empire. Indeed, it is clear that many Labour ministers hoped that withdrawal from India would be followed by a reorientation towards Africa, rather as the focus of the Empire had moved, almost two centuries earlier, from North America to India following the American War of Independence. Far from seeking to decolonise Africa, Labour in government looked to follow on the work of the second Labour government and promote colonial development, which involved increasing the economic exploitation of the colonies (see Chapter 5). In this, it had some success, but the rather grandiose hopes of Bevin, in particular, that exploitation of British Africa's resources would allow Britain to approach superpower status proved false.[53] By 1951 more Labourites were beginning to question the future of the Empire/Commonwealth. Even at that stage, however, there was no plan for wholesale decolonisation: that would only really begin under Macmillan's Conservative government in the aftermath of the 1956 Suez Crisis.

Policy with regard to America and Europe was more variable in this period. At first, the signs coming from the USA were not too favourable. The abrupt ending of Lend-Lease in 1945, and the perceivedly harsh terms imposed by the Americans in granting a loan to Britain in 1946, suggested that there was the possibility of a repetition of the US's post-1919 retreat into relative isolationism.[54] As civil war raged in China, there were voices within the Republican Party advocating an 'Asia First' strategy. One result of this uncertainty was that a small group of ministers made the secret decision in 1946–7 to develop a British atomic bomb as an independent nuclear deterrent.[55] Another was that Labour worked hard at European reconstruction. The party machine took great pains in trying to help the Labour and Socialist International, both to revive itself and to identify 'legitimate' social democrats across the continent.[56] The TUC, for its part, also sought to promote strong native labour movements by encouraging the revival of free trade unionism.[57] Such efforts were far from futile, and indeed their successes encouraged those who wished to see Europe stand as a third force between America and the USSR, such as the authors of the 1947 pamphlet *Keep Left*. But even at this stage, it is worth noting, there were very few Labourites indeed who were genuinely close to the Soviet Union.[58]

By 1947, however, it was becoming clear that Europe would not be allowed to escape the attentions of the two superpowers. Responsibility for the outbreak of what was soon to become known as the Cold War continues to be debated.[59] But the indisputable fact is that by the end of 1947 Europe was beginning to look like two rival armed camps. The Soviet Union helped to impose increasingly obvious Communist regimes in its sphere of influence, and the Americans responded by giving Marshall Aid to the states of western Europe. In this exercise, Britain sat more obviously with the USA than with the still partly prostrate states of the continent, and the partnership of the two countries was cemented in 1949 with the establishment of NATO. By this time, moves were beginning towards greater integration among the Western European states, with the establishment of the Council of Europe (1948) and the Schumann Plan (1950), but most Labourites were happy to leave such experiments to their continental counterparts, although a few federalists were much more favourable.[60]

Essentially, therefore, the Attlee government set the tone of British foreign policy for the next twenty years. But once in opposition after 1951, Labour found that the wider world bit it with regularity. The party leadership gave broad support to the ongoing construction of the superstructure of the Atlantic alliance. It backed the continuation of the Korean War which had begun in 1950, West German rearmament, the creation of the South East Asia Treaty Organisation (SEATO) in 1954, and the decision to develop the hydrogen bomb in 1955. Nor did it try to develop any thorough-going critique of British imperialism. However, it would have been one thing to take up these stances in government, but it was quite another to do so in opposition. What might have seemed regrettable necessities if coming from a Labour government were seen by many Labourites, and not just those on the left, as being much more problematic with a Conservative government in charge. Furthermore, foreign policy became a useful proxy for other issues within the party, not least for the Bevanite movement that grew up in the early 1950s.[61] Dissent on foreign policy issues could be a coded way of expressing dissatisfaction with Attlee, the lack of progress on domestic policy, trade union domination of the party, or whatever. The ultimate result was bitter division within the party. Worse still, perhaps, Labour could be portrayed as 'soft on Communism' at a time when the Cold War was very cold indeed. The development of the H-bomb, for example, led in 1958 to the creation of the Campaign for Nuclear Disarmament (CND). CND was a sincere, and for a time powerful, movement, but the involvement of many Labourites in it allowed the party's opponents to portray it as advocating the weakening of the national defences in the face of a significant external threat.

The Suez fiasco in 1956 was ultimately to convince the Conservatives that the Empire/Commonwealth had largely exhausted its utility, and that the future lay instead with the European Economic Community (EEC), which was formed as a body of six Western European states – Belgium, France, Italy, Luxembourg, the Netherlands, and West Germany – in January 1957.[62] Labour was ultimately to come to the same realisation, but it did so more slowly. At this stage, many Labour politicians continued to invest a great deal of physical and emotional effort in the Commonwealth.[63] Although by the early 1960s former colonies were being given their independence at a startling rate, many Labourites continued to believe that the Commonwealth, as a voluntary association of sovereign states, could be a force for the promotion of prosperity and freedom across the whole world. When in 1962 the party leader, Gaitskell, denounced the Conservatives' application for membership of the EEC, he did so on the grounds that it would represent 'the end of a thousand years of history', and especially 'the end of the Commonwealth'.[64] When his successor, Wilson, led Labour to victory at the 1964 general election, he spoke rather grandiloquently of Britain's frontiers as being 'on the Himalayas'.[65]

However, the Wilson government of 1964–70 saw an end to such hopes. Initially, great efforts were made to promote closer Commonwealth ties, and to develop trading and other economic links. However, these became increasingly problematic, and the 1967 devaluation of the pound, carried through for Britain's own financial convenience, also devalued – without any prior consultation – the wealth of the large number of Commonwealth countries that held their reserves in sterling.[66] But pessimism about the Commonwealth's future had already been signalled earlier that year by Wilson's decision to renew Britain's application to join the EEC.[67] Like Macmillan in 1962, he was unsuccessful; but it was perhaps symbolic that in the aftermath of devaluation Callaghan, a great advocate of Common-wealth, was replaced as Chancellor of the Exchequer by the arch-Europhile, Roy Jenkins. The orientation towards Europe had also been encouraged by the increasingly lukewarm relations pervading between London and Washington, as Wilson repeatedly refused American requests for military assistance in the Vietnam War. By 1970, Britain was withdrawing from east of Suez, mainly on grounds of cost at a time when the economy was moving into more difficult times than at any point since 1945.[68] When Labour was defeated at the 1970 election, few would have claimed that its six years in office had seen much in the way of strategic thinking or planning in relation to the wider world; and, overall, it is difficult to dispute John Young's verdict that, although the government 'created a sustainable policy', it did so 'more by muddle and a collapse of alternatives than any long-term vision'.[69]

Wilson's successor, the Conservative Edward Heath, was in no doubt that entry into the EEC was his key objective, and in January 1973 Britain finally entered the Community. In opposition, Wilson had found – as had Attlee after 1951 – that the Labour Party would not accept from a Conservative government policies it might just about have been prepared to swallow from a Labour administration. Accordingly, Labour's stance on the EEC had shifted closer to outright hostility, a factor which promoted the steady alienation of a group of right-wing Labour MPs, associated with Roy Jenkins, and which represented the start of the process that can be seen as having culminated in the formation of the Social Democratic Party (SDP) in 1981. Once back in government, however, Wilson and Callaghan, by now Foreign Secretary, realised they had no alternative but to remain in the EEC, and got this confirmed, following a somewhat cosmetic 'renegotiation' of the British terms of entry, by a national referendum in June 1975.[70] The referendum campaign split the party. In its aftermath, divisions were if anything intensified when Wilson took the opportunity to demote one of the EEC's sternest Cabinet critics, Tony Benn, and so neuter the party's radical industrial policy. Meanwhile, relations with the United States were improved somewhat, especially once Callaghan had succeeded Wilson in 1976.[71]

Back in opposition after the 1979 general election, Labour again moved leftwards. A month or so after the general election, the first direct elections for the European Parliament were held. The extent of continuing antipathy towards the EEC could be seen in the fact that some constituency parties, like North-East Derbyshire, refused to participate in the election campaign, and threatened disciplinary action against any of their members that did so.[72] Such hostility derived partly from xenophobia, but there was more to it than that. There had long been a perception that the EEC was little more than a club of wealthy countries with predominantly right-wing governments. There were fears that the Community would act to prevent a future Labour government from pursuing the kind of autarchic policies that were part and parcel of Labour's radical alternative economic strategy (AES), which included among other things selective import controls, national planning agreements, and steps to deal with multinationals. And there were those who saw the Community, with its limited membership, as actually being inimical to 'true' internationalism.

The swing to the left also brought the issue of unilateral nuclear disarmament back onto the political agenda. The Callaghan government (1976–9) had discussed updating Britain's nuclear arsenal.[73] Ultimately, the Conservatives under Margaret Thatcher decided to update the Polaris nuclear submarine fleet and also allow the Americans to install their own Cruise missiles on British soil. Thatcher's own Cold War rhetoric, as well as the election in November 1980 of Ronald Reagan as American president with an apparently similar combative rhetoric, seemed to suggest an escalation of the Cold War at just a time when the Soviets were themselves, by their invasion of Afghanistan, destabilising international relations. All this gave CND a huge boost in popularity, and within the Labour Party support for unilateral nuclear disarmament grew to a level not seen since the 1960 conference had voted in its favour (the vote had been reversed the following year).

In retrospect, however, Labour's early 1980s swing to the left was not all that dramatic or long-lived. Although the party conference passed a resolution in favour of unilateral nuclear disarmament in 1980, it also passed one in favour of multilateral (that is, negotiated) nuclear disarmament, with the result that the 1983 election manifesto would carry the baffling formulation 'unilateralism and multilateralism must go hand in hand if either is to succeed'.[74] The same conference defeated a motion to withdraw from NATO by the massive majority of 6,279,000 votes to 826,000.[75] Popular attitudes towards the Falklands War of spring 1982 – or at least towards victory in it – gave party leaders pause for thought, although Labour leader Michael Foot's memories of the 1930s allowed him to give broad support to the government in fighting against what he saw as an act of aggression by the Argentine junta, which he characterised as fascistic.[76] None of this, however, was sufficient to avert heavy defeat at the 1983 general election.

Defeat in 1983 was largely taken as a condemnation of the excesses of a 'hard left' which had favoured unilateralism, opposed Europe, and so on.[77] The new leader, Neil Kinnock, was himself considered a 'soft left' figure. Kinnock was a committed unilateralist, and had considerable doubts about Europe. However, a new Soviet leadership, in the shape of Mikhail Gorbachev, offered the new way forward towards the end of the Cold War that unilateralists had once claimed could only come from a British Labour government getting rid of its nuclear weapons. It was increasingly obvious that it would be elsewhere that those issues would be resolved, and the pressure that had built up behind unilateralism dissipated. In 1989, Kinnock dropped Labour's commitment to unilateralism.[78] Similarly, the changing world situation helped to change attitudes towards what is now known as the European Union. In 1987, Labour's election manifesto stopped a long way short of advocating withdrawal; and, with that election bringing yet another heavy defeat, British Labourites, and trade unionists in particular, became increasingly interested in what British workers might gain from closer European integration. When the President of the EU Commission, Jacques Delors, addressed the 1988 Trades Union Congress, he showed how British acceptance of the EU Social Charter would greatly enhance workers' rights. Once seen as a rich man's club that would prevent a Labour government achieving things for ordinary people, the EU was coming to be seen as the friend of the ordinary people against a rich man's government in Britain.[79] At the 1992 election, therefore, Labour under Kinnock adopted a very pro-EU line.

By then, of course, the Cold War was over. Communist regimes in Europe outside the Soviet Union did not survive long after 1989; by 1991 the USSR itself was no more. Labour views of these developments were generally favourable, although the hopes of many Labourites that the countries involved would find a new third way between capitalism and Communism were soon disappointed as they eagerly embraced crude forms of western capitalism. For Labour, however, there were two other points of significance. One was that the decline of an alternative way of organising society – even if an inefficient, oppressive and at times brutal one – left Labour with less scope to imagine really radical change in Britain.[80] The other, however, was far more positive for the party's prospects. Ever since 1917, the Conservatives had been able to trade on the idea that Labour was just the relatively acceptable end of a spectrum that led straight on to Communism. In other words, a vote for Labour risked being a vote for something akin to Soviet Communism. Furthermore, the Cold War had allowed the Conservatives to contrast their own 'patriotism' with Labour's 'weakness' and being 'soft on Communism'. But now that Communism had gone, the Conservatives had lost a great cry against Labour. In this way, once again, developments in the wider world had a significant (and in this case positive) impact on Labour's fortunes.

To an extent that is often unrecognised, therefore, changes in the wider world made the ground propitious for a rebranding of Labour, even without the promptings of Labour 'modernisers'. The accession to the leadership of Tony Blair in 1994 was seen by some as a return to the modernising tendencies of the late Kinnock years after the rather more conciliatory leadership style of John Smith (1992–4).[81] Initially, Blair's focus was on the party, and then on domestic policy. Waves of rhetoric came and went, but little of substance was said that was new regarding the wider world. To many, it seemed that the most likely outcome of a Blair premiership would be closer British involvement in European integration, moving beyond the 1992 Maastricht Treaty towards something closer to federation, along with a single currency of which Britain would be a member. However, there were indications in other directions, even in the period before 1997. For one thing, New Labour derived a great deal from the American example of Bill Clinton's New Democrats, combining as they did a commitment to social justice with a willingness to be tough with those thought to be trying to take advantage of the state and the community.[82] Clinton's election and re-election as US president in 1992 and 1996 meant that there was almost certain to be a complicating closeness of Anglo-American relations so far as Anglo-European relations were concerned. Furthermore, the more attention was focused on issues like a federal Europe and a single currency, the more it became clear that they could well be vote-losers; and this did not sit easily with New Labour, which was concerned perhaps above all else to minimise its commitments to issues seen as divisive or potentially vote-losing. Finally, the mood-music that would lead to the new Labour Foreign Secretary, Robin Cook, declaring in favour of an 'ethical' foreign policy shortly after the 1997 election suggested that Labour's leaders still believed that Britain was of greater importance in world affairs than its immersion into the European project would have allowed.[83]

In the immediate aftermath of the Cold War there had been a good deal of loose talk about the future. It was, declared some commentators, *The End of History*: liberal democracy had emerged victorious and the world would now be a more peaceful place. There was much talk of a 'peace dividend' as governments could slash expenditure on defence. It rapidly transpired, however, that things were going to be more complicated than that. To an extent that is still not always fully recognised, Blair's years as Prime Minister from 1997 onwards were characterised by British forces being on active service somewhere in the world. Many of these engagements were small in scale, and not all that significant in themselves. Nonetheless, Blair developed, from an early stage, an awareness of, and, arguably, a liking for, the deployment of British troops.[84] The outgoing Conservative government of John Major had been very reluctant to get too closely involved in the messy aftermath of the collapse of Yugoslavia, for example, and its Foreign Secretary, Douglas Hurd, had set his face against 'the straightforward, violent solution to international problems'.[85] However, events in the former Yugoslavia – and especially in Bosnia – became so appalling that there was widespread support for some form of intervention. This intervention, under the aegis of the United Nations but with a strong British element, was eventually seen as successful in bringing peace and restoring order. Similar efforts, in Kosovo in 1999 and Sierra Leone in 2000, were also broadly successful.[86] This all suggested that Major and Hurd's pessimism had been bogus, flawed, or both. Meanwhile, memories of the easy victory of the UN coalition in liberating Kuwait from its Iraqi invaders in 1991, combined with feelings that the Iraqi dictator Saddam Hussein should have been overthrown at that point, became increasingly heard in both Washington and London.

All this might not have mattered had it not been for the narrow victory of George W. Bush in the US presidential elections of 2000. Bush was known to think little of the wider world, but had around him two groups whose views, although in some ways contradictory, were worrying for the Blair government. On the one hand, there were isolationists who suggested that America should draw in its horns and concern itself far less with the wider world. On the other, neoconservatives argued that the USA should seek to intervene widely in the world to overthrow perceivedly hostile regimes, regardless of world opinion.[87] What both groups shared was contempt for America's allies. Blair clearly believed that for America to 'go it alone' in either of these directions would be disastrous for Britain and the rest of the world, and appears to have believed that the best way of preventing such an outcome was to give close support to the general lines of US policy, while at the same time seeking to strengthen 'doves' against 'hawks' in the administration.[88] However, Blair's approach changed as his relationship with Bush warmed, particularly in the aftermath of the 11 September 2001 Al-Qaida terrorist attacks on New York and Washington D.C. Britain supported the invasion of Afghanistan, and when that went well, with the Taliban government being rapidly overthrown, pressure began to build for an attack on Iraq, even though the evidential basis for links between Saddam and Al-Qaida was, to say the least, questionable. When the attack was launched in March 2003, there were numerous questions about the veracity of the evidence that had been used by the Labour government to justify the invasion and Britain's involvement in it. They remain to be answered, and it now seems certain that Blair's achievements in office will be overshadowed, for a time at least, by his decision to go to war in Iraq. Meanwhile, prospects of closer European integration have receded, with the growth of antipathy towards the European 'project' in a number of states and also the development of hostility towards Britain for its close support of highly controversial American policies.

The Iraq War certainly did little to help Labour at the 2005 general election. While Liberal Democrat hopes of major gains from Labour in inner-city constituencies with large numbers of Muslim voters proved exaggerated, Labour support among such voters did diminish somewhat, and it became clear that the party had upset significant numbers of its core supporters, whether Muslim or not.[89] But by that stage the party organisation and membership were in such a weakened state that they could effectively do nothing to protest within the party, and many had no alternative but to join anti-war demonstrations. Even so, it seems that the departure of Blair as party leader will need to be followed by some sharp action to revive the party's spirits in the run-up to the general election due by mid-2010.

In many ways, therefore, the Labour Party has felt the impacts of the wider world deeply. It was helped ultimately by the First and Second World Wars, but damaged by the Cold War and, most recently, by the Iraq War. The often arcane nature of foreign policy, and the need for it to be made (at least when in government) very often in a hurry, and in response to unexpected circumstances on the basis of incomplete information, has tended to restrict the potential of the wider party to influence policy-making. But Labour MPs, and at times Cabinet members, have also often had to be by-passed, as can be seen, for example, in the Attlee government's decision to go ahead with a British atomic bomb. But even if they had been consulted, Labourites might have struggled to come up with coherent alternative policies. The party leadership has often had to think on its feet where the wider world was concerned. Armed only with first principles, Labourites have often found it hard to discern the 'right' path in international affairs, and this means that we, as historians, sometimes look in wonder and confusion at the stances that were taken up on various issues at various times. It is also worth remembering, though, and as this Introduction has tried to indicate, that Labour's relationship with the wider world was not just about foreign and imperial policy. For example, international economic trends have impacted upon the domestic economy, contributing to the economics of boom or bust; trade union membership, so important in terms of Labour Party membership, structure, and funding, has been directly affected by such trends. Similarly, political and economic ideas have flooded into Britain from the outside. It has really only been possible to mention a few examples above, but such ideas have played a significant part in the party's development. In short, the relationship between Labour and the wider world has been complex and multifaceted.

III

This complex and multifaceted relationship is reflected in the essays that make up the substantive part of this volume. The first four of them focus on the period before 1945. In the first chapter, John Shepherd offers a detailed account of the first Labour government of 1924, suggesting that the government's record in the fields of foreign and imperial policy was broadly positive. Next, Casper Sylvest analyses the making of policy in the period between 1918 and 1931 in a chapter on Labour's Advisory Committee on International Questions (ACIQ), showing how it 'functioned as a "school" of internationalism within the Labour Party' in that period. In the third chapter, Jonathan Davis offers a challenging analysis of Soviet influence on Labour's interwar political thought, arguing that the USSR became a 'key definer' of that thinking. Some of these influences were positive, he suggests, but most were negative. Then, in Chapter 4, Paul Corthorn gives a detailed account of Labour in the era of the Nazi-Soviet Pact (1939–41), showing the profound impact that that period had on the nature of Labour's internationalist thinking.

The next four chapters focus on aspects of Labour's relationship with the wider world in the period between the end of the Second World War and the later 1960s. In Chapter 5, John Callaghan offers an important reappraisal of the Attlee governments' foreign policy, showing that it was 'predicated on the maintenance of Britain's Great Power status on the basis of its Empire-Commonwealth', and he shows how American attitudes moved from hostility toward British imperialism to an acceptance of the Empire-Commonwealth as a useful adjunct in the fight against Communism. This is followed by two chapters that are largely centred on the 1950s. In the first of these, Robert Crowcroft revisits the controversy over West German rearmament, and shows the extent to which the disagreements within the party were much more complex than a simple matter of left versus right; in doing so, he offers a useful corrective to accounts that present Labour Party politics in such 'either-or' terms. In the second, Richard Toye and Nicholas Lawton emphasise the extent to which Labour's responses to affluence in the 1950s and early 1960s were conditioned by 'a Cold War discourse which was prevalent in British democratic socialist circles at the time, but which has since been neglected in the historiography': for example, they argue, it influenced Wilson's 1963 'white heat of technology' speech. In Chapter 8, David Fowler analyses the neglected theme of the international student revolts of the 1960s, and demonstrates how the Labour government tried to deal with the perceived threat of foreign activists who, it was feared, were fomenting unrest in British universities.

The last two chapters come closer to the present day. In Chapter 9, Ann Schreiner looks at press and Labour reactions to the break-up of Yugoslavia, and shows how the Blair government, once in office from 1997 onwards, adopted policies similar to those advocated in the left-of-centre press earlier in the decade. In the final chapter, Mark Phythian offers a frank, critical, and incisive appraisal of the performance of Blair and his government in relation to the Iraq War, showing in particular how Blair used Kosovo as a guide to action in Iraq, and also the extent to which 'the case for war was . . . assembled after the decision for war had been taken'. It forms a salutary end to the volume, and suggests that Labour's relationship with the wider world is not likely to become much more straightforward in the very near future.

1

A GENTLEMAN AT THE FOREIGN OFFICE: INFLUENCES SHAPING RAMSAY MACDONALD'S INTERNATIONALISM IN 1924

John Shepherd[1]

In January 1924, on the defeat of Stanley Baldwin's Conservative ministry, Britain's first Labour government took office – even though it could not command an overall parliamentary majority. Ramsay MacDonald surprisingly took on the dual role of Prime Minister and Foreign Secretary, despite the warnings of the King. Only Queen Victoria's Prime Minister, Lord Salisbury, in the late nineteenth century, had also served at the Foreign Office. MacDonald's decision demonstrated the priority he gave to the conduct of international affairs during his first short-lived administration. Since then, Labour's relations with the wider world have been seen as one of the ministry's few achievements during only 287 days in office and to have played a significant role in the evolution of Labour's international policy in the post-war years.[2]

After asking MacDonald to form an administration, George V famously recorded in his diary 'Today 23 years ago dear Grandmama died. I wonder what she would have thought of a Labour Government!'[3] The King's comment reflected deep concern in governing circles about the fate of Britain and the British Empire in the hands of socialists and trade unionists closely associated in their minds with the evils of Bolshevism. Moreover, for those shaken by the Russian Revolutions in 1917, this inexperienced minority administration overseeing British interests around the globe was also led by a former pacifist, who had opposed British participation in the First World War, and had never served in government. During the previous six weeks, a period of minority Conservative government, various hare-brained schemes hatched mainly among Conservative politicians to keep their party in office had come to nothing.

As Britain's first Labour Foreign Secretary, Ramsay MacDonald – the illegitimate son of a Scottish servant, Annie Ramsay, and John MacDonald, a ploughman – made a striking contrast to his Conservative predecessor – certainly in terms of background and personality. He succeeded the wealthy and most widely travelled Cabinet minister until then, Lord Curzon. In 1923 the former Viceroy of India had been coping, with some success, with the threatening diplomatic and political crisis caused by the French occupation of the Ruhr and the provocative encouragement of separatist movements in Germany.[4] To solve the vexed question of Franco-German relations in Europe became the immediate and overriding concern of Labour's new Foreign Secretary.

Over thirty years later, Nye Bevan, Labour's shadow Foreign Secretary, told the 1958 annual party conference that on first becoming an MP in 1929 he discovered at Westminster 'a prevalent myth . . . to the effect that although the Labour Members of Parliament could reasonably be expected to know something about engineering, or about mining, there were two subjects on which they were completely ignorant: foreign affairs, and how to make war. It was always understood that those were the special pre-rogatives of the Tories.'[5]

In 1924 expectations were high among Labour supporters at the prospect of their party in power, in contrast to senior members of the British Civil Service, British Intelligence and governing classes who were distinctly uneasy with socialist figures, rather than familiar bourgeois politicians, at the helm. On first meeting his new Prime Minister, who had to be 'sworn to the Privy Council', the apprehensive George V raised the singing of the revolutionary 'Albert Hall songs' (*The Red Flag* and *The Marseillaise*) at Labour's victory rally and appealed to MacDonald 'to do nothing to compel him to shake hands with the murderers of his relatives'.[6]

In 1920 Winston Churchill had characteristically told his enthusiastic audience in Sunderland that Labour, without any constructive programme and identifying with class rather than national interests, was 'quite unfitted for the responsibility of Government'.[7] His taunt to the Labour leaders – subsequently repeated in public speeches – echoed down the post-war years. MacDonald held an adamantine conviction that his Labour administration had to be seen as moderate, respectable and responsible in high office. At Labour's 'Victory Rally' on 8 January 1924, where the singing of hymns interspersed revolutionary songs, MacDonald not only evoked the world of the socialist pioneers, such as Keir Hardie, William Morris and Edward Carpenter, but 'had [also] come to say a difficult word to an enthusiastic audience. The word was *moderation*.'[8] Addressing the House of Commons on 12 February 1924, MacDonald spoke in careful generalities about the

European question and the League of Nations. Nor would he be drawn on how his policy might differ from his predecessor.[9] After going through his memorandum on foreign policy, unemployment and the budget with future senior Cabinet members, before taking office he had noted 'Unanimous that moderation & honesty were our safety. Agreed to stand together.'[10] In this respect, they succeeded admirably. As a future Labour Prime Minister noted about the 1924 administration: 'Cartoonists and countesses were united in feeling that these men were safe and conformist.'[11]

The conduct of international affairs was the global stage on which Labour's fitness to govern would be demonstrated for humankind to see. In surveying Labour's relations with the external world, this chapter analyses how MacDonald and his ministers managed European and imperial questions during a difficult period of minority government, and the interplay of conflicting influences on Labour's policy decisions in a world still reeling from the destructive effects of the Great War and the forces it unleashed. Central to this discussion is the question of how a seemingly socialist administration on taking office responded to the elitist traditions and conventions of British foreign and imperial policy.

In the immediate post-war years, Labour had condemned the punitive peace imposed by the allies on Germany under the Versailles Treaty and the harmful effects of reparations on the dislocation of international trade, as well as Allied intervention against the new Bolshevik regime in Russia. The new League of Nations was at first viewed in Labour circles with suspicion as an organisation of victorious allies rather than a democratic people's assembly. Former ally France was now perceived as the dangerous expansionist power in Europe – as was confirmed in 1923 by the French occupation of the Ruhr. For those on the left, the rise of Labour offered a new vision in domestic affairs after the empty promise of making Britain 'a fit country for heroes to live in', and also in external affairs as they sought to build a new world after the carnage of the First World War. Labour was free from any association with the 'old diplomacy' of the political elites blamed for the outbreak of international conflict and had consistently called for the revision of the Versailles Treaty.

Instead, Britain's first Labour government was a significant stage in the development in the 1920s of Labour's own foreign policy, increasingly centred on the role of the League of Nations in international affairs.[12] In 1924 the arrival of a Labour government pledged to open diplomacy, the League of Nations, international disarmament and ending the arms trade introduced a significant fresh dimension to British politics, not only during a major period of realignment in domestic politics after the collapse of the Lloyd George Coalition government in 1922, but also in international diplomacy in Europe and elsewhere in the wider world.

I

In 1951 Norman Angell, Labour MP, close associate of Ramsay MacDonald in the Union of Democratic Control (UDC), and Nobel Peace Laureate, defined the Labour leader as a Victorian Liberal in international affairs. 'I doubt if he had worked out in his mind a foreign policy which differed from the somewhat naïve optimism of the old Liberal who was satisfied with political laissez-faire in the international field, sustained by moving rhetoric about the wickedness of armaments, the balance of power, secret diplomacy, and so forth,' he argued. As evidence, he cited the growing apprehension of Arthur Ponsonby, MacDonald's socialist Parliamentary Secretary at the Foreign Office, that Labour policy 'would soon be indistinguishable from that of the more woolly-headed Conservatives'.[13] In April 1924 Ponsonby pressed Angell and his colleagues at Westminster to influence MacDonald's forthcoming parliamentary statement on foreign policy along more socialist lines:

> Without criticising the policy he has pursued, attention might be called to omissions and what is being felt in I.L.P. [Independent Labour Party] circles . . . a syllable of sympathy of Germany . . . a more distinct pronouncement in general differentiating our attitude towards the whole international situation – League of Nations, international disarmament from the Tories.[14]

By the 1920s Ramsay MacDonald was indisputably Labour's dominant figure and the party's main political strategist in widening Labour's appeal as a modern political party among the social democratic movements of Europe. In 1924 MacDonald gave more detailed attention to foreign and imperial issues in office, rather than domestic matters. The significant influences on his attitude to international affairs can be traced through his contributions as a democratic socialist writer, his foreign travels and his close and active association with the Second International in the pre-war and post-war years.[15]

As an Edwardian progressive in politics, MacDonald's editorship of *Socialist Review* and his political writings – including 13 titles between 1905 and 1921, such as *Socialism and Society* (1905), *Socialism and Government* (1908) and *Socialism: Critical and Constructive* (1921) – revealed the evolution of his political outlook, an intermingling of radical and socialist thought influenced by Eduard Bernstein and other continental revisionist figures.[16] Much of this writing demonstrates MacDonald's ideas about the organic growth in society that, to some extent, underpinned his approach to foreign affairs. As Foreign Secretary, MacDonald could bring a cerebral and realistic perspective to the practicalities of international policy. 'In domestic affairs, we and our own wills alone are concerned; in foreign affairs, the convenience and policy, the opinion and wills of foreign Governments have to be taken into account,' he observed.[17]

An instinctive internationalist, MacDonald was one of the few Labour politicians before the First World War – along with Keir Hardie and Arthur Henderson – to speak in parliamentary debates on foreign affairs. In 1900 the fledgling Labour Representation Committee (from 1906 the Labour Party) was primarily concerned with the domestic interests of trade unions and working people. International matters attracted the interest particularly of Ramsay and Margaret MacDonald. Their Lincoln's Inn Field home served as the party's first London office and also as a lively political salon attended by political figures from Britain and abroad. In a series of important world tours, the MacDonalds investigated political and social conditions in Australia, New Zealand, the United States, Canada and South Africa until Margaret's tragic early death in 1911.[18]

However, foreign travel and influential overseas contacts were not, perhaps, restricted to a few early Labour leaders, as is sometimes thought. In 1934 William Maddox identified at least 25 leading Labourites he considered influential on the party's foreign policy – though he realised that this was difficult to gauge precisely. One interest this group shared, whether as parliamentarians, trade unionists, journalists or academics, was overseas journeys, as well as regular opportunities to attend international conferences and visit foreign countries as British representatives. A few within Labour ranks – Norman Angell, Frank Hodges and Sidney Webb – had studied abroad, and so had the former Liberal Imperialist, Robert Haldane, Labour's Lord Chancellor and chairman of the Committee on Imperial Defence (CID) in 1924.[19]

Labour's international policy in the interwar years has been the subject of debate among historians, particularly on how far it could be accurately described as 'socialist' – whether its conduct was influenced by socialist theory and values or inherited from nineteenth-century radical liberalism. During the October 1924 election the journalist and political commentator George Glasgow – probably the first of MacDonald's contemporaries to assess his spell at the Foreign Office – was impressed by his fresh approach while maintaining continuity in policy. Aware of Labour's pacifist and anti-imperialist origins, he concluded that MacDonald was a success on the international stage 'as British foreign policy is traditionally pacific and pro-gressive'. But Glasgow went no further than attributing MacDonald's successful performance to substituting 'co-operation and goodwill for bicker-ing and force as the motive in contemporary diplomacy' at a time of high tension in international affairs.[20] In 1937 Clement Attlee was more precise about the influence of socialism in Labour's approach to the external world. He recalled: 'Socialists in all countries are united by a common rejection of the doctrines and ideals of militarism and imperialism.' Before 1914 there was little to separate Labour's foreign policy from the radical wing of the Liberal Party. But in 1924 Labour had a 'well-considered policy' based on working for world disarmament and the international peace-keeping role of the League of Nations. Labour's international policy, with collective security at its heart, was essentially 'socialist' – as socialists were largely agreed on its aims, principles and implementation.[21]

After the Second World War, Elaine Windrich's survey of Labour's foreign policy benefited from interviews with Labour Party members, including prominent socialists in the 1945–50 government (the first with an overall majority), such as Clement Attlee, Aneurin Bevan, Jennie Lee and Herbert Morrison. According to the author, *British Labour's Foreign Policy* was an account of 'a socialist experiment in the international field' though Labour's conduct of international affairs had been consistently based on distinct principles inherited principally from nineteenth-century radicalism and working-class internationalism. It was this unbroken continuity with a radical past that made a Labour or socialist policy distinctive from its Conservative and Liberal predecessors.[22]

Michael R. Gordon's *Conflict and Consensus in Labour's Foreign Policy 1914–1945* was the most incontrovertible attempt to identify the distinctive socialist character of Labour's policy built on four key principles: internationalism, international working-class solidarity, anti-capitalism and anti-militarism.[23] Similarly, Kenneth Millar also examined the effect of socialist ideology on Labour's foreign policy while affirming a significant inheritance of radical-liberal theories.[24] Both surveys raised the issues of what was socialist about Labour's foreign policy and how could it be defined? A belief in internationalism and workers' rights, which transcended national boundaries, were common important principles though these were often ideals, rather than the bases of formulated policy. More recently, during a period of 'New Labour' government and an ethical foreign policy, Stephen Howe has interestingly suggested that the 'British Labour Party has never had a distinctive foreign policy' or a world outlook shaped by socialist prescriptions.[25] A more appropriate description would be a set of ethical stances inherited from Victorian radical liberalism. Rhiannon Vickers has recently written that Labour's internationalism was a different stance in foreign affairs, compared to conventional *realpolitik*, but lacked 'any socialist ideology as such'. Instead it was influenced by 'radical liberal thinking' and 'a Christian-socialist, Nonconformist streak among party members'.[26] In various scholarly studies, Henry R. Winkler has analysed the significance of Labour's internationalism in the interwar years. He has emphasised the key roles of Ramsay MacDonald, Arthur Henderson, and those associated with Labour's Advisory Committee on International Questions (ACIQ), in gradually shaping a Labour foreign policy based on the League of Nations and the need for collective security.[27]

II

While in 1924 Ramsay MacDonald took office without any previous ministerial experience, or having led a major organisation such as a trade union, his political outlook on foreign and imperial affairs nevertheless had been shaped over more than twenty years. Amongst the leading Labour politicians in the early 1920s, he possessed a notable grasp of foreign affairs and had been one of the major British socialists associated with the Second International in the pre-war years. While out of Parliament in 1918–1922, he made considerable efforts to rebuild the Second International as a democratic socialist alternative to the new Communist Third International controlled from Moscow. MacDonald had been a foremost participant at the important Berne Conference in February 1919 – held at the same time as the Peace Conference in Paris. There he advocated an alternative role of a League of Nations composed of democratically-elected representatives from the different national parliaments, rather than an elite gathering of monarchs and mandarins like the Holy Alliance of the nineteenth century.[28]

In August 1914 MacDonald had resigned as chairman of the Parliamentary Labour Party (PLP) over his party's decision to support British participation in the war. He joined with other dissenting radical and Liberal politicians to establish the UDC. This initiative was not another stop-the-war organisation but a pressure group that sought a just and peaceful settlement to the war, opposed secret diplomacy, and vigorously advocated the parliamentary control of British foreign policy.[29] MacDonald also wrote on international questions and played a significant post-war role in denouncing the punitive peace settlement imposed on Germany under the Versailles Treaty. It is not surprising therefore that MacDonald eventually took the Foreign Office himself. MacDonald's Parliamentary Private Secretary (PPS), Clement Attlee, who also became Under-Secretary of War, realised the significance of foreign affairs in 1924 to the internationalist Labour leader. 'I do not think that MacDonald had envisaged having to take office, and the Party programme, *except on foreign affairs*, was very much a minority document', he recalled.[30]

In assembling his government, MacDonald had several posts with responsibilities for international matters. As his critics pointed out, he did not always choose ministers with the appropriate background such as the denial of the India Office to Josiah Wedgwood, to the disillusionment of Indian nationalists. Instead, Wedgwood had to handle the wave of strikes in Britain as Chancellor of the Duchy of Lancaster. As his Parliamentary Under-Secretary at the Foreign Office, MacDonald chose the aristocratic socialist and peace campaigner, Arthur Ponsonby, his former associate in the UDC. Educated at Eton and Balliol, Ponsonby was a seemingly appropriate choice. He spoke French and German owing to earlier diplomatic service in Constantinople and Copenhagen. After a spell at the Foreign Office, he had entered Liberal politics as Henry Campbell-Bannerman's Principal Private Secretary and was one of five Liberal MPs to speak out against war in 1914. As a member of the Bryce group, he had worked on proposals to establish a League of Nations.[31]

According to his account, Ponsonby was also influential in making certain that MacDonald took over the foreign affairs portfolio in 1924. After hearing at the *New Leader* office in December 1923 that MacDonald had J. H. Thomas in mind as Foreign Secretary, he wrote pointedly to MacDonald: 'The incredible seems about to happen. We are actually to be allowed by an incredible combination of circumstances to have control of the F.O. [Foreign Office] and to begin to carry out some of the things we have been urging and preaching for years. To give this job to J.T. is simply to chuck the opportunity away.'[32] It was probably a most decisive intervention in persuading MacDonald to go to the Foreign Office. Later at his remote Scottish retreat, Lossiemouth, during Christmas 1923, MacDonald carefully pored over the report in the *Manchester Guardian* that Thomas wanted the Foreign Office, since his union had bankrolled the impecunious Labour Party to the tune of £10,000.[33] Instead, MacDonald moved Thomas, the former General Secretary of the National Union of Railwaymen, to the Colonial Office, where his new surroundings suited his growing penchant for the high life. His Whitehall office was the most magnificent of those occupied by the new administration, spacious enough for a cricket pitch and ostentatiously decorated with the portraits of celebrated British imperialists responsible for the greatest empire in the world.[34]

One of the distinctive features of Britain's first Labour government was the appointment of ministers from outside the Labour ranks, who could hardly be considered as socialist influences on Labour's internationalist policy. From Lossiemouth MacDonald had written to Thomas: 'Since coming up here, I have been going very carefully into the details of an administration . . . The mass of appointments for which we have no one absolutely qualified, is perfectly appalling – Whips who must attend in Court Dress, etc., etc. It would take me six months to straighten it all out and would entail hundreds of interviews . . .'[35]

MacDonald had told Henderson, a very likely Foreign Secretary whom he tried to keep out of the Cabinet, of his desire to consider non-Labour outsiders. In this respect, MacDonald's key contact to recruit from outside Labour ranks was Lord Haldane, the former Liberal Imperialist, Secretary of State for War (December 1905 – 1912), who readily advised on appointments to the service ministries and the House of Lords. In 1924 Haldane became Labour Chancellor and chaired the CID. He also suggested the Tory and former Viceroy of India, Lord Chelmsford, who became the First Lord of the Admiralty. A bevy of former Liberals – Charles Trevelyan (Education), Noel Buxton (Agriculture) and Josiah Wedgwood (Chancellor of the Duchy of Lancaster) brought an important influx of radical liberalism, particularly influential in foreign and imperial affairs.

As Secretary of State for India, Sydney Olivier, a founding member of the Fabian Society in 1884 and one of the original Fabian essayists in 1889, was preferred to Wedgwood given his diplomatic career as acting Colonial Secretary in British Honduras and Governor of Jamaica.[36] By accepting a peerage in 1924, the new Lord Olivier strengthened Labour's slender representation in the House of Lords. According to Sidney Webb, Wedgwood was the cause of occasional dissent within the Cabinet over Olivier's policy in India, though a standing 'Indian Committee' (consisting of Olivier, Richards, Chelmsford, Trevelyan, Wedgwood and Webb) met frequently and even compiled the telegrams Olivier sent to India.[37]

Sidney Webb took a particular interest in how the 1924 Labour Cabinet functioned and behaved. 'The Cabinet found itself under a constant pressure of business, even although it sat for three hours once or twice a week, and was seldom troubled by MacDonald with foreign affairs', he noted. Foreign affairs remained mainly the province of the Prime Minister who brought his colleagues up-to-date every few weeks on European issues. Interestingly, the Cabinet gave greater attention to imperial business, particularly in connection with India.[38]

In 1924 the attitude of the senior Civil Service – recruited from broadly upper-class backgrounds – towards a new set of mainly inexperienced Labour ministers was an important factor in how the minority administration functioned in office. In 1924 the mandarins at the British Foreign Office initially welcomed the arrival of Ramsay MacDonald to replace the outgoing Conservative Foreign Secretary, Lord Curzon with his reputation for tetchy working relations. Taking up his new role, MacDonald noted perceptively: 'I must take care. I think I have good men. Curzon apparently treated them badly and the F. O. was on the edge of broken health & revolution. Gentlemanly treatment will do much.'[39] Except over the Dawes Report, where he was always directly involved, MacDonald usually left his civil servants alone to prepare the early memoranda on policy, taking direct control over the final stages. The First Secretary of the Western Department, Alexander George Montagu Cadogan, welcomed the new style of co-operation: 'It's odd that we should have had to wait for the Labour Party to give us a gentleman.'[40]

In particular, defence also caused some early concerns for the British Civil Service with a fledgling Labour administration pledged to reduce armaments while defending Britain and the British Empire. The pacifist Stephen Walsh had been chosen for the War Office, though his deputy was Major Clement Attlee, who had served with distinction and been wounded in the First World War. Even before Labour took office, Maurice Hankey – the most influential contemporary senior civil servant as Secretary to the CID and Cabinet Secretary – had journeyed secretly to MacDonald's Hampstead home to discover the attitude of his new master towards the Cabinet Secretariat and the CID. He later recalled that MacDonald 'pointing to his bookshelves, told me that General Smuts had said that he possessed one of the best military libraries in London'.[41] However, MacDonald was acutely aware of the influence that senior civil servants might wield over inexperienced and busy ministers where policy was concerned. 'I begin to see how officials dominate ministers. Details are overwhelming & ministers have no time to work out policy with officials as *servants*; they are immersed in passing business with officials as *masters*' he observed.[42]

In 1924 the composition of MacDonald's administration reflected – albeit imperfectly – the coalition of different interests and conflicting rivalries within the Labour Party as a whole. From 1900, Keir Hardie's Labour alliance of socialists and trade unionists broadly defined the shape of the new party for the next thirty years. However, with its different conglomeration of identities – Fabians, the Independent Labour Party (ILP), trade unions and trades councils, plus the influx of radicals from the ailing Liberal Party – Labour remained more of a protest movement until its post-war reorganisation and modernisation made it the main opposition party at Westminster in 1922.

During these years, Labour's foreign policy reflected the differing beliefs and political outlooks of the various groups that constituted the Labour Party at Westminster and in the constituencies. As Labour's first Prime Minister and Foreign Secretary, whose career had started in the era of Gladstonian Liberalism, Ramsay MacDonald was – at different times – a member of the Social Democratic Federation, the ILP, and the Fabian Society. Of the medley of groups at the Foundation Conference in 1900, the Fabians displayed the least interest in international affairs, except the question of British imperialism over which MacDonald left their divided ranks during the conflict in South Africa.[43]

In 1924, the trade unions were the major interest group that bankrolled the party through the political levy and held high expectations of an incoming Labour government on wages, unemployment benefits and similar domestic matters. As Rhiannon Vickers has written, through their links with their counterparts overseas and with a large international department, the unions also had an important influence on the Labour Party's foreign policy during the first half of the twentieth century.[44] Of Labour's 'Big Five' Cabinet ministers in 1924, Thomas, J. R. Clynes and Henderson, who was Labour's representative at the League of Nations Assembly at Geneva in 1924 and Foreign Secretary in the second Labour government, were former leading trade unionists. Outside Parliament, Ernest Bevin, General Secretary of the Transport and General Workers' Union and later Foreign Secretary in the post-war Attlee Labour government, was the dominant figure in the trade-union world and prominent in the industrial disputes which faced the 1924 government on taking office. By the 1930s he was part of a significant partnership with Walter Citrine, General Secretary of the Trades Union Congress (TUC) and the Labour politician Hugh Dalton in moving Labour foreign policy away from pacifism towards rearmament.

The ILP – the largest socialist group affiliated to the Labour Party – had been actively associated with the Second International in the cause of international and working-class solidarity. Strongly anti-imperialist, the ILP opposed the post-war settlement based on the League of Nations and reparation payments. In the post-war years, as Robert Dowse has shown, a two-fold division gradually developed in the ranks of the ILP between the internationally-minded ex-Liberal politicians, who had recently joined the party, and the vociferous ILP Clydesiders, who displayed scant regard for parliamentary behaviour in the House of Commons by raucously taking 'the slums into Parliament'.[45] By 1923 the rift – over the relative significance between international and domestic affairs – was apparent between the intellectual section of the ILP and the Clydesiders at the ILP annual conference. The internationalist and anti-militarist Charles Roden Buxton, proposed the return of the French-occupied Ruhr to Germany, but the Clydeside group insisted the German coalminers were less deprived than their counterparts in West Scotland.[46] Others in the ILP, such as the chairman Clifford Allen, saw the significance of pacifying Europe in tackling unemployment at home. In 1924 MacDonald appointed only John Wheatley from the Clydesiders to a Cabinet post. Relief tinged with some understandable anxiety was reflected in MacDonald's diary note: 'Wheatley finally fixed. Necessary to bring the Clyde in. Will he play straight?'[47]

Many of MacDonald's appointments had been associated with the UDC. It had provided an important channel for dissident Liberals with their radical heritage and international outlook to switch their political allegiance to the Labour Party.[48] In 1924, the UDC claimed to be strongly represented in the new Labour administration. However, the Ponsonby Protocol introducing a period of 21 days for the scrutiny of treaties was regarded as a disappointing initial advance to parliamentary control of foreign policy.[49] In particular, the leading figure in the UDC, E. D. Morel, who was bitter at not becoming Foreign Secretary in 1924, remained openly critical of the Labour leadership, the direction of Labour foreign policy and the influence of the permanent senior Foreign Office officials.[50] He was the voice for those in the party who believed firmly in the parliamentary control of foreign affairs for which he pressed without success. The Prime Minister's friendly approach to the French, the continuation of German reparations, as well as MacDonald's refusal to call a conference to revise the Versailles Treaty, were all roundly censured. 'Ramsay MacDonald was undisguisedly jealous of Morel. The latter mistrusted the former and was nervous about his frequent temptations to compromise or vacillate,' Ponsonby noted about his former UDC colleagues.[51]

As Casper Sylvest demonstrates in Chapter Two of this volume, Labour's ACIQ, established in 1918, provided a significant forum for the evolution of the party's foreign policy in the interwar years. With the Fabian economist Leonard Woolf as its secretary, the ACIQ brought together a wide range of academics, intellectuals and politicians with varied outlooks on international relations. In particular, Arthur Henderson increasingly drew on its memoranda and briefings on international relations. He became the main architect in moving Labour's policy from its early doubts about the League of Nations to a realistic acceptance of its place as a world peace-keeping body backed by an effective and enforceable system of collective security in international relations.[52] However, during 1924 the ACIQ had fewer meetings and MacDonald was very much his own man as Foreign Secretary. He did, however, draw on policy briefings from various sources – notably senior government officials and his contacts with academics – including probably the important ACIQ debate over the Draft Treaty of Mutual Assistance (DTMA).

During the 1920s various intellectuals, such as R. H. Tawney, Harold Laski, G. D. H. Cole and Leonard Woolf, also had a significant influence on socialist thought and policy. As the renowned editor of the ILP *New Leader*, H. N. Brailsford, a highly experienced journalist in world affairs, took a critical interest in Britain's first Labour government. Despite his differences with the cagey MacDonald, he welcomed his premiership, endeavoured to act as an intermediary between the Labour leader and Khristian Rakovsky, the Soviet *charge d'affaires* over diplomatic recognition and provided

Ponsonby with a précis of the supposedly secret clauses of the Franco-Czechoslovak treaty. But despite praise in the *New Leader* for MacDonald's recognition of the Soviet Union and his promotion of European peace, including the Geneva Protocol, the newspaper's constant criticism of Labour's lamentable domestic record and the continuation of Conservative imperial policies only earned MacDonald's unremitting fury. Brailsford was an acclaimed socialist journalist of international relations, though his direct influence in 1924 was distinctly limited with a Prime Minister determined to shape and conduct his own foreign policy.[53]

III

In January 1924 Ramsay MacDonald was photographed on his first visit to Chequers working at his desk on international problems. Of immediate importance was the menacing European state of affairs arising out of the French occupation of the Ruhr that had threatened the international order. In January 1923, French and Belgian troops had occupied the heavily industrial Ruhr, the main region of coal, iron and steel production, after Germany had sought a moratorium on reparations and had technically been in default on reparation payments. At the same time, as part of the French premier Raymond Poincaré's policy of hammering Germany, a combined industrial commission of French and Belgian engineers and technicians – the *Mission Interalliee de Controle des Usines et des Mines* (MICUM) – had seized control of strategic Ruhr mines and factories.[54] In Britain the government and opposition parties condemned the French occupation of the Ruhr. Within the British Labour Party, many figures denounced the former ally's expansionism, rather than Germany – perceived as afflicted by a punitive peace settlement imposed by the Treaty of Versailles. The international Reparations Commission had set up two specialist committees to seek some resolution of Germany's financial problems highlighted by the Ruhr crisis. In the November 1923 general election, Labour had fought on a programme that advocated the revision of the Treaty of Versailles, particularly over the thorny issue of reparation payments. Interestingly, during Christmas 1923, Sir John Bradbury, the main British representative on the Reparations Committee, was a solitary visitor to Lossiemouth, where the Labour leader was contemplating the implications of forming his first administration.

In 1924, MacDonald brought an innovative approach to easing Franco-German rivalry by allaying French concerns over security. 'Have made up my mind as to policy. France must have another chance. I offer co-operation but she must be reasonable & cease her policy of selfish vanity. That is my first job. Armaments and such problems that are really consequences must wait. The "weather" must be improved,' MacDonald noted as his foremost objective.[55] As he informed his Cabinet, MacDonald's decision to write openly and personally to Poincaré contravened normal Foreign Office diplomacy.[56] D'Abernon, British Ambassador in Berlin, who warned MacDonald of the rise of the extreme right in Germany, reported 'your letter to Poincaré has been well received here and is thought the strongest statement'.[57] Sensitive to French fears over security, MacDonald had also been warned that the *impasse* in Franco-German relations threatened European trade.[58] A more assured MacDonald noted: 'M. Poincaré & I can agree. I hear the Experts will present a unanimous & satisfactory report. Then the chance will come.'[59] However, he was aware of the opposition to reparations among the left in his party who favoured a more equitable treatment of Germany.

On 9 April 1924 the Dawes Report was published with recommendations on the financial instability of the Weimar Republic, halting German hyperinflation and a resumption of reparation payments to the benefit of European trade. It proposed that Germany return to the Gold Standard and agree to a revised schedule of reparation payments underpinned by a foreign loan of £40 million.[60] MacDonald's skilful diplomacy secured the international acceptance of the Dawes Report within a matter of weeks.[61] By 24–25 April Belgium and France, affected by an ailing currency, also largely agreed to the Dawes Plan and to end the occupation of the Ruhr. After the French general election on 11 May, the more co-operative Edouard Herriot, the radical Mayor of Lyon, replaced Poincaré. MacDonald discovered that left could talk to left. Negotiations at Chequers on 21–22 June between the two leaders brought a large measure of agreement on implementing the Dawes Plan.

In July 1924 MacDonald achieved similar success for his chairmanship of the Inter-Allied Conference in London attended by delegations from Britain, France, Germany, and the USA to discuss the implementation of the Dawes Plan. On 16 July the Labour leader opened the proceedings in his room in the Foreign Office, setting the tone with a conciliatory address to the delegates gathered to bring peace to Europe. As MacDonald put it, only an acceptance of the Dawes Plan could provide a durable peace on the European continent. The rise of militarism was the direct result of the failure of nations to resolve the inflammatory issue of reparations.[62]

However, not all of the Inter-Allied Conference was smooth sailing. From time to time the realities of international matters exposed the rifts and divisions within Britain's first Labour government. The attitude of Philip Snowden, Labour's pro-German Chancellor of the Exchequer, risked the financial and reparation concessions proposed in the Dawes Scheme.[63] 'S[nowden] has been terribly clumsy today & has negotiated like a drill sergeant giving orders. H[erriott] was furious & protested against one of us openly on opposing in a hostile way the findings of the Inter-Allied Conference,' MacDonald noted angrily.[64] In fact, the French delegation threatened to withdraw after more squabbling with a truculent Snowden over reparations and the details of the French withdrawal of troops from the Ruhr. Despite these squabbles, on 15 August, Herriot agreed to the withdrawal of French forces from the Ruhr starting on the day of the final agreement.

On 16 August 1924 the Inter-Allied Conference concluded with the important decision to carry out those parts of the Dawes Report that applied exclusively to Germany, as well as arrangements for German economic and financial development, and sanctions on German failure to pay reparations. Though he had not consulted the party, MacDonald was prepared to continue reparations in order to placate France and secure the withdrawal of French troops from the Ruhr. As MacDonald informed the ILP Conference at York at Easter 1924, 'Here is Europe's chance. Put it into operation all at once. Finish the job and bring peace and security to the Continent.'[65]

MacDonald believed that the Inter-Allied Conference was the outstanding moment of Britain's first Labour government and the pinnacle of his own political career. 'We are now offering the first really negotiated agreement since the war . . . ', though he continually added the reservation 'We have a long way to go before we reach the goal of European peace and security.'[66] Within weeks of taking office, MacDonald's diplomacy in his dual role won significant praise. On 20 March Thomas Jones, Assistant Secretary to the Cabinet, told Lord Astor and J. L. Garvin that 'the P.M's position in the country is distinctly high'.[67] Lord Esher confessed to Jones: 'It is no business of mine, but I think all this talk about the P.M. being unable to combine the F.O. with the P.M.-ship is twaddle.'[68] Maurice Hankey told Jan Smuts, the South African Premier, that MacDonald was 'an admirable Prime Minister, but I must qualify it by saying he would be if he could devote all his time to it. I am told he also has all the makings of a most admirable Foreign Secretary.'[69]

Moreover, the senior mandarins within the Civil Service believed that MacDonald was an accomplished minister compared to the inept Leader of the House, Clynes. MacDonald also won approval from the former Under-Secretary at the Foreign Office, Robert Cecil: 'As for foreign affairs MacDonald appears to be carrying out the policy which I have always wanted. Great friendliness to France coupled with a real effort to make peace even though it costs us a good many concessions. He really is doing a great deal for the League as well,' the stalwart of the League of Nations observed.[70] He wrote to Gertrude Bell, the English archaeologist and influential 'oriental secretary' to the British High Commission in Iraq: 'If he [MacDonald] can only remain in office for a few months, I do not ask for more, we may get foreign affairs relatively straight.'[71]

Nevertheless, MacDonald faced difficulties over foreign policy and defence – particularly for a more democratic conduct of international policy – from within his own party especially from the strong contingent of ILP MPs and the radical members of the UDC now in Labour's ranks. In opposition, Labour had condemned the post-war international order based on the Versailles Treaty and punitive German reparations. Parliamentary control of foreign policy, allied to a deep suspicion of Foreign Office mandarins, was a key demand of those on the left who wished to sweep away the traditional basis of British foreign policy.

There were rumblings of discontent from time to time in the ranks of the PLP over domestic and foreign policy. On 4 June the PLP Executive expressed its 'deep regret that, in view of the unanimous support given by the Party to the request that time should be granted for the discussion of the motion on Parliamentary Control of Foreign Relations, the Government has not seen its way to accede to the request'. The executive appealed to the government to reconsider its decision, if necessary by prolonging the parliamentary session by one day.[72]

MacDonald only attended two of the CID meetings. Haldane, who took the chair, made Labour's first statement on defence policy in Parliament. The new administration reviewed the decision of the Baldwin ministry to build eight new cruisers. After a Cabinet dispute, principally between Snowden (against more armaments) and Chelmsford (defending the Admiralty), only five cruisers and two destroyers were commissioned. Though this provided work at a time of mass unemployment, it did not quell the rumblings on the Labour backbenches. With Conservative votes the government won by 304 to 114 on the Naval Estimates – though 14 Labour members went into the opposition lobby. On defence matters, the Labour government came under attack from its left-wing backbenchers, but a number of minor revolts were soon over.[73] However, the government stopped the defence construction of Singapore started by their Conservative predecessors, primarily because Haldane, on behalf of the CID, wished to build up the Western European defences.[74]

The PLP as a whole remained loyal to the MacDonald administration, although a significant group of Labour backbenchers were altogether opposed to the reparations payments. The continuation of reparation payments and the parliamentary control of foreign affairs were to dominate the thinking of Labour backbenchers as the first Labour government failed to act on these two questions when confronted by the realities of the Inter-Allied Conference. MacDonald saw the discussions in London as a major opportunity to work for the continued peace of Europe that could not be wasted despite the difficult problem of reconciling German and French differences.

Mutterings also came from British trade union leaders about the likely adverse effects from the continuation of reparations. Most aggrieved were the miners who were annoyed about the threat to British coal production and the likely impact on coal production levels and their industry's share of world trade. Despite the presence of former miners William Adamson, Stephen Walsh and Vernon Hartshorn in the 1924 Cabinet, Herbert Smith, the Yorkshire Miners' leader and President of the Miners' Federation, complained bitterly about the Labour government's lack of consultation over the Dawes Report. 'We would not have expected it from the Tory or the Liberal Government,' he declared resentfully.[75] However, despite such misgivings, MacDonald had brought a fresh initiative to European diplomacy but elsewhere the Labour administration had little time or demonstrated any inclination to alter their predecessors' policies.

In Europe, more difficulties arose over the DTMA. This scheme had emanated from the fourth session of the League of Nations Assembly in 1923 and proposed that signatory nations would combine against an aggressor state to secure future European peace and security. France welcomed the DTMA as a guarantee of French security, but it aroused considerable opposition in Britain within governing circles and the British Labour movement. In this case, wary of the military implications, MacDonald drew willingly on the briefings of his service chiefs. 'As for the treaty of mutual guarantee, I must not hide from you the fact that all my experts of navy, army, air force and Foreign Office are opposed to it,' MacDonald told Herriot – only to receive his famous response: 'My country has a dagger pointed at its breast within an inch of its heart.'[76]

Instead, MacDonald kept his assurance to Herriot to consider other options by attending the Fifth Assembly of the League of Nations in September, where he delivered a powerful and sparkling address on achieving peace and security in Europe. 'If we had the beginnings of arbitration . . . what a substantial step forward it would be! If large nations and the small represented here to-day would only . . . create the right commission, and inspire it with the determination that we had in London that no obstacle would baulk us, the success of the commission would be assured within a year,' he promised the delegates.[77] By contrast, Herriot put a dampener on the proceedings by reminding the delegates that arbitration could only go hand-in-hand with general disarmament to ensure European peace and security. In these circumstances, MacDonald was prepared to consider other possibilities such as the possible adoption of the 'optional clause' in the League Covenant to refer disputes to the Permanent Court of Institutional Justice.

Three weeks after MacDonald had left Geneva, the Assembly of the League of Nations adopted 'The Protocol for the Pacific Settlement of International Disputes' – a 21-clause pact popularly known as 'The Geneva Protocol' that had been hammered out principally by Eduard Beneš (Czechoslovakia) and Nicholas Politis (Greece), supported from the British delegation by Arthur Henderson, increasingly the advocate of collective security, and the pacifist Lord Parmoor. The Geneva Protocol offered a test of aggression in international affairs and a system of collective security backed by a range of sanctions to curb aggressor nations. Clement Attlee recalled that the significance of the Geneva Protocol 'was to strengthen League action by outlawing war, increasing security by making more precise the pledges of joint action against an aggressor, and by providing for the compulsory settlement of all disputes between League members'.[78] However, in 1924 there were divided ranks within the Labour Cabinet as to whether aggression could be readily defined in international affairs and the place of coercive sanctions. Henderson and Parmoor joined a somewhat unenthusiastic MacDonald in favour of the Geneva Protocol. Snowden, Wedgwood, Haldane and Chelmsford argued firmly against ratification owing to likely British military commitments – especially for the Royal Navy. Previously, the service chiefs had raised similar objections over the DTMA. A hesitant Labour government therefore did not ratify ratified the Geneva Protocol before it fell from office in October 1924 and the Baldwin government adopted different security proposals at the Locarno Conference in June 1925.

IV

In 1924 Labour's relations with the wider world included governing the vast British Empire which covered a quarter of the world's five continents – two hundred colonies which stretched from London to Gibraltar, through the Suez Canal to Aden, Colombo, Singapore, Hong Kong and beyond to British possessions in the vast Pacific Ocean. In terms of territory, the far-reaching British Empire – coloured imperial pink on British maps appeared even more extensive to those who consulted contemporary atlases based on the Flemish cartographer Gerardus Mercator's projection.[79] When Ramsay MacDonald kissed hands with George V, the King–Emperor ruled over more than four hundred million subjects: Indians and Africans, Arabs and Australians, Canadians, West Indians and Malayans.[80] After the First World War, the British Empire had expanded to include mandated territories under the League of Nations: Iraq, Palestine and Transjordan, as well as Tanganyika and parts of the Cameroons and Togoland.

In 1924 there was little change in Britain's strategic dealings with the wider world. Practical realities of international relations and defence had to be balanced against ideological commitments to open diplomacy, arms reduction and arbitration in international disputes. While Labour's Advisory Committee on Imperial Questions, composed of colonial experts and intellectuals who advocated native rights and self-government, Labour politicians, such as MacDonald, supported the doctrine of trusteeship and steady progress to self-government.[81] As the new Colonial Secretary, Thomas, demonstrated, an implicit racial hierarchy underpinned this attitude to imperial questions with the White Dominions at the top and Africans at the bottom.[82] During the 1920s, Labour maintained the British Empire while increasingly evolving a foreign policy based on the League of Nations and pooled collective security. Labour ministers at the Foreign Office, the War Office, the Colonial Office and the India Office, had previously denounced armaments and the evils of imperialism. Now they were in power and accountable for British naval supremacy over global sea routes essential to the safeguarding of India and the security of the British Empire. At the same time, there had been significant changes throughout the world as the United States withdrew into isolationism. Self-governing Dominions with independent delegates at Versailles were openly reluctant in the 1920s to be drawn into conflicts in Europe. Britain's ailing economy, with mass unemployment and the loss of overseas investments, could no longer prop up worldwide defence commitments.

The First World War had also radically altered the state of Indo-British relations. Large numbers of troops from the colonies and Dominions had fought in the British armed forces, which in turn led to a militant upsurge of nationalism in India and elsewhere. No single event sent greater shock waves around the British Empire than the Amritsar Massacre, when Brigadier-General Dyer's troops slaughtered nearly 400 Indians and wounded more than 1,000 in the holy city of the Sikhs. During the interwar years, the Congress Party – the main Indian organisation calling for home rule and independence since 1885 – sought an end to British rule, a demand that led to Mahatma Gandhi's campaign of civil disobedience. However, during the First World War and the early 1920s, the British only granted some minor concessions to those demanding moves to independence.

Keir Hardie and Ramsay MacDonald, who set the course for Labour thinking on colonial issues, had each visited India before the First World War and viewed the chronic poverty as a definite product of British Imperialism. MacDonald's book – *The Awakening of India* (1910) – had been directly influenced by his experience of the sub-continent. MacDonald reasoned that India should be granted 'wide liberty to govern herself in all her internal affairs'. But like many Labour politicians in the 1920s, who were anti-imperialist without alternative solutions, he saw no way but to govern India through British rule for the foreseeable future.[83]

In opposition the Labour Party had been strongly anti-imperialist and in favour of national self-determination for subject peoples. Nevertheless, such views did not extend to the granting of independence for India once Labour took office. Gandhi was released from prison in January 1924, but only after considerable public pressure following his serious illness. Instead, as part of a bipartisan approach that reflected responsible government, MacDonald and his ministers believed in the careful evolution towards self-rule within the British Commonwealth that, commencing with the Morley-Minto Reforms (1909) had led to the Montagu-Chelmsford Report (1918) that formed the basis of the Government of India Act (1919).

During the interwar years India remained the symbolic jewel in the British Crown. There were powerful political, social and economic reasons that prevented the immediate granting of full independence. Despite a deteriorating position, the net balance in trade in 1924 still stood at £75 million in Britain's favour. Politically, ending British rule in India was tantamount to Britain losing her Empire and becoming 'straight away a third-rate power'.[84]

In 1924 MacDonald made clear his government's policy in India. To his party's opponents – from Indian nationalists and their socialist sympathisers in the British Labour Party to Tory grandees determined to preserve the British Empire – he declared that: 'No party in Great Britain will be cowed by threats of force or by policies designed to bring Government to a standstill; and if any sections in India are under the delusion that this is not so, events will sadly disappoint them.'[85]

Elsewhere in the world, Labour's cautious approach to imperial affairs also stressed continuity with Conservative policy rather than political change. In Parliament Labour ministers – particularly Lord Thomson and William Leach – came under pressure over the RAF bombing of native villages near Basra in Iraq in its peace-keeping role against border tribes under the British mandate of Mesopotamia.[86] The unrelenting campaign by the *Daily Herald*, under the management of the East End socialist MP, George Lansbury, against this British action which had killed 146 men and 127 women coincided with the public announcements at the close of the successful Inter-Allied Conference. There was an angry reaction from MacDonald, who suspected the newspaper – which had been under the ownership of the TUC and the Labour Party – of conducting a campaign on behalf of British Communists.[87]

After visiting the Middle East in 1921, MacDonald wrote about his experiences in Egypt and Palestine in *A Socialist in Palestine* in which he showed considerable respect for pioneering Jewish socialists and drew favourable comparisons with his version of socialist philosophy recently published in *Socialism: Critical and Constructive*. As an anti-imperialist, MacDonald adopted a realistic stance on the prickly question of Arab-Jewish relations in Palestine – support for the continuation of the British mandate, but evolution towards eventual independence for both communities. MacDonald's views on Palestine were influential in his party, despite some active lobbying in the early 1920s by both Jewish Labour MPs and Arab groups. In 1924 Labour policy in office was to maintain a non-partisan national commitment in Palestine under the British High Commissioner, Lord Samuel.[88] In Egypt, where there had been a British presence since 1882, Labour continued existing policies, though MacDonald's attempt to get an agreement with the Egyptian government over the tense question of the control of the Sudan foundered in an abortive set of talks held in London between 15 September and 3 October 1924.

V

One of the first actions of the incoming Labour government in February 1924 was to grant *de jure* recognition of the Bolshevik regime in the Soviet Union, followed by the announcement of a conference in London to straighten out unresolved differences between the two countries. MacDonald's policy of rapprochement with the USSR – to which the Labour leader was committed before taking office – contrasted noticeably with his uncompromising opposition to British Communism at home. In the 1920s, under MacDonald's leadership, the Communist Party of Great Britain's applications to affiliate to the Labour Party were firmly refused and individual Communists were eventually barred from Labour Party membership, attending as conference delegates and standing as party candidates. MacDonald had found much to sympathise with in the Menshevik regime on his visit to Georgia in 1920, unlike the new Soviet system visited by other Labour politicians.[89] However, realistically, he appreciated that the Soviet Union had to be brought back into mainstream European affairs, as well as the benefits to employment in Britain that would accrue from an expansion in Anglo-Soviet trade.

MacDonald only opened the proceedings of the Anglo-Soviet negotiations, as he was still heavily involved in the Inter-Allied Conference. The protracted and difficult dealings with Khristian Rakovsky, the formidable head of the Soviet delegation, were therefore in the hands of MacDonald's deputy, Arthur Ponsonby. He took up the claims of British bondholders about tsarist debts to bondholders with his Soviet counterpart in addition to negotiating a commercial agreement advantageous to British trade in East Europe.[90] However, it soon became apparent that only a financial loan of £30 million, probably guaranteed by the British government, would seal a commercial pact. Ponsonby kept his chief informed, but over the weeks his admiration was transformed into growing disenchantment at MacDonald's aloofness and methods of working.[91] On 30 July, after discussing the Ponsonby memorandum, the Cabinet agreed to recommend this course of action to Parliament.[92] Under the Ponsonby Protocol, these treaties were laid before the House of Commons for 21 days to be ratified after the parliamentary summer recess.

As Parliament reassembled on 30 September over the Irish boundary dispute, the Labour government's international policy and its association with the Soviet Union soon led to the downfall of MacDonald's first ministry.[93] Labour's opponents united to attack the promised loan in the Anglo-Soviet Treaties and the administration's mishandling of the withdrawn prosecution of J. R. Campbell, the acting Communist editor of the *Workers' Weekly*, for publishing an allegedly seditious appeal to British troops. The government's defence was to emphasise the commercial benefits to trade and European peace by a restoration of international relations with the Soviet Union.[94] On 22 September Asquith, the Liberal leader, denounced the treaties as 'crude experiments in nursery diplomacy',[95] though he realised there was a strong likelihood that bringing down the minority Labour government would lead to a third general election in three years for his ill-prepared party. An obdurate MacDonald stood his ground over the Soviet treaties. On 26 September he noted: 'I am inclined to give the Liberals an election on it if they force it.'[96] The next day at Derby he declared: 'An agreement with Russia on these lines . . . is now an essential part of the Labour Party's policy and if the House of Commons will not allow it, the House of Commons had better censure us.'[97] Ponsonby had advised him about the rifts in the Liberal ranks over the treaty: '[T]o reject a Treaty would be unprecedented – a most serious step to take. At the general election which would follow they would be split finally and irretrievably.'[98]

On 1 October at a party meeting the Liberals' decision to oppose the loan guarantee made the downfall of the first Labour government, and another general election, highly likely.[99] Four days later, Austen Chamberlain, the Conservative Shadow Foreign Secretary, wrote to his sister Ida: 'Meanwhile . . . I take it that we are in for a general election. I think the Govt. will be beaten on Wednesday [on the Campbell Case] – I only wish that they would accept that defeat – then, if they last so long, beaten again on the Russian Treaty . . . I find myself absolutely unable to predict what will happen.'[100] In the end, the bungled handling of the Campbell Case in October 1924 was the specific issue – made a vote of confidence at Westminster by MacDonald

– over which Britain's first Labour government fell, rather than the Anglo-Soviet Treaties. Suspicion of Communist leanings had arisen immediately Labour assumed office. This reaction to Labour in power still dogged the party during the 1924 election campaign in shape of the notorious fake Zinoviev Letter, published only five days before polling by the Tory press with allegations of a Bolshevik insurrection in Britain. This 'Red Letter' scare entered Labour mythology as the cause of the party's defeat in October 1924. Remarkably, the authenticity of the Zinoviev Letter, and conspiracy theories about White Russian émigrés, British Intelligence, the Foreign Office and the Conservative press, were still the subject of an official Foreign Office investigation after New Labour's 1997 election victory. In the main, the Zinoviev Letter has been remembered in Britain in contrast to the forgotten first Labour government and Ramsay MacDonald's creditable performance in international relations.[101]

2

'A COMMANDING GROUP'? LABOUR'S ADVISORY COMMITTEE ON INTERNATIONAL QUESTIONS 1918–31

Casper Sylvest[1]

> No Labour Party can hope to maintain its position unless its proposals are . . . the outcome of the best Political Science of the time.[2]

Looking back on his time during the interwar years as secretary for Labour's Advisory Committee on International Questions (ACIQ), Leonard Woolf (1880–1969), a man hardly prone to instinctive optimism, argued that the committee 'did influence the Party's policy occasionally in important ways'. However, Woolf's view of the influence of ACIQ was generally bleak; what the committee did achieve was 'nothing commensurate with the amount of work we [the committee] did'.[3] This view contrasts with that of David Mitrany (1888–1975), a Romanian Jew who became the foreign affairs editor at the *Manchester Guardian* in the years immediately following the First World War. Writing his intellectual autobiography in 1975, the renowned internationalist and functionalist who was a member of ACIQ during the 1920s passed the following verdict: '[I]n 1918 I was invited to serve on the newly formed Labour Party's Advisory Committee on International Affairs [*sic*], a commanding group which at the time included some of the party's leaders and a variety from within and without the party with an interest in foreign affairs.'[4] What are we to make of such judgements? Existing historiography displays the same pattern of divergence with respect to the ACIQ, although scholars that have studied the committee closely tend, inevitably perhaps, to accord it more significance. Thus, to A. J. P. Taylor the committee was 'a sort of rival foreign office'.[5] Similarly, W. P. Maddox claimed that the party was 'heavily dependent' on

ACIQ and that the committee directly formulated policy through its memoranda.[6] Others are more pessimistic.[7] In this chapter, I will contend that the committee was indeed a 'commanding group', but the reasoning behind this conclusion is perhaps less conventional: although ACIQ did have a traceable impact on the formulation of specific policies, I will argue that its wider significance lies in it being the first forum in which the Labour Party could debate and resolve (if only temporarily) its internal differences over international policy. This conclusion should not be taken to mean that other institutions were not also important for the development of Labour's foreign policy. Obviously, there was much overlap between organisations like the Union of Democratic Control (UDC) and the League of Nations Union (LNU) and the ACIQ. However, the historiography of left/progressive politics in this period has focused perhaps too exclusively on the peace movement and too little on the contribution of political parties.[8]

Since its inception the British Labour Party has defined itself as inherently and genuinely internationalist. Ninety years apart, two party leaders – Ramsay MacDonald and Tony Blair – described Labour's internationalism as 'natural' and 'instinctive'.[9] Such claims to continuity are always suspect. 'Internationalism' is a chameleon that changes with the political circumstances of the time; as a progressive ideological label the term has certain rhetorical advantages, but these may obscure its political content. It is therefore not surprising that historians are wary of claims that Labour's international policy has been consistent. Thus, in a recent centennial study of the British Labour Party, one scholar has maintained that '[i]t is arguable that the British Labour Party has never had a distinctive foreign policy'.[10] At one level this is obviously correct. The party has always been, and continues to be, riven by internal debate over foreign policy. Nevertheless, in the turbulent period between the wars the British Labour Party took advantage of a distinctive internationalist ideology which encompassed and accommodated these differences, and the developments of this period have set the terms of much debate within the party since then. This is especially the case with regard to the vexed question of the use of force: to what extent can a political party claiming commitment to an ethical foreign policy use military force? In our time the Labour Party continues to debate this question. Competing factions often base their arguments on unspoken assumptions that the authentic foreign policy legacy of the Labour Party is either pacifist and ethical or else a pragmatic mixture of realism and idealism. These internal conflicts over the meaning of internationalism have been integral to, and perhaps also constitutive of, the very internationalism that defines Labour's international outlook.

Most studies of Labour's international policy in the interwar years emphasise the dramatic (and well-known) developments of the mid- and

late-1930s, when, following heated discussion, the party came out in favour
of military sanctions and grudgingly came to accept rearmament in the face
of totalitarianism.[11] The 1920s, on the other hand, are often regarded as a
relatively calm breathing space interposed between the conflicts preceding
and following it. Henry Winkler has done much to question this narrative.
He argues that the decade following the Great War was crucial in the
development of Labour's international policy: it was during these years that
Arthur Henderson, aided primarily by Hugh Dalton and the ACIQ, confronted and to some extent convinced or silenced other internationalists
within the party, among them the party leader Ramsay MacDonald.[12]
Winkler's meticulous work and its implications have been overlooked,
receiving little attention in one of the recent accounts of Labour's international policy.[13] Drawing on and extending Winkler's work, this chapter
pays particular attention to ACIQ's influence on international political
debate within the Labour Party in a more general and subtle sense. Against
the background of a short discussion of the general features and attractions
of the ideology of internationalism for the British Labour Party, it is argued
that the vitality and composition of the ACIQ as well as the wide range of
issues that it dealt with in this period demonstrate how the new salience of
international issues in the interwar years was reflected within the party.
Finally, the essay discusses the ways in which the committee came to play a
central role in the conceptualisation and development of a distinctive yet
comprehensive ideology that should inform Britain's relations with the
wider world.

I

Viewing internationalism as a relatively open-ended and malleable ideology
is helpful in reaching an understanding of Labour's international outlook in
the 1920s (and beyond) as well as for appreciating the importance of the
ACIQ in this respect.[14] Caution is necessary here. While there is no doubt
that internal discussion, and even discord, makes it harder for the historian
or political scientist to discern a distinctive ideology, to argue that there is
no coherent Labour 'attitude' towards international politics is an exaggeration. Obviously, if it is possible to identify a distinctive internationalist
ideology, and if that encompasses some basic agreement, it may not stretch
beyond a certain ethical disposition towards the solution of international
political problems. But that is not necessarily a disadvantage. In fact,
ideological disagreements within political parties often possess the particular
advantage that they point to the fault lines *as well as* the tacit agreements.

    In late nineteenth- and early twentieth-century Britain, internationalism
appealed to progressives of all sorts and carried almost exclusively positive

connotations.[15] As always when we encounter political concepts, centrality and ambiguity go hand in hand, and internationalism was a multivalent concept. It was sometimes (and still is) viewed as a process, indicating an increase in transactions across national borders (social, cultural and economic) and pointing towards a 'destination' where states would be thoroughly interdependent. Yet restricting the concept of internationalism to this meaning obscures the fact that many politicians and intellectuals, while proclaiming that we are moving towards an internationalist world, harbour(ed) a political agenda about the desirability of this development. Although there are exceptions, it is therefore often assumed that increasing interaction among nations is a positive development leading to some kind of understanding, stability or, in a more ambitious vein, perpetual peace. At the time these processes were often exemplified by Free Trade or the development of international law. If one is interested in the structure of political ideologies the question that becomes immediately apparent is the extent to which this process can be supported, furthered, and/or helped by its promulgators. Answers to such questions can in turn tell us something about the assumptions underlying such arguments; assumptions about categories like human nature, (international) politics, and history.

By introducing the ideology of internationalism in this way, three points can be made. Firstly, at an abstract level, internationalism can be viewed as a political ideology that aims at transferring order and justice in some form – often associated with domestic politics – to the international domain.[16] Secondly, beyond this admittedly very general definition there is scope for considerable variation. The strategy of individual internationalists for realising their objectives as well as the particular configuration of a desired end-state can vary a great deal. Of particular importance for grasping the internationalism(s) prevalent within Labour is that some internationalists are extremely wary about employing military force, while others regard it as a necessary option in any sound internationalist doctrine. Further, some internationalists might look forward to a basically cosmopolitan world that leaves no room for nations or states, while others regard the nation or the state (or both) as the crucial building block. Thirdly, this working definition of internationalism saves us from stigmatising internationalism as a distinctively socialist or liberal creed. This is particularly important in analysing the internationalism of the British Labour Party, which was never exclusively socialist, in the continental tradition, nor, of course, liberal. This does not mean that ideas associated with socialist or liberal internationalism – whether in the shape of the cosmopolitanism of Marx and the Internationals or in the shape of liberal economic or rights-based arguments – had no impact on the Labour Party; they certainly did, but the party's internationalism cannot fit into these categories. In that sense, Labour's internationalism is *sui generis*.

Against this background it might seem both fruitless and conceptually quirky to attempt to analyse the internationalism of a diverse political party in a period that is renowned for its international political instability. Yet party politics is – as all politics – a complex and often contradictory affair. Thus, in the early decades of the twentieth century the ideology of internationalism was not only a popular political slogan, it was also a battle-ground for the development of a progressive foreign policy. On the face of it, this might seem discouraging, but I will suggest that it is exactly what makes ideological analysis interesting. With these clarifications in mind we can now turn to the ACIQ, its background, membership, and working methods.

II

The establishment of the ACIQ in 1918 should be seen in the context of the trend towards professionalisation in British society, and in the context of the reorganisation of the Labour Party that took place in the latter part of the Great War.[17] As John Vincent has famously argued, the Liberal Party, as it began in the 1860s, was not as such an organisation, 'but a habit of co-operation and a community of sentiment' built on the pillars of 'the new cheap Press, militant Dissent in its various forms, and organised labour' all of which were exploited cunningly by Gladstone.[18] Only gradually over the next 50 years in British politics did formal party structures and organisational patterns emerge, but the forces making for professionalisation of politics arguably accelerated in the early decades of the twentieth century. This was not only because of the heightened status of 'political intellectuals' – a development closely connected with a Fabian longing for facts and science – but part of wider pattern in British society.[19] Labour, being a relatively new party, had to consider and develop a party organisation that could keep up with modern British politics. These pressures were already felt prior to the war, when many of the organisational reforms that were implemented in the new constitution were anticipated

Yet it was not until 1918 and after his resignation from the War Cabinet, that Arthur Henderson returned to the organisational tasks of the party that aspired to become truly national.[20] One crucial and relatively new element in his approach to these questions was the Labour Party's perceived need for 'brains'; intellectuals had to be drawn into the party to support the development of sound policies.[21] Not all factions of the Labour Party had such a benevolent attitude to 'intellectuals', the trade union scepticism and sometimes even hostility to 'intellectualism' is well known. Henderson, however, found a natural ally in Sidney Webb, who was deeply involved in the reorganisation of the party. As Ross McKibbin has argued, '[t]he idea of small committees of specialists advising the national executive on all aspects of policy came from Henderson's time in cabinet office, from the experience of the war emergency committee, and, to a lesser degree, from the working traditions of the Fabian Society'.[22] Eventually nine advisory committees were set up, but the call for an advisory committee on international questions was already voiced at the 1917 party conference: 'in view of the confusion of opinion as to Foreign Policy', a resolution called for the establishment of an 'Advisory Committee, whose duty it shall be to specialise upon Diplomatic questions and Foreign Policy.'[23] The committee was not established until 1918, but it is probable that this committee, focusing on the most vital political problem of the day, fuelled support for other similar committees.

Thus, by 1918 the Labour Party had the explicit ambition of drawing on the best available political science of the day. To what extent did Labour succeed in relation to international questions? In an institutional sense, they could not. In 1918 there was no self-conscious academic discipline of International Relations.[24] Yet international questions had for a long time been discussed and debated among progressives of all sorts. Propagandists, pamphleteers, politicians, men of letters, self-styled intellectuals and academics had both prior to the war, and especially following its commencement, devoted much time to international politics mainly through the peace movement and its various organisations.[25] Parts of the written results of this effort did attempt to treat the subject 'scientifically'. Some of the most important figures in this respect were Norman Angell (1872–1967), Henry Noel Brailsford (1873–1958), G. Lowes Dickinson (1862–1932), and Leonard Woolf, all of whom became active members of the ACIQ.[26] Although we should be wary of applying our notions of social science to this period, many writings originating from this group did – alongside their often explicit political purposes – go some way towards 'theorising', and they definitely tried to systematise available knowledge. Against this background, it is hardly surprising that these figures, despite only one of them holding academic positions,[27] are widely regarded today as being the British forefathers of the academic discipline International Relations.[28] Retrospectively, at least, Labour seems to have recruited the right people.

Nevertheless, advisory committees were never thought to be ivory towers of intellectuals, occasionally able to supply some needed facts. The idea was also to have intellectuals, party staff and politicians working together in the making of policy. Although both Keir Hardie and Ramsay MacDonald were active in the pre-war peace movement,[29] the general interest of the party in foreign affairs was peripheral. Labour nodded in various directions: towards both socialist internationalism and its vision of worker solidarity and the radical tradition in British international thought. In the years prior to 1914, Labour had developed 'a fairly consistent line over foreign affairs . . . criticising the increasing division of Europe into armed camps, favouring *rapprochement* with Germany and advocating greater openness in the conduct of foreign policy'.[30] But on the whole, international matters were given less thought or importance than furthering the immediate interests of the Labour movement in Britain.[31] This was all to change dramatically during and after the war, for a number of reasons. The way the war was interpreted on the left of British politics – by supporters as well as by opponents – moved international problems to the forefront of the political agenda. Moreover, a number of discontented Liberals turned left at a time when Labour took over the role of the Liberal Party as the second tier of the two-party system. These developments constituted an opportunity for the system of advisory committees to make intellectuals, politicians and the party bureaucracy work closely together.

Thus, international problems were invested with a new significance within the Labour Party, and there were also more people in and around the party to deal with these problems. This is reflected in the variety of people affiliated with the ACIQ in the period 1918–1931. In the table below I have constructed three categories of affiliation with the ACIQ and listed some of the more prominent persons that participated in the work of the committee (Table 1).

Although the first group is obviously the most important for understanding the political developments within the committee, it should be noted that the three groups were roughly of equal size, each consisting of between 45 to 60 people. This demonstrates that the advisory committee was a vibrant forum in which more than 150 people, including more than 60 MPs, participated in one form or another over the span of 13 years. However, the core members of the committee – judged not only by their presence at meetings but also by their contribution and expertise on international questions, especially after 1922 when the committee debated the need for a 'League foreign policy' – were clearly Angell, Philip Noel-Baker (1889–1982), Noel Buxton (1888–1960), Charles Roden Buxton (1875–1942), Hugh Dalton (1887–1962), Dickinson, William Gillies (1884–1958), Mitrany, and Woolf.[33] In addition, Arthur Henderson, despite not participating in the committee's meetings, was presumably well aware of its business. In 1918 he had amended the original proposal for the establishment of ACIQ (drafted by Woolf), and stressed that the ACIQ should advise the Executive Committee '*through me* upon current international developments'.[34]

TABLE 1 – Persons affiliated with the ACIQ, 1918–1931[32]

Prominent persons in this group	
1. Present at one meeting in more than three separate years	Mr. Norman Angell, Prof. P. Noel-Baker, Prof. C. R. Beazley, Dr. E. Bentham, Mr. H. N. Brailsford, Mr. C. Delisle Burns, Mr. C. R. Buxton, Mr. Noel Buxton, Mr. G. D. H. Cole, Mr. Hugh Dalton, Mr. G. Lowes Dickinson, Mr. W. Arnold Forster, M. W. Gillies, Miss A. Susan Lawrence, Mr. Ramsay MacDonald, Mr. D. Mitrany, Mr. O. Mosley, Mr. A. Ponsonby, Mr. Sidney Webb, Mr. L. S. Woolf, Mr. G. Young.
2. Present at one meeting in more than one year but less than four separate years	Mr. J. L. Hammond, Mr. G. Lansbury, Mr. E. D. Morel, Prof. Bertrand Russell, Mr. S. Saklatvala, Mr. Arnold Toynbee.
3. Present at meetings during one year only	Mr. A. Greenwood (MP), Mrs. Sidney (Beatrice) Webb, Mr. A. E. Zimmern.

Usually the committee met fortnightly to discuss a prepared memorandum and/or current international political developments. The turnout for meetings varied. In the early years, this was sometimes a problem, and a few meetings were cancelled as a result. However, the most experienced members soon learned when it was important to be present. Thus, at a meeting in 1927, when a debate raged over military sanctions and disarmament, no less than 18 people were present. Often members were aware of the main subjects of discussion at coming meetings. Memoranda seem to have been prepared by people who took special interest in a subject or alternatively by whoever had the time and resources. However, some of the most interesting memoranda – for example on the peace terms and the party's attitude towards the League of Nations – stemmed from small sub-committees in which Angell, Brailsford and Woolf often figured. The memoranda varied in quality and length, which reflected the vast range of issues that the committee subjected to scrutiny. It was in the nature of the committee's work that there were papers on specific contemporary international political problems (the coal situation, the supply of milk, famine in Europe, the Ruhr situation, and so on) alongside more general and principled themes like the peace terms, the League of Nations, the signing of the optional clause (in the Statute of the Permanent Court of International Justice), and the overall foreign policy of the party. To some extent this diversity was both the strength and the weakness of the committee, and it goes some way towards explaining why an institution like the ACIQ proved particularly helpful within the Labour Party. It brought in experts and their much needed facts, which in turn attracted other experts. This cycle ensured that the committee was competent and that there was a valuable intellectual exchange.

However, the ACIQ also experienced setbacks. At the outset advisory committees were under little direct control. On the one hand this freedom was beneficial, because the committee could devote its energies to the subjects that its members deemed most important. On the other hand, relative independence also entailed the risk that the work of the committee would not be utilised properly or might simply be overlooked. This seems to have been the case in 1920, when a letter to the Executive Committee complained that '[w]e are far from being satisfied that the best use is being made of the work done by this Committee. In particular it stands in no relation to the Parliamentary Party, and is unable to give effective help.'[35] In retrospect, Leonard Woolf also remarked that many members were 'habitually disappointed with result of their labours'.[36] Until 1920 the ACIQ's work was coordinated by G. D. H. Cole, the provocative guild socialist in charge of the Labour Research Department, who certainly did little to restrain or control the committees.[37] The committees were responsible to the National Executive and the General Council, but it was unclear how much policy-initiative they had, and generally it seems that the system had limited effect as MPs and the party in general failed to utilise it properly.

Relative independence was ended during the first Labour government, when the National Joint Council decided that 'the Committees did not have the power of independent access and their work was to be supervised more closely by the two executives in the future'.[38] Also, it is important to stress that the ACIQ faced political constraints, especially during the first Labour government. According to David Mitrany, '[i]t was hard on the Committee that it was left virtually dormant during the short life of the first Labour Government because Ramsay MacDonald felt it improper to let the view of an unprofessional body meddle in the making of foreign policy'.[39] This was all to change when Arthur Henderson went to the Foreign Office in 1929: 'he sent word that he would welcome any papers or views and would let his Under-Secretary, Dr Dalton, come to us whenever the Committee might be concerned about some particular issue'.[40] Thus, the preconditions for the committee actually meeting its objectives varied considerably over the years.

III

When the ACIQ was established, the main fault line among internationalists was whether the war had been legitimate, and as we shall see, many differences that arose in the first few months of the war, resurfaced later and continued to structure ideological debate within the committee and the party at large. Yet this should not blind us to the considerable ideological unity in ACIQ. Unity was, paradoxically perhaps, especially strong in the years immediately following the war. Thus, the committee reflected internationalist ideology in a broad sense; so broad, arguably, that it could attract all shades of opinion within the party. There is no shortage of internationalist refrains from this period, but one is particularly helpful in teasing out what this ideological convergence consisted of. In 1915, Arthur Greenwood (1880–1954), who was later to become deputy leader of the Labour Party and a member of Churchill's War Cabinet, had just left an appointment as lecturer in economics at Leeds University and moved to London where he became secretary to the Council for the Study of International Relations. Examining the political philosophy of the German historian Henirich von Treitschke (1824–96) in the pages of the *Political Quarterly*, he argued that it led to three deductions about the state:

> [F]irst, that the State is supreme and that there can be no organisation above it; second, that 'might is right'; third, that the rule of law is impossible. The opposing view considers the State as the political organisation of a nation (or a group of nations) contributing its quota to the progress of mankind, reaching out beyond the confines of the State to humanity, implying organisation for peace and not for war. The two views are diametrically opposed: one is competitive, the other co-operative; one is undemocratic in essence, the other democratic; one stands for the rule of force, the other for the rule of law; one represents national individualism, the other national socialism. The second conception takes us along the along the road towards inter-nationalism. The kernel of the word internationalism is 'nation'; it has, however, been frequently misused in the sense of cosmopolitanism.[41]

Although Greenwood did play a role in the development of Labour's foreign policy in the interwar years, it was not a major one.[42] Yet, this quotation captures the most important themes necessary for understanding the international political ideas of the Labour Party in the decade following the Great War. By analysing Greenwood's hymn to internationalism I want specifically to make two related points: firstly, the internationalist convictions that dominated the ACIQ from the outset were not confined to

Labour ideology (however that might be defined). Rather, prior to and during the Great War, internationalism constituted an attractive set of beliefs about the pressing problems of international politics that cut across party lines, although it was mainly to be found among progressives. Secondly, while the positive content of the internationalist ideas that dominated the ACIQ are undoubtedly important, when Liberals, socialists and radicals joined hands within the Labour Party its negative dimension – that against which internationalist ideas gained their identity – became, perhaps inevitably, the most striking feature of this ideology. To some extent it was possible for internationalists to gloss over their internal differences by employing a breathtaking set of oppositions in order to define their creed. As a consequence the kernel of internationalism was openness in foreign policy (against the secrecy of traditional diplomacy), the rule of law (against autocracy), a peaceful attitude in international politics (against the belligerence of aristocrats and militarists), a moderate nationalism (against its vulgar patriotic form at home and abroad), and, above all, a political moralism that recognised duties to other nations and humanity at large (against Germans, the designers of the vindictive peace, and/or imperialists of all sorts). Beneath this simplistic and negative creed we find an over-arching orientation towards 'peace' – a rather under-theorised concept at the time – and a steadfast belief that progress for humankind, despite the enormous setback represented by the war, was possible and necessary. These oppositions were invariably reflected in the work of the committee: memoranda were produced on reform of the foreign services, disarmament, and on 'A Deliberative Assembly as Part of the Machinery of the League of Nations', and so on. Especially in the early years, when Labour did not yet face the opportunity of government and when the vindictive peace settlement was concluded at Versailles, an ethical internationalism along these lines was dominant.[43] Thus, during and immediately after the war, internationalists generally supported the idea of a league of nations. After such a league had become reality in what was perceived to be a perverted form, internationalists generally mocked it. Thus, in July 1920 a letter from the ACIQ argued that the League was condemned to 'a shadowy and hypocritical futility' as a result of its obligation to administer 'these impossible Treaties'.[44]

The differences among the leading members of the ACIQ became clearer as the 1920s unfolded. Initially, as one would expect, the most obvious difference was between those internationalists who had supported the war and those who had (with varying degrees of intensity) opposed it. As with so many other foreign-policy splits within Labour in this period, Arthur Henderson and Ramsay MacDonald epitomised these positions. Yet, as we saw above, at least until 1922–23 these internal differences among internationalists played a minor role. When they could no longer be glossed over, the ACIQ became the battleground where the principles guiding Labour's international policy were debated. A recent study of the Labour Party in the 1920s focuses on the various identities that made up the party and which set the terms for concord and conflict.[45] This approach is helpful for our purposes, but some caveats should be kept in mind. Firstly, like the identities structuring domestic and party-internal debates, the internationalist identities within the Labour Party were far from stable or clear-cut. Secondly, the two types of identities are not homologous. Although one party identity (e.g. 'trade union') might often lead to a particular internationalist identity, this was never a one-way street. Nevertheless, I will try to indicate the most important internationalist identities inside (and outside) the ACIQ in the mid-1920s. This is important, because these identities continued to structure party debate right up to the Second World War (and arguably we still find resonances of these today). In this sense, the ACIQ was a crucible, or perhaps more accurately a laboratory, of internationalist debate within the Labour Party.

At the risk of simplifying the ideological debate, it is helpful briefly to sketch these identities according to their institutional/ideological roots, their leading promulgators, and their attitudes towards the most important international political problems of the day – the League of Nations and the relationship between security and disarmament.[46]

TABLE 2 – Internationalist identities in the Labour Party in the 1920s

Identity	Institutional, ideological origins	Promulgators
Isolationist (liberal)	UDC, ILP	MacDonald, E.D. Morel.
Pacifist	Peace movement generally, religion, UDC	Ponsonby, C. R. Buxton (Lansbury)
Pragmatic (liberal)	1) War-time intellectual debates, LNU/UDC 2) Trade unions (support for/acceptance of the war)	1) Woolf, Angell, Dickinson 2) Henderson (Dalton, Ernest Bevin, Walter Citrine).

Here I can only illustrate (rather than demonstrate) the characteristics of these identities. *Isolationist (liberal) internationalism* was to a large extent a legacy of the UDC's war-time programme, which rested on severe criticism of existing practices but only some rather vague thoughts about the implications of a future reconstruction of international politics. Both of its leading promulgators inside the party (and occasionally inside the ACIQ) displayed a rather curious mix of internationalism and isolationism. They supported the League of Nations, but not necessarily as a political institution vested with powers to enforce its decisions. Rather, this strand of internationalism believed in peace as resulting from interaction between nations rather than governments. In short, the League was viewed more as an *arena* than an institution. As MacDonald argued in 1924, '[i]n the whole of our policy we should aim at bringing all the nations of Europe into the companionship upon which we are to depend for the fullness of our international life – including trade and commerce – and peace'.[47]

Pacifist internationalism had strong affinities with isolationist internationalism, but it was distinct in the sense that it saw disarmament and the renunciation of military force as the overriding ideological objective of internationalism. Arthur Ponsonby and C. R. Buxton both exemplify this position in the 1920s, which in the 1930s was promulgated in more religious terms by Lansbury. In the mid-1920s pacifism (strictly speaking an anachronistic term, which was not yet associated exclusively with the renunciation of military force) was forced to confront the problem of security. This dilemma was expressed forcefully in 1927 by C. R. Buxton, when in a memorandum to the ACIQ, he asked '[s]hould we reconsider our attitude on the whole question of Military and Naval Sanctions? Many of us would give a great deal to be able, conscientiously, to make a pacifist declaration . . . We cannot do so because we are supporters of the Covenant.'[48] This strand of internationalism was a formidable, if subtle, obstacle to the pragmatic strand, which saw security – and with it the obligations of the covenant – as a precondition of disarmament and peace. As Leonard Woolf argued in his autobiography, '[t]here was within [the Labour Movement] a strong pacifist element, derived in part from the tradition of the traditional internationalism of the Labour and Socialist movements of the nineteenth century, and in part from the strong liberal contingent which, with the break up of the Liberal Party after the war, had joined the Labour Party . . . The [pacifist] dilemma and the disagreement were for years habitually and discreetly ignored or glossed over.'[49] Already in 1927, David Mitrany, another influential intellectual, predicted that 'the Labour movement is likely to be split on this issue, unless the various strands are reconciled in time'.[50]

The third *pragmatic (liberal)* strand of internationalism continuously attempted to win over the two other groups to their position by phrasing their policies in terms that appeared acceptable. Often, arguments in favour of sanctions were discrete, stressing the obligation of the Labour Party to the League of Nations as a general idea. The precondition of these arguments succeeding was the development of a 'League foreign policy', the debate on which was instantiated in the ACIQ in 1923 following a memorandum on the League of Nations drafted by Angell, Morel, Young and Woolf. Yet even before that time, Woolf and Angell demonstrated their support for the League and its sanctions. In *The Fruits of Victory* (1921), for example, Angell argued that '[c]oercion has its place in human society, and the considerations here urged do not imply any sweeping theory of non-resistance'.[51] Similarly, in relation to disarmament Woolf argued in a memorandum in 1922 that,

> [t]he guarantee which the league must give its members is as follows:- It will guarantee each of its members that all other members will come to its assistance, if it is subjected to any act of aggression or warlike act . . . by any other state which has refused to submit or has not submitted a dispute to pacific settlement in accordance with the League's obligations. It is only if the League has . . . established this universal guarantee that it can then proceed to a large and universal measure of disarmament.[52]

Neither Woolf nor Angell was unswervingly tied to this position over the following years, and they certainly, if only occasionally, discussed the sanctions of the League as if they were merely hypothetical. To some extent this can be explained by their attempt to win the support of other factions of the party or the peace movement. However, some equivocation in their internationalist beliefs – between instinctive sympathy for the pacifist message and the no-nonsense, pragmatic defence of the League – cannot be ruled out. On the whole, however, there is little doubt that during the 1920s Woolf and Angell emerged as supporters of Arthur Henderson – the ghost of the ACIQ – who from as early as 1919 argued for a system of 'pooled security'.[53] Throughout his career, Henderson 'combined a sensitivity to trade union priorities with a concern for party unity',[54] and this seems also to have been the case with respect to international questions. As a supporter of the war (like the trade union leaders), he tried slowly to persuade various sections of the party. Although bypassed as Foreign Secretary in the first Labour government, he finally had his time in the second, when his aide Hugh Dalton and intellectuals in the ACIQ had largely managed to win over opinion to pragmatic internationalism.[55]

IV

It is important to stress that the ACIQ was of a different nature than organisations like the UDC or the LNU. It was less public, and it sought to influence policy making in a much more direct, but also more subtle, way. Thus, when one member, George Young, referred to the committee and its preparation of a programme (presumably on foreign policy) in public, '[t]he Committee drew attention to the fact that the Committee is an advisory committee to the Executive Committee and the documents prepared by the Committee are confidential'.[56] In fact, there was an air of privilege and secrecy to be found in some of the early memoranda contributed to the committee, and there is no question that the members of the committee thought that Labour was being informed by the best political science of the time. The ACIQ readily accepted that it had this potential. Thus, it was not only argued that '[t]he common criticism, by those who are opposed to Labour, that the Labour Party is totally uninstructed in Foreign affairs is, to say the least, curiously uninformed',[57] but also that the reason foreign policy was so unsatisfactorily controlled and conducted was that 'we English would always sooner be governed by a gentleman than a genius'.[58] This self-confidence on behalf of the committee and its members gradually faded, but this should not distract us from the political and ideological importance of the committee.

A close study of the minutes and memoranda of the ACIQ offers support for the conclusion that the ACIQ – and especially its leading intellectuals – was helpful in developing a 'League foreign policy' which included support for (military) sanctions against recalcitrant powers, i.e. a system of collective (or pooled) security.[59] Yet, the ACIQ arguably performed a role of even deeper significance. This emerges if we make a distinction between immediate and underlying influence. 'Influence' is notoriously difficult to trace in any kind of history, and perhaps especially in political and intellectual history. What amount of personal association, political convergence, or intellectual sympathy is required before we can pass a verdict of influence? The impossibility of supplying any adequate answer to such a question should make us cautious. Yet by emphasising social structure – understood as institutionalised restraints and opportunities, and institutionalised methods of debating and altering interests and arguments – we are directed towards a kind of influence that is different from the immediately detectable.[60] The influence of the ACIQ was underlying in the following sense: the committee provided a testing ground for ideological arguments and for internal party debates on foreign policy, which in turn prepared the various strands for the ideological debates that were to come. In short, the ACIQ functioned as a 'school' of internationalism within the Labour Party.

Yet it was not an indoctrinating school; rather, within certain limits, members of the ACIQ had to write their own textbooks. This meant that the fault lines among internationalists were identified, and that ways of overcoming or neglecting them were developed. Despite the disagreements on foreign policy in the interwar years – where sometimes one internationalist identity, sometimes the other, had the upper hand – there was a constant appeal to a shared ethical internationalism. Thus, the committee performed a central role in conceptualising and constantly negotiating a distinctive yet comprehensive Labour ideology with regard to international politics. It is in this sense, I will argue, that the ACIQ can rightfully be termed 'a commanding group.'

No aspect of the ideological inheritance of the British Labour Party remains so elusive and little understood as the party's approach to the wider world. Although the analytical value of the label 'idealism' is highly suspect, as I have argued elsewhere,[61] academics, political analysts and newspaper editors often use this term to capture the party's international policy. Thus, when Tony Blair's government entered office in 1997 and proclaimed that it would supply 'an ethical content to foreign policy and [recognise] that the national interest cannot be defined only by narrow realpolitik', this initially seemed to confirm a certain settled, if vague, interpretation about Labour and foreign policy.[62] However, Blair's actions and policies since the proclamation of this policy (of which we hear little these days) could, and have been, interpreted both as deviating from or supplying a missionary element to that ethical foreign policy.[63] Often these divergences centre on the use of force. How is the use of military force compatible with an ethical foreign policy, if at all? The debate over this question is heated and polemical. Yet, when we encounter the claims to tradition voiced by the participants in such debates – claims about Labour's pacifist, pragmatic, or even realist heritage – we should acknowledge that these claims themselves can claim a long heritage. As I have argued in this chapter internal conflicts over Labour's foreign policy are longstanding, and we continue to find rudiments of earlier debates in contemporary political argument. This kind of political debate among fellow internationalists is integral to Labour's international outlook. Finding the right balance between ethics and force is an intricate problem, and it would be unrealistic, and indeed politically naïve, to expect the Labour Party to resolve it any time in the near future.

3

LABOUR'S POLITICAL THOUGHT: THE SOVIET INFLUENCE IN THE INTERWAR YEARS

Jonathan Davis

There has always been a tendency in the Labour Party to look to the wider world to see what lessons could be learned from other social democratic and socialist parties. In recent history, Tony Blair turned to Bill Clinton's Democrats and Paul Keating's Australian Labor Party in the 1990s and New Labour was born. After the First World War, Labour used the German SPD as an organisational model.[1] And after the revolutions in Russia in 1917, Labour focused its attention on the construction of Soviet socialism in the former land of the tsars. In the interwar years the USSR became a key definer of Labour's political thought as its gradualist socialist traditions were challenged by the radicalism of the Soviet experiment. Yet because of the ways Labour used the USSR in the interwar years, the challenge from revolutionary socialism *confirmed* rather than replaced Labour's fundamental beliefs. This was a crucial period in which the Soviet Union played a hugely influential role in shaping Labour's political identity, which remained largely unchanged until the 1980s.

Labour's political thought was shaped by many traditions including Fabianism, Labourism, ethical socialism, radical Liberalism and Marxism, and this led to the emergence of a loose collection of socialist ideals rather than a distinct socialist philosophy.[2] This allowed the party to march forward under the all-embracing banner of 'socialism', even though socialism itself was interpreted in many different ways. It is therefore unsurprising that Soviet socialism would also share this trait, and the USSR became all things to all people: trade unionists were interested in workers' control; economists questioned the virtues and possibilities of a planned economy; feminists assessed whether women's lives had been improved. Soviet socialism also promised freedom to Labour's libertarians, equality to egalitarian socialists and even socialism 'from above' to advocates of a managed transfer of power. However, while many saw the Soviet Union as a model socialist state which could be used as a positive example of how to build socialism, Ramsay MacDonald had little time for Soviet socialism, completely rejecting the extremism of Bolshevism after his trip to Menshevik Georgia in 1920.[3] In the 1930s, moderate party members (including the leadership that was guided in no small part by the trade unionists Ernest Bevin and Walter Citrine) portrayed the Soviet Union as a demon dictatorship that shared much with Nazi Germany and was therefore a danger to liberal democracy. Labour's pragmatists believed that this had to be made safe before any steps towards socialism could be taken, if indeed that was the aim.

As most party members saw Parliament as the only legitimate source of governing and of implementing Labour's programme, the means of change were rarely questioned. The real differences of opinion often concerned capitalism – should Labour work to reform or replace it? This question became even more relevant to British socialists after the Russian Bolsheviks swept tsarism and the emerging capitalist system away. This gave a more radical edge to Labourites' discussions about what they would do when they got into power. Pragmatists advocated a more cautious reform programme than the idealists would have liked, as left-wingers were united by the ideal of replacing capitalism, although not necessarily by the details of what would come next. However, 'socialism' tied moderates and radicals to the Labour Party, and, as one pamphlet declared in 1939, '[i]t is indeed true that Socialism is the basis of the Labour Party's faith'.[4]

Whether Labour was a socialist party by 1939 is open to question, but it is certainly true that by the end of the 1930s its political thought was more defined than it had been since 1931, and this was because of the ways in which Labour responded to the Soviet Union when it was in and out of power. There were three main ways that the USSR helped to define Labour's own ideas, all of which are assessed here. The first response was pragmatic, characterised by Ramsay MacDonald's approach to international affairs when in government. Although the Soviet Union's employment of undemocratic practices was contentious, it was a secondary concern when considering the state of Britain's economy or the precarious nature of post-war international relations.

The second response was clearly positive, as Soviet socialism inspired Labour's political thought where economics and foreign policy were concerned. Labour's economists assessed information about Stalin's Five Year Plan and what it could offer Britain's economy and workers, while the Soviet Union's entry into the League of Nations was wholeheartedly welcomed. Yet this attitude concerned Labour's moderate leadership and this provoked the third response, as Bevin, Citrine and Arthur Henderson used the USSR in a distinctly negative way. They rejected various advances from the Kremlin-backed Communist Party of Great Britain (CPGB)[5], as its revolutionary politics were alien to Labour's own reformism. The leadership also had to counter the Tory allegations that Labour was little more than a British Bolshevik party. This meant that, in some ways, Labour defined itself by proving what it was *not*, thus helping it to confirm its gradualist, reformist nature. The USSR was used as a warning against extremism, and party members were urged to reject Communism in all its forms.

The USSR was a constant factor in the party's decision-making process throughout the interwar years. It played a key role as Labour's political thought became clearer, and what emerged was a party that defined itself largely by what it *rejected* from the Soviet experiment. However, this does not suggest that the USSR offered no positive contributions to Labour's political thought, but rather that the negatives outweighed these positives.

I

Soon after the first Russian revolution in February 1917, more than one thousand socialists from all over Britain gathered in Leeds for a special convention where the end of tsarism was celebrated and Labour's relationship with Russian politics entered a new phase. The *Daily Herald* sponsored the Leeds meeting, claiming that it would hail the Russian Revolution as the 'first representative gathering of the British Labour Movement to express unqualified approval of what the socialists of Russia have accomplished'.[6]

Although the Labour Party was not officially represented, Ramsay MacDonald and Philip Snowden both attended, and they were both excited about being there. MacDonald congratulated the Russians for their revolution, and declared that this would allow the initiative once again to pass back to organised labour in Britain.[7] He was reflecting upon a mood that had inspired what the *Labour Leader* called 'Magnificent Labour Demonstrations in Britain', referring to Glasgow as the 'British Petrograd'. The newspaper claimed that 'Glasgow and Petrograd, the Clyde and the Neva, were linked together . . . in the bonds of International Brotherhood.'[8]

Philip Snowden claimed that the meeting in Leeds was a ' . . . spontaneous expression of the spirit and enthusiasm of the Labour and Democratic Movement'.[9] British workers' attitudes had shifted leftwards during the First World War and the Russian Revolution added to this more radical mood at demonstrations and meetings. According to Bill Jones, Leeds 'marked the catalytic effect which events in Russia were having upon Labour's thinking, particularly on foreign policy'.[10] Yet despite the wave of militancy, the Labour Party retained its belief in reformist politics and parliamentary tactics, and Lenin's seizure of power in October did little to change this.

The response from Labourites to the second revolution was less enthusiastic. Jones notes that there was a general feeling of regret that 'the frail flower of Western-style democracy should have been crushed so soon . . . '[11] The Webbs found the aggressive nature of Bolshevism alien to their approach while J. R. Clynes described the Bolsheviks' methods as 'vicious, unjust, tyrannical and dictatorial'.[12] Lenin's victory did inspire Labour however, as the overtly socialist demand for workers to have the 'full fruits of their industry' and the 'ownership of the means of production', was made in Clause IV of the party's new constitution. This has been interpreted in different ways, being seen as nothing more than a cynical means of staving off revolution,[13] the culmination of the various strands of Labour's socialism, complementing the existing ideas and practices,[14] or a way of breaking with the Liberals that offered a generic promise of reform to 'a disparate constituency that included sceptical trade unionists, workers who might be drawn to the new Communist Party and middle-class "progressives"'.[15]

These interpretations are all relevant: the timing of Clause IV certainly suggests that its socialist content was a reaction to Lenin's actions in Soviet Russia, acting as a way of preventing calls for more radical (even revolutionary) politics from Labour reformers. But it was also a confirmation of the general ideals of the Labour Party that sought to draw upon Labour's varied traditions whilst appealing to as many groups as possible.[16] This was evident in *Labour and the New Social Order* which promised employment, nationalisation, social welfare and education for all. It is of course debatable whether the Fabian Sidney Webb – who had a big hand in the drafting of both Clause IV and *Labour and the New Social Order* – would have gone quite so far had Russia not taken such a dramatic turn to the left.

While Soviet socialism was already influencing Labour's ideas, the actions of the British government in the Russo-Polish War inspired Labourites to come to the aid of their eastern comrades, as after the First World War they accepted that Russian matters were for Russians to deal with. This was first reflected in the 'Hands off Russia' campaign that included the London dockers' refusal to load munitions onto the *Jolly George* ship bound for Poland, as these weapons were part of the Allied contribution to the intervention against the Bolsheviks. And it continued as members of the Trades Union Congress (TUC)-Labour Party delegation who visited Soviet Russia in 1920 blamed the intervention for the country's problems (although Ethel Snowden also made it clear that Bolshevism was not the answer to these problems).[17] From this came the Councils of Action, established by the trade unions to enable organised labour to stop any further anti-Bolshevik military activity in Poland. The British labour movement was clear – Soviet Russia must be allowed to deal with her own situation.

This was an instinctive revival of the international solidarity that had suffered so profoundly before and during the First World War. Yet Ramsay MacDonald, Labour's first Prime Minister, did not make dealing with the Soviet Union a cornerstone of his foreign policy because of a shared sense of socialist internationalism. Instead he looked at the situation in a much more pragmatic way, seeing the USSR as a country that could bring vital trade to an economy still suffering from the effects of the war. MacDonald was primarily concerned with solving the problem of unemployment in Britain and helping to stabilise the post-war peace in Europe through the League of Nations, and he saw the USSR as an important part of his plans to achieve these aims. The resumption of economic and diplomatic relations with the Kremlin was therefore considered crucial, and MacDonald told Khristian Rakovsky, the head of the Soviet delegation to Britain, that he had been 'advocating the recognition of the Soviet Government for some years' and it was therefore 'a source of personal gratification to me to receive you here to-day'.[18] However, this was not because of a shared socialist ideology but rather because it had something to offer Britain.

MacDonald was praised by the Soviets for his actions. Maksim Litvinov, the deputy Commissar for Foreign Affairs, told *Izvestiya* that MacDonald not only understood the diplomatic problems of the Soviet government, but that he had come to an appropriate conclusion.[19] And, going on something of a charm offensive, the Soviet Foreign Minister Georgy Chicherin spoke warmly about MacDonald, Keir Hardie and Britain in general. In an interview with the *Manchester Guardian* he used phrases like 'long-sighted statesmen' and 'unbreakable friendship', and he claimed that '[w]orking-class opinion and enlightened political thought are the two forces which brought about the present admirable result'.[20]

The government fell before a deal could be concluded, but the negotiations gave Labourites valuable experience of talking with the Kremlin, which was something that they could call upon when they returned to power in 1929. By that time, more Labourites had witnessed the construction of Soviet socialism for themselves, including Walter Citrine who visited the Soviet Union in 1925 and George Lansbury who went in 1926. They followed the second TUC delegation to the USSR which journeyed there just after Labour fell from power in 1924. The delegates' report added to Labour's knowledge of the Soviet system, and offered encouragement to those seeking to bring the Soviets in from the cold. It also contributed to Labour's economic ideas, as the Soviet economy had left behind the extremism of War Communism (as witnessed by the first delegation in 1920) and moved towards a more mixed economy, known as the New Economic Policy (NEP). This saw a certain amount of private trade return to the Soviet economy whilst the state retained control of the commanding heights of the economy such as large-scale strategic industry, banking and transport.[21]

Labour's travellers considered this an improvement when compared with the situation in 1920 when the more extreme policy of War Communism was still in place. They saw NEP as the first and most fundamental compromise of the Soviet regime, claiming that it had 'real vitality and stimulates the economic recovery that peace has now made possible'.[22] The idea of government intervention in the economy was gaining support in Labour's ranks as it was argued that the war years showed how planning in the economy was more beneficial and reliable than market forces. The controlled reintroduction of markets to the Soviet economy meant that its form was more social democratic than Communist and therefore became even more appealing to Labour's gradualist socialists. This interest in less radical interventionist economics was even more evident in the 1930s once the Great Depression began to end, as Sweden and the United States offered models more suitable to Labour's politics.

Labour's political thought was shaped in many ways by its dealings with the Soviet Union. It accepted some aspects of the Soviet project but rejected others, as many Labourites accepted that the USSR was developing socialism economically but rejecting it politically.[23] This understanding of the Soviet system significantly defined Labour's ideas as it was influenced by the economic side of Soviet socialism far more than it was by the political side: it could embrace the concept of planning and state intervention in the economy, but it could never accept revolution as a way to achieve power or soviets as a way of running society, and this fact became even more evident in the 1930s.

But there was still widespread support for closer links with the Soviet Union in the 1920s, and after the breach in diplomatic relations with the USSR in 1927, Labour made it clear that it would restore relations and renew trade talks at the first opportunity. *Labour and the Nation* stated that a Labour government would remain opposed to Soviet interference in other nations' domestic politics, but would also take immediate steps to establish diplomatic and commercial relations with the USSR, to ' . . . settle by treaty or otherwise any outstanding differences, and would make every effort to encourage a revival of trade with Soviet Russia'.[24] And the party's 1929 general election manifesto declared that Labour would re-establish diplomatic and economic links with the Kremlin. The *New Leader* echoed

MacDonald's hopes, calling for diplomatic relations to be restored 'first, because it is a simple act of justice and common sense; second because the development of Russian trade is urgently needed; and third because normal relations with Russia are so essential to peace'.[25]

Interestingly, there was no mention of a shared interest in socialism from this left-wing newspaper, which offered pro-Soviets like Anna Louise Strong a platform from which to sing Stalin's praises. This suggests that there was a realisation from some in Labour's ranks that a practical policy pursued by both sides was all that could be hoped for. Similarly, Soviet foreign policy was becoming concerned less with the desire to spread revolution and more with the need to acquire manufactured goods. In a move that vindicated MacDonald's policy of working with the Kremlin, the Soviets welcomed British industrialists to Moscow just prior to the election in 1929.

The Labour supporting *Daily Herald* devoted much space to this visit, believing that 'important negotiations were to be entered into'[26] and Ernest Remnant of the Trade Delegation said that they were 'naturally hopeful of success'.[27] The Soviets welcomed the arrival of representatives of British industry to Moscow,[28] but Georgy Pyatakov, the acting Chairman of the Soviet State Bank and member of the People's Commissariat for Finance, commented that any future trade between the USSR and Britain was impossible without the restoration of normal diplomatic relations. *Pravda* also hoped that the delegation would conclude that the resumption of diplomatic relations was essential.[29] Ramsay MacDonald agreed, stating that '[e]veryone knows that British engineering and other manufacturing concerns are not merely desirous of obtaining Russian orders, but are positively anxious to get them. It is all a question of conditions.'[30] He said that it was Labour's contention 'that the fullest and most complete diplomatic intercourse should be resumed at once'[31] as this was the only way to have any complaints satisfactorily met.

The 1920s was a decade in which Labour made some progress, particularly in establishing itself as the main party of opposition and also in foreign affairs. While no concrete achievements were made where Anglo-Soviet relations were concerned, the fact that negotiations took place at all with an 'outcast' state was a significant step forward. It also helped that Labour was dealing with a socialist state, and the ways that the party dealt with the Soviet Union reflected its overall political thought which embraced both ideology and pragmatism. Which one of these governed the party's actions depended upon which individual or group was in control at the time. But one thing is clear – Labour's ideas and actions could be influenced by outside forces such as other models of socialism, and in the interwar years the USSR played a defining role in Labour's political thought.

II

Despite the rivalry between Arthur Henderson and Ramsay MacDonald, when the latter chose his second Cabinet in 1929, Henderson was sent to the Foreign Office to continue the pro-Soviet policy that had been so important in 1924. The USSR's markets were still seen as an answer to British economic problems, and working with the Kremlin, rather than against it, seemed to be best for the wider cause of peace and stability. Henderson's knowledge of Russian affairs, and his desire for peace through the League of Nations, shaped Labour's foreign policy until the government fell in 1931. He maintained that 'Russia, with its vast population, cannot be permanently ignored; only by diplomatic and other intercourse with her will it be possible to bring her once more into the family of nations.'[32] Like his Prime Minister, the new Foreign Secretary sought to use the USSR in a largely practical way to solve unemployment in Britain and help pursue peace and stability in Europe.

There were early problems for Henderson where dealing with the Soviet Union was concerned. The first was an issue for the Home Office to deal with, but one that had a possibility of derailing Henderson's hopes for the USSR. Stalin's nemesis Leon Trotsky applied for political asylum after he was exiled from the Soviet Union. While liberal leftists and socialists called for Trotsky's wish to be granted, the Kremlin would have perceived his acceptance as a hostile act. While Labour was wary of offering residence to a figurehead of the internationalist movement who had been a fierce critic of the party's leaders in the early 1920s, it would also have been impossible to negotiate seriously with Stalin's Foreign Ministry while simultaneously giving refuge to his greatest political rival. It was believed that successful negotiations with the USSR would bring their own rewards for the good of Britain as a whole.

Henderson also had to deal with constraints from his own Chancellor and leader. Philip Snowden needed to prove that this government could not be accused of scaring the City, and therefore ruled out credit loans to the USSR, while MacDonald promised that the government would not permit the exchange of ambassadors without the approval of Parliament. Henderson disagreed with this approach but knew that he could not go back on this statement without running the risk of being attacked in the press. Dalton felt that MacDonald was wrong to give this supplementary answer to the House, but realised that, for the same reasons that Henderson gave, the Foreign Secretary could not go back on it. Despite his doubts, Henderson conveyed this message to Valeryan Dovgalevsky, the USSR's ambassador to France, when they met in London in July. Dovgalevsky replied with the disappointing news that the Kremlin did not expect the question of resuming diplomatic relations to be dependent upon resolving the issues of tsarist debts and Comintern propaganda, and left Britain without further discussion.

The final problem Henderson had to contend with came when King George V made it clear that he was upset that official relations had not been restored before the term 'ambassador' was used (Henderson and Dovgalevsky used the term when they met). The King was not pleased at the thought of friendly courtesies being given to ministers from the USSR who 'if they did not actually plan, certainly approved of the brutal murder of the King's first cousins, the late Emperor and Empress of Russia'.[33] The Foreign Office replied on Henderson's behalf, reminding the King that the majority returned to the House of Commons represented the importance in ending Soviet isolation.[34]

Henderson was intent on pursuing this line and his Soviet policy was concerned with the short-term aim of concluding a trade deal that would help Britain's economy, and the long-term aim of strengthening the League of Nations which he believed would be the case if the USSR joined the body. These aims reflected the reformism of Labour's politics overall which was a mixture of short-term needs and long-term hopes that would be achieved through gradualist methods. Henderson's first significant breakthrough came with Parliament's agreement to the exchanging of ambassadors in November 1929. The Soviet Union sent Grigory Sokolnikov, whilst Henderson's choice of Ambassador in Moscow followed a pragmatic line, as he chose the experienced diplomat Sir Esmond Ovey instead of a Labour politician. According to Andrew Williams, Ovey played an important role in shaping Labour's attitudes to the Soviet Union for the rest of its admini- stration. Williams claims that there was 'no evidence that Henderson doubted the truth of his despatches', that he had a 'great impact on Beatrice Webb's drift during 1930–31 towards the Soviet Union' and that he was in an ' . . . almost unique position for feeding information to the Labour Government'.[35]

With diplomatic relations restored, Henderson concluded his final task in April 1930 with a trade agreement that saw the USSR take up to £7 million of British goods while Britain took £34 million of Soviet goods. However, to maintain its economic relationship with the Kremlin, some Labourites were forced to relegate their principles and the party's traditions, as they ignored stories about religious persecution and slave labour in the USSR that were featured in the Labour press[36] and also in official correspondence from inside the country. These stories challenged Labour's ethics and principles, and forced ministers to turn a blind eye to the allegations in the press about the nature of the Soviet regime.

For example, in July 1930 Ovey wrote to Henderson from Moscow concerning the *chistka* (purge) of party workers in the CPSU. Commenting on a report from Grigory Ordzhonikidze, the Commissar for the Workers' and Peasants' Inspectorate, Ovey wrote that the purges had led to 51,000 state employees being removed from their posts. While he claimed that the 'system has certain obvious merits' (he doesn't say what these merits were), he added that 'it may easily prove in practice to be a dangerous one and is likely to lead to serious injustices . . . The idealism of the members of the "chistkas" may easily become subordinate to personal motives, and the temptation to turn a man out of his job in order to secure it for one of themselves, must be a severe one.'[37] Ovey clearly understood the nature of the Stalinist purges before they had even come close to their more infamous consequences.

The fact that the Labour leadership ignored the evidence presented to them concerning Stalinist practices highlights the MacDonald government's liberal pragmatism, as on the one hand Whitehall had to maintain trade links and diplomatic relations with the USSR whilst on the other Labour accepted that a nation had the right to conduct its own affairs (arguably the starting point for the 'Hands off Russia' campaign), even if this went against many of Labour's long-held beliefs of religious tolerance, workers' rights and political democracy. It was a difficult position to hold and the approach clearly caused problems.

Andrew Williams notes that there was 'a dialectic' between Labourites who believed that there may have been some truth in the allegations and those who were only concerned with the possible impact on domestic issues. Snowden and MacDonald, 'found themselves in the second category' while Henderson 'was in the first', and 'he probably went through agonies of conscience until he persuaded himself of the lack of truth in the allegations. A lot of people fell into both categories.'[38] Of course, a small number of people chose to believe everything that the Soviet propaganda machine fed them and ignored anyone opposing them. In the face of rising unemployment and fascist aggression in the 1930s, this ambiguous attitude to the USSR remained, for the most part, the same.

III

The contrast between how Labour used the USSR between 1929 and 1931 and after the MacDonald era could not have been greater. Both Labour governments had used the USSR in a pragmatic way, as a solution to specific problems. But after MacDonald formed the National government the party instinctively moved to the left, as if deliberately to define itself by embracing everything that their former leader was not. There was a need for the party to come out definitely in favour of socialism, and as Marx's prophecy concerning capitalism's collapse seemed ever more relevant after the Wall Street Crash, the extreme economic conditions encouraged Labour to turn to more ideological answers. This saw the Independent Labour Party (ILP) disaffiliate from the Labour Party in 1932, favouring a more radical socialism than that offered by Labour even in the initial post-MacDonald excitement. The USSR became a socialist beacon of hope in a sea of capitalist despair. It was once again more than just another country with which to trade, and many Labourites used it to find answers to the economic desperation and fascist threat.

This coincided with the need to reorganise the party after the 1931 crisis. According to Andrew Thorpe, Labour had three possible roads it could travel. It could accept that the 1931 election result could be 'written off as an aberration, a defeat due solely to special causes';[39] it could retain its gradualist approach to social reform, but clarify its relationship with capitalism; or it could call for a radical programme that rejected the old 'MacDonaldite belief in Socialism emerging painlessly from the success of capitalism' which now 'seemed nonsensical'[40] with the economic strife and the rise of fascism in Europe and Britain. The party temporarily opted for the third and most radical choice. Continuing with its traditional gradualism at that time was not a realistic approach for a party in need of a radical fix to aid the move away from the 'uninspiring . . . bankruptcy of gradualist socialism'[41] that had failed during the economic recession. Left-wingers argued that the 1931 result was the inevitable consequence of accommodating capitalism – a suggestion that was willingly accepted by many in the party. And in such a radical climate, the Soviet Union was more appealing than ever.

Yet while Soviet socialism was welcomed by many as a model of socialism in practice, it was seen as a threat to Labour's gradualists, and the initial rejection of MacDonaldism ended by the mid-1930s once it became clear that capitalism was not finally collapsing. After much initial enthusiasm for the Soviet Five Year Plan, Labour's moderate leaders used the Soviet Union and the increased activity of the CPGB to reaffirm its belief in parliamentary politics and gradual reform. However, this fight against Communist influence in the Labour movement was made harder for Bevin and Citrine by the fact that moderate leaders like Dalton (and even to some extent Citrine himself) found positive aspects in the Soviet economy, such as a lack of unemployment and a socialised industrial base.

This meant that the area in which the Soviet Union had its most positive influence on Labour's ideology was economics. Many Labourites examined the Five Year Plan and its consequences when they visited the USSR. Scores of travellers journeyed east in the 1930s, often returning with stories of happy workers and peasants who were building a new type of society. Of course others such as Malcolm Muggeridge and Walter Citrine did not share this optimism, failing to find a workers' paradise. Citrine argued that Stalin's Communist Party had become a new ruling class and confidently told factory workers in Moscow that what they called socialism was 'something which I cannot recognise as Socialism. It is certainly not Social Democracy.'[42]

Although Citrine found trade unions acting as agents of the state and no political freedom in the USSR, even he believed that a socialist economic base was being constructed (despite his concerns about the lack of workers' input or rights). Hugh Dalton shared this view, and state ownership of the means of production and planning was taken by many to mean socialism. And although Dalton found Soviet ways unsuitable for Britain in many respects, he did believe that there were lessons to be learned from the USSR. According to Ben Pimlott it was Dalton's visit to the Soviet Union in July 1932 'more than any other event in his own life' that 'fundamentally altered his attitudes towards domestic policy' as until then he had 'given little serious thought to the possibility of re-structuring the economy'.[43]

Dalton visited the USSR as a member of the New Fabian Research Bureau (NFRB) delegation in 1932 and this had a profound influence on both him and Labour's economic ideas. His experience of the Soviet economy was all the more important as he became Chancellor of the Exchequer in Clement Attlee's post-war government, which broke with the economic orthodoxy of Philip Snowden with its support for government intervention in the economy. This widespread interest in intervention led many to see Soviet planning as a solution to the problems brought on by capitalist slump at its absolute worst. G. D. H. Cole suggested that this interest crossed party lines, claiming that the Soviet Plan was a 'powerful influence on capitalist as well as socialist thought' as 'a good many people are ready to admire everything about the Russian Five Year Plan except the Socialist foundation on which it rests'.[44] In the extreme economic climate of the early 1930s it is not surprising that the Five Year Plan was seen as a shining example of a planned economy.

Upon their return, the NFRB delegates produced the report *Twelve Studies in Soviet Russia* which gave details of how planning could work. Dalton came back from the USSR convinced that it was 'better to have a plan than not',[45] claiming that 'I had caught a quick but vivid glimpse of a quite new world. And this remained with me an abiding influence.'[46] He said that he was strengthened in his belief that, 'for a community as for an individual, bold and conscious planning of life is better than weak passivity and the tame acceptance of traditional disabilities, that trial and error is better than error without trial'.[47]

One of the things that most impressed both Dalton and Citrine was the absence of unemployment in the USSR and this was something that Dalton returned to on a number of occasions, obviously affected by the dire economic situation he witnessed in Britain. He noted that most Soviet citizens looked better fed than unemployed miners back home. 'People here, I was told, were "paying a tremendous price for rapid industrialisation". But in Durham they were paying a tremendous price for nothing at all – except unemployment.'[48] Dalton claimed that the demand for labour, 'particularly in the industrial centres, is in excess of the supply, and no one need remain for more than a few days without a job. For the present at least, unemployment has been planned away.'[49]

While Dalton enthused about the 'formidable material apparatus' that 'has set going a unique type of industrial revolution . . . in its speed . . . and its planned Socialist basis',[50] he tempered any excitement with a look at the particular problems of planning. He claimed that this formidable apparatus was not organised or handled 'with any degree of efficiency' as it seemed that for most workers, 'the standard of living had fallen during the period of the Plan, partly owing to its inefficient execution, but partly because consumption has been deliberately sacrificed to construction, and light industry to heavy'.[51]

One reason for this was that the 'technique of planning has been developed empirically. There is, as yet, very little theory behind it', but he accepted this because the 'method of trial and error has been courageously applied.'[52] The exact opposite bedevilled Labour in the 1930s – members had all the time they needed to theorise about solutions to the world's problems, but no opportunity to put these solutions into action as the party as a whole stayed out of power until after the Second World War.[53] However, Labour used this long time out of office to debate and argue about policies, about its beliefs and about the very nature of its ideology. As such the 1930s became a key formative decade where Labour's socialism was concerned and the Soviet Union was a crucial definer in this process.

As part of the wider NFRB delegation, Dalton secured much information about the nature of planning in the USSR, and the lessons learnt whilst there influenced Labour's thought on economic policy in this period as 'the word "planning" took on a central place in [Dalton's] vocabulary' as 'the objectives of planning in the Soviet Union [including maintaining full employment and raising the standard of living] . . . were desirable in Britain'.[54]

Dalton was convinced that only the adoption of 'the principle of economic planning on Socialist lines' would bring the 'solution of our economic troubles'[55] and it is therefore unsurprising that Labour's 1934 programme *For Socialism and Peace* emphasised planning and the need for a socialised industrialised basis. Public control over the major industries such as steel, coal and water was now firmly part of the Labour programme. While there was no specific reference to the Soviet plan as such, its influence was clear, and this is not surprising given the fact that it was drafted by Hugh Dalton. *For Socialism and Peace* committed Labour to the idea that industry should be converted 'from a haphazard struggle for private gain to a planned national economy owned and carried on for the service of the community'.[56] The talk now was of industry being a 'public service, democratically owned and responsibly administered'.[57]

But while Dalton regarded the USSR as a system that could offer ideas to British socialists, it was clear that these ideas would need to be tailored to fit British conditions and also Labour's reformism. While the Bolsheviks had seized Russian industries from their tsarist owners, Labour spoke of compensation and rejecting violence in *Labour and the Nation*, thus highlighting the huge differences in the means advocated by Labour and those used by the Bolsheviks to achieve change. But the years of interest in Soviet planning helped to shape Labour's thinking on planning and intervention in the economy. It gave the party's economists an existing (though unfinished) model to research and learn from. But Labour's aims were still clearly at odds with Soviet socialism, and as capitalism stabilised, Labour's thinkers turned their attention to other interventionist governments which provided less radical challenges to the system. Franklin D. Roosevelt's New Deal in the United States and Sweden's social democracy softened the harsh edges of capitalism, and offered gradualist plans that sat more comfortably with Labour's own reformist socialism.[58]

Dalton retained his interest in the Soviet Plan but began to consider the differences between socialism and planning. In 1935 he wrote that socialism was 'primarily a question of ownership, planning a question of control or direction' and noted that planning was 'not necessarily in the public interest' as there could be 'private planning towards private ends and social planning towards social ends'.[59] For Labour, the general purpose of planning was 'to wage peaceful war on poverty, insecurity, social inequality, and war itself'.[60] Labour would focus on the immediate problems with no definite promise of socialism in the future. This was entirely in tune with Labour's social democratic traditions and also reflected the definition of Swedish social democracy outlined by the economic writer George Soloveytchik, who claimed that they were 'interested not in class warfare, but in general welfare'.[61]

However, the initial examination of the Soviet Five Year Plan inspired a positive response that led some party thinkers to advocate planning of some kind in Britain. Labour's advocacy of governmental intervention in *Labour's*

Immediate Programme contained measures to improve workers' standard of living, including raising wages and improving the Health Service. In terms of Labour's long-term aims G. D. H. Cole claimed that this 'was a substantial programme, not far short of what the Labour Government of 1945 was actually to put into effect'.[62] Although this party programme was not really a direct assault on the capitalist system with the aim of implementing socialism, there was a strong socialist element to it, and also 'concrete plans for the implementation of most of its policies, whereas earlier programmes had been expressions of wishes rather than plans of campaign'.[63]

By the end of the decade the belief that the next Labour government could or would introduce socialism had largely given way to the acceptance that the Keynesian approach was better than a full-scale assault on the capitalist system. But Labour's general thought now revolved around the idea that planning of some form was necessary and better than the anarchy of the free market. This allowed the long-term aims of the party to get caught between advancing to socialism and settling for a planned capitalism, and from here the mixed economy that Attlee successfully managed was born. The economic debates of the 1930s, the models the party explored and the altering conditions in this decade allowed Labour to emerge with a plan of what it wanted to do, replacing the loose collection of ideas that had guided the factions before the 1930s, and there can be little doubt that the Soviet Union was a positive exemplar in Labour's economic thought. It was the first model that the majority of party members turned to when the question of planning arose, and it instructed them in the art of planning not just an economy, but a whole society. This concept of changing the entire system appealed to more than just the economists in the party, as the idea offered hope that capitalism could be transformed in some way. In its guise as a teacher of how to plan, and as a leader out of the economic crisis of the 1930s, Labour used the Soviet Union in a positive way, as it defined the boundaries of Labour's notions about planning.

IV

It was not only in the economic sphere that Labour saw a positive use for the USSR, as many on the left also assumed that it would be part of the fight against Hitler and expansionist fascism. Moderate left-wingers welcomed the USSR's entry into the League of Nations in 1934. Hugh Dalton claimed that the Soviet Union's decision was a 'timely reinforcement to the Collective Peace system'[64] and that '[n]o friend of peace, least of all if he be a socialist, can have heard this news without a thrill of joy and hope'.[65] Left-wingers like Cripps demanded that the USSR be defended if and when attacked by Hitler. This was seen as part of a wider ideological threat to international socialism as Cripps believed that hostile capitalist states would inevitably use anything in their power to continue the struggle for supremacy of the world's markets.[66]

However, a third option made it clear that one of the most important elements of the party's international policy was to ensure stability and peace in the world. Liberal democracy had to be made safe before any transition to socialism could be considered. Arthur Henderson argued that the Soviet Union and socialism were not necessarily an integral part of Labour's plans, claiming that it had never made a policy of promoting a stable peace through permanent political institutions 'dependent upon a universal or a general change in the existing social order'.[67] Indeed, *Labour's Foreign Policy* declared that '[f]or the fulfilment of its aims, both at home and abroad, the Labour Party needs Peace throughout the world' and that Labour 'never held that the attempt to secure international co-operation must await the triumph of Socialism throughout the world'.[68]

With a section of the left denying any need for an ideological unity with the USSR on the international stage, similar demands made to counter domestic fascism caused considerable concern for the party's more moderate leaders. Communism was now challenging Labour in a more direct way than ever before – it was one thing for Labour to use the USSR as a teacher from afar, quite another to allow advocates of Soviet ways open access to its membership. Labour feared that Moscow would use any form of Labour-CPGB alliance to gain mass access to the party membership.

Documents from the recently opened Comintern archives in Moscow demonstrate how well founded Labour's fears were in the first half of the 1930s. The Executive Committee of the Communist International, the IKKI, claimed that the role of the Third International in this period was to ' . . . show the role of the Labour Party as the chief social supporter of the bourgeoisie' and how it 'weakens and divides the working class by . . . enchaining it to "constitutional methods"'. It concluded that the 'Labour Party acts as an accomplice of Fascism.'[69] This highlights the problem for Labour: unity on the streets was necessary to fight fascism (as was proved in Cable Street in 1936) but such unity carried with it the risk of losing party members to the far-left and also of losing middle-class voters who perceived Labour as something it was not – a revolutionary socialist party with undisclosed links to Moscow.

To disprove this Bevin and Citrine, amongst others, led pragmatic Labour's fight back against the revolutionary entryists. Growing worried at the grassroots members' activity with other socialists in the anti-fascist united front, the moderates' view was made clear by Citrine. When presented by the ILP with the possibility of a united front against fascism, he replied '[r]eaction cannot be fought by the methods of Dictatorship'.[70] Any call for unity against fascism that included the CPGB was bound to provoke a fierce backlash from Labour's right-wing, especially as the Comintern – which now offered the rhetoric of reconciliation after the end of its 'Third Period' – was still adamant that it was 'faced with the responsibility that this bunch who control the reformist movement in this country are now the chief obstacles to any tremendous advance'.[71]

Moscow ordered the CPGB to cite German Social Democracy 'as an example of how Democracy leads to Fascism and only the policy of class struggle leads to Socialism'.[72] It claimed that the Labour Party was deceiving the working class in its claims that a united front already existed in the Labour Party, arguing that:

[w]e must explain to the workers that there are two kinds of united front – with the capitalists, or a united front of working class struggle. The Communists are fighting for the workers' united front, but the leaders of these organisations are sabotaging this struggle and making a united front with the capitalists.[73]

Labour maintained that the Comintern 'remained bitterly hostile to . . . the democratic basis of Socialist Parties such as the British Labour Party'[74] and launched a campaign against all forms of Soviet influence, as Labour's moderate figures sought to reaffirm its traditions of gradualism, parliamentarianism and social democracy. The fight against Communist infiltration and influence saw Labour define its political identity by proving what it was not, using the USSR to define its political thought and actions *as a whole*. Pamphlets such as *The Communist Solar System* and *Communist and Other Organisations* were aimed at rank and file Labourites and added more flesh to the bones of Citrine's statement about reaction and dictatorship. The message remained unchanged from the previous decade – even in the face of the fascist threat Labour should have nothing to do with the CPGB. But it now went further than before, denouncing all extremist elements in British politics as no different from one another.

In a sustained offensive against a united front and Communist infiltration and influence in Labour's ranks, the National Joint Council (NJC), representing the Labour Party, Parliamentary Labour Party and TUC, published *Communist and Other Organisations* in June 1933, listing the organisations that were nominally independent of the CPGB but which it claimed were under the influence of Communists. These included the National Minority Movement, the National Unemployed Workers' Committee and the Friends of Soviet Russia. The NJC pointed out that

Communists established apparently innocent organisations with the specific purpose of recruiting Labour Party members and trade unionists who did not realise they were hostile to the Labour Party.[75] Ernest Bevin added to the anti-Communist campaign, arguing that Labour should have no unity with the Communist Party as their tactics were:

> . . . repugnant to decent people, and certainly repugnant to our tradition in this country. Whilst I feel, like many others, that the parties of the 'Left' have a contribution to make, that contribution cannot be made whilst they resort to all these underground and stupid methods.[76]

The Communist Solar System: The Communist International reiterated the warning against united front action by reinforcing the traditional reformist ideas of the socialist and trade union movement. It claimed that the Communists, together with the Nazis, were 'fertile in the manufacture of grievances, notably when the workers were employees of a municipality with a Socialist majority', and that the united front 'was the battle cry of Communism at war with German Social Democracy and Trade Unionism. It was a slogan and nothing but a slogan.'[77] The point was to reinforce the idea that Communism and Communist parties were not compatible with the Labour Party, as they believed in a different type of socialism and politics to Labour whose objective was 'to organise and maintain in Parliament and the country, a definite and independent political party'.[78]

In *Democracy versus Dictatorship* the NJC argued that all dictatorships were the same, thus rekindling the party's argument from the 1920s when Communists called for a dictatorship of the proletariat. *Democracy versus Dictatorship* was a call for workers everywhere to strengthen the Labour Party so that it could lead the fight against fascist or Communist dictators.[79] And it was an affirmation of the party's 'belief in constitutional principles and its opposition to Communism and Fascism alike'.[80] Ultimately it emphasised the type of organisation the Labour Party was and would continue to be.

This campaign had two purposes. The first was for these documents to uncover Communist activity in Labour's ranks and to ensure that Labourites knew that such activity was neither acceptable nor compatible with Labour's ideas. The second purpose was to ensure that Labour Party members did not ally themselves with Communists and thus risk giving Labour's opponents on the right any reason to be able to portray the party as a British Bolshevik party – an allegation the Tories had consistently made to discredit Labour. This was a powerful – if untrue – charge that forced the party's leaders to be careful when considering their actions: move too far to the left and risk losing middle-class votes; move too far to the right and risk being out-flanked by the Communist Party on the left. In 1939, one party pamphlet claimed that an alliance with the Communists 'would bring some few thousand votes . . . but it might well drive millions into the arms of Mr. Chamberlain's camp'.[81]

Labour argued against a popular front government claiming that it would be 'inherently weak and unstable, divided in its outlook on both home and foreign fronts. Its failure would discredit and endanger democracy in Great Britain.'[82] It stated that the inclusion of the Communist Party in a popular front would be 'an electoral liability' and was 'undesirable, impractical and would meet with electoral disaster'.[83] Even supporters of bringing the Soviet Union into an international anti-fascist alliance, such as G. D. H. Cole, claimed that an alliance between the CPGB and the Labour Party 'would be, for us, like a partnership between an elephant and a flea'.[84] Labour reinforced its own electoral beliefs through its rejection of an alliance with the CPGB, and the party's position was clear — it would pursue progressive reform through Parliament rather than through anti-capitalist protest and industrial action. It thoroughly rejected any extra-parliamentary activities advocated by the far-left. Despite all the problems Labourites had with MacDonaldism, the party ultimately returned to the words of its former leader, who years earlier had written that '[a] workman was not fully organised unless to his weapon of trade unionism he added to it the weapon of the ballot box'.[85]

Labour's fundamental beliefs in parliamentary rather than revolutionary democracy, in reform over revolution, in compensation rather than expropriation and in 'political' rather than 'industrial' tactics, were never seriously threatened by the Soviet influence. These beliefs were, however, confirmed by Labour's reaction to the actions of the Comintern, the CPGB and the Soviet Union, all of which were used by Labour as a negative definer of its ideas. In this way, by proving what it was not, Labour confirmed what it was.

The USSR was sometimes portrayed as a less aggressive or more progressive dictatorship than Nazi Germany, but party members were still reminded that it was a dictatorship nonetheless. It was constantly highlighted to Labourites who flirted with Communism, or who openly advocated a united or popular front with the CPGB, that the leaders in the Kremlin and workers, soldiers and peasants in the country answered to only one man who ruled over the USSR like a tsar. The title of Labour's 1933 pamphlet *Democracy versus Dictatorship* left little to the imagination, and this case was helped by news of the Show Trials later in the decade as countless old Bolsheviks fell victim to the Stalinist system.

Stalin's attack on his old comrades during the purges proved to be the start of a reassessment of the USSR for some leading figures. H. N. Brailsford condemned a 'terror based on lies'[86] noting that the 'purge of the Communist Party . . . recalls Hitler's slaughter of his rivals'. He described the trial as 'a relic of the Middle Ages, worthy of the Inquisition rather than a Socialist tribunal'.[87] Clement Attlee also wrote about the use of violence, noting that '[i]n Soviet Russia to-day, fifteen years after the cessation of foreign intervention, the method of terrorism continues, as may be seen from the trials of the Trotskyists'.[88] An editorial in the *Daily Herald* stated that the judicial methods used during the trials were 'worthy of Tsarism'.[89]

The *Manchester Guardian* journalist Malcolm Muggeridge, who reported from Moscow in the early 1930s, wrote that in the USSR the:

> . . . total abandonment of Law, and its replacement by terrorism, was obscured by the ostensible application of humanitarian principles to the punishment of non-political offenders. The fact that many were shot without a public trial for unspecified reasons of state, did not deter earnest advocates of penal reform from holding the Soviet Government up to admiration for having abolished capital punishment.[90]

And Walter Citrine wrote that the purges:

> . . . made a spy of every man on his neighbour . . . it was the duty of every worker to keep an eye on the actions and words of his fellows, and to report anything which seemed to be hostile to the interests of the working class. That is why no Communist dare argue independently, or criticise his leaders, or their policy. He is so anxious not to be regarded as a 'deviationist', that when confronted with any question he asks himself, 'What is the true Leninist line? What would Stalin say?' To argue with a Russian Communist is to argue with a gramophone record of Stalin.[91]

Stalin's abusive actions against his own side now made it more difficult for Labour's socialists to cite the USSR as a successful example of socialism. Stalinism proved that it went against some of the fundamental beliefs of the party's socialism – egalitarianism, freedom of expression and religious tolerance. While not everyone in the party and the wider movement was convinced of the trials' legitimacy, some still stubbornly refused to abandon the Soviet Union as Europe's saviour from Hitler. A letter in the *Daily Herald* insisted on political co-operation with the Kremlin in the 'interests of peace and the defence of democracy'.[92]

It took one last blow from Stalin finally to betray those Labourites who were still clinging to the idea that the USSR was on their side, as the Nazi-Soviet pact was signed by Vyacheslav Molotov and Joachim Von Ribbentrop in August 1939. However, this showed that the USSR's leaders could be just as pragmatic as Labour's, as it was a short-term policy designed to buy the USSR time to fight off the expected Nazi attack. It also proved to be only a temporary cessation of support for the Soviet people and their government, as Labourites once again offered their backing to the Kremlin when Hitler invaded Soviet lands in June 1941 and Hitler proved to be the greater of two evils.

V

A climate of extremism can breed extreme responses, and this was certainly the case where the Labour Party and the Soviet Union were concerned in the interwar years. Context is therefore very important when assessing Labour's relationship with the Stalinist dictatorship in this period. Even after capitalism stabilised and the USSR became less of an economic ideal, it was still seen as an important factor in opposing Hitler. This suggests that there was a relationship between crises and support for the USSR, allowing many Labourites to turn a blind eye to the more disturbing stories that emerged from the USSR.

Labour knew about things like the purges when it was in power for the second time, but chose not to concern itself with the internal politics of the Soviet Union as it could jeopardise what it was trying to achieve in terms of economics and peace. This was a constant in the party throughout the 1930s as British socialists found hope – of varying degrees – in the Soviet Union. The shocking news of the Nazi-Soviet pact brought this to an abrupt end, devastating many of Labour's socialists and vindicating its social democrats.

This highlights the different ways in which the Soviet Union was used by, and influenced, the Labour Party. When it was in power, Labour was less concerned with the USSR being a socialist system, but out of office, ideology again became more important. Where the Soviet Union was used as a model for specific ideas such as economics, or as part of the campaign for peace in Europe, it proved to be a positive influence for socialists. In the 1920s party members had called for state intervention in the economy, and by the 1930s, because of lessons learned from the Soviet Union (and the less aggressive progressive countries) Labour accepted that the state did indeed have a clear role to play in the economic life of the country. This in turn laid the foundations of the post-war National Health Service and Welfare State. However, Labour still argued that because of different conditions it would need to do things differently from the Soviets.

At the same time Labour confirmed its faith in the parliamentary path rather than opting for more industrial methods which may have seemed natural had they allied with the CPGB. By remaining a parliamentary party Labour proved that its various gradualist traditions were stronger than its revolutionary ones, even though the latter had a powerful model to follow. But this was not, and could not be, the Labour way. By using the Soviet Union to define its political thought, Labour emerged as a confident social democratic party – albeit one with many socialist members that often acted as its conscience – and its gradualist and reformist tendencies were confirmed rather than replaced. Despite Winston Churchill's claim that the Socialist movement in Britain ' . . . was from beginning to end a foreign minded movement' that ' . . . had been lifted bodily from Germany and Russia',[93] Labour's socialism was governed by its own traditions, leaving Clem Attlee to state in 1937: 'I do not think that Britain must follow the Moscow . . . road.'[94] Ultimately, the USSR was rejected as a model for the Labour Party, but the process of this rejection confirmed Labour's fundamental beliefs – its gradualism, its parliamentary tactics and its political thought – thus creating a party that was socialist in principle but social democratic in power.

4

THE LABOUR PARTY IN THE ERA OF THE NAZI-SOVIET PACT, 1939–41

Paul Corthorn[1]

The announcement of the Nazi-Soviet pact on 23 August 1939 shattered an assumption which had come to underpin the Labour Party's foreign policy: that the Soviet Union was opposed to the rise of international fascism. Later the same year the Soviet invasion of Finland prompted the Labour Party to argue that the Soviet Union was now even imitating Nazi methods of 'imperialist' territorial aggrandisement. As the Labour Party threw its support behind the British war effort, it also took pains to plan for the peace. Alongside domestic reconstruction, the Labour Party reconsidered its ideas about the desirable form that the future world order should take. The challenge facing the party was considerable. World war provided the opportunity to devise fresh schemes or to revisit older ones. Yet the Labour Party's task was made markedly more difficult because it could no longer rely on the Soviet Union as its principal international ally, a role it had increasingly assumed during the 1930s. By examining Labour thinking at this time, it is therefore possible to locate more precisely the Soviet Union's place in the party's views of the wider world at this critical juncture.

It is clear that for Labour fellow travellers the era of the Nazi-Soviet pact marked a watershed, albeit in a variety of ways. The elderly Sidney and Beatrice Webb were initially shocked but clung desperately to their faith in the Soviet Union. For Victor Gollancz, John Strachey and others in the Left Book Club the pact prompted them to begin to reject the Soviet Union. On the other hand, D. N. Pritt became the most famous Labour apologist for the Soviet Union at this time, publicly defending the Soviet invasion of Finland and being quickly expelled from the party as a result.

For the rest of the Labour Party, for whom the Soviet Union was not a central point of reference in the same way, the Nazi-Soviet pact has to be understood within a wider domestic political and foreign policy context. Trevor Burridge has charted the party's decisions to support the war in September 1939 and to agree a cross-party truce but not to enter Neville Chamberlain's government.[2] He has also examined in fine detail Labour's role in Chamberlain's downfall in May 1940 and its subsequent involvement with Winston Churchill's coalition.[3] The development of a patriotic stance towards the war, especially from 1940, has received persuasive treatment by Stephen Brooke.[4] This coincided with the Nazi-Soviet pact but was, of course, not directly prompted by it. In a similar manner, the eclipse of Labour's pacifist contingent, led most notably by the former party leader George Lansbury, also occurred during the opening stages of the war. This marked the culmination of a process begun in the mid-1930s and owed more to the wider features of the 'People's War' than it did to responses to the Soviet Union.

Labour's ideas about international post-war reconstruction have also been subject to close scrutiny. Yet the emphasis has, for understandable reasons, been firmly on the future treatment of Germany.[5] Not only did the issue of Germany go on to assume critical importance after Hitler's defeat in 1945 but it also remained at the centre of Labour's collective consciousness well into the 1950s, as debates over the rearmament of Germany in a Cold War context divided the party. Moreover, this focus on Germany reflected contemporary concerns in 1939 and 1940. Not only was Britain actually at war with Germany, but it had also long been held in progressive circles that the harshness of the Treaty of Versailles, which concluded the First World War, had provided the circumstances that allowed Hitler to come to power. There was a strong desire not to make the same mistakes again and, as a result, to think clearly in advance about the future – even at a point when British success in the war appeared far from certain.

Yet the prominence given to Germany in some accounts of international 'War Aims' has meant that other aspects of Labour's attempt to rethink its international outlook have received less attention. In particular, the party's ideas about international post-war reconstruction have been far from fully related to its swiftly changing views of the Soviet Union. This is despite the fact that Labour's discussions about federalism at this time were, in part, actually prompted by the Nazi-Soviet pact.

An attempt to understand the relationship between these developments requires more than just an examination of foreign policy in a narrow sense: instead it necessitates an analysis of Labour's internationalism.[6] There is no doubt that a rhetorical commitment to internationalism has been central to

Labour's public identity at many points in its history. But what exactly does internationalism mean? In one sense, it concerns the broad aspiration to transcend national boundaries in an attempt to find solutions to international issues. It is, therefore, about the shape of the future world order and the role of international organisations. In another sense, Labour internationalism carries distinct connotations of certain values.

In her recent overview of Labour foreign policy in the first half of the twentieth century, Rhiannon Vickers argues that despite the rhetoric of socialism, Labour's internationalism has drawn heavily on liberal internationalist traditions. These have emphasised the need to impose order into a system of international anarchy. Labour's support of the League of Nations is a classic example of that outlook.[7] More detailed work by R. M. Douglas has identified the outbreak of the Second World War as a turning point in Labour's internationalist thought. He has argued that it forced Labour to abandon its radical liberal internationalism and to begin to embrace either the emerging 'muscular' internationalism of the United Nations or some kind of European Federation.[8]

This chapter analyses closely Labour's changing views of the Soviet Union during this key moment in the evolution of its internationalism. It builds on an understanding that the Stalinist purges between 1936 and 1938 had already prompted a criticism of Stalinism – involving an explicit comparison with Hitler's regime – tentatively to emerge across the party, only to be obscured in the immediate pre-war years by an emphasis on the Soviet Union as a key ally.[9] The chapter focuses in particular on Labour's internationalism as a reciprocal relationship between domestic and international values.[10] This approach serves to reveal the precise ways in which the Soviet Union was central to Labour's international outlook. It suggests that, despite important differences, there was also significant common ground between the Labour left and the Labour centre right, thus challenging accounts such as Bill Jones's which have asserted that these ideological divisions are the central story in Labour's relationship with the Soviet Union.[11] Above all, the chapter contends that, despite its discussion of federalism, the Labour Party as a whole never fully reconciled its internationalist vision to a world in which the Soviet Union was not an ally.

<h1 style="text-align:center">I</h1>

The Labour Party's overwhelming response to the announcement of the Nazi-Soviet pact was one of shock. As news of it emerged, Hugh Dalton, a leading figure on Labour's National Executive Committee (NEC), and Arthur Greenwood, the deputy Labour leader who was acting as leader during Clement Attlee's absence through illness, raced over to the Soviet

Embassy 'to demand explanation' from Ivan Maisky, the Soviet Ambassador.[12] When more detail was revealed, it did indeed look like a complete 'reversal of Russian policy',[13] a 'bitter and unexpected blow to peace'.[14]

There was wide agreement across the range of Labour opinion. Walter Citrine, the moderate General Secretary of the Trades Union Congress (TUC), was 'profoundly shocked',[15] as was the left-wing Barbara Betts (later Barbara Castle).[16] This was why the pact was a 'catastrophic blow' for the left-wing intellectual Harold Laski who, as his friend and political associate Kingsley Martin later recalled, had 'regarded the Soviet Union as a sure bulwark against fascism and the leader of the world's forces making for socialism'.[17] For the Labour Party, the Soviet Union's pact with Germany did more than change the geopolitical landscape or represent a disastrous failure of British diplomacy to build an alliance with the Soviet Union. It brought into question the deeply-held conviction that the Soviet Union would always be on the 'right' side.

By the mid-1930s, Soviet involvement with the League of Nations was central to Labour's foreign policy. The Labour Party's commitment to the League of Nations itself had developed gradually since the middle of the Great War. By the mid-1920s the League of Nations was viewed as a mechanism for achieving international security through a system which provided collective security and sought, in the longer term, to facilitate worldwide disarmament.[18] At this stage, the Soviet Union was outside the League, viewed with suspicion by its leading member states. Yet in the early 1930s the Labour Party began actively to press for the Soviet Union's involvement in the League, and indeed warmly welcomed its entry in 1934.[19] The following year, as the Labour Party debated the use of League of Nations sanctions against Italy, the fact that the Soviet Union was firmly backing collective security became central to the case in favour of sanctions.[20]

After 1935, with the League of Nations discredited following its failure properly to implement sanctions against Italy, the Labour Party began to base its demands for collective security directly on an alliance with the Soviet Union. Indeed, in September 1938, the Labour Party was left utterly dismayed that Chamberlain had completely by-passed the Soviet Union during the Munich Crisis.[21] As the threat from Hitler increased in early summer 1939, Dalton argued that 'an arrangement with Russia should both be made and proclaimed'.[22] And on 27 June, the trade-union dominated National Council of Labour (NCL) appointed Dalton, Citrine and Herbert Morrison, the influential NEC member who was also leader of the London County Council, to consult the Chamberlain government on various matters of international importance, especially negotiations with the Soviet Union.[23]

Crucially, by this time the Labour left – loosely grouped around the *Tribune* newspaper – was also portraying the Soviet Union as a key strategic international ally, in the same way as official Labour Party policy. Earlier in the 1920s and 1930s the Labour left had embraced an overtly pro-Soviet outlook, seeking to emulate it domestically and urging a future Labour government to align with it internationally. As the international crisis deepened, however, and the Labour left sought wider alliances at both home and abroad to defeat fascism, it began to present the Soviet Union as an essential immediate ally.[24]

Despite their initial surprise, some on the Labour left soon began to explain the Nazi-Soviet pact by placing responsibility for it on Chamberlain. In doing so, the Labour left was building on its anti-capitalist critique of the National government which had epitomised its stance during the 1930s. *Tribune* was quick to condemn Chamberlain's failure to build bridges with the Soviet Union.[25] Aneurin Bevan, the fiery Welsh miners' MP who had been expelled from the Labour Party in March 1939 for his involvement with left-wing defiance of official party policy, even called for renewed efforts to reach agreement.[26] Betts later recollected how she was influenced by Bevan and became sympathetic to the Soviet Union's difficulty in making sense of British intentions.[27] Ellen Wilkinson, MP, was another left-winger who – in the immediate aftermath of the pact – placed the blame firmly on the National government for excluding the Soviet Union at Munich and for sending only a low-level Foreign Office official to discuss a potential alliance in summer 1939.[28]

While these criticisms of the British government had some resonance, based as they were both on anti-capitalist sentiments and on the natural role of an opposition party, they were not so powerful as to diminish much of the criticism of the Soviet Union. Labour's official newspaper, the *Daily Herald*, could be expected to indict the Soviet Union. It forthrightly asserted that 'the British Government's attitude on numerous occasions, disastrously wrong as it has been, provides no justification for Russia's complete betrayal of the principles for which she appeared until last week to stand so firmly'.[29] It was perhaps equally unsurprising that Dalton privately pondered if the Soviet Union was 'ever sincere in their negotiations for a Pact with us and France', even though he accepted that 'British conduct, as seen from Moscow, was throughout most suspicious and unsatisfactory.'[30] The position adopted by H. N. Brailsford – a stalwart of the Labour left – was arguably more significant in this respect.

Brailsford accepted that the British government bore a large part of the responsibility for the outbreak of the war. In his view its manifest reluctance to involve the Soviet Union at critical moments had only 'increased Moscow's suspicions'. Brailsford also linked this more widely to the National government's dangerous inaction in international affairs, criticising not only its acquiescence in Hitler's demands at Munich but also its policy of Non-intervention during the Spanish Civil War of 1936–1939. Even so, Brailsford was clear that this 'cannot justify what Stalin has done . . . He has gone out of his way to make an unprovoked attack on Poland easy and safe.'[31]

Yet critical views of the Soviet Union did not at this point permeate Labour's official policy statements. The NEC manifesto published on 1 September and the TUC General Council's declaration submitted to the TUC Congress meeting on 4 September both omitted any reference whatsoever to the Soviet Union. Instead they focused on the imperative of resisting Nazi Germany so that 'liberty and order' could be 're-established in the World'.[32] In a context where Britain was at war with Germany, such an emphasis was entirely logical. Nevertheless, it also implicitly indicated Labour's uncertainty about the Soviet Union's position and its subsequent desire to tread cautiously.

II

The Nazi-Soviet pact played an important part in initiating discussion of 'federalism' as the desirable end result of a 'constructive inter-nationalism'.[33] The League of Nations, and the liberal international values it represented, had been discredited well before the outbreak of war. What made the circumstances of late summer 1939 so unsettling was not just the actual fact of war but the realisation that it had come about in such a way that the Soviet Union could no longer be counted as an international ally. Thinking about future international reconstruction, Brailsford was utterly despondent about having to work 'without the help from Russia on which we had counted'.[34] Laski was likewise emphatic that the Soviet Union had 'thrown away . . . a share in the moral leadership of the world', necessitating the need to find 'a new orientation of world direction'.[35] In this context, demands for federalism, which typically involved a signifi-cant reduction in national sovereignty, quickly gathered momentum. Indeed, Brailsford was soon arguing that most 'of us will feel that this war has ended in failure unless it results in creating at least the nucleus of a Federal Union'.[36]

At this early stage of the war, it fell to prominent left-wing intellectuals – Brailsford, Laski and Kingsley Martin, the editor of the *New Statesman* – to adumbrate these federalist ideas. The Wilsonian liberal ideals that had underpinned the League of Nations were now portrayed as wholly inade-quate. As Brailsford put it, this was because they had accepted 'the old-world notion of the absolute independence of all Sovereign States'.[37] Martin agreed, contending that: 'We must talk not of a League of sovereign nations . . . of self-determination, but of a federal government.'[38] Likewise, Laski wrote frankly of the need for 'the abandonment of national sovereignty'.[39]

The principal justificatory purpose of a 'federal union' was that it would have the power to remove the underlying causes of wars – an aim of the initial League of Nations idea. Brailsford's conviction about the need for some kind of international organisation had long lineage. He had taken a great interest in the burgeoning League of Nations idea during the Great War and had then tentatively explored the practicality of a federal authority in *Property or Peace* in 1934. Now that war was underway, he frankly argued that the 'authority we require must be what the League never was: a super-National government. It is not enough to arbitrate disputes; we want to remove the causes that lead to disputes and wars.'[40]

The Labour Party had long considered the causes of war to be international economic inequality. The proposed federal union was a means of eradicating this problem. Laski advocated a 'fundamental change in the economic relationship of states' that went beyond merely ensuring 'access on equal terms to raw materials'.[41] Brailsford envisaged the federal union providing 'economic security by controlling the flow of international trade', as well as a means 'to pool our economic resources'.[42]

While economic security was the federal union's *raison d'être*, international security – through an international police force – was also important. Brailsford argued that it was to 'its forces, and not to our national army and fleet, we must look for the defence of our own shores'.[43] Just as in the mid-1930s, a 'central police force' was readily portrayed as a means of ensuring national disarmament, Labour's long-held foreign-policy objective.[44] In the 1920s the Labour Party had sought to achieve multi-lateral disarmament by putting in place League of Nations security and arbitration procedures. The deterioration of the international environment in the 1930s necessitated more reflection on how exactly the League would restrain an aggressor state. In 1933 the Labour Party argued for the first time that an international police force should form the basis of the League's 'pooled security' that would, in turn, facilitate disarmament.[45] Such ideas were, however, quickly abandoned and disappeared from Labour debate for the rest of the 1930s. In 1934 an official Labour Party report acknowledged that in the interim period before an international League police force replaced national armed forces, Britain might have to use its own military forces to support the League in restraining an aggressor.[46] In 1935, of course, this prospect became a reality. Following a heated debate at the party conference, the Labour Party decided to support the National government in applying sanctions against Italy, which had been defined as an aggressor by the League of Nations for its invasion of Abyssinia.[47]

Despite the Soviet Union's absence, the federation was to comprise only progressive states. This was consistent with the Labour Party's central internationalist commitment to the interaction of national and international values. After meeting Laski, Patrick Gordon Walker described what he had in mind as a 'socialist Federal Union'.[48] Brailsford was even more explicit about what he considered essential. He argued that:

> Some common political and social outlook must unite its members. It is nonsense to say that the internal affairs and the political systems of our neighbours do not concern us. Their foreign policy grows out of their internal political system. If they aim at economic self-sufficiency or start persecuting their minorities, they can upset our way of life.[49]

It was also very emphatically 'a Federal Union in Europe'.[50] Brailsford was clear that the United States would not become involved, having become disillusioned with European power politics after the First World War.[51] Laski was one of those in the Labour Party who was most interested in American politics and who took a favourable attitude to President Franklin Delano Roosevelt and the New Deal. Significantly, he too considered that US involvement was highly unlikely.[52]

III

On hearing news of the Soviet invasion of Poland, which took place on 17 September, a range of Labour figures compared Soviet foreign policy to that of Nazi Germany for the first time. Greenwood forthrightly argued that the Soviet invasion had taken place 'on grounds which cannot be justified and which have been used previously by Hitler as excuses for his monstrous outrages'.[53] This was a clear reference to the fact the Soviet Union had cited Polish provocation as the reason for its invasion, just as Nazi Germany had done. The *Daily Herald*'s editorial was equally critical, pointing out that the invasion was 'in direct defiance' of the 1932 non-aggression treaty between the Soviet Union and Poland (thus drawing attention to the obvious parallel with Hitler's disrespect for international agreements) and making the same wider comparison as Greenwood between the Soviet Union and Nazi Germany:

> Russian Communism joins German Nazism in the scramble for plunder. The country which has set – which we once all believed would set – an example to the whole world in social justice and international fair dealing embarks upon war for the naked purpose of

territorial gain. Cynically, the decision is clothed in phrases struck directly from the Nazi mint . . . There is and can be no justification for what Russia has done.[54]

Altogether, Labour criticism of the Soviet Union now reached such a level of intensity that Harry Pollitt, the CPGB General Secretary, spoke publicly of the 'vile anti-Soviet elements in the Labour Party leadership'.[55] Moreover, the CPGB Central Committee was even giving credit to the idea that the 'Labour party would have come out for a declaration of war on the Soviet Union if it had not been for the restraint exercised on them by government quarters.'[56] Sir Stafford Cripps, the controversial leader of the Labour left in the 1930s who had been expelled from the Labour Party in January 1939, also recorded privately 'the anti-Russian feeling in the Labour party'.[57]

Criticism of the Soviet Union was not, however, uniform. Some – such as Gordon Walker – were less quick to condemn the Soviet Union. Nonetheless they still found themselves completely exasperated by Soviet actions. Noting that 'Russia justifies this on same sort of arguments that Germany uses for her invasions', Gordon Walker wrote ominously that this 'needs thinking out'.[58] Others on the Labour left were plainly more sympathetic to the Soviet position. In late September Cripps emphatically insisted that 'Russian policy is the continued development of socialist power in Russia.'[59] And in early October he argued that the peace offer made by Nazi Germany and the Soviet Union, despite being based on an acceptance of their territorial gains in Poland, should not be dismissed out of hand.[60]

The position adopted by Dalton cut across the divisions between the more critical Labour centre right and the more benevolent Labour left. Dalton initially found the news of the Soviet invasion of Poland 'very shattering'. However, as a hard-headed expert in foreign affairs who had never exhibited the same kind of emotional attachment to the Soviet Union as some in the Labour Party, he soon 'wondered whether a Russian elbow around Romania would now shut off Germany from that country'. For this reason he told Greenwood that 'Russia should not be publicly slanged too much at present'.[61] Dalton clearly felt very strongly about the issue. He urged Rab Butler – Under-Secretary of State at the Foreign Office – that 'Russia should not be treated with high pique',[62] and he suggested to Anthony Eden at the Dominions Office, that the government should not be 'too passive nor cultivate any sense of moral rectitude or bruised pride as regards Moscow'.[63]

A further strand of the Labour response also provided the basis for agreement across the party. With Poland effectively partitioned between Nazi Germany and the Soviet Union by 22 September, the NEC now became greatly concerned with the safety of the Polish socialist leaders in Soviet-occupied territory.[64] This, of course, mirrored their concern for socialist leaders in areas occupied by the Nazis over the past few years. The NEC had sent a message of goodwill to the Polish socialist movement earlier in September.[65] During the course of October, the NEC entered into a heated correspondence with Maisky over the issue.[66] The NEC's International Sub-committee probed the issue further with Jan Stanczyk, the General Secretary of the Polish Miners' Federation who had taken office in the new puppet Polish government, during his visit to London.[67] The International Sub-committee also authorised its secretary, William Gillies, and Citrine to ask the Foreign Office to make official representations to the Soviet government about the matter[68], which they duly did at a meeting with Lord Halifax, the Foreign Secretary, on 23 November.[69]

IV

Following the Soviet invasion of Poland, federalist ideas gained wider currency in the Labour Party. 'With Russia helping the enemy',[70] Brailsford continued to advocate a 'federal union' involving militarily 'the creation of a single international force', together with international co-operation on economic re-organisation.[71] Others were less clear that some kind of federal project was necessary but still called for a substantial rethinking in the international sphere. Francis Williams, the editor of the *Daily Herald*, emphasised only the need for 'international law',[72] but nonetheless identified the same hindrances to peace as the advocates of a federal solution. He contended that there would 'be no real peace in the world until those principles of international equity, of common opportunity and of social justice which Labour has so long urged are established'.[73] Philip Noel-Baker urged that it was imperative that 'a strong international organisation is created'.[74] On the Labour left, C. P. Trevelyan, who had defected from the Liberal Party to the Labour Party after the First World War on foreign-policy grounds, proposed 'a revitalised League of Nations, with definite power to limit the sovereignty of all states'.[75]

Significantly, party leader Attlee now began to endorse schemes of federal re-organisation. Broadcasting on 10 October, Attlee made clear how a link between domestic and foreign affairs underpinned his internationalist out-look and pushed him towards a federal solution. He argued that 'the principle that we are all members of one another applies to foreign as well as home affairs'. He was emphatic that 'the people of other countries are our concern'. Discussing Hitlerism, he argued not only that 'lawless aggression should be stopped', but that it was 'the denial of social justice in the countries of Europe which has been one of the chief courses of the present condition of things'. Attlee identified social justice as comprising 'political, religious and personal liberty' including 'the rights of free speech, of conscience and of citizenship'. At this stage these arguments led Attlee to contend that 'no lasting peace can be established without a close unity among the European peoples, economic co-operation, disarmament and collective security'.[76]

By the time he spoke at the Caxton Hall on 8 November, a speech quickly printed as *Labour's Peace Aims*, Attlee had developed these ideas into specifically federalist ones, arguing that 'Europe must federate or perish'. Mirroring the points made earlier by Laski and Brailsford, Attlee contended that this involved, above all, 'recognition of an individual authority superior to the individual states and endowed with power to make them effective, operating not only in the political, but in the economic sphere'. Attlee was adamant that there would have to be 'an international force, possessed of such overwhelming strength that no would-be aggressor would dare to challenge it'.[77] In making this case, Attlee returned to the advocacy of an international air force, a subject on which he had written in 1934.[78] So far as economic policy was concerned, Attlee related his plans for federalism to Labour's commitment to economic planning, which had occupied a central place in its programme since 1931.[79] 'Bold economic planning on a world-wide scale' ensuring 'equal access for all nations to markets and raw materials' was strongly advocated 'to meet the post-war situation, and to avoid in the future recurrent economic crises'.[80]

At this point a call to end imperialism assumed a central role in the discussion of federalism. Attlee argued that 'there must be an abandonment of imperialism'.[81] Brailsford wanted Britain to take the lead: 'Let us offer to transfer to the Federal Union the whole of our dependent Empire, together with our mandated areas, and let us ask the French, Dutch, Belgians, and Portuguese to do the same.'[82] Yet this brought into sharp focus subtle differences in views about British imperialism. Attlee was actually quite positive about it, arguing that the 'British Commonwealth of Nations shows how it is possible to have unity with diversity, and to bring together peoples of different races and languages while preserving the freedom of all.'[83] For Brailsford, however, Britain's 'moral weakness in this war is that we enter it an Empire' which meant the 'first step towards winning this war is to complete the liberation of India'.[84]

These debates over British imperialism also revealed that some Labour thinkers had yet to formulate a full understanding of Soviet expansionism – an issue that would come to the fore in the early stages of the Cold War. Despite his forthright criticism of the Soviet regime, Brailsford argued that while its control of Poland was about power it was 'not imperialism in the sense in which we must use that word when we think of India or Kenya' because there was 'no Russian owning class to exploit this territory'.[85] Clearly, criticism of the Soviet Union sat alongside continued respect for the fact that, in some economic senses at least, the Soviet Union remained a socialist state.

The federal union that the Labour Party discussed remained emphatically a European one. This was clear not just in Attlee's and Brailsford's schemes, but also in that of the Labour left intellectual and former Guild Socialist G. D. H. Cole, who expressed his support for a federation in November 1939, advocating:

> a complete pooling between the constituent states of all armed forces other than local police . . . a complete internationalisation of all colonial territories . . . an internationally-elected Parliament, chosen directly by the people, and a responsible International Executive, headed by a popularly elected International President, with powers broadly similar to those of the President of the United States.[86]

Crucially, Cole stated that there was 'no chance of America coming in, and . . . an attempt to include the Far East will only wreck it at the outset'. He did not grapple directly with the changed position of the Soviet Union. Instead, he benignly suggested that he did 'not think that it can include the Soviet Union, both because the Soviet Union would refuse to come in on any terms practicable for Western Europe, and because bringing in the Soviet Union would involve bringing in Asia as well'.[87]

V

The Labour Party responded to the Soviet invasion of Finland on 30 November 1939, which had been immediately preceded by Soviet claims of Finnish provocation, by comparing its foreign policy to that of Nazi Germany, just as it had after the Soviet invasion of Poland. Some on the centre right of the Labour Party now took these parallels further by arguing that the Soviet Union was imperialist in the same way as Nazi Germany. The *Daily Herald* was emphatic that the Soviet Union was operating on 'the brutal imperialist doctrine that might alone is right',[88] and was thus prepared to assert that: 'The Union of Soviet *Socialist* Republics is dead. Stalin's new imperialist Russia takes its place.'[89] Greenwood not only described the Soviet invasion as 'imperialist and militarist', but went so far as to argue that of 'the acts of aggression in recent years, this last is perhaps the most unjustifiable'.[90]

Others on the Labour left were more cautious about defining Soviet actions as 'imperialist'. Martin was a case in point. Nonetheless, he still contended that the invasion was inspired by 'national expansion and power politics'.[91] Likewise, Brailsford did not label the Soviet Union 'imperialist' – no doubt because he had been working to develop a careful distinction between capitalist and 'socialist' expansion. Nevertheless, Stalin's 'unprovoked attack on Finland' led him to dismiss the Soviet Union as a 'totalitarian state like another', a 'verdict we had hitherto refused to register', involving a denial of 'the international creed of socialism' and even a return to a Russian nationalism where 'Peter the Great has been reinstated as the national hero.'[92]

Despite these differing nuances, a great deal united the Labour reaction – in ways that again related to the connections between domestic and international values. At this point many in the party linked their interpretations of the Stalinist purges to the Soviet Union's international policy. To Brailsford the Soviet claims of Finnish provocation were 'as puerile as the tales that Stalin produced to justify the purge of his internal enemies'. It was the 'intellectual degradation' within the Soviet Union which, together with its actions abroad, left 'no answer to the charge that his [Stalin's] system and Hitler's are politically akin'.[93] Francis Williams identified the purges as a turning point: 'I think Socialist sense came to an end when Stalin secured complete control and murdered all those who had been the pioneers of the new order.'[94] This insight undoubtedly underpinned the way in which the *Daily Herald* integrated the attack on Finland into its overall analysis:

> Socialism is . . . a belief that between nation and nation as between man and man there should be justice and honourable dealing and a respect for the integrity of the weak no less than the strong. Stalin's Russia sets all that aside in international affairs as it earlier set aside all democratic freedom in internal affairs.[95]

Cole made it clear how the values that states adopted internally were central to any war aims. He argued that for the Labour movement in Britain one of the 'chief war aims' was the preservation of 'certain habits and institutions which are of permanent value' despite having been 'built up under a capitalist system which has been rapidly becoming obsolete'. Cole identified these as 'the value set on individual liberty and federation, within fairly broad limits, of difference of opinion and behaviour; the freedom, still within limits, of speech and writing, and the freedom to organise voluntarily for a host of purposes and causes of very sort and kind'. Cole was emphatic that while the Nazis had 'trampled' on these values, the people in 'barbaric Russia' had frankly 'never possessed them'.[96] At the time of the purges, Cole had expressed no opinion about them, not wanting to undermine the international anti-fascist cause.[97] With the Nazi-Soviet pact and now the invasion of Finland, such international restraints no longer existed for Cole and many others in the Labour Party.

Laski was a conspicuous exception. Despite having criticised the purges publicly in 1938,[98] he now urged against condemning the Soviet Union's actions too strongly because he continued to envisage the Soviet Union as an essential long-term ally. On 7 December he wrote to an American associate, explaining his reasoning:

> I have a job keeping our own fools from rushing into fantastic denunciations instead of careful explanations; above all the job of making them see that Russia will recover sanity by the impact of our wisdom and magnanimity, not by the shriek of a betrayal which fear prevents her from understanding. She is like a burglar who unintentionally commits murder to prevent the burglary from being found out. But the less we renounce and the more we clarify, the more the chance I see of getting the right forces in the long run on our side.[99]

This outlook explains why, in February and March 1940, Laski became involved in a heated debate over the nature of the internal Soviet regime with the young centre-right Labour economist Evan Durbin, who had just published *The Politics of Democratic Socialism*. During the purges Durbin had begun privately to stress 'the tyrannical nature of the Stalinist regime'.[100] Now he publicly compared the Soviet Union's domestic regime with that in Nazi Germany. He argued: 'Imprisonment without trial, torture without trial, execution without trial, and the punishment of the perfectly innocent friends and relatives of mere suspects, are regular practices in Russia and Germany alike.'[101] In contrast, Laski could not accept 'that torture is used by the Soviet government as a deliberate instrument of policy as it is used by the Nazi Government'.[102]

There is little doubt, however, that Laski's careful approach to the Soviet Union was not widely shared by the Labour Party as a whole in the aftermath of the invasion of Finland. The NCL quickly produced a manifesto, which took a highly critical stance towards the Soviet Union and marked Labour's first official pronouncement on Soviet foreign policy since the outbreak of the war. Issued on 7 December, the manifesto was adopted by the NEC later in the month.[103] It expressed 'profound horror and indignation' at 'the Soviet Government's unprovoked attack upon a small state'. It was clear that 'Soviet imperialism has thus revealed itself as using the same methods as the Nazi Power against which the British working class is united in the war now raging.' The manifesto also made explicit the reason behind Labour's strong reaction, arguing that it 'repudiates utterly' the claims of the Soviet Union 'to be the leader of the world's working-class movement, guardian of the rights of peoples against their oppressors, interpreter of socialist principles, and the custodian of international peace'.[104] To emphasise this point, the NCL identified itself with the plight of Finland, building on an approach already taken publicly by Greenwood.[105] The manifesto noted the 'splendid achievements of the Finnish nation in social legislation and in the building up of a trade union, co-operative and political organisation of the working class on the foundations of true democracy'. It also went so far as to call on the 'free nations of the world to concert measures for giving all practicable aid to the Finnish nation'.[106] In effect, it was asking them to act indirectly against the Soviet Union.

VI

The Soviet invasion of Finland also brought about calls for a federal union from different Labour Party quarters. Prompted by a growing awareness of the 'danger of Stalinism', Francis Williams at the *Daily Herald*, who had previously held back from endorsing anything more than a general need for international law, now embraced the possibility of a 'new League or federation'. He demanded 'a genuine effort to build a new world order' involving 'machinery for international co-operation which, unlike the League of Nations, shall be economic as well as political'.[107]

This outlook necessitated a change in the *Daily Herald*'s attitude to the existing League of Nations, which, despite looking increasingly ineffectual after 1935, had remained in existence. During this period, the *Daily Herald*, like the Labour Party itself, had placed less and less emphasis on the League. Now, however, it warmly welcomed the League's decision to announce its disapproval of the Soviet Union. Even before the League of Nations Council expelled the Soviet Union on 15 December 1939, the *Daily Herald* gave the League its full backing, contending that, so far as the all-important future international organisation was concerned, 'the more there is to build on, the better'.[108]

Furthermore, at this point, Morrison, who was famously uninterested in foreign affairs,[109] made a rare venture into that arena. He did not define his plans as federalist but they clearly shared a great deal with those that explicitly were. Morrison urged that 'the nations must come together and tackle international economic problems, including the problem of colonial possessions, on international lines, even if this means the limitation of national sovereignty' and necessitated 'international control of arms manufacture and armed forces'. Against the backdrop of Soviet aggression,

THE LABOUR PARTY IN THE ERA OF THE NAZI-SOVIET PACT   101

Morrison asserted the key Labour internationalist tenet that 'the governments that dominate at home are often the peace breakers abroad'. For this reason he sought to apply the same policies in both the domestic and international spheres: he aimed to 'organise the industry, trade, commerce and raw materials of the world with the idea not of bolstering up the special privileges of any class or group, but of achieving a higher standard of life for all'.[110]

VII

As spirited Finnish resistance prolonged the Soviet invasion, the question of how the Labour movement would respond assumed greater importance. In late December 1939, it was decided to appoint two representatives, Barbara Ayrton Gould from the NEC and William Holmes from the TUC General Council, to the newly-established Finland Relief Committee.[111] More significantly, on 10 January 1940 the NCL received an invitation to visit Finland from its trade union and Labour movements. The NCL accepted, sending Citrine, Noel-Baker and J. Downie as the TUC, Labour Party and Co-operative representatives respectively.[112]

This Labour delegation, which arrived in Finland on 24 January,[113] aroused considerable internal controversy. On the NEC's International Sub-committee, Laski put forward the 'possibility of the delegation proceeding to Leningrad to consult with representatives of the USSR government'.[114] Laski's reasoning was that if 'they had been refused, that would have been a final condemnation of Stalin; if they had been accepted, at the best they might have mediated.'[115] A lengthy discussion ensued but, in the end, Laski's proposal was defeated.[116]

Soon real fears began to develop about the prospect of British involvement in a war against the Soviet Union. For Labour this was a deeply emotive issue, dating back to 1920 when the Labour movement, in the Jolly George incident, had threatened direct action as the British government looked to step up its intervention in the civil war in Russia against the Bolsheviks by sending weapons to Poland. After this point, until the mid-1930s, the Labour left in particular had been deeply suspicious that the capitalist states would attack the Soviet Union, perhaps even through the machinery of the League of Nations. This was the longer-term background to Attlee's concern in mid-January 1940 that the on-going Soviet-Finnish struggle might, at a time of 'phoney war' in Western Europe, serve those 'forces in this country' that would like 'to switch the war away from its real objective'.[117] Anthony Crosland feared a similar scenario: that the 'unexpected prolongation of the war . . . has given time for anti-Soviet feeling to reach an unprecedented pitch, and, even more important, it has given the forces of world capitalism an opportunity of firing their first broadside against the USSR'. In particular, he was concerned about the repercussions if the capitalist states were 'to raise the banner of help for Democratic Finland',[118] the very issue that would soon polarise Labour debate.

The range of Labour opinions over Finland revealed much about the Soviet Union's contested place in the party's internationalist thinking. Attlee accepted that Soviet Communism 'in its methods of repression, brutality and dictatorship it is only too like Nazism'.[119] He also openly 'deplore[d] the defection of the USSR'. Nonetheless, he retained an underlying hope that 'even yet it may range itself against fascism'.[120] As a result, Attlee continued to emphasise the need to 'widen the scope of international order' but refrained from mentioning the plight of Finland.[121]

This was a subtly different approach to that taken in the NEC's statement *Labour, the War and the Peace*, which was published on 9 February. Significantly, Attlee had not voted in favour of this policy document, which had been drafted by Dalton, because he did not 'like the balance of it'.[122] In addition to calling for the 'utmost effort to the overthrow of the Hitler system in Germany', the document reiterated much of the party's thinking about the need to 'establish a new Association or Commonwealth of Nations, the collective authority of which must transcend, over a proper sphere, the sovereign rights of separate states'. Crucially, however, it went beyond merely criticising the Soviet invasion of Finland and asserted that the party 'should regard the extinction of the free Finnish democracy as an intolerable disaster for civilisation'.[123]

The divisions within the movement were further heightened by the publication of the report of the NCL Delegation to Finland in March 1940. The report took pains to celebrate Finland as 'a free and democratic State in which personal liberty and civil rights are the foundation of national life' and to lavish praise on its system of parliamentary democracy within which the Social Democratic Party, as well as the trade unions and co-operative movement, operated. Significantly, the report argued that Finland 'had the same right to receive arms and volunteers that the Labour Movement always demanded for the Spanish Government'.[124] Notwithstanding the disingenuous nature of this claim given the NCL's decided ambivalence over Spain, this was a provocative argument.[125] Directly confronting the contention 'that to ask for help for Finland was to work for war with Russia', it asserted boldly that 'had such a danger existed it could have been removed at any time by Russia ceasing her aggression and withdrawing her troops from Finland'.[126]

Dalton was also forthright in accepting the possibility of a war with the Soviet Union as his confrontation with Maisky in mid-March 1940 shows.

Dalton strove 'to strike a note of frank and friendly intimidation'. He clearly judged that the situation had changed greatly since late September when he had urged that the Soviet invasion of Poland not be criticised too harshly. Dalton now told Maisky that Soviet aggression against Finland was 'disgraceful and indefensible'. He questioned which territories the Soviet Union would attack next, stating that he was 'unpleasantly reminded of Hitler's actions in the Sudetenland, which was followed, only a few months after, by the conquest of all of Czechoslovakia'. Boldly, Dalton stated: 'We don't want war with you – I repeat that our purpose is to kill Hitler – but if you force us into it, we shall not run away.'[127]

It was against this background, and in a context where the NEC would soon invite the Finnish Social Democratic Party as fraternal delegates to the annual party conference,[128] that a substantial part of the Labour left lent their support to an open letter opposing war between Britain and the Soviet Union. On this occasion, Brailsford, Trevelyan and the Webbs joined Liberals such as Richard Acland. Arguably in order to hold such a coalition together (which in terms of personnel mirrored the various popular front campaigns of the late 1930s), the letter emphasised some strategic military considerations for the British Empire of fighting a war against a large state such as the Soviet Union. Nonetheless, Labour internationalist considerations, which linked foreign and domestic policies, were at the forefront of the letter's concerns. Envisaging a British attack on the Soviet Union, it argued that 'no matter what errors the Soviet Union has committed, a very large section of the people of this country – especially the workers, who have been watching with sympathy the vast social and economic experiments of the Soviet Union – would interpret the action of our rulers as an attack upon Socialism'.[129] Laski was not a signatory of the letter, but he clearly feared a war with the Soviet Union for the same underlying reason. As Martin later put it, Laski considered that the 'socialist purpose at home involved maintaining, even at great cost, a friendly attitude towards the Soviet Union'.[130]

VIII

The Labour Party's reaction to Pritt's defence of the Soviet invasion of Finland further revealed that, in crucial respects, its international outlook still rested on the assumption of an alliance with the Soviet Union. Ahead of its meeting on 20 March 1940, the NEC prepared a memorandum intended to meet Pritt's claim that since the Labour Party conference had not yet had the opportunity to debate the issue, members of the Labour Party were free to voice their own opinions. In response, the NEC argued that 'on no other subject has the Annual Party Conference laid down more clearly what its attitude is than to the armed aggression of one state upon another'.[131]

Significantly, however, the NEC memorandum exposed the outdated nature of Labour's thinking on international affairs. The memorandum cited the 1934 policy documents *For Socialism and Peace* and *War and Peace* in support of 'collective action' taken by the British government against a 'peace-breaker'. These documents were, however, constructed at a time when the League of Nations was a credible international organisation and when the Soviet Union could be counted on to play a significant role in it. Both policy documents sought to undermine the war resistance resolution, which explicitly provided for the use of a general strike against the National government, and had been passed at the 1933 party conference on the motion of the left-wing Socialist League. The League, which was involved in a power struggle with the moderate majorities dominating Labour's NEC and the TUC General Council, was opposed to any involvement in a 'capitalist' and 'imperialist' war and, in the longer term, sought the establishment of closer economic and political relations with the Soviet Union.[132] Crucially, therefore, when Henderson introduced *War and Peace* at the 1934 Labour Party conference, he drew attention in particular to the Soviet Union's recent entry into the League of Nations. Henderson powerfully argued that even the Soviet Union recognised 'it may sometimes be necessary to co-operate with capitalist states for the preservation of peace' and went on to secure *War and Peace*'s passage by an overwhelming majority.[133]

Pritt's defence was not, of course, based on these points. Indeed, most of the debate focused on his unwillingness to accept party policy on Finland prior to its endorsement by the party conference. Pritt further argued that he retained a certain freedom of action, having opposed the passage of the NEC's statement, *Labour, the War and the Peace*, in February. These technical arguments did not, however, carry much weight on the NEC which moved to expel Pritt because of his inability to follow agreed party policy and his affinity to the CPGB. Susan Lawrence proposed an amendment, which was seconded by Ellen Wilkinson, to postpone any decision until after the party conference. In the event, however, the amendment was lost by an emphatic three votes to 17, with Laski the only other member lending it his support.[134]

Pritt's expulsion was, therefore, as much about party discipline to check the domestic threat from infiltration by Communist sympathisers as it was about rival views of the Soviet Union. Yet this too challenged the way in which Labour understood the links between Communism in Britain and in the Soviet Union, allowing a more critical view of the latter to develop.

Domestic anti-Communism had developed in the Labour Party during the 1920s as the CPGB sought to infiltrate it through a variety of methods. Anti-Communism continued to pervade the Labour Party, and particularly the trade union movement, in the 1930s, being epitomised by a suspicion of British Communist attempts to 'make mischief'[135] and involving a condemnation of them as 'tools of Stalin'.[136] The Labour Party had rejected the CPGB's applications for affiliation and had been quick to introduce disciplinary action against those associating with the CPGB, such as the Socialist League during the Unity Campaign of 1937.[137] Anti-Communism continued into the war. The CPGB quickly moved from initial support for the British war effort as an anti-fascist crusade to a condemnation of it as an 'imperialist war' on 5 October. At this point Pollitt was removed from the leadership in favour of Rajani Palme Dutt and official CPGB pronouncements defended the Soviet position at every stage. Even before the CPGB's volte face, the NEC had already rejected the CPGB's latest application for affiliation,[138] and on 20 December it devoted considerable energy to discussing Communist activity within the constituency parties.[139] Early in 1940 Attlee dismissed the CPGB as 'the dummy of the ventrilo-quist Stalin',[140] but this accusation now carried very different connotations than it did in the 1930s. Then, of course, fierce anti-Communism had sat alongside more favourable attitudes to the Soviet Union as an invaluable international ally. Yet since August 1939, the distinction between views of domestic Communism and views of the Soviet Union had become much finer. Communists had often been criticised for following the Soviet line, which was held to be fundamentally unsuitable to British circumstances. Now it was considered that the Soviet stance was not just wrong for Britain but also in the widest international sense.

IX

The advance of Hitler across Western Europe in April 1940, together with the Soviet control of Finland established the previous month, reduced the critical attention that the Labour Party gave to the Soviet Union. Demands to open discussions with the Soviet Union now increased. On 17 April Laski asked the NEC 'to explore without delay the possibility of rebuilding effective relations with the USSR'.[141] The proposal was shelved but the idea gathered momentum in left-wing *Tribune* circles with Cripps and George Strauss playing a central role.[142] Yet the only concrete outcome of these moves was that later in May 1940 Cripps, who had sought to act as a mediator since the start of the war, was sent to the Soviet Union as British Ambassador.

After the Labour Party entered the Churchill coalition in May 1940, it became markedly more restricted in its freedom to debate its own international policy.[143] This, together with the imminent threat of German invasion, prompted a wave of patriotic feeling to dominate Labour's international outlook. These sentiments, which contributed to the notion of the 'Peoples' War', had already begun to emerge in the Labour Party. Indeed, in February 1940 Durbin had stated that it was 'worth our while to die in order to preserve the way of life that has become natural to us'.[144] Martin later recalled how the 'desperate hour of 1940 called forth a great wave of patriotism', which he shared with Brailsford and Laski and meant 'putting aside . . . deep political differences with Mr Churchill, because . . . we had chosen our "captain" in a life-and-death struggle and that for the moment all that mattered was survival'.[145]

Against this background, the Labour Party conference in late May 1940 struck a decidedly ambiguous note. It endorsed the NEC's report which comprised its previous critical statements on the Soviet Union made since August 1939. Yet it also passed a resolution moved from the floor which contended that 'the defence of the Soviet Union is of vital importance to the cause of World Socialism'. This pledged 'the Party to oppose all forms of capitalist intervention against the Soviet Union of Russia' and to 'support no policy which might make friendly relations with the Soviet Union more difficult of attainment'.[146] The same uncertainty overshadowed the debate about Pritt. In line with the NEC's grounds for expulsion, Noel-Baker denounced Pritt for acting like one of the 'secret members' of the CPGB. He did, however, assert that 'all our hopes of Socialism depend on whether we can make an international system by which aggression shall be restrained' and express the hope that 'Russia will even yet come back and help us.'[147]

Throughout the rest of 1940 and into 1941 the Labour Party largely refrained from discussing the Soviet Union and instead concentrated its efforts on checking the Convention Movement which had emerged in July 1940, was led by Pritt and supported by the CPGB, and sought a negotiated peace with Nazi Germany.[148] At this same time, the Labour Party's debates over federalism saw an increasing division between those who sought a militarily strong United Nations and those who placed their hopes in a distinctly European federation.[149]

<h1 style="text-align:center">X</h1>

The Nazi invasion of the Soviet Union on 22 June 1941 dramatically changed the situation once again. The following day Attlee spoke of how 'we and the Russian people are fighting a common enemy'.[150] On 25 June the NCL sent 'warm greetings to the Russian people' and pledged 'its assurances of support in their effort to defeat the fascist enemy'.[151] By the end of July, as the Soviet Union suffered the full onslaught of the Nazi offensive, the

Labour Party and the TUC placed 'on record their warm appreciation of the great efforts of the Soviet Union in the common struggle against Hitlerism'. Welcoming 'the fullness of the co-operation which has developed between Great Britain and the USSR', they argued that a 'common understanding between their peoples' was a 'necessary condition of an enduring peace'. [152] At a time when British popular attitudes to the Soviet Union were enormously favourable, it was clearly a relief for the Labour Party to re-install the Soviet Union as an integral part of its struggle to defeat fascism.

At the same time, however, these developments served to re-introduce a distinction between positive views of the Soviet Union and more critical views of the CPGB. This allowed the Labour Party to separate what it saw as the particular merits of the Soviet Union from the disruptive tendencies of British Communists. Attlee commented that: 'We have always opposed the Communist Party in this country and have found it impossible to reach any basis of agreement with them. But we have always held that it was for the Russian people to choose the system of government which suits it.'[153] Meanwhile, the *Daily Herald*, alluding to the Convention Movement, argued that the CPGB had 'sought in recent months to interfere with the nation's war effort'.[154] And the joint statement from the Labour Party and the TUC in late July, which had been so full of praise for the Soviet Union, warned frankly that 'no association with the Communist Party' was possible because it had 'taken every opportunity to obstruct and weaken the national effort' and possessed an 'irresponsible and unstable character' which was not suited to 'the needs and purposes of the British people'.[155]

Even so, it was the re-integration of the Soviet Union in a positive manner into Labour's worldview that was most noticeable at this juncture. With internationalism viewed, at one level, as exchange between states, Laski argued that both Britain and the Soviet Union had much to gain from a close relationship. Indeed, he contended that:

> political offences apart, we have much to learn from the Soviet Union in all matters concerned with civil and criminal justice, including prison treatment. We have much to learn about the treatment of backward peoples, especially in the matter of education, where I think, broadly speaking the Russians are fifty years ahead of anything we can show in India or in Africa . . . We have much to learn, thirdly, about the proper place of scientific research in national organisation.

In return, he argued that Britain could 'demonstrate that, in a really creative way, the intellectual ceases to be an intellectual if he is forced to don the uniform of a particular creed'.[156]

Writing in late summer 1941, Cole adopted a similar position. He argued frankly that the 'ruling consideration for us, in this new phase of the war, must be that the Soviet Union is, by virtue of its basic economic and cultural institutions, a Socialist country, and therefore necessarily the principal rallying point for the forces of socialism throughout the world'.[157]

XI

It is clear that the era of the Nazi-Soviet pact was not a turning point for the Labour Party in the dramatic way that it was for Gollancz or Strachey. Earlier responses to the purges had already led many in the Labour Party to make uncomfortable comparisons between the internal regimes in the Soviet Union and Nazi Germany. Yet the Nazi-Soviet pact did more than just provide an opportunity for the expression of more critical views of the Soviet Union which had been inhibited earlier in the 1930s because of the Soviet Union's role as the principal means of checking the international threat from fascism. Instead the pact posed a serious challenge to the basis of Labour's internationalism.

As the Labour Party struggled to adjust to a world in which the Soviet Union could no longer be relied upon as an ally, ideas about federalism, involving a significant reduction in national sovereignty, were embraced to a much greater extent than ever before. These federalist ideas had emerged initially on the Labour left but, following the Soviet invasions of Poland and Finland, they were endorsed across an increasingly wide range of Labour opinion.

The various federal schemes had different emphases. They did, however, typically draw on older ideas about the need to eradicate international economic inequality through access to raw materials and the control of international trade. They also often involved the creation of an international police force, an idea that had been regularly mooted in the early 1930s. Yet, overall, the plans were decidedly thin on detail[158] – largely because they were produced quickly in response to the new and unsettling international circumstances created by the Nazi-Soviet pact. Most obviously, very little was said about which states would actually form the federal union. It was usually described as a federal union in Europe which might also include former imperial territories. Laski and Brailsford further proposed that any federation should consist of progressive, if not overtly socialist, states because of the all-important interaction between national and international values. Yet in their schemes the absence of the Soviet Union was greatly conspicuous.

An emphasis on internationalism as a two-way relationship between the international and domestic spheres also casts light on other developments during the early stages of the Nazi-Soviet pact. Soviet territorial expansion in Poland and then Finland led many from across the party's ideological spectrum to link their privately-developed critiques of the Soviet disregard for civil liberties in its domestic affairs with a condemnation of its actions abroad. With both Nazi Germany and the Soviet Union at the forefront of their concerns, demands for social justice within states and political justice between them were frequently voiced as the basis of any future world order. Moreover, a concern for the well-being of political prisoners in areas annexed by the Soviet Union found wide support across the Labour Party.

Yet Labour failed fully to make the transition to a worldview that did not involve a positive role for the Soviet Union. For the Labour left, with its greater affinity with the Soviet Union, this was particularly apparent. Indeed, in March 1940 a large part of the Labour left announced its opposition to British involvement in a war against the Soviet Union on the basis that this would also be an attack on 'socialism' in Britain. Furthermore, while some on the Labour centre right, such as Greenwood, readily labelled the Soviet invasion of Finland as 'imperialist', Brailsford was markedly more cautious. He insisted that it could not be defined as imperialist in the same way as British actions in India because in the Soviet Union there was no capitalist ruling class.

Even the Labour centre right, with its more critical attitudes towards the Soviet Union's foreign policy, had difficulty in adapting to the changed international circumstances. Some still retained a belief that the Soviet Union would eventually return to the 'right' side. Attlee wanted the party to stand aloof from the Soviet-Finnish War for this very reason, and Noel-Baker publicly speculated about the Soviet Union's future role in the struggle against international fascism at the Labour Party conference in May 1940. More significantly still, when the NEC made its case against Pritt's refusal to follow its agreed foreign policy in March 1940, it was forced to fall back on policy statements which had been developed firmly on the assumption of a Soviet alliance.

After the Nazi attack on the Soviet Union in 1941 the Labour Party as a whole quickly re-integrated the Soviet Union into its international outlook. In doing so, it attributed to the Soviet Union tremendous importance not just for achieving victory over Hitler but also, as Cole put it, for making 'socialism the basis of the post-war settlement'.[159] The era of the Nazi-Soviet pact had begun to shake the basis of Labour's internationalism but, with the Soviet Union established as a wartime ally, many painfully discovered insights were soon glossed over. Many ambiguities, therefore, remained as world war turned into Cold War and a Labour government had to face up to a world in which Britain was for the first time pitted against the Soviet Union.

5

THE FOREIGN POLICY OF
THE ATTLEE GOVERNMENT,
1945–50

John Callaghan

For twenty years the Labour Party's thinking about foreign policy had been conditioned by its assessment of the First World War as a catastrophe foretold. The secret world of diplomacy and balance of power politics, in this analysis, allowed a great war to begin almost by accident, though profound forces of militarism, imperialism and nationalism had provided the combustible material which the failure of statesmanship set alight in July–August 1914. The two equally matched sides had then fought each other to a standstill for four years eventually bringing down empires, wrecking economies and promoting social revolutions in the process of mutual attrition. Thereafter the avoidance of war informed Labour's thinking with the paradigm of 1914–18 in mind. At first the whole Treaty of Versailles was denounced for laying down the preconditions for a repeat performance. But the party soon learned to regard the institutions of the League of Nations as the best hope for war-avoidance, while pressing for measures of disarmament. Such beliefs peaked just as the liberal international order, on which they depended, unravelled between the Wall Street Crash of October 1929 and the advent of Hitler in January 1933. Though the party's official line continued to stress war-avoidance through the League and to oppose measures of rearmament – which suggested the return of an arms race and an alliance system redolent of 1914 – it concealed the increasing fragmentation of views within the organisation. The crisis of capitalism suggested to some that only a change of social system could avoid another world war; some talked of the need for collective security through an alliance with France, the Soviet Union and, perhaps, the USA; others continued to stress juridical instruments of arbitration and conciliation through the

League; and there was a revival of interest in economic appeasement drawing upon Britain's colonial resources.

The party continued to reject conscription – in symbolic opposition to British foreign policy – as late as April 1939, when the government introduced a bill in response to the collapse of Prague to German armed forces. In the summer the annual conference debated the international situation along the well-worn paths. The NEC resolution on the international situation talked about staving off the imminent danger of war by the formation of 'a strong group of peaceful powers bound together by pacts of mutual aid against aggression'. It complained about the delay in reaching an accord with France and the Soviet Union and it denounced the betrayal of Spain, Czechoslovakia and the League itself. Action ought to have been taken in 1932, it was said, when the Manchurian struggle had just begun. But appeasement, according to Philip Noel-Baker, one of the party's international experts, had become 'a dangerous pathological complaint' instead of a policy. Belatedly a stand was made with guarantees for Poland and Greece. But alliances, though undoubtedly necessary, did not constitute an active policy for peace. This still depended on a rebuilt League and, as Noel-Baker put it, 'the Labour Party will not abandon, now or ever, the vision of a new world order'.[1] Other speakers in the debate admitted that they still put their trust in 'peace conferences' or the social reconstruction of Europe, or worried that they would soon be fighting so that Britain could retain control of 'Egypt and Iraq and oil' – as William Mellor, former editor of the left-wing *Tribune*, expressed the point.[2] But it was Ernest Bevin who brought most of these concerns together in a widely-reported speech which said that collective security could never be effective unless all the parties concerned had something to secure.

He wanted to know what the causes of the present world disorder were and firmly laid the burden of his explanation on the economic insecurity which had characterised the years since 1918. He suggested that 'the biggest contributor is this country and not Germany, for one of the most potent causes of world disorder has been our dominant financial policy'. He was referring to the policy of deflation, pursued with rigour since 1920. Chamberlain was merely a spokesman for the bankers, the main supporters of appeasement in Bevin's view. The Prime Minister was guilty of trying to fit world events into the requirements of the City of London. Bevin agreed with the main resolution on the international situation in believing in the desirability of a closer relationship with the USA and thought that the quickest way to secure it was through the Empire – the Dominions and Africa in particular – rather than through agreements in Europe. An 'understanding' with the USA might come about by extending 'the great

Commonwealth idea' to make the USA 'a partner, at least economically, even though it may involve a limitation of our [British] sovereignty'. Instead of scrapping the Ottawa Agreement – which had introduced a trading system of imperial preference in 1932 in place of the free trade which the Labour Party had always supported – Bevin thought that it ought to be expanded. Collective security and an 'economic Peace Bloc' would then go together and be extended to all those willing to co-operate, all those who choose 'to come within our preference system' and pool 'the whole of the Colonial Empires of the world and their resources':

> It would bring the 'Haves' together and they would, in fact, be controlling 90 per cent of the essential raw materials of the world. They would also control 75 per cent of the world population and, in fact, would be the great financial and money powers of the world.[3]

Having pooled their arms, resources and economic power the Peace Bloc, as Bevin called it, would be able to 'pilot the world along towards a World Order'. The colonies would be held in trusteeship and the world's resources would be opened up for the benefit of humanity. Bevin's striking vision of a US-UK or US-imperial European condominium over the government of the Free World would have to wait until more powerful politicians reworked the idea in the 1940s, including, of course, Bevin himself. It was an idea he had been working on for some time, in various forms, and one he would return to again as Foreign Secretary.[4]

Leaving aside such specific plans for the moment, Bevin's thinking reflected the enduring tendency of Labour's principal figures to regard the Empire as both a fact of life and a force for good in the world. It is true that under the influence of the radicalism generated in the last year of the First World War, the party had recommended international supervision of colonies south of the Sahara and north of the Zambesi. It even denounced the system of mandates that was actually adopted in 1919 as a fig-leaf behind which imperialism operated as usual. But the 800,000 square miles added to the British dominion after the First World War were rarely mentioned in Labour publicity. Though it continued, as it always had done, to deplore specific acts of repression in the colonies, the Labour leadership treated these as deviations from the benign norm and often talked about the Empire as a voluntary Commonwealth of Nations – in fact as well as in aspiration. Nationalists in India noticed little or no difference in imperial policy on the subcontinent during the two minority Labour administrations of the inter-war period. If the Second World War made a difference to this outlook, it underlined both the difficulties in delaying Indian independence any further and the desirability of hanging on to as much as possible of the rest of the Empire-Commonwealth. Promises of 'jam tomorrow' had been unable to pacify the Indian National Congress in 1942 when the Cripps Mission failed to broker a deal. Nationalist agitation grew again as the imprisoned Congress leaders came out of their jails in 1945. But the war had also confirmed a proposition which no one in public life denied in Britain; Great Power status depended on the Empire-Commonwealth. None of the Victorians in Attlee's Cabinet were anxious to surrender this status, though as upholders of the trusteeship idea Labour's leaders were perhaps more conscious than their Conservative counterparts of international pressures for decolonisation which Franklin Roosevelt had spearheaded since 1942.

The war effort had concentrated official minds on Empire 'development'. Suddenly the received rationale of British imperialism in the interwar years became something more than propaganda as civil servants and Tory politicians adopted Fabian arguments for reconciling British needs of the hour with the duties of trusteeship in colonial economic advancement. Monopolistic trading boards were established in the Crown Colonies and other dependencies in which the British retained control. Local taxes were increased, sometimes as an 'incentive' to work, accompanying production drives. Successful efforts were made to increase production of foodstuffs and raw materials for export at prices fixed below world market levels. Dollar earnings were 'pooled' for the benefit of British spending priorities. Local expenditures in the war effort were borne locally as colonies were awarded frozen sterling credits in return for services and goods rendered. By 1945 Britain owed its dependencies £3,500 million. Under the Labour government the poorest of these dependencies, the Crown Colonies, saw their sterling credits grow from £454 million to £928 million as Britain continued to extract dollar earnings for its own immediate benefit. In short British reconstruction efforts employed a more systematic exploitation of colonies than at any previous time in imperial history.[5] There was development *in* the colonies, but not necessarily *of* the colonies.

I

When Labour entered office in 1945 British armed forces were stretched across Europe and the Middle East and helping to restore European colonialism in Indo-China and Indonesia. There was the new indefinite responsibility of occupied Germany and the commitment, which Churchill made towards the end of 1944, to prevent the Communists from coming to power in Greece. British troops could also be found in Austria and Trieste. In Egypt the presence of about 150,000 British troops and various military bases – including the biggest arms dump in the world – were being questioned by a nationalist agitation which wanted to abrogate the 1936 Treaty. In Palestine and India the problem of maintaining the British presence was on a larger scale still. The navy had commitments in the Pacific, the Caribbean, the Mediterranean and the Indian Ocean. At the end of 1946 over 1.4 million still served in the armed forces. Peacetime conscription was introduced in 1947 and the cost of the armed forces amounted to 15 per cent of national income, falling to 8 per cent in 1948. About half of this cost was composed of imperial commitments such as the 20,000-strong garrison in Cyrenaica (modern Libya), the former Italian colony which Bevin was negotiating to retain as a British base, and the war against Communist insurgency in Malaysia where the British army would perfect techniques later deployed by the USA in Vietnam. The Cold War threatened to increase these costs further still when the Korean War broke out in June 1950 and Hugh Gaitskell was forced to contemplate a defence bill amounting to 14 per cent of national income.

It would be a mistake to imagine these commitments simply stemmed from forces beyond any British government's control. Though it is obvious enough that the Labour government responded to events as and when they occurred, it did so with assumptions, plans and theories. By the time it took office arrangements had already been made at Bretton Woods in association with the US administration to establish institutions for the management of free trade. Similarly a United Nations Organisation (UNO) had been conceived; its Charter was signed at San Francisco in June 1945, shortly before the Labour government was formed. By these means the Anglo-American states sought to preserve peace, advance justice and constitute permanent structures for international cooperation. The wartime advance of the Soviet Union into Central Europe, the emergence of mass Communist parties in Italy, France, Czechoslovakia and Yugoslavia, the post-war instability of Germany and Greece, the progress of the civil war in China, the Soviet presence in northern Iran, and the upsurge of nationalism in much of Asia; all these problems jeopardised both UNO and the Bretton Woods arrangements. US policy-makers in the State Department believed that American prosperity depended on a global application of what used to be called the Open Door policy. Communist autarky stood in the way of this objective, as did the sort of imperial preference schemes that operated within the British Empire. Since 1932 Britain had operated both a sterling area and an imperial preference trading zone based on the Empire. During the war economic necessity made the government receptive to schemes of colonial economic development, as we have seen. When Labour entered office in 1945 these projects were continued with a Fabian gloss. Meanwhile, Foreign Office officials, seemingly unconcerned by massive economic problems at home, worried that if Britain 'ceased to regard [itself] as a World Power' it would 'gradually cease to be one'. Sir Orme Sargent, shortly to become Permanent Under-Secretary, thus advised in July 1945, that 'in the immediate future' Britain had to 'take a stand' in Europe to maintain its interests in Finland, Poland, Czechoslovakia, Austria, Yugoslavia and Bulgaria – all states in which the Soviet Union had a major interest – and maintain 'close and friendly relations with Italy, Greece and Turkey'. To sum up, Sargent advised that 'in the immediate future we must take the offensive in as many of the Eastern countries of Europe as possible'.[6]

II

Friction between Britain and the Soviet Union over the future of Poland and the holding of free elections in the countries under Red Army occupation had already surfaced at Yalta in February 1945. On the other hand, Stalin had also been given to understand that Eastern Europe was a Soviet sphere of influence – Churchill explicitly proposed this arrangement in October 1944 in Moscow. Different interpretations inevitably accompanied these and other deals such as those concerning the future of Germany, the treatment of war criminals, the payment of reparations and so on. Orme Sargent's advice was calculated to increase such friction. Before the result of the British general election was known Attlee accompanied Churchill to Potsdam in July 1945 and witnessed the beginnings of the Cold War as Truman took up the Polish question with Stalin. The wartime alliance was already breaking down now that Germany was defeated and the first successful test of the nuclear bomb – which Stalin was told about while the conference was in session – gave the USA a monopoly of the new super weapon. As early as August 1945, Attlee set up a secret Cabinet sub-committee on atomic energy which he called the 'Atom Bomb Committee', though most of the Cabinet were unaware of its existence. It is evidence of Attlee's conviction that Britain was and would remain a Great Power. His decision marked the beginning of the process by which Britain acquired its own bomb independently of the USA. The first step was taken before the end of the year, though the decision to go ahead and build atomic weapons was left until January 1947, by which time the US had signalled its intention to maintain its monopoly position by refusing to share its secrets with Britain. Parliament first heard a vague allusion to these fateful steps only in May 1948.

The British disposition in foreign and defence policy – bold and confident as it was – was not supported by the underlying economic reality that Labour inherited in July 1945. The war had cost Britain about a quarter of its national wealth and most of its export trade, in addition to saddling it with sterling liabilities of £3,500 million. Exports would have to increase by 75 per cent to correct the balance of payments deficit even if the volume of imports could be kept down to pre-war levels. Rationing was intensified. Lend-Lease was terminated six days after the Japanese surrender yet Britain suffered from shortages of every kind including dollar earnings, manpower and building materials needed for the urgent housing programme. While exports earned just £350 million, total outgoings including military expenditure abroad was running at the rate of £2,000 million per year. A team of officials headed by Keynes – who warned that the country faced a 'financial Dunkirk' – negotiated a US loan in December 1945, subject to Congressional ratification. But this would only become available in July 1947 and, when it came, much of it was frittered away trying to maintain sterling convertibility – a condition of the loan which the USA insisted upon. In the light of these facts the government's determination to maintain Britain as a world power is as impressive as its determination to press ahead with its domestic reform programme, all the more so as the public expectations and pressures which attached to the latter were absent in foreign relations.

Well before the hardening of US attitudes towards the Soviet Union, when Britain's economic problems were still mounting, the new Foreign Secretary, Ernest Bevin, was already following the advice of officials like Orme Sargent and Gladwyn Jebb (assistant Under-Secretary and United Nations advisor at the Foreign Office) that to yield, as the latter put it, 'to any Russian demand would clearly mean that we were not prepared to play the part of a Great Power'.[7] This may account for Jebb's high opinion of Bevin whom he counted as one of the best Foreign Secretaries Britain had ever had. Within two months of taking office Bevin, with Jebb at his elbow, was negotiating at the London Council of Foreign Ministers meeting in September 1945 to acquire British control of the former Italian colony of Cyrenaica in North Africa. The USA favoured an international trusteeship rather than a British military base. Only when Molotov, who agreed to the British proposal, insisted on a Soviet military base in neighbouring Tripolitania did Bevin change tack and side with the Americans. In October, at the Soviet Embassy, Molotov accused Bevin of wanting a British monopoly in the Mediterranean to which the Foreign Secretary replied that Britain could not tolerate a 'new military power . . . across the lifeline of the British Empire'.[8] Molotov had a point, the British claimed 'special strategic rights' in Libya. But Foreign Office officials realised that this argument might not convince the USA. One way round this obstacle was to propose the rapid independence of Cyrenaica so that 'we can conclude with her an alliance such as we have had with Egypt'.[9] British confidence on this score was based on the supposed reliability of Sheikh Idris, the Emir of the Senussi, a local collaborator of the sort that Britain had been accustomed to find in 'independent' Egypt. But other suggestions were considered, such as extending the Senussi writ over Tripolitania. Bevin agreed with the ancient South African sage, General Smuts, one of the originators of the mandates idea, that with the Soviets having already reduced the Balkans to virtual satellites, and now casting greedy eyes on the Persian Gulf, across a weakened and dependent Iran, it was only a matter of time before they occupied 'a commanding position in the Mediterranean' and undermined Britain's Great Power status – if they were allowed a say in any international trusteeship over the former Italian colonies.[10] This had to be blocked at all costs – British control of Gibraltar, Cyprus, Malta, and East Africa was evidently not enough, even though Britain also had troops stationed in Palestine, Egypt and Greece. The Foreign Office was also preparing a case for British control of Italian Somaliland and the Ogaden which would be administered as a single unit together with British Somaliland, but for tactical reasons the idea was not tabled at the Paris meeting of the Council of Foreign Ministers in April 1946.

III

This was not the posture of a Power that was down and out, though behind the scenes both the Chancellor, Hugh Dalton, and the Prime Minister were unhappy about the scale of British overseas commitments and unconvinced by the strategic logic of maintaining such a massive British presence in the Middle East. In March 1946 Attlee had confided to a sympathetic Dalton, while Bevin was negotiating to obtain Cyrenaica, that he was:

> pressing the Chiefs of Staff and the Defence Committee [to take] a large view of his own, which aims at considerable disengagement from areas where there is a risk of us clashing with the Russians. This would mean giving up any attempt to keep open the passage through the Mediterranean in war-time, and to pull out from all the Middle East, including Egypt, and, of course, from Greece. We should then constitute a line of defence across Africa from Lagos to Kenya and concentrate a large part of our forces in the latter . . . we should concentrate a great part of the Commonwealth defence, including many industries, in Australia. We should thus put a wide glacis of desert and Arabs between ourselves and the Russians.

Dalton added that 'This is a very bold and interesting idea and I am inclined to favour it.'[11] This ran completely counter to Foreign Office proposals for increasing British control over the Mediterranean and keeping the UN out. Foreign Office thinking proceeded as if the Prime Minister's reservations did not exist. An interdepartmental committee, for example, reporting shortly before the Council of Foreign Ministers' Paris meeting in 1946, took the same line as Smuts. It particularly disliked the American idea of a five-Power advisory committee to supervise the UN trusteeship of Libya because it would give the Soviet Union a say in the area. The idea that a referendum should be held to test local opinion was dismissed as frankly ludicrous, bearing in mind, as one official observed, that referenda did not always work well even in civilised countries such as Switzerland. Press reports in Cairo, however, were already blaming Britain for obstructing the creation of an international trusteeship for the former Italian colony and, according to the Commander-in-Chief in the Middle East, General Paget, were having a disturbing effect on the already tense situation in Libya itself.[12] Bevin, advised by the Chiefs of Staff that a Soviet presence in North Africa could only 'lower our prestige and lead to unrest among the Arab tribes', went to the Council of Foreign Ministers determined to block the Soviets by proposing immediate independence for both Cyrenaica and Tripolitania. But when the Americans came round to the idea that Italy should resume control, he changed tack again by arguing that 'Cyrenaica was vital from the point of view of the British Empire.' This implicitly confirmed Molotov's suspicion that Britain had all along wanted to turn Libya in to a new Egypt – that is, independent under British military occupation. He was also aware of the British plan for the Horn of Africa, but this was a secondary concern. As late as February 1948 Bevin was still advising the Cabinet in favour of British control in Libya even if this meant giving back Somaliland and Eritrea to the Italians.[13]

The Foreign Office's appetite for additional bases in the Mediterranean was seemingly unaffected by the problems it was facing everywhere in the Middle East and may have been sharpened by the imminent loss of India. Oil was a factor as the scramble for rights between Britain and the USA in Iran and Saudi Arabia illustrated. Bases were also a factor; the Chiefs of Staff advising that the USSR's own oil fields were more easily hit from bases in the Middle East. Then there was the vacuum problem – the Soviet Union, already 'malevolently bent on expansion southwards' into the oil preserves, had to be checked.[14] But Egypt had been repeatedly promised (since 1882) that the British would soon withdraw and there was still no sign of them doing so, despite mounting nationalist agitation. Palestine was coming to be seen as an insoluble problem for Britain and elsewhere in the region the traditional leaders who had always collaborated with Britain were faced with national movements and worse. In Iraq the Communist Party had grown alongside the resurgence of Kurdish separatism. In Iran another Communist Party had become significant especially after the creation of autonomous governments in the Kurdish and Azeri regions which owed something to the continued presence of the Red Army since the Anglo-Soviet invasion of 1941.

Anglo-American differences over the future of Iran tended to fade when the Soviet Union persisted with its claims for oil concessions.[15] Although Truman had acknowledged the USSR's claim on rights of access to the Mediterranean at Potsdam in July 1945, he was accusing it of planning an invasion of Turkey and seizure of the Black Sea Straits in January 1946. Stalin's delay in withdrawing Soviet troops from Iran in March 1946, under the terms of the wartime agreement which Britain and the US complied with, added to the friction. That month Churchill made his Fulton Speech warning of an imperilled 'Christian civilization' in all the countries beyond North America and the British Empire, and the US Joint Chiefs of Staff came to the same conclusion warning that 'the defeat or disintegration of the British Empire would eliminate from Eurasia the last bulwark of resistance between the US and Soviet expansion . . . Militarily, our present position as a world power is of necessity closely interwoven with that of Great Britain.'[16] The Soviet Union withdrew from Iran in April and continued to demobilise its troops so that only three million of the twelve million in uniform remained by 1948. By this time, however, the Soviet Union had responded to the Marshall Plan of June 1947 by tightening its grip on Eastern Europe and the perception and fear of an ideologically-driven expansionist empire was heightened in the West. This may have been a factor in forcing Attlee to revise his views on the wisdom of maintaining, and even increasing, the British presence in the Middle East. Since the spring of 1945 he had expressed scepticism on this issue – opposing the plan for Cyrenaica, favouring international control of the Suez Canal, and expressing doubt on the need for a massive British military presence in Egypt. He observed that from the Soviet viewpoint Egypt was a British satellite and in an age of aerial warfare this was an unnecessary provocation since the strategic argument for British occupation was simply redundant. By January 1947, however, he had backed down from this stance, under pressure from Bevin, who was supported by the Foreign Office and the Chiefs of Staff.[17] The unfolding Cold War ensured that such heretical views would not be taken seriously in Cabinet.

IV

The implications of polarisation in international affairs were clear to contemporaries. Whereas Attlee had once imagined Britain on the eastern boundary of a strategic zone centred in North America, critics of Bevin's foreign policy from within the Labour Party pointed out as early as May 1947 that it committed Britain to forward defences all over the globe, under American leadership.[18] A vocal opposition had taken the view since 1941 that Britain should seek to befriend the Soviet Union, rather than the USA. Others, like the *Keep Left* authors, had favoured a socialist 'third force' via European integration.[19] But these had been minority views, lacking support at Cabinet level, and the larger numbers sympathetic to the Soviet Union melted away as the Cold War intensified, especially after Marshall Aid was announced and Labour's domestic programme received the support of American dollars. Bevin himself was keen to restore Britain's economic independence from the USA – necessarily so for it was obvious that this was a precondition of Britain remaining a Great Power. What is more interesting is how he imagined this could be achieved, and here his ideas of 1939 resurfaced. The scheme he championed envisaged the economic restoration of Western Europe on the basis of a co-ordinated development of imperial possessions, especially on the African continent. As he told the French Prime Minister Paul Ramadier in September 1947, 'with their populations of 47 million and 40 million respectively and with their vast colonial possessions they [Britain and France] could, if they acted together, be as powerful as either the Soviet Union or the United States'. Bevin stressed that 'they possessed between them supplies of raw materials greater than those of any other country' and he was impressed 'by the number of raw materials in which the United States was lacking'.[20]

As this project was developed other imperial Powers were invited to join it, including Belgium, the Netherlands and South Africa, with Bevin calling for the involvement of Italy and Portugal too. It was made clear from the start that West European economic integration was 'wanted for political reasons, such as combating communism', as well as to secure its future economic independence.[21] Immediately after the Soviet Union formally refused Marshall Aid and its conditions, and the Cold War division of Europe had hardened, Bevin and his officials talked of the 'opportunity' which the European Recovery Programme offered to promote 'a union . . . which would have natural cohesion and political reality'. Like the Americans Bevin initially saw a customs union as a necessary step in the restoration of the West European economy and the defeat of Communism.[22] Indeed the US considered that Marshall Aid was to be conditional on such progress and Bevin realised that British co-operation was necessary on this score if Congress was to approve the massive expenditures required. But the British were always clear in their own minds that they wanted nothing to do with a customs union that would compromise the UK's imperial role. The development of colonial resources was seen as 'vital for our long-term viability', in the words of a briefing for the Cabinet Economic Policy Committee.[23] Bevin was perfectly open in his conviction that Britain 'was not just another European country'; as he told the Americans at the International Trade Organisation negotiations in Geneva in June 1947 'through the resources of its empire . . . it could make a contribution to European recovery second only to that of the United States'.[24]

As early as the autumn of 1947 the Treasury, the Foreign Office and Colonial Office were at one in rejecting European union, not only as a threat to imperial preference and the preservation of the sterling area, but also as inevitably involving a supranational authority. On all these counts the imperial role would be weakened and the perceived advantages of the Commonwealth lost. Bevin remained convinced that 'some measure of economic unity' in Western Europe was essential to restore its independence from the USA. But he again stressed to the Economic Policy Committee (November 1947) that control 'over important Colonial territories' was vital to the project since they contained 'resources [which] would be available to sustain this new structure'. Stafford Cripps, the Chancellor of the Exchequer, agreed that 'the first step should be the creation of a Customs Union with the Colonial Empire'. His predecessor Hugh Dalton – a man who was appalled by the thought of 'pullulating, poverty-stricken, diseased, nigger communities' when he was offered the Colonial Office in 1950[25] – agreed that the principal value of any arrangement 'we might enter into with Western Europe lay in the Colonial resources which this might make available to us'. Harold Wilson, President of the Board of Trade, also spoke against a customs union but added 'that it would be inadvisable to appear lukewarm or hostile' to the proposal in view of American support for the idea. In discussion it was observed that:

> The United States and Russia would be critical of any arrangements which appeared to involve the exploitation of Colonial areas in the interests of Western Europe, or any restrictions on the development of multilateral trading. It would therefore be inadvisable in any public statement to lay emphasis on the inclusion of Colonial territories within any arrangements that might be contemplated.[26]

The public statements of Labour politicians were in fact very careful to stress colonial 'development'. Every minister in the government made speeches extolling the virtues of Britain's overseas economic development policies at a time when the net gain of this activity was very definitely

Britain's rather than its colonies', though this was naturally obscured by official rhetoric.[27] Future problems in African colonies such as the Gold Coast (Ghana) and Kenya were related to the socially disruptive policies Britain pursued in the period between the opening of the war and the end of the Labour government, including the doubling of the white settler population in Kenya, the intensification of land theft in that country, widespread shortages and inflation. No doubt Bevin was as sincere as Creech-Jones at the Colonial Office in wanting genuine development in Britain's colonies, if only so that future markets for British goods would be created by rising living standards in Africa. But the capital for major overseas investments could not be found in Britain. Not only was it bedevilled by shortages of every kind in the state sector of the economy, Bevin and the Labour government had no power to direct the flow of private investments. The vast capital outflow from Britain which actually occurred was the equivalent to eight per cent of the national income, but the Dominions took the bulk of it, especially Australia and South Africa.[28] In the Crown Colonies there was net disinvestment. Just £8 million flowed annually under the Colonial Development and Welfare Act, while a far greater flow of value came back to Britain. The ill-fated groundnuts scheme in Tanganyika cost £40 million and £86 million was found between 1945 and 1949 to invest in Malaya's rubber plantations and tin mines, these representing the second and fifth largest dollar earners in the sterling area at a time when Labour was desperate to overcome the dollar shortage. But these large-scale projects were exceptions to the rule. The chief devices for colonial development were the sterling balances, the monopsonist trading boards, the physical controls on colonial commerce, higher taxes, production drives, and emigration. Bevin was thinking long-term, of course, when he set out with his plan to raise British living standards and achieve political independence for Britain by colonial development. He was not even sure of the raw material resources which the Empire possessed and in August 1947 asked for an inventory to be made highlighting those that were scarce in the United States.[29] But the fact that Britain persisted throughout the 1950s in the view that its future prosperity was bound up with the Commonwealth is surely evidence that it was taken as commonsense in the 1940s.

Ministers and officials also speculated on the likely results of Britain remaining aloof from Western European economic integration, noting that even in the short run there could be 'devastating competition from the Continent' in certain basic industries such as steel and chemicals. Some officials feared that if Britain stood alone 'we shall just manage to survive as pigmies between two giants' always dependent on one of them – the USA –

for protection. Robin Hankey, Head of the Northern Department at the Foreign Office, observed that 'we have not had, in practice, sufficient industry to arm the British Empire for the last twenty-five years and in two wars . . . we have only survived because the Americans have made the arms for us and in effect given us the money to pay for them'. Gladwyn Jebb, in the same discussion, talked of the 'dismal choice' of Soviet satellite or poor dependant of the USA which awaited an isolated Britain, but he also saw that 'a Customs Union does not make sense unless it leads on to economic and political union'; this meant losing the Empire and accepting the eventual German domination of Western Europe in perhaps twenty years time. It was seen that 'every long-term economic and strategic argument would seem to be in favour' of European economic integration because it 'would surely offer greater security and stability than any system of military alliances could achieve'. Hankey argued that 'Western Europe as a whole . . . is potentially a Great Power even by modern standards' but he went on to advocate the position which Bevin championed in Cabinet; 'we can, I believe, only meet this situation by actively building up the economic potential of the Empire, and by pressing forward the economic and political reconstruction of Western Europe and also co-ordinating its defence as a whole'.[30]

Bevin obtained Cabinet approval for his plan and persisted throughout 1948 in linking it with resistance to Soviet expansion, mobilisation of African resources and European union to create 'a bloc which, in both population and productive capacity, could stand on an equality with the western hemisphere and Soviet blocs'.[31] It was not until the autumn of 1949 that he reluctantly acknowledged in Cabinet that his imperial 'third force' strategy was dead.[32] In the meantime he learned some hard lessons that had plagued imperial-minded politicians since 1918. There was insufficient political unity in the Commonwealth; the UK could not supply imperial defence requirements on its own; Britain did not possess the capital to develop Africa and the Middle East; and Western Europe could not defend itself without American assistance. The formation of NATO in April 1949 was formal recognition of US hegemony, but its reality had been established during the Second World War and an American 'empire by invitation' was there for the taking in its immediate aftermath. For the British this did not mean that the world role was finished. Bevin only echoed his officials and virtually the whole political establishment in Britain in calculating that it was usually possible to reconcile American and British views and in supposing that as the US took on the burden of global responsibilities it would learn to regard the UK and its Commonwealth as its most reliable and essential friends.[33] Western Europe might well form a Customs Union,

but Britain had too much to lose by submerging itself in a mere regional
project.

V

Withdrawal from India, Ceylon and Burma in 1947; the need for the
Americans to take over in Greece and Turkey in the same year; the scuttle
from Palestine in 1948 – these strategic retreats were not intended to
inaugurate a general de-colonisation process. Disengagement from the sub-
continent was a function of the fact that Britain had faced an effective
national movement there since the end of the First World War. Labour
politicians had individually and collectively expressed sympathy with the
ideal of Dominion status for India since the beginning of the twentieth
century. Conservative politicians had repeatedly legislated for constitutional
change to appease the nationalists, without enduring success. The Second
World War further radicalised the sub-continent and brought US influence
to bear on the debate about India's future. The War Cabinet had considered
the idea that Britain might 'engage in a grand scheme of majestic politics
involving direct appeals to Indian peasants and workers over the heads of an
"unrepresentative" bourgeois Congress'.[34] Even Cripps, friend of India that
he was, thought that:

> If the British Government could enlist the sympathy of the workers
> and peasants by immediate action on their behalf, the struggle in
> India would no longer be between Indian and British on a nationalist
> basis, but between the classes in India on an economic basis. There
> would thus be a good opportunity to rally the mass of Indian opinion
> to our side.[35]

The naivety is staggering but, to be generous, was probably borne of war-
time duress and wishful thinking. But what is one to make of the fact that
Bevin was complaining of a policy of 'scuttle' from India as late as January
1947, when Attlee silenced him in Cabinet by simply asking for 'a practical
alternative'?[36] If this was more wishful thinking so was Britain's initial
negotiating gambit which tried to get something like the settlement
proposed by Cripps in 1942 – that is the retention of a federal India within
the Commonwealth and the sterling area and continuing Indian dependency
on British military leadership, involving the use of Indian armed forces and
facilities for British operations in Southeast Asia. These ambitions were soon
demolished – hence Bevin's complaints and a hasty, improvised withdrawal
took place not dissimilar to the retreat from Palestine a year later and in
acknowledgement of the same problem of ungovernability.

Once the loss of India was seen to be inevitable, the Labour government became more dedicated to the development of the Middle East and East Africa as its replacements, though the original rationale for occupation of these places had been to defend India.[37] The Middle East now became the 'gateway to Africa' and the Indian Ocean which Britain had to defend against supposedly inevitable Soviet incursions. It was also argued that British prestige in the whole of southern Europe, the Balkans and Turkey depended on it and that it was (according to Bevin) of enormous economic value to Britain. As late as the spring of 1948 about 270,000 British troops were deployed in a dozen different countries in the region – this at a time of acute 'manpower' shortage in Britain itself.[38] Advice from the Chiefs of Staff and the Foreign Office, both seemingly oblivious to Arab national sentiment as much as they were uninterested in Britain's economic plight, was adamant that the Middle East was a vital 'strategic reserve' into which the Soviets would inevitably descend in the event of a British withdrawal.

VI

On colonial matters – as in its attitude to nuclear weapons, European economic integration, the disposition to challenge Soviet hegemony in Eastern Europe and the search for economic independence from the USA – the foreign policy of the Attlee government was predicated on the maintenance of Britain's Great Power status on the basis of its Empire-Commonwealth. Growing tensions between the USA and the Soviet Union in the course of 1946, culminating in President Truman's announcement of an American policy of 'containment' of Communism in March 1947, followed by the announcement of Marshall Aid in June of that year, ensured that the basis was laid for a 'special relationship' with the USA – the only Power to have emerged from the Second World War stronger than when it went in. Weak though Britain was, it was substantially stronger than the defeated Axis Powers and France. Its global commitments meant that it could be expected to 'punch above its weight' in the confrontation with Communism. It was for these reasons that the US administration stopped lecturing the British on the evils of colonialism – as Roosevelt had done throughout the war – and began to regard the remnants of Empire as an asset. The suppression of Communist insurgency by the British in Malaysia from 1948 and the successful attempt to pre-empt a Communist victory in Greece from 1944 – not to mention the efforts to restore French and Dutch colonialism in the Far East against nationalist and Communist elements – showed what could be done.

In 1948 Communist parties throughout the world went on the offensive – rhetorical and industrial in Western Europe, military in much of Asia. In

China the Communist armies swept their American-backed 'nationalist' opponents into the sea in the course of 1949. In June 1950 Communist North Korea attacked South Korea with the approval of Moscow. The British military budget already stood at a damaging 7.5 per cent of national income when the Korean War began. Under pressure from the USA, the Cabinet now approved an increase in expenditure from £700 million to £1,800 million for the year, with a further £3,600 million over the next five years. When Hugh Gaitskell became Chancellor of the Exchequer in October 1950 Britain was pressured to raise the projected expenditure to £6,000 million, but the USA finally accepted £4,700 million – or 14 per cent of national income. In the event it was only another twelve months before Labour was ejected from power in the general election of October 1951. Churchill's incoming administration, realising the disastrous scale of the projected defence expenditure, scaled it down. But in the meantime differences over foreign policy within the Labour Party, already evident before the Second World War ended,[39] had flared up when it was realised that the American demands of 1950 represented the price of success for the government's foreign policy. Aneurin Bevan's resignation from the Cabinet was the dramatic signal. A period of exceptional bitterness in the internal politics of the Labour Party was begun, centring on foreign policy.

6

LABOUR PARTY FACTIONALISM AND WEST GERMAN REARMAMENT, 1950–4

Robert Crowcroft[1]

The history of the Labour Party during the 1950s is well-known as witnessing sustained and intensive factional conflict which lasted throughout the decade. This occurred against the backdrop of the early Cold War, with debates about the development of the hydrogen bomb and the prospective rearmament of West Germany giving rise to multiple internal clashes. While these struggles have generated a sizeable literature, there remain gaps in the historiography of the period, stemming largely from the competing and very personal interpretations advanced by Michael Foot and Philip Williams in their biographies of Aneurin Bevan and Hugh Gaitskell respectively.[2] While a considerable amount of scholarship has been carried out relating to the party and the Korean War in the early fifties,[3] there are limitations in the historiography relating to West Germany and the party, particularly in granting the German issue its rightful position in accounting for the factional crises.[4] Previous work has identified German rearmament as a controversy that became central to the conflict between left and right, yet an important series of events *within* the right over Germany, and the ramifications of this for existing understandings of the party between 1950–4, have been neglected. These events took the form of a conflict between two groups – one, led by the veteran Hugh Dalton and comprised of numerous prominent Labour figures, vehemently opposed to German rearmament; the other, under the dual leadership of Chancellor of the Exchequer and rising star Hugh Gaitskell, and deputy leader Herbert Morrison, advocating the remilitarisation of West Germany as an important element of European defence. This chapter will therefore seek to link the West German issue with the other internal struggles that wracked Labour, chiefly a conflict between an alliance of those loyal to Gaitskell and Morrison and the Bevanite group, assembling a more complex interpretation of the disputes than has previously been attempted, and bringing these events to the forefront of an examination of the period.

In spite of the prevailing tendency for historians to perceive Germany as a Bevanite issue, this chapter will show that that group was only peripherally involved with the problem until 1953, and even then were driven largely by their concern for relations with Moscow. It is significant, given subsequent Bevanite claims, that Bevan himself did not demur in Cabinet from the government line on the inevitability of German armed forces. In fact, while apparently not speaking publicly on Germany at this time, in the late forties Bevan does seem to have actually *supported* German rearmament, telling Dalton and Stafford Cripps that Britain 'ought to build them [the Germans] up as much as we could', being a more resistant barrier to Communism than the French.[5] This conversation sheds incriminating light on his future motivations in campaigning against official policy on Germany, suggesting that the Bevanite position may have been predicated on a degree of sheer opportunism and anti-Gaitskellite hostility. Instead, the primary actors during the most important stages of the controversy were a faction, previously unacknowledged in the literature, centred upon the notoriously German-hating Dalton.[6] Their conflict with the Gaitskell-Morrison alliance, also referred to here as the 'Atlanticists', has gone unexamined, representing an important omission in scholarly work.[7] In fact, within the Labour right, activity in opposition to German rearmament occurred vigorously throughout the period. Spearheaded by Dalton, and enjoying support across the party, this faction opposing the recreation of German armed forces was a separate, distinctive entity from Bevanite hostility to Germany, and remained so between 1950–4. Dalton and his supporters were natural denizens of the Labour establishment, but broke with their traditional allies due to their position on Germany. Interestingly, Dalton's prosecution of the effort sits in contrast to the popular image of his declining influence in the early fifties, and although ultimately unsuccessful in decisively changing Labour's stance, his faction did come closer to securing victory, or something approaching it, than did the Bevanites in their own later effort.

I

Prior to 1950, the future political status of occupied Germany was ambiguous yet leaning towards permanent division and the integration of the west of the country into the Western alliance. The outbreak of the Korean War accelerated this process, hastening the need for the West to strengthen its defences against Communism.[8] Hence, from 1950, Britain and America moved cautiously but inexorably towards acceptance of West German armed forces. The notion of a rearmed West Germany was a difficult proposition for Labour to accept, provoking disquiet in both the party and the nation at large. Nonetheless, under the aegis of the Foreign Secretary Ernest Bevin, the government had, by 1950, broadly come to recognise that German rearmament was inevitable in the long term in the context of the developing Cold War. However, it was still widely felt to be a distant prospect. Thus, Britain's early strategy was to ensure that other Allied nations were securely armed before weapons were put in German hands once more. Given that the problem did not seem likely to become an immediate one, the question was not sufficiently contentious at this stage to stir substantial dissent within Labour's ranks. The policy decisions which led to acceptance of a West German contribution to European defence have been well detailed by Dockrill and Mawby, and are not directly relevant to our concerns here.[9] The heightening in international tensions throughout 1950, though, particularly following the beginning of the conflict in Korea in June, precipitated demands from Washington that Britain and France explicitly agree to West German rearmament. Like many, Bevin was reluctant to acquiesce in this, and prevaricated in the negotiations on the issue that took place throughout the year. Yet at the Council of Foreign Ministers in New York in September, American pressure finally compelled him to drop his opposition and formally accept the principle of German armed forces.

However, Bevin had astutely avoided agreeing that Germany should rearm *immediately*. Hence his strategy had been successful, minimising Labour dissent while tying the United States to Europe, the cornerstone of his foreign policy. Concurrently, procrastination on the form of rearmament would ensure that other Allied programmes would be well advanced when the parameters of German armed forces were set. Significantly, many in the Attlee government were even hopeful that German rearmament could be traded outright in return for concessions from Moscow. Moreover, though much of the PLP was unhappy at his support for the creation of military units, this was not yet severe. Even the opposition of Dalton was not particularly energetic at this point, indicating that most Labourites mistakenly felt that the German question still remained a distant, rather than an immediate, issue.[10] With the exception of the possibility of abandoning German remilitarisation for *détente*, the developments also suited the Atlanticist cause. In December, a three-month impasse was resolved with the adoption of the Spofford Plan, proposing that, while the French idea of a European Army would be investigated, German military units were needed at once. Bevin was at first hostile to this as well because he perceived a European Army to be a threat to the Atlantic alliance, but finally accepted it when Washington agreed to abandon its earlier requirement that the German issue be resolved before it would bring more troops to Europe.[11]

As 1951 dawned, the fact that the Americans were now tied to Europe encouraged a group within the Cabinet to attempt to put into effect their plan, suggested above, to derail German rearmament by trading it for concessions from the USSR. The most vociferous of this grouping was Dalton, but it also included John Strachey, Kenneth Younger and, significantly, the Prime Minister.[12] Outside the Cabinet, James Callaghan was also in alliance with the effort.[13] The group seeking a *rapprochement* with the Soviet Union was only a temporary alliance in pursuit of a specific goal, but it did reflect the views of many in the PLP, which was becoming steadily more hostile to the notion of restoring Germany to the capacity of a military power as the issue suddenly became rather less than hypothetical. It should be emphasised, though, that this grouping was not the Daltonian faction that would soon come into existence. It had not launched a campaign against settled Labour policy, merely desiring to amend the next stage of Western defence preparations from an emphasis on German rearmament towards a relaxation of international tensions. The composition of the group – incorporating the leader, denizens of the right and centrists – afforded it considerable political weight. Dalton, in particular, had always been seen as sound on defence, a fact that gave this initiative, and his future efforts, a certain credibility, for his opponents were unable to denounce him as a pacifist. The efforts of the *détente* group met with energetic opposition within the Cabinet from Gaitskell and Morrison, who regarded it as likely to give succour to Moscow. However, given Bevin's reluctance on the issue, these two were the only senior figures who consistently supported rearmament. Consequently, while the government was split, those in favour of seeking *détente* held the stronger position in Cabinet.[14] In his diary, Dalton noted tellingly that party feeling was stronger on Germany at this stage than it was on the Bevan-Gaitskell clash over the British defence budget.[15]

Bevan did offer his support for the *détente* initiative.[16] However, it should be recognised that this occurred against the backdrop of his developing feud with Gaitskell, an active supporter of German rearmament. Furthermore it is hardly surprising that Bevan, instinctively sympathetic to the Soviets, should seek negotiation. Hence, we should not read too much from this. Crucially, he remained silent on the issue of Germany and the Germans themselves, concentrating instead on improving relations with the Soviet Union. In his foreign-policy address at the 1950 party conference in October, he had avoided mention of Germany and concentrated instead upon the Third World, as did Ian Mikardo, one of the hardcore of his supporters.[17]

This bolsters the perception that the Bevanites were not particularly worried about the German issue at this point. If Bevan had been genuinely horrified by the prospect of German rearmament, it is surprising that he did not oppose it here, just two weeks after Bevin had accepted the measure. Consequently, it seems reasonable to suggest that it was his personal feud with leading advocates of German rearmament over the separate issue of the defence budget, as well as his sympathetic view of the Soviet Union, that provides much of the explanation for his support. Ultimately the attempt by Britain to encourage improved East-West relations floundered due to Superpower apathy. If it had been a success, it seems plausible that the subsequent Bevanite rebellion would have been less damaging, as without the German issue to fight over, the Bevanite-Gaitskellite dispute would, at least from late 1952, have lacked publicly acceptable substance beyond the antagonism of the protagonists, exposing the competing ambitions that acted as the real motive power of the conflict.

Dissatisfaction in the PLP was growing stronger, and in late January 1951, despite his own misgivings, Attlee was forced to defend the government's stance on Germany against energetic attack. Dalton was unsurprisingly the most active in encouraging this.[18] Clearly, then, the direction of opinion within the party had shifted away from the Atlanticist position towards that of Dalton. In a bid to defuse the gathering storm over Germany, in early February the Prime Minister set out to the Commons the 'Attlee conditions', in which he insisted that Britain could only support West German armed forces if safeguards necessary to prevent Germany from once more becoming a threat were met.[19] Nevertheless, the worsening dissent on Germany makes evident that, by early 1951, the clashes weakening the government had now spread beyond British defence to encompass the German question as well. However, the Daltonian group had still not taken form during this period, chiefly due to the fact that most of the party – including Attlee – were in favour of seeking either to delay the implementation of rearmament, or drop it altogether. Hence the circumstances did not yet exist for a real split within the right. This would only occur in the summer, when the Atlanticists came to push towards immediate remilitarisation, spurring Dalton and his supporters into action.[20]

There remained no indication of future Bevanite concern with the issue. They had not sought to give the German question emphasis in their growing dispute with the right, nor had they adopted the anti-Germanism that they would later espouse. In his biography of Bevan, Foot attempts to portray this in a less damaging light by arguing that Bevin bulldozed the 'unthinkable proposition' of a rearmed Germany through the Cabinet so quickly that resistance was impossible, while more urgent matters – the British defence programme – meant that Germany provoked little controversy among the Bevanites.[21] However, such an assertion does not withstand scrutiny. While Bevin used his authority to ensure Cabinet support, the fact remains that the decision-making process went on over the course of several months. Bevan and his followers had ample opportunity to resist government policy if they desired. Most damning of all to the Bevanite case is the fact that the Cabinet records reveal that Bevan had not even attended two crucial Cabinet discussions of the issue.[22]

II

Following the April 1951 resignations of Bevan, John Freeman and Harold Wilson from the government following their failure to resist the ascendancy of Gaitskell and his policies, the Bevanite rebellion became relatively subdued over the following months. Yet the problem of West Germany continued to develop. The efforts of those seeking *détente* had collapsed due to American unwillingness to compromise on the agenda for a four power meeting and successful UN counterattacks in Korea that lessened the immediacy of world tensions. Attlee's hospitalisation, the death of Bevin and the furore surrounding Bevan's departure left the government in no state to mount a concerted effort to break the international deadlock. It is evident, though, that the German question was still essentially a disagreement within the Labour right, the Bevanites remaining unconcerned with Germany during the spring of 1951.

Despite the failure of *détente*, the anti-German rearmament forces were not to be outmanoeuvred. In response to increasing support from the Atlanticists for a speedy resolution of the debate, the campaign centred upon Dalton coalesced into a discernible and more cohesive faction. Almost immediately, the right became divided between rival camps in a struggle that would wrack the party establishment for the next twelve months, undermining their ability to resist the growing strength of the main Bevanite rebellion. In early July, Dalton – who was fond of the slogan 'No guns for the Huns' – communicated to Attlee the strength of feeling within Labour that was opposed to rearmament, continuing to push for a strategy of delay.[23] Attlee remained supportive of this line, replying to Dalton that 'I am very much of your view'.[24] Those who advocated remilitarisation attempted to reinvigorate their campaign a fortnight later, when Morrison and Emanuel Shinwell submitted a paper to the Defence Committee urging the necessity of quickly resolving the German question and accepting rearmament.[25] The paper furthermore stated that Britain would have to acquiesce in the European Army proposals in order to secure French agreement. The forces hostile to this, as observed above, held a considerable degree of strength within the government, and Attlee invited Dalton to attend the meeting – a further sign of his support for the Daltonian goal, although his enduring disinclination to become involved in factionalism meant that he was never a member of the group. With Dalton, Strachey, Robens and Ede all opposed to the paper, and Attlee still desiring to proceed very slowly, the Defence Committee was deadlocked, as was Cabinet a week later, and again at the beginning of September.[26] Attlee dismissed the paper as premature, arguing that no immediate action was required. The Prime Minister appears in fact to have been rather strongly in favour of Dalton's position, telling Dalton that 'we mustn't have Germans in uniform'.[27] Ede argued that 'we'll create something we can't control', and Robens was fearful of the 'enormity' of arming the Germans.[28]

Therefore, even with Bevan and Wilson out of office, Dalton was able to muster significant support for the anti-German rearmament effort. This also reinforces the judgement that the Bevanite campaign and the German controversy were indeed separate entities at this point. During the last months of the government, with Morrison proving an unsuitable Foreign Secretary, the collective role of the Cabinet became increasingly important in foreign affairs decision-making, bolstering the potential for Dalton and his supporters to have an impact on policy. These meetings witnessed major rows between the two camps, and it is apparent that the disagreements on Germany were, by mid-1951, precipitating open hostility within the Labour right. That Dalton enjoyed the support of so many leading figures – over a third of the Cabinet – underlines the fact that, though the *détente* effort may have stalled, the reluctance to rearming Germany that existed within the party ensured that his group, and not his opponents, held the greater momentum. Though outside the Cabinet, a key impression gained when studying the Daltonian group is one of the role of Callaghan. Despite being at an early stage of his career, he seems to have been very much the 'second man' of the group, heavily involved in the manoeuvres against remilitarisation, and, by 1954, the only member willing to resign alongside Dalton from the Shadow Cabinet. Whilst not possessing an NEC seat, his membership of the Shadow Cabinet once Labour was out of office did accord him prominence in the debates on the issue, and he frequently suggested that Dalton be the one to put forward the Labour position.[29] Moreover, in this, he appears to have been the organiser of the faction, reaching across to the Bevanites on occasion.

Nonetheless, despite the best efforts of Dalton, it is possible to discern a softening in the administration's opposition to German rearmament in the Cabinet's acceptance that the European Army could, in principle, provide the basis for German armed forces.[30] This decision stemmed from a realisation that, in the long term, it was probably inevitable that Germany would again become a military power, and that the US might not insist on safeguards out of a desire for rapid rearmament. Dalton did, however, secure a success for his line in the refusal of the Cabinet to endorse immediate German equality in NATO.[31] As has been asserted by Spencer Mawby, it does seem feasible to believe that if Labour had not been defeated in the 1951 election, Britain would have been less compliant to remilitarisation than the Conservative government was to be.[32]

But Labour *did* lose the election which took place in October, and returned to full Opposition for the first time in eleven years. Moreover, out of office, the factionalism which had threatened to overwhelm the party was to rage unchecked. The scale of the emerging division within the right is suggested in Freeman's bizarrely informing Anthony Crosland that he believed it to be only a matter of time before Dalton became a Bevanite.[33] While Dalton refuted this, explicitly stating that he did not consider the Bevanites to be even *potential* allies, the fact that the distance between the Daltonian and Gaitskell-Morrison forces had become so great as to engender speculation that Dalton would align himself with the Bevanites, despite his opposition to them on British defence, does demonstrate that the split within Labour's upper echelons was serious indeed.[34] This perception is strengthened by the decline in Dalton's vote in the election to the NEC constituencies section at the 1951 party conference.[35] His support fell by 110,000 votes, intimating that his traditional backers were reluctant to canvas for someone so energetically opposed to the leading politicians of the right, while he was still too visibly part of the Labour establishment to attract votes from those disaffected with the leadership. In fact, the Bevanites actively worked against him in the election, strong evidence of the gulf that separated the two groups.[36]

In December, Dalton used the opportunity presented by his delivering of a party political broadcast to strike at the Labour position on Germany once again.[37] His comments were a well constructed critique of German rearmament, yet cleverly stuck within the boundaries of official policy by emphasising the Attlee conditions. The broadcast represented a further entrenchment of the clash between the Atlanticists and the Daltonians. It is possible to identify here the first signs of Bevanite concern with his efforts, in the rejoicing by Crossman at Dalton's 'ferocious broadside'. On the other hand, that the Bevanites *still* failed to exploit the German controversy indicates that rather than signifying their conversion to the issue itself, Crossman and his group were instead enthused by attacks on those who had defeated them in April.[38]

III

It was another four months until the controversy developed further, as it entered its most critical stage, driving a wedge even more deeply between the clashing factions of the right. In late April 1952, Dalton attempted to persuade the NEC not to give Labour support to a government proposal to resolve the issue by the creation of a European Army.[39] He emphasised the hostility of French and German socialists to the rearming of Bonn and wanted the NEC to clarify the party position, which of course, to Dalton, was a means to criticise further the idea of rearmament. The fears over resurgent German aggression were hardly baseless, for the objectives of the Adenauer government might possibly have included revision of the peace treaties and recovery of the lost eastern territories.[40] The Executive agreed, and Dalton was himself tasked with the drafting of the NEC statement. Attlee and Morgan Philips were also involved in the process.[41] Morrison had the chance to join the drafting team, but, suspecting that he would be outnumbered by opponents of rearmament, refused.[42] In view of his later attacks on the statement, it would perhaps have been prudent for him to be involved and use his influence as deputy leader to outweigh Dalton and attempt to shift Attlee's position. In not doing so, he offered Dalton an opportunity to deliver a serious blow to those who supported the creation of a German military. The statement produced by Dalton was a classic piece of political manoeuvring, re-emphasising the Attlee conditions – and, like his broadcast, remaining within the boundaries of party policy – but including what amounted to a declaration that Labour had no confidence in the Adenauer administration, and therefore by implication in German rearmament itself.[43] It further weakened the position of the Gaitskell-Morrison forces by asserting the necessity of delaying the creation of military forces until after German elections and negotiations with the Soviets, another effort to exchange German armed forces for *détente*. The resolution was adopted by the NEC, twenty votes to three.[44] Besides Morrison, one of those opposed was Griffiths, who had previously supported the Daltonian line.[45] Another member of the Daltonian group, Robens, also moved away over the issue. It is apparent that they retreated out of fear for the damage that the split within the right was inflicting, Robens warning Dalton 'don't piss into the wind'.[46] Nonetheless, Dalton's statement was a major success for his group, for the position of the faction was now backed by the authority of an official declaration.[47] Moreover, that Dalton had achieved this without Bevanite involvement again reinforces the assertion that the Daltonian and Bevanite campaigns were distinctive entities. Crossman described the statement as a 'really clever piece of Daltonian politics', as the Atlanticists would be forced to abide by a ruling that they were opposed to – the very thing that the Bevanites were so castigated for failing to do.[48]

Those who advocated rearmament were furious, denouncing the statement as 'caucus rule' and accusing Dalton of 'sabotaging' the NEC, further deepening the divide.[49] Morrison remained adamant that policy on Germany should not be changed, and thus demanded that the statement not be given effect until the Shadow Cabinet had discussed it.[50] At the same time, the dispute within Labour's upper echelons was compounded when, much to the delight of the Bevanites, those who desired a German defence contribution threatened to defy Standing Orders if it came to a vote.[51] The hostility within the right continued for a fortnight, until a foreign affairs debate in Parliament on 14 May. Despite his own opposition to German armed forces, Attlee had come to realise that the NEC declaration had fatally split the party establishment, and consequently abandoned the position adopted by Dalton's NEC statement and instead supported Eden's European Defence Community (EDC), the currently favoured vehicle for effecting the remilitarisation of Germany.[52] He tried to balance both sides of the argument in his speech, but nonetheless could not hide the fact he had failed to bring Labour out against rearmament. This was a sizeable turnaround and victory for the Gaitskell-Morrison forces, due wholly to Attlee's concern for unity. For the Daltonian group, though, the alteration in policy was a sudden, and bitter, defeat. Bevan followed Attlee in the debate, and chastised the leader for ignoring the NEC resolution.[53] However, the contents of his speech stuck to his usual concern with relations *vis á vis* the USSR, reinforcing the perception that the Bevanites were motivated by a very different international analysis than was Dalton.[54] The latter was aggrieved, predicting that Britain would be 'railroaded' into accepting rearmament with none of the Attlee conditions attached, and resolved to fight on.[55] He, Callaghan and Robens, despite the fears of the latter over a split, worked closely together in attempting to engineer a Labour vote against ratification.[56] In his hour of defeat, Dalton did, for the first time, perceive the Bevanites as allies, supporting their PLP motion that the leadership must observe the NEC statement.[57]

As it appeared increasingly unlikely that Labour would oppose ratification of the new Paris Agreements, creating a European Army and, by extension, permitting German armed forces, Dalton began to consider resignation from the Shadow Cabinet. He knew that such a move would have a significant impact, serving to rally his supporters and enabling him to criticise the policy openly.[58] That Dalton – previously confining his opposition to within Labour's inner councils – was on the verge of coming out vigorously against the direction of the party makes apparent how serious the split had become. Callaghan attempted to talk Dalton out of resigning on the grounds that it would only aid Bevan's revolt.[59] The tensions also affected Dalton's relations with his protégé Gaitskell. They had an 'unsmiling' meeting, with Gaitskell accusing Dalton of being a 'fence-sitter' and the veteran warning his pupil that he was becoming Morrison's 'Jack in the Box'.[60]

The climax of the struggle over the Labour stance on Germany occurred in late July 1952, and witnessed a change in the fortunes of the Daltonians as suddenly as events had turned against them two months earlier. At a Shadow Cabinet meeting on 24 July to decide the response to the imminent acquiescence by the Conservatives to the Paris Agreements, Dalton again argued that the PLP should accept the policy on Germany set out by the NEC in April.[61] He stressed that while most of the Shadow Cabinet may have supported Morrison and Gaitskell, the feeling amongst the rest of the PLP was rather different.[62] The great divide that separated the Dalton and Bevan positions is made evident by the meeting of the full PLP that occurred immediately afterwards.[63] At this critical juncture, with the two sides manoeuvring for advantage, Bevan amazingly resurrected the arguments of the previous year over the *British* defence scheme and engaged in a row with George Brown.[64] Furthermore, Dalton said afterwards that he was 'embarrassed' by Bevanite support, an indication that he did not consider his faction to be operating alongside the Bevanites.[65] He also complained of attracting the hostility of right-wingers who mistakenly associated him with their Bevanite adversaries.[66] At the Shadow Cabinet meeting the following week, the Daltonians' warnings of majority feeling inspired sufficient wavering members to shift position, and, consequently, the Shadow Cabinet chose to oppose ratification of the Paris Agreements.[67] This moved the party back towards the line that Dalton had engineered with his NEC resolution. The Shadow Cabinet also authorised him to write an Opposition amendment to the government motion to ratify.[68] This was very much along the lines of the NEC statement, with another paragraph added to placate those who favoured rearmament, emphasising the necessity of strong defences. Yet this does not obscure the fact that the Daltonian group had dealt their opponents an important defeat. At the meeting of the PLP that occurred the following day, angry supporters of rearmament complained at being forced to vote for a policy that was in opposition to their views, conduct that permitted the Bevanites a certain amount of glee that their enemies were constrained by their own Standing Orders.[69] When a vote was taken, the party approved Dalton's amendment by 141 to ten, and the vote against ratification by 131 to 27.[70] It was indeed a 'personal triumph', as Dalton's allies told him.[71] In fact, this was the most substantial success achieved by any faction in the long campaign against German rearmament that ran from 1950–54. The tendency to perceive the efforts of Dalton as a mere subsidiary to a larger Bevanite struggle over Germany is erroneous. That it was accomplished wholly by the Daltonians rather than the Bevanites suggests that standard historiographical interpretations of the German question as being centred upon the latter group should therefore be revised.[72] The more well-studied rebel faction achieved no comparable successes in their own efforts.

However, the split damaged Dalton at his political base. Those who advocated remilitarisation set their faces against him, and, this being the case, he lost his NEC seat at the annual Conference in the autumn.[73] Following the events of mid-1952, the German question, both because of the lack of progress between Western governments, and because Dalton had achieved a temporary settlement, faded from view for the next year. Moreover, given Dalton's gradual withdrawal from the centre of Labour Party affairs following his removal from the NEC, as well as the clarion call presented by Bevanite success at the Conference, the fissure within the right over Germany became less intense, as the former opponents pulled together in order to resist the attempts at a Bevanite takeover. Henceforth, the schism between the clashing groups of the right opened only occasionally, and where it did so the efforts of Dalton and his supporters were rather more closely tied to those of the Bevanites than before.

IV

German rearmament returned to the fore during the autumn of 1953, but now took the form of another clash between the Bevanites and the Gaitskell-Morrison forces, rather than a dispute within the right itself. The Bevanite's actual agenda remained a linked dual concern with thwarting the policies of their enemies in the party and constructing better relations with the USSR. Consequently, we should refrain from perceiving the developing Bevanite involvement in Germany as the successor to the Daltonian effort. It may have been so in terms of being a group operating in opposition to acceptance of West German rearmament, but the reasons behind their doing so were different. The Daltonian campaign had been focused on an international issue, and became a struggle within Labour only due to the competing positions of the Daltonian and Atlanticist factions. In contrast, the Bevanite campaign was intended at least as much for internal consumption as it was concerned with the international environment. The Daltonians, though still strongly opposed to the notion of a rearmed Bonn, were only peripherally involved. Throughout 1953, Dalton's diaries rarely mention the issue, and he did not repeat his energetic performances in the Shadow Cabinet of the previous year. This was a symptom of his declining interest in politics generally.

In September 1953, the Bevanites tabled a resolution to be submitted to Conference, typically denouncing the ideological obsession with Communism, but also calling for Labour to come out against 'resurgent German nationalism'.[74] It is here possible to detect the first indications of their exploitation of fears over the spectre of Nazism.[75] It marked a departure from their previous stance of avoiding angering the Soviets – which was easily portrayed as appeasement by their opponents – and a move towards Dalton's angle of attack instead. This was perhaps likely given the success that Dalton had experienced in conducting his efforts in an anti-Germanic manner. Coupled with their conciliatory view of the USSR, such a stance would afford the Bevanites two distinct platforms – and hence two audiences – from which to attract support. Four days beforehand, *Tribune* began the campaign, denouncing Adenauer's supporters as the 'same people who were content to lick the jackboots of the Nazis'.[76] Such a shift in the language employed is important, signaling a movement towards the vitriol that lay in the near future. Whereas previously the Bevanites had refrained from adopting such a posture, instead concentrating on the need to preserve peace, they now tapped into emotive fears of German aggression. The scale of Bevanite scare-mongering in exploiting anti-Nazi prejudice is unsurprisingly concealed by Foot in his biography of Bevan.

Yet, the proposed Bevanite Conference resolution was rejected by the rest of the Executive.[77] Moreover, the Daltonian group continued to stand apart from these events. The eventual resolution, while something of a compromise following the line set out in the Attlee conditions, actually swung the advantage on Germany towards the Gaitskell-Morrison camp.[78] In stating that the remilitarisation of Germany should not occur until efforts towards unification and neutralisation had been exhausted, the resolution provided those who advocated the measure with the opportunity to declare that negotiation had failed due to Soviet intransigence and to press ahead with the creation of German armed forces.[79] That it expressed concern at the 'resurgence of reactionary German nationalism' does not obscure the fact that while it may have sounded Bevanite, it actually accorded the Atlanticists an important edge.[80] The careful wording ensured that it passed Conference near-unanimously, but in reality it meant that those who favoured rearmament now had command of policy.[81] They began to exploit this as soon as an opportunity to do so presented itself. In February 1954, the Atlanticists attempted to engineer a resolution supporting the EDC. They believed that the failure to achieve agreement with the Soviet Union on Germany would encourage sufficient Labour MPs to recognise the necessity of German armed forces, expecting to pass the resolution comfortably.[82] Dalton now briefly returned to the fray, having heavily criticised Adenauer the previous month.

In a newspaper article, he had warned that Adenauer would revert to the 'traditional German foreign policy that we know so well' and was preparing to make a stand against the Atlanticists before he suffered a slipped disk in his spine.[83] In the Shadow Cabinet on 16 February, representatives from both the Bevanite and Daltonian factions spoke against acquiescence to rearmament, but with Dalton absent due to his injury, Bevan, Callaghan and Ede were unable to overcome Gaitskell and Morrison.[84] In addition, the Atlanticists now held the support of Attlee, having convinced him that the German question would no longer provoke rancour.[85] Consequently the Shadow Cabinet voted to recommend the resolution to the full PLP.[86]

However, by the time of the PLP meeting on 23 February, it was apparent that the pledge to Attlee that there would be no split was inaccurate.[87] Hence the leader characteristically backed away, supporting the Atlanticist resolution but arguing that remilitarisation need not be undertaken immediately.[88] The meeting witnessed dramatic speeches by both sides, but it was unmistakable that, as in 1952, much of the Labour Party was opposed to rearmament. Nonetheless, when a vote on a Bevanite resolution calling for further negotiations with Moscow was taken, the Daltonian members of the Shadow Cabinet, Callaghan and Ede, accepted collective responsibility and opposed the motion. This was important, for the result was very close, the Bevanites being defeated by just two votes.[89] If Dalton had been present, it seems likely that he would have abstained, if not actually voted for the Bevanite resolution. In such circumstances, the Gaitskell-Morrison forces would have held a majority of just one vote against the Bevanite position, or even been defeated if Dalton had persuaded Callaghan and Ede to join him in voting with the Bevanites. His injury was thus one of those comparatively minor incidents that in fact shape the course of historical events. The Atlanticist motion on Soviet intransigence was passed by a barely improved margin of 113 to 104, hardly a resounding approval of the remilitarisation of West Germany.[90] The episode was repeated the following day at the NEC, with the six Bevanites being buttressed by five other supporters. That these were all union leaders, most significantly Jack Cooper and Edwin Gooch, demonstrates that the problem engendered disquiet within the right that spread well beyond the Daltonians.[91] The Bevanite resolution was again defeated by just two votes, thirteen to eleven.[92]

In the summer, the Bevanites took the most energetic step of their campaign thus far with the publication in August of the *Tribune* pamphlet *It Need Not Happen*.[93] Employing alarmist language, the Bevanites asserted that German military units would be 'Nazi-led and Nazi-trained' in another effort to utilise xenophobia in order to win support.[94] According to the Bevanite line, German militarism and American behaviour rendered a World War 'inevitable'.[95] Yet this only served to reveal the faction's actual agenda, the improvement of relations with Moscow via the resurrection of a common enemy in the Nazis. In contrast, Dalton's own position did not turn upon rhetoric over Nazism, but German nationalism broadly. To Dalton, all Germans – including German socialists – were dangerous.[96] The significance of the Bevanite campaign on Germany must be questioned, though, for it is apparent that the highpoint of the controversy had in fact passed two years earlier; the Daltonian group had retreated from involvement due to the Bevanites' distortion of the issue. Moreover, the Bevanite effort was effectively torpedoed the same month as the pamphlet was published, when the French Parliament rejected the EDC. This rendered many of the arguments employed by the Bevanites obsolete, swinging momentum once more towards the Atlanticist position and preparing the ground for a way out of the quagmire. The NEC produced a statement to be submitted to Conference, intended by the Atlanticists to bind the party to remilitarisation.[97] This resolution, introduced by Attlee in a bid to minimise opposition, reiterated the original 'conditions', but stated that a German defence contribution must be made as soon as possible – in essence, rearmament within a NATO context.[98] It is noteworthy that the debate saw no Bevanite attacks on the policy, even from those who were not members of the Executive.[99] If the Bevanites had been genuinely exercised by the substance of the German question, it is inconceivable that they would have not made a stand. The resolution was passed, albeit by just 250,000 votes.[100]

Yet, this seeming conclusion to the problem in fact precipitated the final outbreak of conflict within the right. On 21 October, the Western allies announced that they had concluded a settlement of the West German question, and accordingly all that remained was for the agreements reached a month earlier in Paris, stating that the country should have sovereignty restored and undertake rearmament as a member of NATO, to be ratified by the parliaments of the nations concerned. With the issue now being fought once again on the undiluted issue of German nationalism, Dalton returned to the fray in a last attempt to shift the party's position, gathering around him those members of the group still willing to break with the rest of the right. Only Callaghan and Ede pledged to throw their weight behind him, the others feeling bound by the Conference decision.[101] They spent several days developing a course of action, planning to invoke a precedent set during the 1936–7 Service Estimates row that allowed the Shadow Cabinet minority to express their views to the PLP.[102] Dalton and Callaghan intended to resign if this was not observed.[103] On 8 October, Dalton met Attlee privately and found him, as during 1952, cool to the prospect of a remilitarised West Germany.[104] The two agreed that one possibility was for Labour to abstain on the Paris Agreements.[105] Dalton expected to be defeated, acknowledging that the party had grown weary of the issue, and that there was a general perception that the Scarborough Conference had settled the matter.[106] At the Shadow Cabinet the next day, only four members – the three Daltonians and Wilson – spoke against supporting the Paris Agreements.[107] Dalton's efforts to win the right to speak against them met with resistance from Morrison and Gaitskell, the latter telling his patron simply not to attend the party meeting.[108] Dalton instantly dismissed this, threatening to resign.[109] The split within the Labour right that had existed in 1952 had begun to open up once more. It should be noted, however, that this was largely the responsibility of Gaitskell and Morrison for their attacks on Dalton, he having made efforts to be amiable and avoid a row.[110] The prospect of a senior figure resigning at this crucial moment – Dalton was not bluffing – was too serious a risk, and thus a compromise, permitting those opposed to abstain in the PLP meeting as long as they did not actually speak against the majority, was put forward and gained support.[111] Gaitskell and Morrison were both against this, but Attlee overruled them, and Dalton and the others reluctantly agreed.[112] After a two-day PLP debate, the official line for ratification of the Paris Agreements was carried by 124 to 72.[113] While the sizeable vote against ratification reveals the continuing divides, Dalton felt it a 'very bad result', and blamed the Bevanites for discrediting the German issue by associating it with their personal campaign against the Gaitskell-Morrison camp, a final parting shot in the 'alliance' between two factions.[114]

Bevan initially determined that the Bevanites should flout official policy by voting against rearmament in the Commons, yet characteristically changed his mind when threatened with disciplinary action.[115] In abandoning their opposition to German armed forces in order to escape sanction, the Bevanites had done their credibility a great deal of harm. Furthermore, the extent to which their struggle was about personalities and power rather than principle is evident in that, in not opposing the agreement, the group was even willing to disregard their favourable view of the Soviets and acquiesce in the rearming of a nation that would make another war 'inevitable'. Dalton recorded that the Bevanites had committed 'suicide'.[116] Following years of mutating policy, then, Labour had finally ended its troubles over the rearmament of West Germany. Securing an approach based upon strong Western defences, the Atlanticists had achieved the aims for which they had fought against both the Daltonians and the Bevanites.

V

The question as to why the Daltonian group and their campaign has been so obscured in the previous literature is an intriguing one, and worth considering. The activities of Dalton certainly challenge the perception of him at this stage as being purely a patron of young politicians. Instead, he remained an important factional figure. The reason for the group's lack of acknowledgement by scholars perhaps resides in the aforementioned mythology that surrounds the period, namely that of the Bevanites struggling against a robotic party establishment, and which has had the effect of diverting attention from other events that were occurring simultaneously. Further explanation can be posited in that the Daltonian group suffers by comparison, as a political faction, with the Bevanites. The Daltonians unquestionably lacked the organisation of the more prominent rebels. This was confirmed to the author by Callaghan, who stated that the Daltonian group was not on a 'large-scale' like the Bevanites.[117] It is perhaps understandable that Callaghan would not wish to acknowledge fully the faction of which he was a member, representing as it did a significant challenge to party orthodoxy at this time of internal upheaval.[118] Yet, by any definition of political factionalism, Dalton and his supporters do indeed warrant being identified as a distinctive group within Labour. As Callaghan accepted, they worked together in attempting to alter the direction of policy on Germany, speaking in support of a common line and manoeuvring in concert against the Atlanticists – the standard activities of a faction.[119] Political groups generally lack the organisation displayed by the Bevanites. Most factions, especially on issues such as this, are comprised of politicians working together in pursuit of a desired objective. It is only the exceptionally well-organised nature of the Bevanite group that has prompted scholars to perceive the Daltonian campaign as a minor episode and simply attach it to the Bevanite struggle. In fact, the split within the Labour right was an important series of events during the period. Moreover, although the reliability of Dalton's diaries has sometimes been called into question, with regards to the subject of this chapter, there is a strong degree of corroboration between them and the other chief sources, notably official records and the diaries of Crossman and Gaitskell. Indeed there are actually no contradictions between them in their coverage of the events described here. Given the accuracy and weight of this material, it seems evident that the Daltonian-Atlanticist conflict should be accorded appropriate consideration in the history of the party during the early 1950s.

This chapter has sought to postulate a more complex picture of the reality of Labour factionalism in this period, moving away from the mythology-loaded interpretations that have previously predominated and examining a hitherto neglected episode. Existing work has only partially acknowledged Dalton's efforts, and has tended inextricably to link them with Bevan's own hostility to remilitarisation, positing a Bevanite-Daltonian alliance. Yet the two were separate entities, with Dalton's initiative reaching its high point in mid-1952 and the Bevanites' own only becoming important afterwards. Dalton and his group were distinct from the Bevanites in being motivated by genuine concern with the German issue, whereas, as previously noted, the Bevanite line was an opportunistic one, influenced by their enmity towards the United States and an appeasing attitude towards Moscow. By comparison, the Dalton faction was pro-NATO and hostile to the Soviets. Furthermore, whereas Dalton was driven by xenophobic anti-Germanism, it is far from clear that the Bevanites subscribed to this view. The rhetoric of Nazism that they were willing to employ – which exactly paralleled the Moscow line – indicates a rather different motivation. They hoped to facilitate an improvement in relations with the USSR, and were not particularly concerned with German nationalism at all. Interestingly, members of the Daltonian group appear not to have shared all of Dalton's opinions, in fact holding concerns similar to those of the Bevanites, namely over East-West tensions stemming from the creation of German armed forces. That they felt this way, but were consistently hostile to the Bevanites nonetheless, reinforces the view that their split with the Atlanticists was indeed separate from the Bevanite struggle. The conflicts within the Labour Party in this chapter are all marked by a connection to events beyond simple domestic politics, namely the broader international setting. That the wider world has so often been a significant element in internal disputes, providing a symbolic and emotive impetus to clashes between antagonistic groups, means that we should identify this linkage between the two arenas as a central feature of the party's history. The events detailed here would suggest that study of the factionalism that wracked Labour in this period should now be shifted away from prevailing concentrations upon a simple 'left-right' ideological conflict between rival groups centred upon Bevan on the one hand, and Gaitskell and Morrison on the other, towards a more nuanced appraisal of the internal divisions, both in terms of policy and, crucially, personality.

7

'THE CHALLENGE OF CO-EXISTENCE': THE LABOUR PARTY, AFFLUENCE AND THE COLD WAR, 1951–64

Richard Toye and Nicholas Lawton

The 1951–64 period was both an age of 'affluence', in which the Western democracies experienced economic growth, full employment, and increased availability of consumer goods, and one of 'competitive coexistence', when the opposing sides in the Cold War battled for the allegiance of under-developed countries. For the Labour Party, three successive general election defeats were followed, in 1964, only by the narrowest of victories and a difficult period in office. Contributing to this poor showing were the factional and ideological conflicts that wracked the party in the years before 1963, and which were disguised rather than resolved thereafter, during the initial period of Harold Wilson's leadership. Those disputes were dramatised in the personal rivalry between Aneurin Bevan and Hugh Gaitskell, and in the high-profile controversies over nationalisation and unilateral nuclear disarmament. Such problems were compounded, some historians have argued, by Labour's hostility to the cultural trappings of affluence, creating a sense of alienation between the party and an electorate that was becoming better and better off. Important as these phenomena were, they cannot be fully comprehended save in relation to a Cold War discourse which was prevalent in British democratic socialist circles at the time, but which has since been neglected in the historiography.

This 'Cold War-affluence' discourse linked domestic economic performance and the country's international solvency with questions of consumerism, as well with science, technology, post-colonialism, the provision of overseas aid, and relations with Europe. Its central tenet is encapsulated, briefly, in the words of one of its key proponents, Richard

Crossman MP. He told the 1961 Trades Union Congress that the Cold War was typically presented 'as a struggle between, on the one side, totalitarian planning and, on the other side, unplanned, unjust, unequal affluence'. As long as the battle was fought in these terms, he argued, a Communist victory was inevitable, because, presented with such a choice, people would opt for controls (which, he implied, would provide economic security) over freedom. Therefore, the 'only choice today is between totalitarian Communism and democratic socialist planning, and if you will not swallow the second your freedom will not be preserved'.[1] Crucially, then, the discourse did not merely articulate a set of beliefs about the political economy of international relations, but also served a powerful rhetorical function. If the analysis it contained was accepted, it followed that an interventionist domestic economic programme was not merely desirable from the point of view of those it would benefit directly, but was a compelling necessity from a global perspective.

The 'Cold War-affluence' discourse, although very important, was not, it should be emphasised, all-pervasive or utterly ubiquitous within the party. Certain aspects of it were heavily contested, most notably by the influential revisionist politician Tony Crosland. (It may be observed that Crosland clearly considered the point of view he was seeking to refute to be well established and influential.) Moreover, it was subject to a host of inter-pretations. All the same, the extent to which figures from different wings of the party engaged in it, albeit with often very different emphases, is remarkable. It is vital for historians to take this discourse into account, not only to provide the necessary context for understanding Labour attitudes to affluence and the East-West struggle, but also in order to understand the party's whole view of Britain's place in the wider world. This was, of course, a time when the UK's great power status, as measured in traditional military and territorial terms, was in the throes of collapse. Yet if the nation were, through practical example, to demonstrate the superiority of 'democratic socialist planning' to both 'totalitarian planning' and 'unplanned, unjust, unequal affluence' it would not merely succeed in making a point about economics. It would also make concrete its longstanding claim to inter-national moral leadership as a third power in a bipolar world. This pattern of thought therefore had a close relationship to debates about national decline, and how to reverse it.

Labour attitudes to the 'Affluent Society' have received much attention in recent years. Historians have, on the whole, judged the party quite harshly. According to Lawrence Black, for example, 'Labour's politicisation of affluence defined the electorate so critically, meant it was apt to slight those it was seeking to both better and represent and thus struggled to create a supportive electorate.'[2] Although the argument may at times be overstated, there is certainly a strong element of truth here. However, as Stefan Schwarzkopf has noted recently, those who have written on British debates about consumption (in contrast to historians of Germany and the USA) have rarely invoked the Cold War in their explanations. He suggests that 'the emergence of post-war "affluent Britain" cannot properly be understood' without reference to it.[3] This is undoubtedly right as regards the Labour Party's attitude to affluence, and the converse is also true. Without reference to the question of affluence and related aspects of political economy, our understanding of Labour's attitude to the Cold War will also remain partial.[4]

A complete description of the discourse we have identified, and the details of its undoubted connection to internal party power struggles, is not possible in the space available.[5] Our aim in this chapter is simply to demonstrate its existence, and delineate some of its main features, with reference to arguments made, in particular, by Bevan, Crossman, Crosland, Gaitskell, Wilson, as well as by the economist Thomas Balogh. (Balogh, a Hungarian émigré, was to become one of Wilson's key economic advisers, and one of the most important intellectual exponents of the Cold War-affluence discourse.)[6] We conclude by showing why, after the discourse reached its apotheosis in Wilson's famous 'White Heat of Technology' speech of 1963, its themes were later sidelined in the run-up to the 1964 election. Arguably, however, it did find a continuing reflection in some key initiatives of the first Wilson government, not least in relation to economic planning, the role of science, and overseas development.

Although archival sources play some part in establishing our case, we rely mainly on books, pamphlets, speeches and newspaper articles. We make no apology for this. Important as the papers of organisations and individuals often are, what one might call 'archival fetishism' can lead historians into error, by leading to an excessive focus on the mechanics of policymaking and the petty internal disputes to which it frequently gives rise. This can lead to the role that politicians play in establishing the contours of public debate being obscured, and, to a degree, the differences between them being emphasised at the expense of the things they have in common. It would be idle to deny that the Labour Party in this era was faction-ridden, that the atmosphere within it was often poisonous, and that this was a source of electoral weakness. All the same, as well as the defeats of the 1950s, there is the victory of 1964 to be explained. As the 'Cold War-affluence' discourse played a significant part in the development of the 1964 Labour platform, it may be a factor that can help achieve this. An examination of it can also help us identify the beliefs that those, generally left-wing, figures who subscribed to it in its full form shared with those 'revisionists' who endorsed certain important parts of it. In this sense it also provides some explanation for the fragile unity which developed in the run-up to the 1964 election under Harold Wilson's stewardship.

I

Discourses linking issues of domestic welfare (in the broadest sense) with national security concerns have occurred at various times and places throughout history. The Cold War was, of course, a cultural and economic conflict as much as it was a military one. The economic aspects were stressed in the March 1947 Truman Doctrine, in which the US President pledged his country's support to 'free peoples who are resisting attempted subjugation by armed minorities or by outside pressures . . . I believe that our help should be primarily through economic and financial aid which is essential to economic stability and orderly political processes.'[7] Similarly, 'Point 4' of Truman's 1949 inaugural address called for 'a bold new program . . . for the improvement and growth of underdeveloped areas'.[8] Many British Labour politicians were sympathetic to this 'progressive' aspect of Cold War policy. In the debate on the Budget of 1950, for example, Leslie Hale, MP for Oldham West, noted the importance of developing underdeveloped territories. 'The pointers of ethics are not only pointing to the path of change but also the pointer of expediency, the economic pointer, [and] the pointer of science' he argued. He went on to suggest that 'economic nationalism leads to war, [and] that under-development leads to communism and to the uprisings of the undeveloped people'.[9] A few days later, Richard Acland MP developed the point, noting that an aid programme on a sufficient scale would be very costly, and would require from the British people common sacrifices for the common good. This justified the continuation of the Attlee government's policies of economic interventionism and domestic austerity. For, if the West was 'involved in a contest of infinite duration' and if 'it must be our primary purpose to make to it the greatest material contribution we can' then 'the coherent and purposeful ordering of society' – which Acland considered to be the fundamental aim of the Labour Party – had become, more than ever, 'a major necessity'.[10] Later, Hale and Acland gave help and encouragement to Harold Wilson in his writing and activities in connection with world economic development.[11]

Other figures also invoked Cold War concerns in arguments about home policy. A key example is the controversy over the 1951 Budget, in which Hugh Gaitskell, as Chancellor, introduced health service prescription charges, prompting the resignation from the government of Aneurin Bevan, Harold Wilson and John Freeman. Gaitskell believed the charges were essential in order to help pay for the large-scale rearmament programme triggered by the outbreak of the Korean War the previous year. Towards the end of his Budget speech he argued:

> The popular urge to relax, the pressure for higher living standards, the absorption with domestic issues, are all powerful influences which weaken the will to re-arm . . . It has happened many times in history that democracies have played, while dictatorships have prepared.[12]

Bevan, in his resignation statement, naturally took the opposite line: that living standards and social services should not be prejudiced by excess defence spending.

> It has always been clear that the weapons of the totalitarian States are, first, social and economic, and only next military; and if in attempting to meet the military effect of those totalitarian machines, the economies of the western world are disrupted and the standard of living is lowered or industrial disturbances are created, then Soviet Communism establishes a whole series of Trojan horses in every nation of the western economy.

He went on to argue, moreover, that the government's post-1945 social reconstruction programme had enabled Britain, by the end of 1950, to assume 'the moral leadership of the world'.[13] (This advantage was, he thought, now being thrown away, as the government allowed itself to be dragged behind the wheels of US diplomacy.) Bevan's comments are noteworthy as an example of an idea that was to remain influential in the 1951–64 period. Labour's proposed economic and social reforms were not merely desirable in their own right, but would, if implemented, allow Britain to act as an exemplar. They would demonstrate to the economically underdeveloped yet politically 'uncommitted' nations of the world that there existed a palatable alternative to development on Communist lines or capitalist 'exploitation' of the underdeveloped, in the form of planned social democracy.

After the party's loss of the October 1951 general election, some of these pre-existing patterns of thought were reformulated into the rhetoric of opposition. This adaptation was influenced by major developments in the Cold War. The death of Stalin in March 1953, and the end of the Korean War that July, led to a phase in which the Soviets were less overtly confrontational. Their new doctrine of 'competitive co-existence' was particularly associated with Nikita Khrushchev, although some of its elements were in place before 1955, the point by which he emerged as leader ahead of his rivals.[14] The strategy had two prongs. First, there was the courting of underdeveloped countries through economic aid. This was particularly significant in view of the emergence of the Non-Aligned Movement, headed by China, Yugoslavia and India.[15] Second, there was the attempt to demonstrate the superiority of the Soviet economic system over capitalism. The launch of the first *Sputnik* in 1957 was the most dramatic symbol of what that system was capable, but the authorities also put considerable emphasis on improving the lives of their own citizens, not least in terms of housing and domestic technology. Hence the seminal nature of the 1959 'Kitchen debate', in which Khrushchev and US Vice-President Richard Nixon argued over the merits of their countries' respective technological achievements.[16] Many Labour thinkers were amongst those who regarded the Soviet efforts at 'peaceful competition' as a serious threat to the West.

Harold Wilson was one of those who felt alarm, even though he felt the new regime would be easier to work with than that of Stalin. In May 1953, he paid a return visit the Soviet Union, where he had previously conducted bilateral trade talks when in government. In a speech that October, he said that 'One of the things which most impresses a visitor to the Soviet Union is the speed of their industrial development.' He admitted that the Soviets had devoted too many resources to heavy industry and not enough to agriculture, yet, he argued, the West could not afford to ignore 'the spectacular increase in production and productive capacity'. Moreover,

Since the war Russia has been seen as a military rather than an industrial rival. We have devoted so many of our resources to countering her military power that we are in danger of ignoring her growing industrial power . . . we shall ignore the economic implications of her growing industrial potential at our peril.[17]

Such thinking flourished over the ensuing years into a wide-ranging Cold War critique.[18] Wilson's intellectual development along such lines was enhanced by repeated visits to the USSR as part of his private consultancy work.[19]

Wilson was by no means alone in perceiving Soviet economic performance as a threat. Some, like Thomas Balogh, believed that, once allowances had been made for Soviet exaggeration, a growth rate of between six and ten per cent per annum could be estimated.[20] (Although the Soviet growth rate was to decline significantly from the 1960s onwards, Balogh's estimate was probably a tolerable guess as to what was happening in the 1950s.)[21] This produced serious pessimism, at least on the left of the party. Richard Crossman, writing in 1960 argued that, 'Progressively year by year we shall see that, judged in terms of national security, scientific and technological development, popular education, and, finally, even of mass living standards, free enterprise is losing out in the peaceful competition between East and West.'[22]

As Jim Tomlinson has noted, a number of right-wing Labour figures shared the view that the Eastern Bloc economies were successful, although some doubted that high growth rates could be maintained in the longer run.[23] Douglas Jay, for instance, said in 1956 that 'The evidence suggests strongly that Russian production is increasing at about 10% per year . . . At that rate, the real standard of living in Russia may equal ours in perhaps fifteen years.'[24] In 1960, Tony Benn noted that Jim Callaghan 'had come back from Czechoslovakia convinced that socialism does work'.[25] There were, it should be noted, some, like Tony Crosland, who were much more sceptical – a point which will be returned to below. And of course, all of those concerned, on both wings of the party, found the Soviet *political* system repellent. The essential point is that the belief that totalitarian planning could be economically successful – and thus potentially appealing to underdeveloped countries – was not merely a left-wing hobbyhorse.

II

The assumption that the Soviet bloc posed an economic as well as a political threat was often present in Labour criticisms of Conservative economic policy. After 1951, the Tory government had pursued a policy of economic decontrol, and rationing came to an end within three years. A common way of attacking this policy – which was, after all, likely to be popular with voters – was to suggest that this was likely to jeopardise the possibility of higher national income in the future. The result of reducing restrictions on consumption, including through the relaxation of import controls, was recurrent balance of payment problems, it was argued, to which the government responded by curtailing economic activity, in the classic pattern of 'stop-go'. The balance of payments was restored at the cost of slowing growth. (Jay observed; 'As soon as things get better, people want to relax, and as soon as they relax, things get worse.')[26] To put it another way, 'affluence' was an illusion, for the distribution of too much jam today was undermining the prospect that yet more jam (or perhaps worthier things) would be produced tomorrow. This was regrettable not merely because growth was desirable in itself but because the resulting economic stagnation would weaken the West in the Cold War. Labour's manifesto for the 1955 election argued that there could be no lasting peace until the gap between industrialised Western countries and 'the peasant millions' of Asia and Africa had been addressed. Moreover, 'In order to strengthen our Welfare

State still further and at the same time to play our part in assisting the under-developed areas of the world, our own production must rise every year. Only a government prepared to plan the nation's resources can do this.'[27]

Balogh was one of those who argued on such lines. There were two aspects to his thinking. Firstly, he urged that the only way to tackle the growth problem was to increase the rate of investment and thus of productivity and technical progress throughout the West. This, he argued in an essay written at the end of 1955, would restore strength, in particular, of Britain, and hence her ability to provide aid to poorer countries and to moderate US policy. 'The fulfilment of our moral obligations and the safe-guarding of our political influence would then no longer lead to continuous embarrassment.'[28] This fed into the second aspect of his thinking, namely that only by leading a planned world economy could Communism be defeated. Balogh felt that the operation of the world economy exploited the weakest economic powers by ensuring downward pressure on the prices of primary goods, preventing any accumulation of wealth by such nations, wealth that was required for investment in education, industrial development and infrastructure. Balogh felt that 'aid' was insufficient, because the Third World would be appalled at the capitalist 'system' and turn towards a system which was more economically 'humane' and not subject to violent market forces. Only a world organisation led on social-democratic lines could moderate capitalist exploitation and Communist expansionism. The perfect solution was therefore a new 'Commonwealth' initiative which would not only alleviate poverty and safeguard freedom, but would also restore the economic and moral power of Britain in the world as a new 'Third Force' in the Cold War. Such ideas may have been utopian (and Balogh's own enthusiasm for them ebbed gradually until 1964 as a result of decolonisation and Conservative dismantling of the Sterling Area), but they appealed to many in the party. Balogh's ideas would later be picked up and developed by Richard Crossman, who, like him, would play a significant role under Wilson's leadership.

The 'Cold War-affluence' discourse was, however, strongly contested. An articulate and systematic challenge to it was launched by Tony Crosland, in his important revisionist work *The Future of Socialism* (1956). He argued that, even on the questionable assumption that Soviet growth figures were as high as many people claimed, it was doubtful whether these rapid rates would continue in the future. He believed that as Soviet society developed, there would be increasing demands for the 'fruits' of development (i.e. the development of an 'affluent society'). Resources would then no longer be devoted, as they were during the Stalin years, to industrial and military development, and instead allowed to flow into 'less productive' consumption. Thus he noted that it was important to distinguish between economic growth and increases in consumption. A higher rate of growth was not necessarily desirable, as it might be achieved only at the cost of greater inequality or by attacks on workers' rights. By contrast, he considered that 'a sustained and rapid rise in home consumption' should be a 'central socialist objective', and would have been very discontented with a rate of growth inadequate to support such a rise. 'But', he argued, 'our present rate of growth can hardly be called inadequate on these grounds, since on reasonable assumptions it will double the standard of living in 25 years. This is not bad going; and it scarcely seems worth chafing if other countries make prodigious efforts and do rather better.' (He was clearly right that Soviet growth would not be sustained, but arguably somewhat complacent about British growth.) Given that, in his analysis, British growth was thus likely to prove adequate for purely domestic purposes, he went on to examine the political and strategic reasons for fearing Soviet economic power.

First he considered the military implications. Fear of these, he thought, reflected 'a rather obsolete, pre-atomic approach'. Even if it were believed that the West would be outstripped in total industrial output, this was unlikely to revolutionise the balance of power, because success depended on stockpiles of H-bombs and the development of new military techniques. There was, he claimed, no reason to think that achievement in these spheres was a simple function of steel output, nor did it seem that the West was lagging badly. (This of course was pre-*Sputnik*.) He then considered an alternative argument, that the faster Soviet rate of growth and the accompanying rise in living standards would increase the attraction of Communism for the peoples of underdeveloped countries. 'But the people of these countries will hardly judge the relative prosperity of Russia and the West by comparing small differences in their respective rates of growth, of which they will in any case not, for the most part, be aware.' A more credible argument, he thought, was that the ability of Russia and the West to give aid to the under-developed areas was a function of their respective rates of growth. Yet he doubted that, even if it were, a slower Western rate of growth would necessarily have disastrous political consequences. This was because countries' choice of alignment in the Cold War might depend more on foreign political rather than on foreign economic policy, that is 'on the political "image" of Russia and the West respectively which is built up in Asia and Africa'. From this point of view, he concluded 'British policy in Cyprus or Kenya may be more significant than the exact amount of economic aid.'[29] Proponents of the Cold War-affluence discourse naturally agreed with Crosland on the importance of having an 'ethical foreign policy' although that term was not then in use.

III

It should be remembered that although *The Future of Socialism* was an influential work, that influence took some time to develop.[30] Crosland was out of Parliament when it was published, and therefore it makes sense to turn to the views of his friend Hugh Gaitskell for a further exploration of the revisionist outlook on these issues at this time. Gaitskell, who defeated Bevan and Herbert Morrison for the leadership of the party in December 1955, was a more significant figure than Crosland (in terms of practical politics if not intellectually). As such he did not have the same freedom to suggest that the British growth rate, under Conservative economic stewardship, was actually perfectly healthy. At any rate, the line that he took was more ambiguous than Crosland's. In a conference paper given shortly before he became leader he cast doubt on Soviet statistics. He also echoed Crosland's views by arguing that, as the Soviet Union's living standards improved, the rate of betterment might slow down, because, as she caught up with the West, her population would be less likely to save so much, invest so much and work so hard. Therefore he did not argue for the demonstration effect – that is, the idea that Britain must show that social democracy could deliver growth in order to reduce the appeal of totalitarian planning to the Third World. But he did stress the need to appeal to the underdeveloped countries by granting political freedom to the remaining colonies and by offering aid in varying forms. Indeed, 'it is in these uncommitted areas, most of them economically backward, that the economic no less than the political challenge to freedom is greatest, and that the effort needed to meet it must therefore be correspondingly all the more energetic and sustained'.[31]

Crosland would not have dissented from these views. But, after a year as leader, Gaitskell developed his ideas in a manner that reflected the Cold War-affluence discourse rather more strongly. He did so in lectures he gave at Harvard, published in 1957 under the title *The Challenge of Co-existence*. He noted that 'the uncommitted areas', including India and the Arab nations, offered a favourable field for the expansion of Communist power by non-military means. 'Undoubtedly, the emphasis placed by the Russians in the new co-existence era is upon propaganda, diplomacy, economic penetration, rather than direct military assault', he said. 'This is what they mean by "competitive coexistence"'. Furthermore:

> communism, in the ideological war, starts with considerable advantages in these territories. They are all countries which desire to see a higher degree of industrialisation and economic planning, planning which it is generally admitted must in such cases be carried

out by the government. They have heard of spectacular accounts of the success of the Russian economic policy over the past thirty years and particularly the last ten years . . . In the typical liberal economies of the West, although there may be, and indeed is, substantial economic progress, it is not associated so directly with governments and it seldom receives the same degree of publicity.

Gaitskell, then, was steering a path between the Crosland line and that advanced, most conspicuously, by Balogh. In his view, the West was experiencing economic progress, but there was still a Communist demonstration effect of sorts. He also argued that, in underdeveloped nations, 'Many customs have to be altered if productivity is to increase' and that 'These changes can undoubtedly be forced through far more easily by a dictatorship than under democratic conditions.'[32] Again, because he shared Crosland's belief in the economic success of 'affluence', he did not claim that economic planning in Britain was essential in order to show that democracy could in fact deliver the goods. As such he rejected the Balogh solution of a world planning body based on the Commonwealth, and instead continued to emphasise colonial freedom and economic aid as the appropriate remedies.

These same emphases were present in Labour's manifesto for the 1959 general election. Although the document did claim that 'Britain in these last years has been outpaced by almost every other industrial nation', it did not highlight the USSR in particular, or argue that this lagging-behind would have consequences for the Cold War. The party did believe 'in extending the Socialist concept of the Welfare State to all the peoples of the world' and hence its commitment to an expanded aid budget. Moreover, 'At this historic moment a British Government with a clear policy based on the ethical principles of Socialism can exercise a decisive influence for peace. Hundreds of millions of people throughout the world still look to Britain for moral leadership and eagerly await the result of this General Election.'[33] Still, one would be hard pressed to argue that the manifesto was steeped in the Cold War-affluence discourse. After Labour's heavy defeat, though, it took on a new salience.

Two factors played a part in this. The first of these was that nervousness about British economic performance – the phenomenon that Tomlinson has dubbed 'declinism'[34] – reached a critical mass in the early 1960s. The intellectual ferment that resulted was by no means restricted to the Labour Party, but extended to a growing band of professional economists and to the Treasury, and was reflected in Conservative 'planning' initiatives such as the establishment of the National Economic Development Council (NEDC). Relative decline was of course a reality: in 1961 Germany and France both overtook Britain in terms of income per head.[35] There were also intellectual influences from outside, notably J. K. Galbraith's *The Affluent Society* (1958). This book, which contrasted American society's 'private affluence' and 'public squalor' had succeeded in capturing the imagination of the US public, in the midst of the questioning and anxiety that followed the launch of the first *Sputnik*; for it now appeared that the USSR was able to make a much more purposeful use than the USA of a much less productive economy.[36] It struck a chord in Britain too. Crosland declared himself 'wholeheartedly a Galbraith man'.[37] Richard Crossman also approved of the book.[38] Balogh's favourable review of it located Galbraith's arguments firmly in their Cold War context: 'Only ruthlessly clear thinking and reform can possibly safeguard the survival of the West against the imminent technical advantages of the Communist menace.'[39] And Michael Shanks, a Labour-sympathising journalist, echoed not only Galbraith's title but also his themes, in his 1961 'declinist' classic *The Stagnant Society* (inspired by a visit to the East). 'In everything that makes life valuable and worth living, Western democracy has the edge on Communism', he argued. Nonetheless:

> Athens was in every way a finer society than Sparta, but she did not gain the victory. She lost because she wasted her talents in fratricide and frivolity, whereas Sparta husbanded and refined hers with the same single-minded persistence which Soviet Communism, with all its defects, demonstrates today.[40]

The second factor contributing to the new prominence of this type of discourse was its potential as a weapon in internal party debates. The 1959 defeat prompted much soul-searching and plenty of recriminations. Gaitskell concluded that it was time to drop Clause IV of the party's constitution, which committed it to pursuing 'the common ownership of the means of production, distribution and exchange'. Left-wingers, however, thought that dropping nationalisation would be a betrayal of socialist principles, and Gaitskell was defeated. During the party conference debate on the issue Bevan invoked the threat of Soviet economic power as a justification for retaining the Clause. 'The so-called affluent society is an ugly society still', he argued. Moreover, 'The challenge is going to come from Russia . . . The challenge is going to come from those countries who, however wrong they may be – and I think they are wrong in many fundamental respects – nevertheless are at long last being able to reap the material fruits of economic planning and of public ownership.'[41]

This view was summed up with great vividness by Michael Foot, in his comment on the 1959 election: 'While placards on every hoarding were prophesying the doom which nationalisation would bring, while Labour leaders were lisping their much too mild peeps in favour of the principle of public ownership, a nationalised rocket hit the moon and another circled it.'[42] Crossman now emerged as a key exponent of such thinking. His ideas were developed in a reply to an article by Tony Crosland, published in *Encounter* in April 1960, which had attacked the left-wing attitude to nationalisation as 'schizophrenic', and which had deployed arguments about the Cold War similar to those made in *The Future of Socialism*.[43] Crossman lambasted Crosland for his 'failure to observe the terrifying contrast between the drive and missionary energy displayed by the Communist bloc and the lethargic, comfortable indolence of the Western democracies'.[44] He laid out his ideas further in the follow-up pamphlet *Labour in the Affluent Society*, and elsewhere. He believed that affluence could not be sustained, and that its end would create a radicalised electorate ripe for a socialist programme.[45] He also believed the international situation strengthened the case for economic planning in democratic industrialised countries. 'In peacetime, overall planning is jettisoned', he argued in 1961. 'Western freedom means today that no Western government has either the right or the power to take the decisions necessary for winning the Cold War until a hot war has actually begun. In the 1960s this is the strongest argument for socialism.'[46] In this he echoed the earlier views of Balogh by arguing that although the West retained the economic potential to defeat the East, any 'hot' war would come via conventional weaponry, and not H-bombs as Crosland argued, due to Mutually Assured Destruction. Only by preparing a strong industrial base capable of mounting a conventional war would the West have true military as well as economic security.[47] Crosland felt this approach smacked of millennialism.[48] His fellow revisionist Roy Jenkins felt that Crossman had set out with the aim of justifying nationalisation come what may, and had then constructed an ideology, based on an extreme interpretation of the Soviet threat, in order to do so.[49]

But although left-wingers did invoke the Soviet threat in order to justify public ownership it would be unfair to dismiss its use as wholly opportunistic. Bevan's remark about the 'ugly' nature of affluence is telling. It clearly did reflect the kind of hostility to cultural change – or at least aspects of it – that Black and others have identified as prevalent on the left. Linking the weaknesses of acquisitive Western society with the 'challenge' posed by the USSR was a useful rhetorical figure, but it also reflected Bevan's real and longstanding admiration for Soviet economic achievements.[50] Consider too Crossman's criticisms of advertising. This aspect of affluence was also found ethically suspect by many other Labour figures, including

Crosland, Morrison and Bevan, because of its role in promoting materialism.[51]
There was, however, also the issue of efficiency, which Crossman for his part
emphasised, arguing that one of the advantages of Soviet planning was that
it removed the need for 'wasteful' advertising.[52] Casting the 'efficiency' of
Communism as a threat or challenge allowed proponents of the Cold War-
affluence discourse to praise elements of its economic system whilst
condemning its political cruelty and despotism. The praise appears, on the
whole, to have been as genuine as the condemnation, and thus the discourse
cannot be dismissed merely as a weapon in Labour's internal battles,
although it in part fulfilled that function.[53]

IV

Bevan's death in July 1960 recast the Labour landscape, but Gaitskell's
troubles were not at an end. At the party conference that year he was
defeated by advocates of unilateral nuclear disarmament (although the
decision was reversed in 1961) and shortly afterwards faced a challenge
from Wilson for the leadership. Although Wilson was defeated, he
remained an influential power in areas which were crucial in the 'Cold
War-affluence' discourse, as Shadow Chancellor and subsequently Shadow
Foreign Secretary. Wilson had, of course, resigned with Bevan in 1951 over
Gaitskell's rearmament budget, and had continued a dalliance with the
'Bevanite' left throughout the 1950s (maintained via links to Balogh and
Crossman). His position as the left's standard-bearer had been
strengthened by Bevan's death. His influence may help explain the fact
that the Cold War-affluence was now increasingly reflected in the party's
official programme.

Labour in the Sixties, drafted prior to the 1960 conference, has been seen
as the starting point for later policy developments in the run up to the 1964
election.[54] Its authorship is to some extent in doubt. Crossman (who was at
this point Chairman of the NEC) claimed to have written it, although
others, including Wilson, may have been involved too.[55] But rather than
endorsing the pamphlet to the party conference, as was usual, the NEC
instead recommended it should be approved under the name of the General
Secretary Morgan Phillips, thus removing collective responsibility for its
proposals and argument. Steven Fielding suggests that this had come about
because neither left nor right either fully agreed with the document or
wanted to reject it completely.[56] Written at roughly the same time as
Crossman's Labour in the Affluent Society, the document showed, on the one
hand, evidence of the 'millennialist' approach that Crossman expounded and
about which Crosland was sceptical. It argued that 'our socialist beliefs will
be vindicated in the 1960s, as it is ever more clearly seen that the new post-

war *capitalism is creating its own insuperable problems* and that, in the epoch of scientific revolution, *democracy, if it is to survive, must plan its resources* for the common good'.[57] Moreover,

> There is the basic economic problem of ensuring that sufficient of our resources are allocated to capital investment and industrial development. Here again we are lagging not only behind the Communist countries but behind our chief capitalist competitors as well . . . But instead of extending public ownership and control, the Tories pour out ever larger sums of money to big combines, unaccountable to Parliament.[58]

On the other hand, *Labour in the Sixties* also paid heed to many of the revisionists' preferred views on the future. It talked more about 'western competitors' than 'communist' ones, and about economic 'control' as well as 'public ownership'. Indeed, in contrast to its statements about the 'insuperable problems' of capitalism, it said that 'full employment and some growth in prosperity' was 'in contemporary conditions . . . almost inevitable'.[59] Therefore, the claim in *Tribune* that the pamphlet marked the 'death knell of revisionism' was a considerable exaggeration.[60] However, the document does signify that certain ideas typically associated with Wilson's leadership – for example, the connection between 'scientific revolution' and the Communist challenge – were gaining some purchase even during the Gaitskell era. Its Cold War-affluence discourse elements thus offer further support for Ilaria Favretto's contention that this period marked, in the party's programme, 'the beginning of the contamination of pure centre-right revisionist arguments with centre-left technocratic ones'.[61]

What may loosely be described as centre-left ideas took hold more firmly in the *Signposts for the Sixties* (1961). This is unsurprising given that Wilson was appointed Chairman of the Home Policy Subcommittee just before preparation for *Signposts* began.[62] That Wilson's hand was at the centre of such work can easily be demonstrated. Wilson's own 'Four Year Plan for Britain' (published in the *New Statesman* in March 1961) and a further policy document which was written by the Home Policy Committee and signed by Wilson (*Science and the Future of Britain* (1961)) both reflected the 'Cold War-affluence' conclusions of the 'centre-left'. Much in the same way as the 'Four-Year Plan', *Signposts* played up strongly the idea that capitalist democracy was facing a 'crisis', and that economic planning in Britain was an essential way to safeguard political freedom.

> We live in a scientific revolution . . . In such an epoch of revolutionary

change, those who identify laissez-faire with liberty are enemies, however unwittingly, of democracy. The enlargement of freedom which we all desire cannot be achieved by opposing State intervention but only by assuring that national resources are wisely allocated and community services humanely planned.[63]

Another argument gaining prominence within the party at this time cast further doubt on the virtues of modern 'affluence', which was portrayed as a dangerously short-termist option. One pamphlet suggested: 'we must postpone that television set for the bathroom so that we can be sure of having enough to eat in the 'seventies.' Whereas much British investment had been devoted to the area of consumer goods, it was claimed elsewhere in this pamphlet, too little had been devoted to capital goods. It was said to be the latter 'which make possible the major advances in production techniques and the volume of output'. It was anticipated that the demand for producer goods would probably increase, whereas Britain would meet stiff competition in the consumer goods field.[64] This, it was believed, meant that it would be best for Britain to focus on selling 'hard' industrial products to developing countries, and especially the Commonwealth, rather than on attempting to sell 'soft' consumer goods to industrialised, and especially European, countries, that were already making such goods themselves. The intellectual debt to Balogh was apparent.[65]

Therefore it is not surprising that during 1961–2 the question of potential British entry to the EEC gained prominence in the debates about the economics of the Cold War. One important argument was that membership would compromise Britain's ability to plan her own economy – creating the dynamism associated with 'hard' industry – and thus rise to the Communist challenge. Balogh made this type of claim, and its overall thrust also found more politically weighty endorsement.[66] Gaitskell's predecessor, Clement Attlee, articulated his own concerns in a speech in the House of Lords. He said that it was important to consider 'what is going to be the result of this country's joining with countries that are essentially capitalist countries'. He noted that the Communist bloc appealed to 'the debatable countries of Asia and Africa' through the cry of anti-colonialism, and that EEC countries such as France, Holland and Belgium had unfortunate colonial records. It was important, therefore, to consider what the repercussions of joining were likely to be on the British Commonwealth. Attlee's combination of an argument for the demonstration effect of a dynamic British social democratic economy with the suggestion that Commonwealth countries might feel politically and/or economically 'deserted' if Britain joined was notable:

Now I am not afraid of Communism. I think that we shall meet it. But we shall meet it only if we have a dynamic as strong as the Communist dynamic, and I do not think we shall get that if we go back to the old capitalism, still less the old imperialism. The biggest contest in the world today is ideological. Which way will the nations of Africa and Asia go? We have to be very careful that they do not feel we are deserting them, because they will look to Communism.[67]

Wilson – who could be described at this time as a noncommittal Eurosceptic – also invoked the Cold War in debates over membership. On one occasion he challenged Harold Macmillan to give details of how safeguards for the Commonwealth's trading future could be combined with British membership, 'because it really is nonsense for the Prime Minister to talk about a holy war against Communism . . . if he is wantonly embarking on a course which by undermining, for example, the Commonwealth Sugar Agreement and the Citrus fruits arrangements will knock out the props which underpin the prosperity of struggling colonial economies'. He also emphasised that, by alienating the Commonwealth, EEC entry might jeopardise Britain's supposed ability to help resolve the Cold War. 'We have a rôle to play in the world, perhaps a decisive rôle, at some historic moment; in building a bridge between East and West – between America and Russia, perhaps America and China, and we must search our hearts and ask whether going in, or not going in, will best help in that rôle.'[68]

Abandoning the Commonwealth, it could even be argued, would destroy the potential for a 'socialist' world alternative, and thus the possibility of bringing the two ideologically opposed Cold War blocs together. (Labour had long been keen to encourage the newly independent countries to undertake socialist planning.)[69] In 1964, one writer in the revisionist journal *Socialist Commentary*, which had been scornful of 'third force' ideas during the 1950s, suggested that Britain should lead a 'middle course in social philosophy', between Soviet beliefs and the American way of life. It should 'take the initiative in establishing an order that combines what few, if any, have up to now been able to achieve – personal freedom and socialism'. This meant acting as a bridge between the US and the USSR. The influence of centre-left ideas seems to have become widespread by 1964.[70]

Gaitskell in his famous 'thousand years of history' speech to the 1962 party conference did not go quite that far. He did, however, echo some of Wilson's arguments quite closely. He came down firmly against EEC entry, declaring it would mean the end of the Commonwealth. Moreover, 'the existence of this remarkable multiracial association, of independent nations, stretching across five continents, covering every race, is something that is potentially of immense value to the world . . . for together we can, I believe, make a great contribution to the ending of the cold war'.[71] He also argued that Britain needed to remain free to plan her own economy. He did not make the explicit argument that such planning was essential in order to combat the Soviet threat, and therefore he was not endorsing the Cold War-affluence discourse in its full form. Nonetheless, he had made enough concessions in a left-wing direction to gain himself a warm response, from, amongst others, Wilson. (He also of course pleased right-wing anti-Marketeers like Jay, whilst displeasing enthusiasts such as Jenkins and Bill Rodgers.) Hence Dora Gaitskell's well-known remark: 'But all the wrong people are clapping.'[72]

V

When Wilson took over the leadership, after Gaitskell's death in January 1963, important elements of his economic approach were already established within the party. These included not only an emphasis on planning, but also concern with Commonwealth links.[73] But although Gaitskell had recognised 'the challenge of co-existence', and although he believed in economic planning in Britain, he had not made the argument that the latter was necessary *in order to meet the former*. This was what Wilson did – most famously in his 1963 'White Heat' conference speech. The speech was a *tour de force*, in which he defined Conservative affluence as a kind of soft option, which threatened to prevent Britain meeting the Soviet challenge. Thus, far from abandoning earlier views, Wilson gave full voice to his earlier 'Four Year Plan' beliefs. Yet at the same time he appeared to suggest that, under a Labour government, Britons would be *more* affluent, as their living standards shot up:

> only if technological progress becomes part of our national planning can that progress be directed to national ends.
>   So the choice is not between technological progress of the kind of easy-going world we are living in today. It is the choice between the blind imposition of technological advance, with all that means in terms of unemployment, and the conscious, planned, purposive use of scientific progress to provide undreamed of living standards and the possibility of leisure ultimately on an unbelievable scale.

He argued it was imperative that Britain must produce more scientists, as the USSR was radically outstripping her in that regard: 'the sooner we face up to that challenge the sooner we shall realise what kind of a world we are living in.' Furthermore, he said, many of the country's existing scientists were 'deployed, not on projects that are going to increase Britain's productive power, but on some new gimmick or additive to some consumer product which will enable the advertising managers to rush to the television screen to tell us all to buy a little more of something we did not even know we wanted in the first place. This is not strengthening Britain.' One might think that the British people would in fact have welcomed a few gimmicks and additives as part of their 'undreamed of living standards', to help them while away the leisure they were to experience 'on an unbelievable scale'. Yet the gap in the logic was significant only insofar as it shows how successfully Wilson's rhetoric melded the 'national security' critique of affluence with claims that were more obviously voter-friendly. He reached a ringing conclusion: 'Because we are democrats, we reject the methods which Communist countries are deploying in applying the results of scientific research to industrial life, but because we care deeply about the future of Britain, we must use the resources of democratic planning, all the latent and underdeveloped energies of our people, to ensure Britain's standing in the world.'[74]

The Cold War-affluence discourse had come to full fruition under Wilson's leadership. He skilfully blended 'revisionist' aspirations for a Labour Party focused on material wealth with one based on planning and an 'ethical' world policy. This was in contrast to Gaitskell's approach. The latter's failure to embrace the 'Cold War-affluence' discourse in its full form meant he had backed away during 1960–1 from giving full exposure to the 'Science' aspect of Labour's policies. This aspect implied a more interventionist approach to the economy and society at a time when Gaitskell was still reeling from his failure over Clause IV. It is thus doubtful that a Gaitskell election platform in 1964 would have been both as rousing to the party faithful and as unifying as that developed under Wilson's guidance.

The 'White Heat' speech was reminiscent of John F. Kennedy's call 'Let's get this country moving again', made during the 1960 presidential election, in which the Democrats suggested that Republican economic complacency had weakened the US in the fight against Communism. Given the seeming success of that approach, and his own reputation as 'the British Kennedy', it might appear surprising that Wilson did not continue to harp on the theme of the Soviet threat in the run-up to polling day in 1964. Yet not only did he fail to do so, but there are few obvious traces of the Cold War-affluence discourse in the Labour election manifesto. The focus on 'purposive planning' and the application of science was a crucial element of the Labour campaign. But it was not justified on the basis of the Communist challenge, even though that had provided much of the original rationale for adopting such ideas in the first place. This can be seen in Wilson's new tendency to play up the threat posed by German and Japanese economic competition, without mentioning the USSR or China.[75] He did make a brief reference to the Cold War in his final election broadcast, in response to the launch of the Soviet *Voskhod* 1 spacecraft: 'We are faced with the formidable industrial and technological challenge from the Soviet Union and other countries. We have had a reminder today with the new Soviet spacecraft. Faced with this kind of challenge, we cannot, as a nation, afford to neglect the development of a single child.'[76] Yet he could certainly have made much more of this had he wished, and this single reference was aimed more at supporting educational reform rather than economic planning.

Indeed, he had emphasised the Soviet threat much more strongly when, earlier in 1964, he had visited the USA. (While there he collected an honorary degree from Bridgeport University, and published a book on *The Relevance of Socialism* for US consumption.)[77] He noted that, 'There is one thing we must understand. If we are scared away from demanding economic planning, then others will step in with their more rigid and dictatorial versions. The struggle for the soul of Asia is a struggle between the democratic socialism of India and the totalitarian Communism of China.'[78] He also stressed other aspects of the Cold War-affluence discourse, and, in his book, wrote that 'It is no accident that the success of the post-war Labour Government produced the virtual elimination of Communism as an effective political force in Britain.'[79] It seems likely that Wilson was anxious to couch his arguments in these terms in order to strengthen his anti-Communist credentials and reassure a nervous American administration that a Labour government would not be weak on Communism, either at home or abroad. But why, then, the neglect of these themes when he was back in Britain?

One possible explanation is that the Cold War-affluence discourse had been used in a purely instrumental way, in order to get the party to accept a centre-left, interventionist economic agenda. Once this had been achieved there was no longer a need to discuss the Cold War threat as often as before, particularly given that, as the Crosland Crossman exchange in *Encounter* had shown, the 'Communist challenge' argument was potentially divisive. There is, however, rather more direct evidence to support the theory that Wilson was making a straightforward electoral calculation. As Fielding notes, from the moment Wilson became leader, his preoccupation was not to jeopardise the party's electoral chances.[80] Research for the party found that domestic issues rather than foreign or defence issues favoured Labour.[81] Indeed, Wilson cancelled two speeches that he was planning to make on foreign affairs during his 'New Britain' tour early in 1964.[82] On one occasion Tony Benn wrote in his diary that Wilson had 'decided not to do foreign affairs because it is domestic issues which really pull in the support'. Subsequently Benn, together with Peter Shore, decided that the Labour leader should speak on foreign affairs, the UN, and aid to underdeveloped countries. Wilson was unconvinced. 'I put it to him that a foreign affairs speech was necessary if only to influence opinion formers', Benn recorded. 'But he would not have it . . . He is almost more closely tied to the Gallup polls than Hugh Gaitskell was.'[83] Gallup's findings did indeed show that 63% of people surveyed mentioned a domestic issue first, compared with the 28% who mentioned a foreign or defence problem.[84] Labour candidates reflected these preoccupations in their election material and speeches, which obviously reduced the number of possible avenues to discussion of the Communist threat.[85] In his own speeches during the campaign itself Wilson did in fact place considerable emphasis on the need to tackle world poverty, even though this was not an obvious election winner, and he also spoke of the importance of the Commonwealth.[86] However, his nods in the direction of the Cold War-affluence discourse were restricted to generalities such as 'If you stand still at home, you stand still all around the world.'[87] Shortly after the polls shut on 15 October, the news came through that Khrushchev had been overthrown. But the explicit link between his doctrine of 'collective coexistence' and Labour's critique of affluence had been displaced from party rhetoric some months before.

Although the Cold War-affluence discourse was not prominent during the 1964 campaign itself it was nonetheless of significance. This is because it clearly played an important role in the adoption of Labour's 1964 economic programme, with its emphasis on planning and the Commonwealth, even though, after 1963, that programme was 'de-linked' from the Soviet threat in party rhetoric. (The exception, as has been seen, was Wilson's American visit.) This is true regardless of whether the 'Communist challenge' argument was used in a purely instrumental way, or whether, as seems more likely, it was advanced because it was believed sincerely, but was then nonetheless played down for tactical reasons as the election approached. Indeed its effect seems to have lasted beyond the election. As Tomlinson has noted, it is often forgotten (due to the later EEC application) that during the 1964–6 government Wilson pursued various routes to bringing the planning of the Commonwealth and Britain together through Trade Conferences in order to build a new socialist world order.[88] Moreover, the establishment of the new ministries of Overseas Development, Technology, and Economic Affairs may be seen as a reflection of key parts of the Cold War-affluence discourse. Therefore, Labour views on affluence cannot be fully understood without reference to the Cold War, just as the party's approach to the Cold War during 1951–64 cannot be understood without reference to affluence.

VI

Taken together, these issues also cast new light on 'declinism'. 'In the US there was much concern with growth rates relative to the USSR, and the idea that success in the growth race would be crucial for the underdeveloped countries' choice between capitalism and communism', Tomlinson argues. 'But while there are echoes of this kind of strategic debate in Britain, the concern with growth there was primarily more parochial and narrow', being linked more with domestic issues and the British 'standard of living'.[89] Yet, within the Labour Party, the strategic debate was considerably more than a mere echo of the US one. Thinkers and politicians from both wings of the party engaged seriously with 'the challenge of coexistence'. Right-wingers tended to believe that the challenge could be met through aid to the Third World, greater colonial freedom and – if they opposed entry to the EEC – the maintenance of Commonwealth trading links. Left-wingers (if that category is thought to include Wilson) believed in such remedies, but they also went further. They argued that Western economies needed to improve their growth rates through planning in order to meet the Soviet challenge *and* provide increases in standards of living on top.[90]

The concern for the underdeveloped countries, shared throughout the party, was commendable, even though Labour's record in office on development policy turned out to be weak.[91] Other aspects of the discourse now appear mistaken, and even downright peculiar. Consider, for example, Wilson's suggestion in his 1963 conference speech that research into the production of 'little simple one or two-horsepower steam engines', as an alternative to consumer goods, would help Britain meet the Soviet challenge.[92] And the assertion, made by right- as well as left-wingers, that Britain had a major role to play in ending the Cold War, appears delusional, if perhaps harmlessly so. All the same, however misguided they may in some ways have been, the Labour politicians who engaged with the Cold War-affluence discourse cannot be convicted of having purely parochial instincts. Their rhetoric did gain a narrower domestic focus as the discourse faded out of view during 1964. This, however, seems to have been caused by a thoroughly realistic assessment of the genuine parochialism of the British electorate, rather than by an inherent lack of willingness to take note of developments in the wider world.

FROM 'DANNY THE RED' TO BRITISH STUDENT POWER: LABOUR AND THE INTERNATIONAL STUDENT REVOLTS OF THE 1960s

David Fowler[1]

During the 1960s the Labour Party was led by one of the most academically brilliant students of his generation – Harold Wilson. 'J. H. Wilson', as he was then known, graduated from Oxford University in 1937 with a first-class degree in Politics, Philosophy and Economics (PPE) and gained first-class marks on all of his finals' examination papers. Wilson was not a student radical in his years as an undergraduate at Jesus College, Oxford (he was regarded by his contemporaries as a swot); but he did read the work of 'radical' economists such as J. M. Keynes and his Economics tutor was astounded to discover that, just before sitting his finals, he read the whole of Keynes' revolutionary new work *The General Theory of Employment, Interest and Money* (1936) and absorbed it.[2] During his two Labour governments of 1964–1970 Harold Wilson was responsible for a period of enormous university expansion. Eight new universities were created during these years – Sussex, Kent, Warwick, Lancaster, East Anglia, Essex, York and Stirling – and 29 polytechnics. In fact, the student population increased at a faster rate under Wilson than under any previous prime minister.[3] Moreover, these students were eligible for state maintenance grants as of right and these grants enabled students from working-class backgrounds to go to university. They also made it possible for more affluent middle-class students to drive cars; some driving all the way to Paris in May 1968 to offer support to the Paris students in their disputes with their universities.[4] Wilson himself regarded his greatest achievement of these years as the Open University, which he pushed through Cabinet and Parliament himself during 1965 and 1966.[5] But it was in his second period in office, from 1966–1970, that Wilson's Labour government was drawn into the international student revolts that had spread from the University of California, Berkeley in the United States in 1964 to Paris, London and Northern Ireland by 1968 and 1969.[6] This chapter is concerned with the Wilson government's handling of the international student revolts of the 1960s in two senses: first, its understanding of international student conflicts in the wider world and, second, its handling of the student demonstrations in Britain during the late sixties, in which international students were perceived as the prime movers.

Very little is known about the Labour government's views on the students of the 1960s and no monograph has yet appeared on this intriguing subject. Historians do not have much material to work from in published form. Harold Wilson, for example, does not refer to the student revolts at all in his detailed study of these years *The Labour Government 1964–1970: A Personal Record* (1971). Two of his distinguished biographers, Ben Pimlott and Philip Ziegler, do not shed any light on this subject either. Austen Morgan's biography of Wilson has an amusing reference to Tony Benn's positive attitude towards students. Benn, who was MP for Bristol South East in the sixties and a junior Cabinet minister, wanted to get to know the students at Bristol University and visited the university in June 1968. He attended lectures on revolution, Black Power and Vietnam, and recorded in his diary that he found his visit an enjoyable experience. He wrote: 'I realised all of a sudden that for three and a half or four years I have done absolutely no basic thinking about politics. I have just been a departmental Minister . . . I thought they asked a lot of important questions and I enjoyed it.'[7] About a year later, Benn took part in a student 'sit-in' at a student flat in Bristol and passed on his impressions of the students he encountered to the inner Cabinet at Chequers. What was said at this inner Cabinet meeting is unclear; but it is clear from all the secondary sources available that Harold Wilson recorded few of his own thoughts about youth, or university students, of the late 1960s. Furthermore, Steven Fielding's recent study *Labour and Cultural Change*, volume one of a three-volume series on *The Labour Governments of 1964–1970* tends to confirm Wilson's own reticence over youth; though he is reported to have lost his temper with one long-haired 18-year old in Bristol who heckled him, telling him: 'You're too young to know anything.'[8]

We know more about the student protesters' views of Harold Wilson. One of Wilson's biographers, for example, describes him as 'an icon of failure' among the radical students of 1968.[9] We know that, during the Grosvenor Square demonstration outside the American Embassy in March

1968, the student leader Tariq Ali scribbled a note to the Prime Minister and put it through the letterbox of Number 10 Downing Street. 'Dear Harold', he wrote cheekily, '100,000 people came to tell you to stop supporting the Americans (in Vietnam) . . . What about it? Yours TA . . .'[10] Kenneth Morgan even makes the bold claim that the student protesters of the late sixties forced reforms on the Labour government; most notably, the reduction of the age of majority from 21 to 18 passed in 1969 (although a government report, the Latey Report, had recommended this back in 1967).[11]

The following discussion of Labour and the international student revolts of the late 1960s draws on a rich vein of primary material on British student protests, and official reactions to them, held in The National Archives, London. It also involves research on contemporary publications, ranging from the prolix discussions in *Hansard* (severely truncated here) to the widespread coverage the student protests received in the national press (discussed below) and to the many often incisive articles on student power that frequently appeared in contemporary journals such as *The Spectator*, *New Statesman*, *The Listener* and others. The chapter is in two parts. In the first section, the focus is on just two months during 1968, May and June. During this two-month period the international student movement quite literally came to London. In this section, I want to explore a widely-publicised event during May and June of 1968 – the visit to Britain of the charismatic and highly articulate leader of the May '68 student revolt in Paris, Daniel Cohn-Bendit (renamed by the British press of the period 'Danny the Red').[12]

This significant event of the 'British 1960s' led to an even more significant event – a major BBC TV documentary examining the international student revolts shown on prime-time television and eliciting much discussion in the press, in British universities and within the British political establishment. Indeed, as will be discovered, the government and the security services were far more directly involved in this visit than any historian has so far suggested.[13] The whole visit was carefully monitored by the Home Office, and the Home Secretary at the time, James Callaghan, met Cohn-Bendit for discussions.[14] The Home Office's Special Branch was also closely involved, trying to monitor the threat of student revolution throughout British universities.[15] What this case study makes possible is an exploration of the Labour government's thoughts on the student protests of the late sixties, a neglected subject, and it will enable us to reach judgements on surprisingly neglected questions such as how far the Labour Party was seeking to understand student demands (as suggested by Tony Benn's own experiences with students)? Was the Labour Party well informed about student protest movements in the wider world and indeed in Britain? Did

Labour regard the whole question of student radicalism as an international or European phenomenon, somehow spreading to Britain in the late 1960s? Moreover, did the Labour Party conduct its own research on how student radicalism spread from one country to another?

In the second section, the focus shifts to a more systematic analysis of the Labour Party's thinking on youth and student affairs in the period from c.1967 to 1970. It asks: how far did the Labour government of these years, and also the government's senior civil servants, see the global student protests of the late 1960s as a threat to the stability of British universities, and indeed to the stability of British society in the so-called 'Swinging Sixties'?

I

Student internationalism and its impact on Britain during the 1960s – both in the universities and on the British political establishment – has not really been taken seriously by British historians. The official historian of the LSE, Ralf Dahrendorf, has described 1968 as 'a quiet year'.[16] Moreover, Colin Crouch, a third-year Sociology student at LSE in May 1968, agrees. When 30,000 students occupied Paris's ancient university, the Sorbonne, and the University of Nanterre in the Paris suburbs for over a month, and were involved in dramatic confrontations with the Paris police leading to five students being killed and to hundreds more being hospitalised, British universities were in a state of slumber in comparison. The clinching evidence, for Crouch, is the lack of interest British students showed in the May '68 events in Paris. When a student demonstration in support of the Paris students was held at LSE during May 1968 it was an abysmal failure. Less than a hundred students turned up in a university which had over 3000 students.[17]

These two retrospective accounts of events at LSE – one from a former Director of LSE (Dahrendorf) and the other from one of its former students (Crouch) – have led political historians examining the wider British picture in the late sixties, most notably Kenneth Morgan, to devote very little attention to the question of whether the British student protests were linked to student protests in other countries. The picture we are given in accounts such as Morgan's recent biography of James Callaghan (*Callaghan: a Life*, published in 1997) and in his earlier survey of post-war Britain, *The People's Peace*, suggests that the British authorities in 1968, from the Home Secretary down, were never seriously bothered about student protest and accordingly left the university authorities to deal with the student discontent, at LSE and elsewhere.[18]

It is clear from the archives, however, that during May and June 1968 the subject of the international student revolt, and its possible effects on British students, was given far more serious attention in Britain – both at West-minster and in the national press – than has hitherto been argued by British historians. A valuable Ph.D. thesis could be written on the subterranean, and intriguing, world of international student networks during 1968. Morgan, perhaps understandably in a work of synthesis, did not probe these networks in *The People's Peace* and neither did he refer to the rich material on British student protest in government records. His account of the student 'revolts' is a 'top-down' approach to the subject which underplays the dynamics of student revolt, especially within the British student movements of the period. An interesting question for historians to answer is how far the worlds of New Left students on the campuses of the United States, on which Doug Rossinow has written a fascinating survey entitled *The Politics of Authenticity*, intersected with the worlds of radical students in Britain and Europe.[19] There is a danger of being overwhelmed by the richness of the primary sources on a single country and losing any sense of whether the students of that country travelled to other countries to preach student revolution. Rossinow, for example, has studied a single state, Texas, and has produced a monograph of almost 500 pages. Moreover, there is not a single reference in this massive study of the American New Left to the most celebrated student revolutionary beyond the United States in 1968, Daniel Cohn-Bendit.[20]

A way into the subject of student internationalism during 1968 is an exploration of reactions within Britain – from politicians, the press and from British university students – to Daniel Cohn-Bendit's visit to London in June. It is an intriguing story that has only been referred to in passing by other historians. Dahrendorf, for example, simply notes that Cohn-Bendit made 'several visits' to the LSE and leaves it at that.[21] It is quite clear from press reactions to Cohn-Bendit's visit, however, that he made a great impact in Britain, positive and negative, in the few days he was here from 11 June to 15 June 1968. Let us now explore why this event is worthy of historical study.

In mid-June 1968, amid dramatic events in Paris, the BBC made a 50-minute documentary on the international student revolts. It was an ambitious and costly media event. Students were flown into London from as far afield as Japan and from Eastern Europe (Yugoslavia, for example) and, in the Western Hemisphere, from the United States and Western Europe. The BBC obviously felt this was a significant news story. They paid all the expenses – airfares, domestic travel and accommodation – of the students brought to Britain to be interviewed for the programme and the programme was shown in a prime-time slot, at 9.05pm on a weekday evening.[22]

Daniel Cohn-Bendit was the undisputed leader of the French student movement in Paris. He had led the original Paris student protest at Nanterre over 'university conditions' (more specifically why male students were not allowed to stay in female students' rooms) and he was also involved in the student occupation of the Sorbonne and of the Odeon cinema in Paris, a building occupied for five weeks during May and June 1968.[23] He was described, even in the liberal English press, as an anarchist. *The Observer* described him as the leader of an extremist 'anarcho-Maoist movement' at Nanterre, where he was a second-year Sociology student aged just 23.[24] What makes Cohn-Bendit such a captivating figure for British historians to analyse is that he spoke fluent English (he was also fluent in German and his father had been German). Moreover, he was a mobile revolutionary. During May and June 1968 he found time to visit both Germany and Britain and in both countries he lectured to university students. He had great presence and spoke like a revolutionary; as if his movement was bound to succeed in the short term. For example, when he and the Paris students occupied the Odeon cinema, expelling the owner Jean-Louis Barrault, Cohn-Bendit told the press: 'Barrault is dead [he wasn't]. We are going to have to start again from the beginning and rethink everything.'[25] He sounded like a committed revolutionary, therefore; he travelled to different countries preaching student revolution and when he reached Britain in mid-June 1968 the British press became transfixed with him; the Labour government also became embroiled in the visit; and Parliament spent several hours debating the international student revolts, as we will discover.

It might be argued that a fracture within the international student movement was there from the beginning. We need only list the student activity around the world during May and June 1968 to see how feeble the British student protests were in comparison with those, for example, in Columbia University in New York, as well as in Paris and throughout Germany. The differences in scale are the most obvious point of difference. Whilst 30,000 students took part in the Paris student revolt in early May 1968, a mere 300 students occupied the University of Hull's administration building in June – around 10 per cent of the student body there.[26] The geographical spread of revolt was another point of difference between Britain and other countries. In May alone there were student protests in 27 cities across Germany. In Britain the only significant activity in that month was a student occupation at Hornsey College of Art in a suburb of North London. The third difference between Britain and elsewhere was in the spirit of the protest. The student protests in the United States and in Paris were bitter and confrontational, and the police were heavily involved. At Columbia over 900 students were arrested during a one-week student occupation. In Britain the protests were more sedate. The Hull occupation only lasted two days and no one was arrested. There was even an air of somnolence among British students. At Bristol University, for example, a student protest held in mid-June 1968 was advertised as a 'sleep-in'.[27]

When Cohn-Bendit arrived at Heathrow Airport at around 11.30pm on 11 June, there were student protests in progress in parts of Britain – though not in London. The student protesters had not, by this point, come to the attention of all Westminster's politicians; as would very soon happen. In Bristol students had set up a 'Free University' and members of the public were allowed in to attend lectures. But these lectures, given by the students, were not free at all. Each lecture cost one shilling to attend (12 pence).[28] There was also a Free University movement emerging in Cambridge and one of its leaders was a second-year English student at King's College called Simon Hoggart. His father was the pioneering Professor of Cultural Studies at Birmingham University, Professor Richard Hoggart. Simon Hoggart would eventually become a *Guardian* television critic.[29] In the week of Cohn-Bendit's visit members of the Free University group in Cambridge had boldly invaded a major university function in the Senate House – the installation ceremony for the new Chancellor, Lord Adrian. One of the group had forced his way into the Senate House and proclaimed to all the senior members attending the service: 'I have an announcement to make. The Free University . . . '. But in mid-sentence he was then forcibly removed from the building and the protest was continued on the streets of Cambridge.[30]

It made a lasting impression on the dons. Some of them even wrote to the press to record their impressions.[31] Indeed when letters by eminent Cambridge scholars such as Professor G. R. Elton appeared in *The Times* the subject of student militancy had obviously become a serious issue in Britain. Elton wrote a long rebuke of the student militants of Cambridge whom he had observed 'yelling in chorus' along the pavements, as the Chancellor and senior dons processed along King's Parade to the University Church, Great St. Mary's.[32] He admitted that, as *The Times* had stated in a report on the incident, there were around 100 militant students at the Senate House demonstration in June 1968 and, clearly rattled that a militant student movement had arrived in Cambridge, he described these militant students (who would have included Simon Hoggart and R. E. Rowthorn who is now a Professor of Economics at Cambridge) as 'insane' and the shouting of slogans as 'ugly'. He offered his own explanations of this student unrest in Cambridge for *Times* readers. The students, he thought, were coming under the influence of 'certain prophets' (whom he did not name) and he implied that the students were being brainwashed by these prophets. (He talked of their 'unlearned idealism' and 'unthinking admiration' for certain prophets). Whoever these prophets were, it is obvious that they were not Cambridge tutors. So, in effect, what Elton was saying was that these militant students in Cambridge had liberated themselves from the moral and academic structures of the university. They were advocating something that had not been heard of in Cambridge before: student power.[33]

Elton's letter to *The Times*, printed on 12 June 1968 (Cohn-Bendit's first full day in Britain) was one among several letters published in *The Times* that brought bad publicity to Cambridge during early June 1968. Another, by Dr W. H. G. Frend of Gonville and Caius College, was even more alarmist than Elton's. It suggested that Cambridge students saw the dons as a spent force and wanted to oust them. Frend saw one banner proclaiming 'Adrian Out, Intellectuals In'. He found this declaration a grotesque insult to one of the most distinguished academics in Britain. No doubt Lord Adrian would have seen it as he processed along the narrow street outside King's College and the University Church.[34]

Letters from Cambridge students also appeared in *The Times* during June 1968. Rowthorn, who was at this point a graduate student in Economics at King's College, wrote in to challenge a statement made in *The Times* by the University of Cambridge's Vice-Chancellor Lord Ashby. Ashby had suggested that students at Cambridge had no interest in sitting on university committees alongside the dons, as students at LSE had been demanding. Rowthorn dismissed this as incorrect. In two Cambridge colleges, King's and Queens', students had not only been campaigning to sit on university committees but had won this concession in one faculty: Economics.[35]

How much Daniel Cohn-Bendit knew about the militant students of Cambridge in June 1968, or about the student protest at LSE in 1967, is unclear. But he did make visits to the LSE during his stay and he might have also received a warm welcome in Cambridge. At the airport he was asked by a reporter what he would do during his one-day stay in Britain. He replied, vaguely, that he might visit his mother's grave 'somewhere in Golders Green' and he wanted to visit Karl Marx's tomb in Highgate Cemetery.[36] His lack of planning is, however, quite understandable. Since late May 1968 he had been too-ing and fro-ing between France and Germany and enduring what can only be described as a disorientated and fugitive existence. At one point, in late May, he had had to dye his red hair black to disguise himself from the French police. His hair was still black when he arrived in Britain. He had also undertaken an arduous trek through woods along the German-French border near Saarbrucken and triumphantly reappeared at the Sorbonne around midnight on 29 May.[37] In short, he was a fearless and seasoned revolutionary student leader when he arrived in Britain in mid-June, having boarded a plane at Frankfurt in Germany. He was an enigmatic speaker; he was self-assured, self-sufficient and seemingly at ease in whichever country he found himself in.[38]

How much the Labour government knew about Cohn-Bendit before he appeared in London is shrouded in mystery. Callaghan does not mention Cohn-Bendit's visit at all in his memoirs.[39] But this may be because it proved such a humiliating episode for the government, at least in the short term. The problem was, as we will discover, the Labour government was never consulted about the visit. The BBC had arranged the trip and Callaghan was forced to react to events at very short notice.[40] Indeed, he was reported to be irate on hearing the news that Cohn-Bendit was in London.[41] Senior Labour politicians had been following the clashes between students and police in Paris with no unanimity of response at all. There was both fear and complacency in ministers' speeches. For example, Denis Healey, Labour's Defence Minister, had told a group of trade unionists in Clacton during May: 'We have heard disturbing echoes from the thirties in the violence and anarchy across the Channel.'[42] Callaghan, on the other hand, dismissed any possible threat of the European student revolt reaching Britain. He told a meeting in Edinburgh during late May 1968 that 'the troubles' on the continent 'could not happen in Britain'.[43]

How far was Cohn-Bendit able to inject more purpose and dynamism into the British student protest? He faced virtually insurmountable difficulties right from the beginning. The first problem was that he was only allowed to stay in Britain for twenty-four hours and when he arrived in a breathless and dishevelled state his optimism about drawing British students into a wider international student movement cannot have been high. But the circumstances of his visit presented excellent potential for doing just this for two reasons. The first is that he was the most famous living student revolutionary in Europe and the British press were fixated with him.[44] Secondly, he had in fact been invited to Britain by the BBC, a global organisation, and he was to appear in a BBC programme with other international student leaders on prime-time television. In effect, if Cohn-Bendit was not able to create a global student movement himself on his tours of university campuses around Europe, the BBC might achieve this outcome for him, by bringing all its leaders together into a studio, allowing them to talk and broadcasting what they said to several million viewers.[45]

It is interesting that the quality press in Britain – *The Times*, *The Guardian*, and *The Daily Telegraph* – followed Cohn-Bendit's movements very closely throughout his stay in Britain. His photograph appeared on the front page of *The Times* for three days in succession on 12, 13 and 14 June. He appeared on *The Guardian*'s front page on 12 and 13 June and on *The Daily Telegraph*'s front page on 12 and 14 June. From the beginning, there was an air of mystery about him and *The Times* referred to him ominously as 'Herr Cohn-Bendit'. The paper knew that he had a German passport and gave its readers the impression that his family roots were Nazi.[46] But all of this was farfetched. Cohn-Bendit's father was a German Jew who fled Nazi Germany in 1933 and his mother was French. Both his parents were dead by June 1968 and so he was an orphan, along with his brother Gabriel.[47]

In his interviews with the British press, Cohn-Bendit revealed to reporters that he had a wry sense of humour and was not in any sense a sinister figure. Asked by a reporter at the airport why he was held at the immigration desk for two and a half hours, he replied: 'They think I am very dangerous, I suppose.'[48] There were all sorts of curious people at Heathrow to meet him, male and female. There were many female students dressed in mini skirts. Tariq Ali, a committed Marxist revolutionary from Pakistan who had been the President of the Oxford Union and was by 1968 a co-editor of *Black Dwarf*, a militantly leftist underground paper, was the first person Cohn-Bendit met as he walked through the airport terminal. The BBC was also there. After being photographed alongside Tariq Ali, both with clenched fists held in mid-air like the Black Power activists in the United States, Cohn-Bendit was whisked away from the airport in a chauffer-driven car by members of the BBC.[49]

On his first night in Britain Cohn-Bendit attended a party at the offices of *Black Dwarf*. Various media celebrities of the day were there such as Kenneth Tynan, the theatre critic, who wore a kimono shirt and Christopher Logue, a left-wing poet (described in *The Guardian* as 'the poet Laureate of the left'). *The Times* was so interested in Cohn-Bendit they sent along one of their reporters, Richard Davy, undercover to observe him at the party. When Davy was identified the proprietor of *Black Dwarf*, Clive Goodwin, decided that a vote would have to be taken to see if the rest of the group wanted *The Times'* reporter to stay, or to be ejected. It was 2am and the guests could not be bothered to vote. Goodwin therefore decided to ask the reporter to leave and he was sent home. But Davy had enough material for an article on Cohn-Bendit, which appeared on 13 June.[50]

Cohn-Bendit's first full day in London, 12 June, was a hectic and important day in his stay. He was under the constant supervision of two groups of people – the student revolutionary movement of Britain headed by Tariq Ali, who in fact had ceased to be a student three years earlier, and Anthony Smith, a producer at the BBC who was making the television programme on the international student revolt. So, for certain periods Cohn-Bendit was kept indoors at the BBC television studios in White City. At other points during the day, he was set free to go wherever he liked. He spent several hours in dispute with the staff at the BBC. He told them he would not make the programme until his visa was extended, and he had a good argument. The other student leaders the BBC had flown in from Europe and other parts of the world were given visas for at least a week and some for two weeks. Why should his last a mere 24 hours?[51] All the press reporters and photographers who spent the day at the BBC studios – there were 100 of them – thought something dramatic would happen. Some suggested that Cohn-Bendit would be kidnapped at the BBC and held hostage until his stay was extended.[52] There was a frisson of student power at the BBC that day. While the fate of Cohn-Bendit and the fate of the BBC's programme were being decided, all the international students stood together in the BBC foyer and sang the Communist anthem 'The Internationale'.[53] This was conducted in the presence of the press reporters and an embarrassed-looking Anthony Smith.[54]

During the day Cohn-Bendit managed to persuade all the other international students at the BBC Television Centre to abandon the programme unless his visa was extended. This was a major embarrassment for the BBC and costly. The organisation had paid 'several' thousands to fly the students over to Britain and a programme that was supposed to be filmed at 2pm on 12 June had still not been made by 7.30pm.[55] Cohn-Bendit, meanwhile, had gone off to meet British students and to lecture at the LSE.[56] He also visited Highgate Cemetery with Tariq Ali and other students and they stood in front of Karl Marx's tomb and sang 'The Internationale' for the second time that day.[57] Interestingly, the LSE was at the centre of the whole Cohn-Bendit saga. It was a Law lecturer there, Michael Zander, who applied to the Home Office during the day asking for Cohn-Bendit's visa to be extended.[58] Moreover, it was another LSE academic, Professor Robert McKenzie, who was to interview all the international students for the BBC TV programme.[59] Two hours before Cohn-Bendit's visa was due to expire the Home Office issued a statement to the press stating that he could stay on in Britain for a further 14 days.[60]

The 'Students in Revolt' documentary was shown on BBC1 at 9.05pm on 13 June. All the British quality press drew attention to the programme the next day. *The Times'* television critic Michael Billington described it as: 'Obviously . . . the one indispensable item on television last night'; but, rather disappointingly, he did not say what he found so indispensable in the programme.[61] In fact, he did not review it at all. It is clear from the other newspaper reports on the programme that it was not really a useful platform for Cohn-Bendit. It was too eclectic and included interviews with 11 other student revolutionaries, each representing a whole country.[62] Moreover, it seems to have done the students no favours. Indeed it was actually harmful to a Spanish student who participated. Martin de Hijas, aged 23, of the University of Santiago de Compostela, was chosen for the programme because he spoke excellent English. But on his return to Spain he was arrested and charged with spreading 'illegal propaganda'.[63]

Cohn-Bendit did not impress *The Guardian*'s television critic Stanley Reynolds, who described him as 'a trendy' and his contribution as 'unclear and vague'.[64] The appearance of the student revolutionaries was also derided by this critic, who described them all as looking like 'chubby schoolboys'.[65] This seems a somewhat sweeping and imprecise criticism. Tariq Ali, for example, was over six feet tall and was of slim build. Moreover, while he was only 24 he wore a thick moustache. He did not resemble a schoolboy in the slightest. If anything he looked older than his years.[66]

However Cohn-Bendit came over in the programme, it did not stop the British press and others talking about him. After the BBC, it was the turn of the politicians. Callaghan was forced to answer questions on Cohn-Bendit in the House of Commons on 13 June. In fact, the Cohn-Bendit visit occupied the politicians at Westminster for several days. There were debates about him in the House of Commons and in the House of Lords. In the latter case one debate about the student protests lasted over eight hours.[67] In the House of Commons, Conservative MPs, including the Conservative leader Edward Heath, gave the impression that Cohn-Bendit was likely to foment a large-scale student rebellion while he was in London. Heath wanted Callaghan as Home Secretary to guarantee that 'firm action' would be taken to control Cohn-Bendit's movements.[68] Another Conservative politician, Sir Walter Bromley-Davenport (MP for Knutsford, in North-West England) thought the whole episode was irresponsible. He told the House:

> At a time when our great ally, the French people, are fighting for their very existence against a communist revolution . . . the BBC . . . bring to this country and offer payment to one of the arch-enemies of free speech and law and order.[69]

Labour politicians were silent in this debate. Given Healey's concern about events in Paris, he might have been expected to say something; but only Callaghan spoke for the government. William Deedes, Conservative, thought the government had 'panicked'. But there was not the slightest sense of urgency in the tone of Callaghan's response. 'I . . . hope that no one will exaggerate . . . this young man's importance', he remarked emolliently.[70]

The House of Lords debate on Cohn-Bendit (also on 13 June) was edgier than the Commons debate. Several speakers believed he was 'a dangerous agitator' and were seriously worried about his potential to destabilise British universities. Lord Boothby wanted to know which universities Cohn-Bendit intended to visit. Lord Molson implored the government to 'give an assurance that if this alien visitor engages in agitation in the universities, his permit . . . will immediately be terminated'. Several questions were tabled in both Houses on Cohn-Bendit; chiefly, on the security threat he posed. (What did Parliament think of Cohn-Bendit's threats to 'use force'? Who would pay for the extra policing? How much would it cost?, and so on).[71]

In addition to the parliamentary debates on Cohn-Bendit, over 30 Conservative politicians signed a petition to the Home Secretary deploring the extension of Cohn-Bendit's visa.[72] Moreover, two sharply-worded motions, both introduced by Conservatives, were put to the House on 13 June, the day after Cohn-Bendit's visa was extended. One of these is worth quoting to illustrate the passion the young Frenchman had aroused in Parliament. Sir Charles Taylor proposed the motion: 'That this House condemns the BBC for inviting a well-known foreign professional revolutionary agitator, already banned from France, to appear on one of their programmes at the expense of the British licence-holder and taxpayer.'[73]

While these debates and questions were being heard in Parliament, Cohn-Bendit was pondering his future. In France, the government had taken control of the student protest in Paris with a vengeance. It had banned all student demonstrations in Paris for the remainder of June to prepare the population for a General Election. It had banned several extremist student organisations, including the 'March 22 Movement' which Cohn-Bendit had led. And it had deported 30 student leaders from France who had been involved in the Paris students' revolt. These deportees included 12 members of the German student group SDS. Cohn-Bendit wondered what the immediate future would hold for him if he returned to France. He told a *Times* reporter on 13 June: 'If I return to Germany or France, I believe my life would be in danger.'[74] At this point, he began to think about seeking political asylum in Britain.[75] But he had little time to think seriously about his future. There were still engagements he had to fulfil such as addressing the students at the LSE.

Cohn-Bendit's visits to the LSE were not successful. At a meeting there on 'Student Power' on 13 June one of the students present asked him his nationality and he refused to answer. He also told them that the French students would not cooperate with any student body that was 'anti-Communist'. Many LSE students heard him speak that day. The main lecture hall was full and loud speakers were used to broadcast his words to students who were crammed in the corridors of the main building. What infuriated LSE students that day was Cohn-Bendit's decision to conduct yet another interview with the press on the LSE's premises.[76] The next day at a student meeting to launch a new revolutionary organisation at LSE, the Revolutionary Socialist Students' Federation (RSSF), the tensions between

Cohn-Bendit and British student revolutionaries surfaced again. One of the organisers of this meeting, James Wickham, told a *Daily Telegraph* reporter: 'The students are fed up with the press foisting leaders like Ali, Cohn-Bendit and others on us.' He added: 'Tariq Ali only represents himself . . . Tariq Ali is not a student. He represents no student organisation. He is just someone who considers himself a revolutionary.'[77] It seems that Cohn-Bendit had been snubbed by the RSSF. He was not at the inaugural meeting at LSE. Tariq Ali was present, but sat at the back and left before the end. The next day, 15 June, as the RSSF meeting continued for a further two days, Cohn-Bendit left Britain, heading for Frankfurt.[78]

Cohn-Bendit's visit to Britain divided politicians. Callaghan had warmed to him and was reassured to learn that one of the places Cohn-Bendit wanted to visit in London was Buckingham Palace. 'I could think of nothing better than that for his education', Callaghan told MPs.[79] He was also surprised to learn from the BBC television programme that Cohn-Bendit did not seem to know all the words of the Communist anthem 'The Internationale'. On seeing Cohn-Bendit stumble through the song, Callaghan made contact with Cohn-Bendit and offered to teach him all the words.[80] We have, then, a strange mood in government circles during June 1968 about international student protest. One of the most prominent European student radicals of the period was treated not as a threat to British university life, but as a tourist. The Home Office handled the whole visit, rather than the government as such, and the key to understanding the Home Office's decision to extend Cohn-Bendit's visa is not to be found in any Cabinet discussion of Cohn-Bendit or in the Labour Party's views of Cohn-Bendit; but most probably in the Special Branch files still unavailable to researchers. He was under constant surveillance during the week of his visit and Special Branch officers were no doubt among his closest guides.

At the other extreme from Callaghan and the Home Office, were leading Conservatives such as Heath, who told the House of Commons: 'This is a matter which has caused grave concern to a large number of people.'[81] It is true that Cohn-Bendit's visit did worry the General Secretary of the National Viewers' and Listeners' Association, Mary Whitehouse. She sent a telegram to the BBC's chairman asking why the BBC was allowing 'the foreign anarchist' to promote his ideas on the BBC.[82] But there is no evidence that large numbers of people were disturbed by Cohn-Bendit. The editorials of all the quality newspapers were either sympathetic or at least curious; but not censorious. For example, even *The Daily Telegraph* welcomed the BBC programme on student protest, reporting: 'the nature and causes of student unrest are a matter of major public interest at the moment, and as such a proper subject for objective and balanced treatment on the air'.[83]

We are left with the impression from the newspaper coverage that the group most hostile, or indifferent, to Cohn-Bendit were his peers – British university students. There was no formal welcome for Cohn-Bendit from, for example, the National Union of Students (NUS). Nor was he invited to the launch of the RSSF at the LSE; a major snub it seems. Far more research is needed on, for example, the spread of information on the international student movement among British students during 1968 and on the so-called 'prophets' influencing the British student body – Herbert Marcuse and others. But it seems very clear from this survey that Daniel Cohn-Bendit was not one of these prophets, who allegedly inspired British student protest during the late 1960s.[84]

II

The Labour government was not greatly concerned with youth affairs, even after student protests started at the LSE in 1967 had spread to other universities in England, Scotland and Northern Ireland during 1968 and early 1969. In the records of central government youth affairs were dealt with, bizarrely, by the Foreign and Commonwealth Office (FCO) until 1970. The FCO had links with only one youth organisation; the British Youth Council, a body set up to represent British youth overseas.[85] Harold Wilson had created a 'Minister of Youth' in November 1968, in the aftermath of the anti-Vietnam demonstrations of that year in March, June and October, but the minister in question, Judith Hart, was ridiculed in Parliament and beyond Westminster for being a Wilson gimmick. The problem was she was a Minister of Youth without Portfolio and neither she nor anyone else knew what her responsibilities were. In the House of Commons she was asked immediately after her appointment, and quite bluntly, to tell the House what she did:

> Mr Marten: . . . could the Prime Minister be a little more explicit about the right honourable Lady's duties, namely, her concern with the problems of youth? What particular aspect of youth – moral, political, social – is she to be concerned with, and how old is youth before it is to get her attention?

> The Prime Minister: She is concerned with all the problems of youth, of all relevant ages.[86]

The minister's work continued to be shrouded in mystery, however, for the remainder of the decade and, as student protests developed, even Labour Party members wanted to know whether she was responsible for students or not. Manny Shinwell asked Judith Hart in February 1969, after a student protest at the LSE, whether she would be setting up an inquiry into student unrest. She gave an ambivalent answer. She claimed, on the one hand, that she was not responsible for student unrest (the Education Secretary Edward Short was); but she also gave the House her own explanation of the causes of the student unrest at the LSE. This was a vague statement, backed up by no evidence, noting that students at the LSE and other universities wanted 'rather more of a share in the management of various aspects of universities'.[87] She does not seem to have known very much about the LSE protest of January 1969. The LSE's students had wanted more student representation on committees some two years earlier and their dispute with the School's authorities had moved onto new territory since 1967. In January 1969 the issue at the LSE was gates. The students had noticed iron gates bolted to walls inside the School and thought it had begun to look like a prison. They had decided to remove the gates with pickaxes and spanners and 30 of them ended up in Bow Street police station cells for a night, later incurring fines in court.[88] Judith Hart was possibly trying to make amends for a provocative speech Edward Short had made in the Commons the previous week when he claimed that American students were behind the protest at LSE and were wrecking, quite literally, a great educational institution.[89]

Judith Hart in fact held two posts in the Wilson government of 1966–1970: Paymaster General and Minister of Youth. Her job of Minister of Youth was held in such low regard in the Cabinet that Peter Shore, her successor as Paymaster General in November 1969, refused to become Minister of Youth as well and the Education Department took over responsibility for all youth-related matters.[90] Several questions can be posed about Judith Hart's work as Minister of Youth. How much information did her department gather on student youth? How did it gather material? Did it have a policy on youth and a view on the student protests?

Hart began her work by avoiding students who were in dispute with their universities. One of her first visits was to a university settlement in Birmingham where she sat and sipped tea and chatted with students in a hotel room. The females sat on a sofa and chairs; she sat in an armchair and the male students sat on the floor or stood. She was photographed at the meeting and the photograph appeared in a local newspaper, the *Birmingham Post*.[91] After chatting to this group of around 12 university students, Hart told the press that the event was 'a most interesting and constructive meeting', giving the distinct impression that it was a very formal meeting. She later wrote back to Birmingham University and asked to be put in contact with just three of the students, though it is unclear in the government records why she selected these three, or what was discussed at the original meeting.[92] What is evident from the official records is that Hart was not instantly popular with young people. Students who were asked to comment on the new Minister of Youth were not very kind. A 21-year old student in Birmingham told a national newspaper *The People*: 'The idea of a Minister of Youth is ridiculous.'[93] A 16-year old student, also from the Midlands, remarked: 'If she's anything like my mum and dad, she won't do any good.'[94] A student from Dudley told *The People*: 'She's too far away. She's out of touch with the younger generation.' This student's negative judgement was quoted in another national newspaper article on the new minister printed in *The Daily Express*.[95] When young people were asked for their suggestions on what the new minister should focus on an amorphous group of schoolchildren, teenagers and university students delivered a long list of policies she could pursue: athletic tracks instead of dance halls ('We don't all want to dance to pop music all night', the minister was told). Another suggestion was that she should deliver better student accommodation. Schoolchildren reported that they wanted more choice over school meals and better lessons.[96] The range of complaints makes it clear that her responsibilities were too broad and that too many different types of young people were part of her remit.

Hart worked closely with civil servants and, though she denied she was responsible for student protest, the civil servants in her department were gathering material on student youth in Britain, and beyond, from very early on in the student troubles of 1968.[97] Judith Hart had a somewhat idealistic approach to youth affairs, making speeches about how 'communication' could be improved between students and their elders[98]; but this whimsical approach was far from being the government's only approach to youth. Her civil servants conducted research on student protests across the world and did ask strategic questions such as whether students were a threat to British society of the late 1960s. The government kept very detailed information on what it called 'the student movement' in Britain, as well as broad statistics on the number of students in a given year. It appears from the material in the government records that the Wilson government was never really worried about student protesters in Britain. But they did feel that in Northern Ireland students could create political instability (as its whole surface area was smaller than Yorkshire and only a million people lived there).[99] This prediction proved accurate and what started as a student movement at Queen's University developed into a 'civil rights movement' of students and adults, and eventually in 1969 the O'Neill government in Northern Ireland collapsed.[100]

The Labour government felt safe knowing that the British student population was quite dispersed and that there were no colossal universities in Britain where students could present a serious law and order threat if discontent spread through a university. There was, for example, no university in Britain on the same scale as the Sorbonne in Paris, which had 160,000 students in 1968. In the whole of Britain there were only 169,000 university students in 1965.[101] Another feature of the British student body that reassured government ministers was that almost all British students (90% in 1968) depended on state grants and, in theory, cutting student grants, or, in the case of international students raising tuition fees, was a form of control the Labour government could exert over the student body if it felt like it. One of the issues at the LSE in 1968 was that the Labour government had raised fees for foreign students.[102] Whether this was a strategy for reducing their numbers in British universities from 1968 is a moot point, but the Labour government never restored these fees back to their earlier level.

A third feature of the British student population that gave policy makers confidence during the years of student unrest is the absence, certainly before 1968, of professional or perpetual students in British universities. Most domestic students received a state grant for three years and then left the universities to pursue careers. It was believed that many of these students were from working-class families and valued the state's contribution to their studies. In other countries, notably the United States and West Germany, students were at liberty to retake courses and stay in the universities for an indefinite period. Some of these students migrated to Britain; such as Paul Hoch who had a Ph.D. from an American university but began another at Bedford College in the University of London.[103] Marshal Bloom, one of the leaders of the student protest at LSE, was another of these seasoned students who lingered on in the universities into their late twenties.[104] Moreover, Tariq Ali who had studied in Pakistan, and at Oxford in the mid-sixties, was still addressing student meetings in London in the late 1960s. Indeed, he led the Grosvenor Square demonstration in London in March 1968. Callaghan referred to him as a 'spoilt, rich, playboy'.[105]

It is tempting to suggest that, without these affluent professional students from abroad, the student protests in London would not have developed beyond the confines of individual universities. Who would have led the British students? The international students, especially those from the United States, some of whom had already participated in 'campus wars' there,[106] brought new techniques of student protest to Britain and devoted much of their time to trying to develop a student movement in Britain.[107]

British civil servants were always primarily concerned with the way British student protest was organised, and whether it posed a threat to law and order rather than with the students' demands. From early on, the Cabinet Office believed there was no evidence that British students had links with student protesters in Europe and the United States.[108] It seemed abundantly clear to them that the student movement in Britain did not spread by design, but through students seeing their European peers on television and imitating them. Ongoing research does suggest that the protest at LSE (possibly an isolated case, but possibly not) was highly organised and carefully planned and international students were the orchestrators.[109] But the role of television, and indeed radio, in spreading knowledge does need to be studied more systematically. One British government official made the acute remark that television had turned student youth in Britain into 'instant internationalists'. At the flick of a switch, they could easily learn about the death of Che Guevara thousands of miles away in Chile, or see students demonstrating in the streets of Paris from their living rooms.[110] As the government civil servants mulled over the evidence from different parts of Britain, they heard nothing that would have seriously worried them. Students were probably too candid for their own good in Britain. One LSE student activist told the *Evening Standard* in May 1968: 'the movement in this country is still very weak. At the moment, things haven't got very much further than individual contacts with overseas movements.' Officials in the Cabinet Office filed this statement with their other correspondence on the student protests.[111]

The idea that American students were behind the British protests, outlined in the Commons by the Education Secretary Edward Short in January 1969, had dawned on the civil servants in the Cabinet Office as early as May 1968. They knew all about the protests at Berkeley in 1964, for example; and were aware that the phrase 'student power' was an American import first used at Berkeley. They also had the names of all the American students who were active in British universities during these years. The Cabinet Office described these American students colourfully as 'informal missionaries of student protest' and they knew that two of these 'missionaries', Eliott Isenburg and Marshall Bloom, were studying at the LSE.[112] They knew that another American activist Michael Klein was at Sussex; that Alan Krebbs and Joseph Berke were at Shoreditch Art College; and they were also keeping an eye on the American friends of Bertrand Russell: Ralph Schoenman, David Horovitz and Russell Stetler who were involved with the Bertrand Russell Peace Foundation. They even recorded that the leader of the militant students at Columbia University in New York, Lewis Cole, had toured British universities in June 1968 – at the time of Cohn-Bendit's visit to Britain.[113]

What made it easier for the government to track so-called student revolutionaries in Britain was that most joined extremist organisations: most notably, the Vietnam Solidarity Campaign (VSC) and the RSSF. All the main student leaders of this period were in one or the other of these organisations. Besides the Americans, David Triesman, a student leader at Essex (now Lord

Triesman) was in the Radical Students' Alliance (RSA) and so was the South African student leader at the LSE, David Adelstein.[114] The British government estimated that there were around a thousand revolutionary students in Britain in 1968 in a student population of 450,000 (which included college students as well as university students).[115] There was some concern that the RSSF advocated 'killing policemen'; but also some comfort in the fact that the membership of the NUS and the Scottish Union of Students (SUS) dwarfed that of revolutionary groups. Together these two moderate student bodies had 400,000 members in 1968.[116]

There was further comfort in the low level of student 'disturbances' in Britain and it is interesting that British civil servants never used more alarmist terms such as 'student revolt' in their communications on this subject. The government could look back over 1968 and identify just a handful of incidents involving students. There had been one death at the LSE when a porter suffered a heart attack during a surge at one meeting. Just one incident was reported from Manchester. A student demonstrator had grabbed hold of the Education Secretary. There was a single incident at Sussex University where an American diplomat had been smeared with paint and more minor incidents elsewhere, which the Cabinet Office did not feel merited any comment other than that they occurred at Regent Street Polytechnic, Liverpool University, Leicester University, Oxford University and Hull University.[117]

By February 1969 the government was under the impression that the student protest in Britain (though not in Northern Ireland) had all but dissolved. The government kept a record of the fact that in the student elections at the LSE in February 1969 all the militant candidates were defeated.[118] A government memorandum entitled 'Student Protest, 1968–69', written in February 1969, also noted with satisfaction that the student union in Essex was taking responsibility for the student protest itself. The students at Essex had voted to reimburse the American diplomat whose suit had been daubed with paint. Moreover, a sit-in organised by the RSA at Essex had had to be abandoned.[119]

The behaviour of the student protesters in Britain was the prime focus of government thinking, but civil servants also discussed the influences shaping student behaviour; in particular, the intellectual influences shaping their thoughts. Two civil servants in the Cabinet Office discussed this in great detail and their exchanges were almost like an academic seminar. The influence of the American author and Berkeley academic Herbert Marcuse was probed in great depth. For example, one of the Cabinet Office's civil servants, named 'R. Jardine', went to the trouble of reading Marcuse's book *One Dimensional Man* (published in 1964), which identified students as the new revolutionary class. Jardine reported back to his colleagues that the book was incomprehensible. He described it as 'technically unreadable' and after consulting with officials in the FCO it was discovered that even in France none of the students who participated in the May 1968 protests in Paris had read a word of Marcuse. Cohn-Bendit supplied this information.[120]

As to the potential of other intellectuals or charismatic leaders to influence British students, the government were always sceptical. Jardine noted that all the heroes of British student protesters were foreign and since they were usually thousands of miles away there was no danger to the British state of these influences developing. In any case, they were emotional affinities rather than serious influences. Che Guevara, Ho Chi Minh and Fidel Castro were all mentioned in student speeches and literature, but the government felt the utterances of these foreign leaders were so vague they were laughable. Jardine noted:

> They (the students) tend to be against authority, and instead of a clear political ideology have heroes (Che Guevara, Ho Chi Minh and Fidel Castro etc) who all tend to be foreign and far away, and whose utterances are suffused with emotion and as vague as anything out of the medieval Schoolmen.[121]

Jardine, a very donnish civil servant who thought a lot about the student protests in Britain, decided that they were not revolutionaries at all, but simply wanted to belong to a community.[122] Colin Crouch, the student activist at the LSE who wrote a Ph.D. thesis about the student revolt in Britain, reached the same conclusion.[123]

By February 1969, therefore, the government thought the worst of the student protests in Britain was over. A government survey was undertaken the same month and 749 university students were asked if they had taken part in a student demonstration in the previous 18 months – during the highpoint of the protests. They learned that 30% of the students had done, but that three-quarters were now 'satisfied with life as a student'. The civil servants rejoiced at this news. One joked: 'the general picture is not such as to cause oldies like me to turn in our graves'.[124] By April 1969, the government civil servants who dealt with youth affairs behind the scenes began to turn their thoughts to the working-class youth of the cities. They had deduced that working-class youths who committed crime were a far greater problem for society than university students. As one put it:

> I suspect that it is the non-student young who are much more

important as a potential social problem . . . What is . . . worrying is
the virtual lack of any worthwhile rapport between society and the
young man who kicks your ribs in the Seven Sisters Road out of sheer
boredom, or stays more peaceably at home filling up the football pools
for lack of any effective encouragement to interest himself in anything
else.[125]

III

More research on the government records may uncover new material on the
student protest in Britain, but it seems unlikely that it will call into
question my argument that at no point were civil servants or government
ministers seriously worried about the student protest movements in Britain.
They seem to have thought the whole subject of youth was too frivolous for
senior civil servants at Whitehall to devote time to. 'R. Jardine', who was
more engaged by the subject than others, and certainly more knowledgeable
than the Minister of Youth Judith Hart, told a colleague in September 1969
he never discovered what Hart was supposed to do. 'We have previously
discussed this question of "youth"', he stated, 'and you are aware that I find
it rather difficult to pin down. Like the elephant it is easier to recognise than
define, and even when identified it is far from clear how it concerns the
government.'[126] After writing some interesting thoughts on the subject and
amassing a lot of material, he confessed that he found the whole subject too
superficial – 'anything one writes on the subject tends to be of the nature of
journalism rather than the more weighty prose that Whitehall is used to'.[127]
We can excuse him this comment. He was not delving too deeply into his
subject and only had to report on student protest, rather than delve into
complex questions such as juvenile delinquency and its causes. Moreover,
since he had found no disturbing evidence of a student movement in British
universities, he was probably thoroughly bored with the subject.

In essence, then, it was senior civil servants within the Labour Party who
were largely responsible for the Labour government's handling of
international student protest during the late 1960s. The Prime Minister,
Harold Wilson, despite being an economic radical in his youth, did not
regard either youth affairs or student protest movements as serious subjects
worthy of his time – except, briefly, in relation to the youth vote and when
the LSE had been forced to close for a month in January 1969.[128] Civil
servants like Jardine found that such was the government's lack of
knowledge about students and youth culture that he and colleagues had to
engage in information gathering from researchers in British universities who
had undertaken research on student movements.[129] In September 1969, the
FCO even sent some of their officials to an international conference on

'Youth in Revolt' held in Trinidad and Tobago.[130] What these officials were interested in was how the international youth revolt was affecting British Commonwealth countries, and so there was a vague sense within the government that somewhere across its far-flung Empire and Commonwealth students might create problems for colonial governments. But closer to home the international student revolts only impinged on British political life fleetingly. Moreover, when the visit of Danny Cohn-Bendit passed without anything more threatening than the BBC's cameras and a few clenched student fists, raised in poses for the cameras, the Labour government forgot about 'student power' and focused on more pressing matters.

HUMANITARIAN INTERVENTION, THE LABOUR PARTY AND THE PRESS: THE BREAK-UP OF YUGOSLAVIA IN THE 1990s

Ann Schreiner[1]

The NATO air strikes against Serbia in 1999 have been described as the 'first war fought in the name of humanitarian intervention'.[2] The British government, led by Tony Blair, gave strong support for the policy, and the Prime Minister was recognised as being a key figure behind the implementation of the military action. These events were a clear assertion of the new approach to foreign affairs that had been outlined by Robin Cook in the days following the landmark 1997 general election.[3] What they revealed was a strong desire for the Labour Party to present itself as a party of government, adopting a viable and identifiable policy in its actions towards the wider world.

However, just a few years previously, at the time of the initial break-up of Yugoslavia, the Labour Party was regularly criticised by important parts of the left-wing press, as being ineffectual in its response to the way in which the Conservative government had handled the earlier conflict. During the early 1990s, and especially during the Bosnian War of 1992–1995, vociferous criticism was made of the way in which the break-up of Yugoslavia had been handled by the 'international community'. Aside from general concerns regarding the lack of intervention, the media also singled out the way in which the Labour Party failed to take a lead in persuading the British government to take a stronger role in the crisis. The later NATO action against Serbia and the British government's participation in such a policy appears to be a reflection of the comments made in the left-wing media some years earlier. This raises questions regarding the way in which foreign policy evolves over a period of time, and also highlights the nature of the relationship that exists between elements of the same political current, in this case the Labour Party and the left-wing press.

I

British left-wing politicians and intellectuals have constantly struggled with the complexities of forming a foreign policy which, in practice, does not betray the principles of their ideology.[4] The gulf between those participating in left-of-centre politics, that is, the politicians, and those located on the periphery, the commentators, has been a repeated feature of debate within international relations. The obvious distinguishing quality of this argument is that those in government discover that their ideological principles are tempered by the realities of national interest. Intellectuals however, being outside of the parliamentary political process, are more easily able to hold onto their defining beliefs, thus the purity of their dogma survives unhindered by external considerations.

The dynamics of the situation in Britain are further complicated by the very broad church that is the Labour Party. As is well documented, the British Labour Party has embraced, and continues to embrace, politicians from a very wide spectrum.[5] One example to illustrate this point is the struggle that dominated the party during the 1980s. Seen as unelectable by the British electorate, the party was riven by factions, from those on the far left to those occupying a more traditionally social democratic position. The culmination of this struggle was the exodus of the so-called Gang of Four, leading to the creation of the Social Democratic Party (SDP). Even today, Labour contains politicians from an extremely wide ideological background. Traditional or old Labour figures, such as Dennis Skinner, sit in the House of Commons side-by-side with their undeniably New Labour colleagues such as David Miliband and Alan Milburn. The divide within the Labour Party – that is, between old and New Labour – falls normally along government and back-bench lines, with those furthest from power usually being the most critical of their front bench. Obviously, under Blair, dissenting figures are unlikely to be placed in the Cabinet.

In fact, there is a long tradition within the Labour Party of internecine debates on the very issue of foreign affairs. For Labour, the apparent dichotomy between ideology and policy in government, or indeed opposition, has continued throughout the twentieth century until the present day.[6] The question of bridging the gap between the aims of a left-wing foreign policy with the realities of office has proved to be endlessly problematic. Indeed, there is a rich seam of literature which explores this very point.[7] Even a cursory glance at the debates that have surrounded the various foreign-policy initiatives of the Labour governments since the 1997 election does much to underline how this particular issue is relevant today.[8] Recent interventions and subsequent controversies in Kosovo, Sierra Leone, Afghanistan and Iraq have all added fuel to the fire on the debate of the characteristics that define an 'authentically' Labour foreign policy. One such important example from the recent past, the break-up of Yugoslavia, provides a useful study of how the principles and priorities of a Labour foreign policy have changed and developed over the last few years. In a wider context, the Yugoslav case gives us the opportunity to examine the responses of the broader left wing; and in so doing, what becomes apparent is the diversity of opinions that exist within just one strand of British political thought. Interestingly, this leads into a broader discussion of the relationship that exists between politicians and the wider left-wing on foreign-policy issues. The Yugoslav example thus offers the opportunity to examine how different elements of the left responded to the same crisis, and to identify how ideas evolved and developed over a decade, and were subsequently adopted as actual policies.

Thus, the aim of this chapter is to analyse how different elements of the British left reacted to the break-up of Yugoslavia in the period 1991–1999. This will develop in two parts. Firstly, it will examine how parts of the left-wing press responded to the earlier events of 1991–1995, focusing on the key theme of intervention during the wars in Croatia and Bosnia. I will position this within the wider context of the British left-wing, by offering some analysis as to how the editorials assessed Labour Party foreign policy during the same period. Secondly, the chapter will examine Labour Party speeches, and parliamentary debates from the period from 1998 to 1999, in order to illustrate the way in which the Labour government reacted to events in Kosovo, and the subsequent NATO intervention against Serbia. It will then be possible to identify the similarities in approach of the later policy of the Blair government with the editorial comment of the various publications in the earlier part of the decade. We will find that the policy pursued in the latter part of the period by the Labour government is evolved from the views espoused by the left-wing media some four years earlier.

Editorials from two left-wing publications will be analysed in this chapter, namely *The Observer*, the Sunday broadsheet, and the *New Statesman*, the weekly political title.[9] The justification behind the selection of these titles is so that the views of what could be termed the mainstream left-wing media intelligentsia can be ascertained.[10] These titles are similar in their general stance to that of the Labour Party. *The Observer* had five editors during the period 1991–2000, and the *New Statesman* had three.[11] Although editorials are not necessarily always written by the editor, they provide an insight into editorial opinion on a selection of topics. Every column will have been formally approved by the editor. Thus, for these reasons, the use of these articles for this chapter offers us the nearest possible consistency in published material available for analysis. For the second part of the chapter, the focus will be on two landmark foreign-policy speeches, one given by the Prime Minister, Tony Blair, and the other by the Foreign Secretary, Robin Cook.[12] These two examples can be seen as an attempt by the New Labour government to signpost its intentions clearly within the international relations arena. After considering these keynote speeches, this chapter assesses how the issue of humanitarian intervention in Kosovo was discussed within the House of Commons by close examination of parliamentary debates as published in Hansard. As I will conclude, there are strong overlaps between the interventionist line discerned in the editorials, and the subsequent policies implemented by the Blair government.

II

The break-up of Yugoslavia during the 1990s was a complicated and violent process; one that did not fit into traditional foreign-policy approaches still looking for a new direction following the fall of the Berlin Wall, and the end of the bi-polar world. The much heralded 'new world order' failed spectacularly to deal effectively with the wars in Slovenia, Croatia and Bosnia. The war in Bosnia especially was a conflict which received a large amount of coverage on television screens but little effective intervention or policy solutions.[13] The Conservative government of John Major, along with those of other leading European states, floundered in its search for a workable approach to the situation. The Labour Party was heavily criticised in the *New Statesman* and *The Observer* for its ineffectual approach to the problem. Although in Opposition, and therefore unable directly to formulate British foreign policy, the party was condemned for the way that it reacted to the ensuing crisis, and the fact that it was seen by commentators as not using an appropriate level of influence in Parliament to change the way in which the government responded to the Balkan wars.

However, events later in the same decade were to provide observers with a strong contrast in Labour's approach to international relations. In 1998, Serbian forces, under the control of Slobodan Milosevic, intensified an ongoing campaign of violence against the majority Kosovo Albanian population within the province of Kosovo. Violence against the local population, together with retaliatory action by the Kosovo Liberation Army (KLA), led to heightened fears for the security of the region. In 1999, following failed peace talks and various ultimatums, the NATO alliance launched an air campaign against Milosevic's Serbia. To many observers, this was driven by Tony Blair and his New Labour government.[14] Indeed, Blair's role in this policy was seen as being crucial to the success of the mission.[15]

The position taken at that time by the Labour government of Tony Blair contrasts sharply with the criticism levelled at his predecessors by the left-wing press. Indeed, editorials from the earlier period offer some sort of harbinger as to the type of policy initiatives that would be pursued by the new Prime Minister during NATO's Kosovo campaign. This raises interesting questions regarding the relationship between ideas that are espoused within the left-wing press, and actual policies that are implemented by a centre-left government just a few years later. To what extent is there a correlation between the two? If one studies left-wing editorials of the early 1990s, that is, those offering a commentary on the initial break-up of Yugoslavia, there is an obvious similarity with the policies which were implemented in Kosovo in 1999 by the Labour government. The issue of cause and effect is obviously difficult to measure. However, an analysis of the two, namely the left-wing editorials from 1991 to 1995, and the actual speeches and policies of Labour Party politicians (1998 – 1999), provides an example as to how ideas evolved from being the deliberations of commentators in the media, to the actual working foreign policy of a Labour government.

III

The editorials commenting on the break-up of Yugoslavia can be divided into two groups, that is: initial responses to events in the former Yugoslavia; and secondly, comments on the use of intervention at the beginning of the Bosnian War in 1992, and the development of that debate throughout the war until 1995. Let us now look at each case in turn.[16]

The *New Statesman* responded to the outbreak of war in Croatia in 1991 by outlining its views on the potential role of a peace-keeping force. Its editorial of 9 August stated, 'some such force remains the best hope of pulling the Balkans back from the brink. It is time for the United Nations to take over where the European Community has so far failed.'[17] Similarly, *The Observer* raised the issue of intervention by highlighting another foreign policy episode of the recent past. It argued that if the British government was prepared to intervene for the Kurds in Iraq, then it should do the same for Yugoslavia. The editorial went on to say that, in this case, the national interest was greater and that Yugoslavia mattered to Europe.[18] Ironically, given what we know about subsequent events, the editorial gave the caveat that any intervention had to be properly equipped with well-thought through operational aims and a clear line of command. This bears little, if any, resemblance to the efforts of the international community in the years 1991–1995.

Initial comments, even before the Bosnian War started in April 1992, succinctly illustrate the desperate nature of what was to occur in the following years. *The Observer* stated, in February 1992, that: 'Once civil war starts in Bosnia it will be too late to send peacekeeping forces; they must be sent before it begins.'[19] Just one month after the start of the war, the newspaper's editorial declared that '[t]his war cannot be allowed to continue. If not a UN peace-keeping force, then a UN peace-*making* operation may yet be needed.'[20] By the end of the first full month of fighting, calls for military intervention were plainly stated in *The Observer*. Fear of a military quagmire and the huge numbers of troops necessary for such intervention were suggested as reasons for the West's inactivity. Frustration at the absence of effective intervention by the international community, in this initial period of war, is apparent in the *New Statesman*'s editorial for 17 July 1992. This piece followed a period of diplomatic activity, President Mitterrand's visit to Sarajevo and the start of the relief effort:

> The illusion of action over former Yugoslavia conceals the abandonment of the Balkans to their fate . . . [T]he UK government – in common with the EC and the international community as a whole – has displayed an uncanny knack for doing precisely the wrong thing at the wrong time . . . What we are seeing is the betrayal of Bosnia.[21]

One month later the world was given hard evidence of the situation in Bosnia, when television pictures of concentration camps were broadcast (6 August 1992). This did much to galvanise debate about intervention, and, as we know, ethnic cleansing was to be a dominant feature of the war.

In reaction to these tragedies, both *The Observer* and *New Statesman* were firm proponents of military intervention in Bosnia. The earlier recognition of Bosnia as a sovereign state meant for *The Observer*, that 'doing nothing' was not an option. On 9 August 1992, the editorial listed four options that it urged Britain to support at the United Nations: namely, the bombardment of Bosnian Serb artillery positions; the supply of arms and weaponry to Bosnian government forces; the sending of investigators to the area to begin enquiries into war crimes; and support to be given to the Bosnian government for its own plans for regionalisation, a unitary state divided geographically not ethnically.[22]

As the conflict moved into its second year, the *New Statesman* reaffirmed its pro-interventionist stance. An editorial in April 1993 suggested that the international community was faced with a choice of allowing aggression and ethnic cleansing to be rewarded, or making a clear commitment to take whatever steps were necessary to halt the killing. 'To do nothing' the editorial argued 'is to be complicit in genocide'.[23] If the international community itself was not prepared to intervene, the editorial argued that the arms embargo should be lifted against the government troops. Calls for intervention were repeated three months later in the July of 1993:

> To intervene or not to intervene? That question has dogged the peace movement and the left . . . since war first broke out . . . The balance of opinion, supported by *NSS*, has been pro-interventionist . . . The subsidiary question, however, has been more difficult to answer decisively. What *form* should intervention take?[24]

One year after *The Observer's* list of four suggestions for the UN, the *New Statesman* tried a similar approach. An editorial, published in September 1993, contained a summary of all of the points that it had mentioned in the previous eighteen months, such as the right to self-defence, the use of air power, and the provision of ground troops.[25] Due to the lack of coherent action taken by the international community, it is little surprise to find that these pro-interventionist journalists continued to publish such editorials in the following year.

The infamous massacre in a Sarajevo marketplace that saw 60 people killed and 200 others wounded in February 1994 was the starting point for yet more pro-interventionist discussion. *The Observer* editorial for 6 February 1994 argued that, whilst calls for retaliation were understandable, the international community needed to think carefully about its overall policy aims.[26] This was linked to the problems of intervening at such an advanced stage of the conflict. Intervention would have to be supported with the use of NATO troops; their presence could be detrimental to the UN humanitarian effort. Thus, the editorial stance was clear; the lack of early intervention in the Bosnian War had created immense problems for dealing with the conflict in its then current form.

The spring and summer of 1994 saw a further period of Bosnian Serb advances on 'safe areas', and the seemingly endless – and fruitless – diplomatic efforts by the international community. Both publications continued their support for intervention. An editorial in the *New Statesman* in the May of that year stated that 'we support intervention by the international community, including, if needs be, military intervention, to ensure that the war in Bosnia is resolved in a way that upholds the values of multi-ethnicity, democracy and respect for human rights'.[27] At the end of July, *The Observer* also repeated its call for intervention, suggesting a combination of safe havens, air strikes, and armed forces to bring the situation under control.[28]

In 1995 the war began to reach its conclusion, and Bosnian Serb advances against the 'safe havens', most notably Srebrenica, acted as a catalyst for further comment from both publications. The fall of Srebrenica in the July to the Bosnian Serbs, and the subsequent atrocities that were carried out, were met with the following comments in the Sunday broadsheet:

> Did we not tell them [the Bosnian Muslims] their homes in Srebrenica were part of a UN designated 'safe' area? And where are their men, all 10,000 of them . . . A united and determined foreign policy could yet startle the Serbs. For now, they have nothing to fear by taking on the world.[29]

The disenchantment shown by both titles for the way that the 'international community' dealt with the war continued to the very end of the conflict. The Dayton Peace Accord, negotiated during November 1995, was described by the *New Statesman* as being 'a shabby compromise'.[30] This particular assessment is wholly representative of the despair and frustration that both titles displayed towards the international community for the duration of the war.

Crucially, both the *New Statesman* and *The Observer* were critical of the Labour Party's stance towards the former Yugoslavia during this time. Throughout the conflict, the *New Statesman* made reference to the Labour Party's lack of participation in the deliberations over intervention. As early as September 1992, an editorial stated that the Labour Party had not debated any issues regarding the war in Bosnia.[31] Two months later, Michael Meacher wrote an article in the publication outlining different ways that the West could help.[32] The editorial response asked why it was left to the shadow minister for overseas development to propose policy for the Balkans. The key question was: 'Shouldn't war in Europe be a matter for the shadow foreign secretary himself – and for the Labour Party at the highest level?'[33] The editorial argued that it was time for a re-evaluation of policy by the left on the issue of international relations. It stated that the left-wing and its view of foreign policy was still framed by the Cold War, imperialism, Suez, Hungary and Vietnam, and it powerfully urged the left to 'look again at the old antipathy to interventionism in world affairs'.[34]

Criticism of the Labour Party was again apparent 18 months later as war continued. In a *New Statesman* editorial from 22 April 1994, the Labour front bench was compared to the Labour Party of the 1930s, which was portrayed as having supported Chamberlain's appeasement of Hitler. The two key Labour politicians with responsibility for Bosnia, that is, David Clark, the Shadow Defence Secretary, and Jack Cunningham, the Shadow Foreign

Secretary, were described as having 'played a consistently craven role throughout the Bosnian war, parroting the government's rhetoric of "civil war" and "warring factions"'.[35] This criticism of the Labour Party illustrates the differences that existed within the British left towards intervention in the former Yugoslavia. Whilst these differences could partway be explained by the fact that journalists *write* about an issue, in contrast to politicians who actually have to *act* on the same issue, the gulf between the two groups was clear to see. However, what is of great interest is that ideas first espoused in left-wing editorials were adopted by the Labour government as a pro-interventionist policy against Serbia in 1999.

IV

The NATO action against Serbia in 1999 was Tony Blair's first prolonged foreign-policy outing, and set important precedents for later initiatives in Afghanistan and Iraq.[36] The pro-interventionist stance that Blair took over Kosovo was clearly at odds with the media representation of the party's actions over Bosnia, but, significantly, was in keeping with the position taken by the *New Statesman* and *The Observer* during that earlier conflict. Indeed, close analysis of key speeches and debates from the period 1998–1999 show just how closely the foreign policy of the Labour government (1997–2001) mirrored the views that were espoused in the two publications in the early 1990s. The impact of the war in Bosnia, and the subsequent failure by the international community to deal with the situation effectively, cannot be understated when looking at the manner in which intervention was discussed with regard to Kosovo. Exorcising the ghosts of Bosnia became a common theme in speeches in the House of Commons with frequent references to how the world had failed the Balkans on one occasion, and how this could not be repeated.[37] What developed was a concerted attempt to deal effectively with a foreign policy problem, and the development of an interventionist foreign policy, around the theme of the defence of human rights.

In May 1997, shortly after Labour's election victory, Robin Cook gave an important speech which has been subsequently remembered for his exposition of an 'ethical foreign policy'.[38] As has been well-documented, this is perhaps an unfair representation of the tone of his speech.[39] Outlining the approach that Labour would bring to international relations, Cook gave a wide-ranging overview of what he saw as being four policy goals that should be achieved by the new government. The first two goals focused on traditional areas of international relations; namely, the security of Britain, and the securing of prosperity for the country through a reinvigorated approach to trade and business. The third goal emphasised a commitment to the quality of life in Britain, emphasising the role that the environment would play in foreign affairs. However, it is the fourth of Cook's points that provides us with the supposedly controversial aspect of the foreign policy:

> . . . the fourth goal of our foreign policy is to secure the respect of other nations for Britain's contribution to keeping the peace of the world and promoting democracy around the world. The Labour Government does not accept that political values can be left behind when we check in our passports to travel on diplomatic business. Our foreign policy must have an ethical dimension and must support the demands of other peoples for the democratic rights on which we insist for ourselves. The Labour Government will put human rights at the heart of our foreign policy and will publish an annual report on our work in promoting human rights abroad.[40]

The remainder of Cook's speech detailed how the government would place heavy emphasis on a new way of implementing foreign affairs. Terms such as 'mission statement' were used to highlight how this approach applied just as much to embassy staff abroad as to those working in Whitehall, from the most junior civil servant to Cook's team of ministers. Cook's speech concluded with the plea:

> My message to all staff is that Ministers need their professionalism, expertise and dedication if we are to achieve our aims and measure up to our benchmarks. I invite them today to work together with us in a joint project to make Britain once again a force for good in the world.[41]

The clarion call for change could be heard throughout Whitehall. Aside from it being a statement of foreign policy intent for a new government, the significance of the Cook speech is that one aspect of it was magnified and seized upon as being the defining sentiment behind New Labour's arrival onto the world stage. Although referring to an 'ethical dimension' of foreign policy, the speech has forever been identified as the time and place where the Foreign Secretary launched his 'ethical foreign policy'. The differences between the two are clearly subtle, but the fine distinction was to be of considerable significance during later controversies of the first New Labour government. The proposed sale of Hawk jets to Indonesia and the Sandline affair in Sierra Leone are just two examples where the nuances of the two terms would be of fundamental importance.[42] In short then, here Cook identified the key principles behind New Labour's foreign policy, and a relatively short speech offered the chance to take just one of the points and use it as a barometer with which to measure the government's subsequent policies and actions.

The extent to which Cook was proclaiming a traditional left-wing foreign policy is problematic. Although in the opening sentences of the speech he made reference to long-held values of internationalism, the central objective of a foreign policy with an ethical dimension – intervention so as to protect human rights around the globe – is much more difficult to identify with the left. The notion of using military action to promote this policy certainly goes against what could be viewed as a traditional left-wing principle, namely anti-militarism.[43] This issue, along with the wider use of military force by the three successive Labour governments from 1997, has continued to be extremely contentious. What is clear, however, is that the interventionist stance mooted here has clear echoes in the earlier extracts from the left-wing media that I have discussed above.

Another important speech was the keynote address given by the Prime Minister in Chicago in April 1999.[44] One month after the start of the NATO action against Serbia, Blair used the occasion as an opportunity to reaffirm both his, and by extension, New Labour's, commitment to a foreign policy based on the bedrock of humanitarian intervention. In a speech that can be seen as of fundamental importance in identifying the defining principles of a Blair-led foreign policy, five areas were examined: namely, Kosovo; global interdependence; globalisation; international security; and politics. It is obviously the comments on Kosovo which are of most relevance here. Blair's speech leaves us in little doubt as to the reasons behind the NATO action against Serbia. He stated:

> No-one in the West who has seen what is happening in Kosovo can doubt that NATO's military action is justified . . . This is a just war, based not on any territorial ambitions but on values. We cannot let the evil of ethnic cleansing stand. We must not rest until it is reversed. We have learned twice before in this century that appeasement does not work. If we let an evil dictator range unchallenged, we will have to spill infinitely more blood and treasure to stop him later.[45]

Blair then outlined five key objectives that NATO would achieve in the area: the end to all military activities and killings; withdrawal of Serb military and paramilitary forces from Kosovo; deployment of an international military force; the safe return of all refugees; and the political rebuilding of Kosovo based on the framework of the Rambouillet talks.

Significantly, Blair's five-point plan was comparable in stance and detail to the editorial line taken in both *The Observer* on 9 August 1992, and the *New Statesman* on 3 September 1993.[46] Both of the publications had offered simplified lists of solutions which we now see, at least in some way, replicated in his speech. Thus, the issues of military action, humanitarian concerns, and long-term plans for the local region were apparent both within the media editorials, and later in the Prime Minister's address. It is also interesting to see Blair refer to the spectre of appeasement; an issue which was readily invoked by the left-wing media at the time of the earlier Balkan conflicts.[47] Now it was Blair who used the negative associations that the very issue of appeasement implies as a justification for his action in supporting the NATO intervention.

The longer that the NATO action continued, the greater the potential difficulties for the military alliance. However, any possible setbacks for Blair were brushed to one side.

> Just as I believe there was no alternative to military action, now it has started I am convinced there is no alternative to continuing until we succeed. On its 50th birthday NATO must prevail. Milosevic had, I believe, convinced himself that the Alliance would crack. But I am certain that this weekend's Summit in Washington under President Clinton's leadership will make our unity and our absolute resolve clear for all to see. Success is the only exit strategy I am prepared to consider.[48]

The strong resolve which Blair displays in stressing that the policy must be carried through to its successful fruition shows a total avoidance of the arguments put forward by those against such military action.[49] For the Prime Minister, there was little doubt that intervention was the appropriate policy for dealing with the Serbian violence in Kosovo. Furthermore, the Prime Minister's position was one that resonated throughout the Labour government's policy statements during the build-up to the NATO air campaign in March 1999.

As far back as March 1998, the issue of Serbian violence in Kosovo was debated within the House of Commons. The Foreign Secretary Robin Cook described 'security operations' in Dreniza, which had led to at least 80 fatalities.[50] Outrage at the situation was stated thus: 'We strongly condemn the use of violence for political objectives, including the terrorism of the self-styled Kosovo Liberation Army. Terrorism, however, cannot be used as a pretext for the indiscriminate use of force against the civilian population.'[51] In this statement, Cook outlined four objectives for an action plan which would attempt to bring the situation under control. This focused on the issue of justice with the establishment of a war crimes tribunal; the introduction of international monitoring in Kosovo, led by the OSCE; Contact Group meetings with representatives from neighbouring states in order to take a regional approach to the situation; and finally, the introduction of sanctions against Belgrade.[52] A ten-day ultimatum was to be issued to President Milosevic, and the Contact Group would reconvene on 25 March to consider his response. At this stage of events, it was not considered that military action itself would be an option. Indeed, in the same speech, Robin Cook appeared to distance himself from such an approach.

[A]ny question of military intervention has not been contemplated, and is not on the agenda. We seek to ensure that we achieve progress that averts the need for military intervention. Nor would such military intervention, if it were to happen, have a simple or uncomplicated impact on the region as a whole. It is much better that we make progress on the strategy that has been adopted by the contact group.[53]

What is of interest here is that the issue of military action was not considered as even a remote possibility. The diplomatic efforts put in place by the Contact Group were seen to be the most successful way to reach a peaceful conclusion to the conflict within Kosovo. This is striking when compared to the resolve shown later when the escalation of the situation made military intervention seem unstoppable. This then is in stark contrast to the earlier period when parts of the left-wing media accused the Labour Party of being ineffectual during the initial break-up and wars in Yugoslavia. What is shown in the front-bench approach to Kosovo is a desire to resolve the situation effectively, even when that meant having to deal with stakes that were constantly being raised. Ultimatums and peace processes were attempted, but when these failed, the government moved to carry out its threat. The military intervention that was espoused by the *New Statesman* and *The Observer* during the earlier wars thus became a reality.

The summer of 1998 saw the Serbian campaign in Kosovo increase. Military offensives against the Kosovo Albanians continued, and attacks were carried out on an almost daily basis. The culmination of this activity was a NATO decision to authorise air strikes on Serbian military targets. Following this threat, Milosevic backed down and agreed to a settlement presented by the American diplomat Richard Holbrooke.[54] In announcing this development, Cook observed that: 'There can be no Member of the House who imagines that President Milosevic would have made such a commitment if the diplomatic efforts backed by the contact group had not also been backed by the credible threat of military action by NATO.'[55] As would be seen less than six months later, the failure of diplomacy would indeed be reinforced with action by NATO, in a concerted effort to bring Milosevic to order. Cook's comments show a determination to persevere with a particular policy, even one requiring considerable long-term commitment. This idea of using a broader strategy to deal with a specific issue has echoes with remarks made in the left-wing media during the earlier Balkan conflicts. A criticism consistently made during that period regarded the seemingly *ad hoc* responses to the ever changing situation on the ground. Here though, Cook's policy bears the hallmark of a broader, less reactive plan, with an emphasis on Britain playing a key role in fulfilling an obligation to ensure the long-term security of the region. This point is reinforced by the following comments from the same debate:

> It would be a grave mistake to imagine that the Holbrooke package marks the end of the international community's pressure on President Milosevic. It is only the beginning of a process that will require the full commitment of the international community to achieve stability, security and reconstruction in Kosovo . . . Britain played a leading part within the international community in putting the pressure on President Milosevic that made these agreements possible. Britain is now demonstrating that we are among the first nations to make a practical contribution towards making a success of the agreements. We will not let up on our efforts until President Milosevic carries out his commitment to withdraw forces, and until the people of Kosovo can return to their homes without fear, can rebuild their villages in peace and can start to construct a self-governing Kosovo without repression from Belgrade.[56]

Just one month later, a debate on 'Foreign Affairs and Defence' tied together the key themes of diplomacy and military intervention, reflecting the Labour policy up to that point in Kosovo. Robin Cook outlined how these two approaches could work together in order to reach foreign-policy goals and aims.

> A dominant theme in the foreign policy of the past year has been the necessity of backing diplomacy with the credible threat of force against those who challenge international stability. Both in Kosovo and in Iraq, that twin-track approach has been successful in securing agreement. However, a necessary feature of agreements obtained by the threat of force is that they are likely to be implemented only if we demonstrate our continuing resolve.[57]

For Cook then, the policy that had been used in Kosovo during the violence instigated by Slobodan Milosevic, that is, diplomacy reinforced with the credible threat of force, was to be a key tenet of Labour's approach to international relations. A dual approach to foreign policy was further emphasised by the Secretary of State for Defence, George Robertson. Robertson reinforced the sentiments espoused by his Cabinet colleague.

> In the Balkans, too, we have witnessed once again the need for action to avoid a catastrophe. The humanitarian disaster that could have occurred in Kosovo has been averted by the intervention of NATO and the international community. The powerful combination of diplomatic pressure and NATO's credible threat to use force has changed the situation in Kosovo for the better. However, it is only the beginning. The effects of ethnic hatred will not disappear overnight, and we must do all that we can to support the search for a political solution.[58]

In this instance then, the dual approach to diplomacy had succeeded. However, despite Robertson's optimism regarding the improved situation in Kosovo, events in the region were about to take a turn for the worse.

At the start of 1999, violence again took hold in Kosovo. In what can be identified as the defining incident, the Racak massacre was seen as the resumption of Serbian attacks against the Kosovo Albanian population.[59] After outlining both the events of the massacre, and the diplomatic efforts that were to be put in place in order to avert further crisis, Robin Cook summarised how the situation could be resolved.

> President Milosevic must be clear that military action last autumn was suspended only because of his agreement to cease fire, to withdraw part of his military units in Kosovo, and to return the rest to barracks. The North Atlantic Council met yesterday and agreed that General Clark and General Naumann, NATO's two most senior generals, should visit Delgrade with a clear message that President Milosevic must comply in full with the agreements he made. On its part, the Kosovo Liberation Army has committed more breaches of the ceasefire, and until this weekend was responsible for more deaths than the security forces. It must stop undermining the ceasefire and blocking political dialogue.[60]

Cook did not explicitly mention the use of a military threat but given Labour's dual approach to foreign affairs, it was undoubtedly an intrinsic part of the search for a solution to the fighting in Kosovo. Nonetheless, in speeches that took place within the same debate, there was an extremely clear realisation of the problems that could accompany any military action. In short, in no way at all was armed intervention seen as being an easy solution to the problem – it was not seen as an option to be taken lightly. Cook himself stated that 'any military action need[ed] to be tied to a clear political settlement'.[61] This echoed a point made by the senior back-bench Labour MP Donald Anderson, who stated that: '[t]he activation of the NATO bombing is unlikely to make any serious contribution to a solution because no military solution will do that'.[62] What was very apparent then was that any military action must only take place if delivered as part of a wider strategy, as we have seen, the so-called dual approach to foreign policy. Indeed, later in the same debate, Robin Cook reiterated this very point.

> Currently, after the experience of the past three months . . . I should be very hesitant about committing ground troops in Kosovo unless there was a clear commitment by both sides to a political track. If we were to commit forces in the current situation, there is a danger that we would end up being the people keeping apart two sides, both of which seem intent on carrying out war and undermining the ceasefire. Those are not circumstances in which peacekeeping can operate. We shall first have to see some evidence of good will, good faith and a strong commitment to a political negotiation.[63]

Although we now know that military action did indeed follow the failed diplomatic efforts, it is clear that there was a wide-ranging strategy aimed at providing a comprehensive solution to the situation in Kosovo. This has clear resonance with the earlier approach outlined by sections of the left-wing media, and provides a stark contrast to the piecemeal approach offered by both the previous Conservative government, and the Labour opposition, at the time of the earlier break-up of Yugoslavia.

However, it is important to note that Cook offered an argument for intervention that was far more sophisticated than that which has been previously suggested in the editorials. Replying to criticism of the government's policy of intervention during the same debate on Kosovo, Robin Cook outlined the precise internationalist role that he envisaged that Britain could play within the sphere of international relations.

> I must tell the hon. Gentleman that there is no question of Britain being the world's policeman, but we are proud of the way in which we play our part and make a major contribution to the world com-

munity. We participate in events in the former Yugoslavia, in Bosnia and in Kosovo as a member of the North Atlantic alliance and as a permanent member of the United Nations Security Council. We cannot expect to retain our position as a permanent member of that council – and the respect that goes with it – and as a major member of the North Atlantic alliance if we are not willing to take part in actions when mounting such actions is deemed necessary.[64]

Thus the nature of New Labour's internationalism is an ethos that sees it at the forefront of international activity. It is a belief that Britain should play a leading part in foreign affairs, with the scope to fulfil what Cook saw as its global responsibility. Of particular interest is how Cook stressed the multilateral nature of Britain's role: Britain is seen as being a key part of a global approach to foreign-policy issues, leading from the front but as part of a collective effort, under the umbrella of various international institutions.

Significantly, support for military intervention was not just popular amongst the Cabinet members themselves; a range of other Labour politicians backed the action. To illustrate this point, if we take just one debate, the occasion where Tony Blair announced the intention for NATO to take military action against Serbia, a variety of Labour back benchers spoke in favour of the plans.[65] Donald Anderson, Bruce George, Clive Soley, and David Winnick all supported armed intervention against Serbia.[66] Similarly, in other debates leading up to the intervention, a range of Labour politicians spoke in favour of the policy, taking their lead from the Prime Minister, but, in so doing, also following views that had been published in *The Observer* and the *New Statesman* in the years that had preceded these debates.

However, it would be wrong to assume that despite considerable back-bench support for the military intervention espoused by Tony Blair and Robin Cook that there was unanimous backing for this policy. Indeed, in a party as diverse as the Labour Party one would expect to see a divergence of views. Although elected as 'New' Labour, and thus pursuing a policy of 'new internationalism', it is perhaps inevitable that the dissenting voices belong very much to the group of politicians that we would not associate with the re-branded part of the party. The most vociferous opponent of the NATO action was the veteran MP Tony Benn. If the policy of Blair and Cook can be identified as 'new internationalist', then Benn's views certainly fall into what could be described as 'old internationalism', or even anti-Americanism, reflecting traditional left-wing reliance on, and support for, the power of the United Nations. Thus, in a debate on Kosovo in October 1998, when the idea of NATO air strikes was discussed, Benn responded:

NATO's threat to bomb Serbia is contrary to the charter of the United Nations which provides that only the Security Council can authorise military action [.] It is contrary to article 1 of the NATO treaty that commits NATO to the United Nations charter . . . Is my right hon. Friend [Robin Cook] also aware that NATO is not the international community, and that to talk as if he and the United States speak for the world is to undermine the authority of the United Nations itself?[67]

Benn's commitment to the United Nations as the means to solving the problems of Serbia and Kosovo and his opposition to military action was repeated on regular occasions within the House of Commons.[68] He can be seen then as symbolising a more traditionally left-wing approach to foreign policy, thus providing an interesting contrast with the views expressed by both the majority of the parliamentary party, and those working on the *New Statesman* and *The Observer* earlier in the 1990s. Another notable opponent to the intervention was Tam Dalyell. Interestingly, the objections to the war that Dalyell raised were to do with tactics and strategy rather than the actual principle of military intervention. Strongly opposed to air strikes, Dalyell raised the issue of ground troops. This was not a popular idea with those charged with forming the policy. The increased danger and risks involved for Allied troops with this strategy meant that air strikes would always be the first option. Dalyell's stance rested on the argument that a bombing campaign would help to unite the very people that it was targeting. He invoked the 'spirit of the Blitz' to emphasise his point.[69] The 'new internationalism' which had its genesis in the exemplary material from *The Observer* and *New Statesman* during the earlier Balkan wars had not spread across the entirety of the back benches.

V

This chapter has shown how different strands of the British left, namely elements of the left-wing media and the Labour Party, reacted to the break-up of Yugoslavia during the 1990s. At the time of the initial conflicts, the strongly pro-interventionist stance taken by the *New Statesman* and *The Observer* was then at odds with the Labour Party Shadow Cabinet. However, this approach has subsequently been mirrored by New Labour, as has been shown by analysis of speeches and parliamentary debates. This is despite disquiet across the wider British left. Additionally, opposition to such a policy emanated from within the party as we have seen here in the contributions from both Tony Benn and Tam Dalyell. A further point that has been considered here is Robin Cook's approach to internationalism. As has been demonstrated herein, he showed a commitment to the implementation of a long term diplomatic strategy, involving international institutions. However, his approach to diplomacy was underscored by an acceptance to use military force if necessary. The notion of Britain playing a leading role in foreign affairs certainly ties in with the views voiced by the *New Statesman* and *The Observer* at the time of the earlier wars in Croatia and Bosnia. Instead of listening to the cry, 'something must be done', what Cook demonstrated was a will to 'do something'. Whatever the successes of the NATO intervention in Kosovo, what was shown in the months before the bombing began was an acknowledgement that a coherent policy existed; one with a choice of outcomes, either peace through diplomacy or resolution through military action. This contrasts with the way that parts of the media had criticised, earlier in the decade, a series of seemingly random Labour responses to events in Croatia and Bosnia.

Thus, the chapter has analysed, in one specific case, the divisions that emerge within the left when it addresses issues relating to its actions in the wider world. The British left is such a broad coalition that it is notoriously difficult for it to reach a consensus on foreign policy. Yet the policies towards the former Yugoslavia advocated by parts of the media in the earlier part of the decade were later adopted as the foreign policy of the Labour government. The issue of cause and effect is, of course, difficult to measure with fine precision but the overall direction in which official Labour policy evolved is clear.

A final irony is worth noting. The NATO action against Serbia, which began on 24 March 1999, was the culmination of the Labour government's dual-policy approach to foreign affairs. It also embodied the attitude towards military intervention that had appeared in elements of the left-wing media much earlier in the same decade. Nevertheless, at this juncture both *The Observer* and *New Statesman* were, in varying ways, critical of the path taken by the Labour government *vis à vis* intervention over Kosovo.[70] Therefore, perhaps what any study of the relationship between the media and politicians really reveals is that it is much simpler to offer an opinion than actually to implement a particular policy.

10

FROM CLINTON TO BUSH: NEW LABOUR, THE USA AND THE IRAQ WAR

Mark Phythian

Tony Blair's support for the Bush administration's war to remove Saddam Hussein from power in Iraq represents a defining moment in Labour Party, British, and world history. The task of explaining this support is likely to generate one of the most keenly contested debates in the history of the Labour Party's approach to the wider world. This chapter brings together several factors that together help explain the Blair government's support for the US war. The first is structural in character, and relates to the increased presidentialisation of British politics, a process that created the necessary space in which Blair could offer his support. If British government has become increasingly presidential, then we must direct at least some of our attention to the personal and political beliefs of the individual at its head. Hence, this chapter also considers Blair's personal beliefs and emerging world view as sources of his government's decision. The allure of the US and the extent to which it represented a model for the architects of New Labour is also clearly important. Once in office, it proved impossible for New Labour to see that the US and UK could have divergent interests – after all, both the New Democrats in the US and New Labour in the UK promoted the same values, one set consciously modelled on the other. The fact that the events of 11 September 2001 (9/11) occurred relatively soon after the transfer of power in the US from the Democrats to the Republicans meant that there was little time for events to challenge Blair's conviction, forged during the Kosovo campaign, that the US and UK had the capacity to work together militarily and diplomatically to uphold the values they held in common. In any case, Blair found it easy to forge a working relationship with the new Republican

President. Having analysed the sources of Blair's decision, the chapter goes on to illustrate how these factors came together on the road to war in Iraq. The question of why Blair acted as he did also begs subsidiary questions. One of these is whether there was anything particularly new about this aspect of New Labour policy-making? This issue was so divisive and damaging to Blair's own position that when Bush suggested a summit meeting with Blair a week before the war was to begin, 'Blair's people were concerned about the Prime Minister leaving the country for even eight hours because of the Maggie Thatcher precedent.'[1] Hence the question posed by historian Ross McKibbin as to why 'a man usually so risk-averse was prepared to take so many risks with the unity of the Labour Party', and his own position, over this issue.[2]

I

Since 1997 the presidentialisation of British politics, a process clearly underway during the Thatcher years, has gathered considerable momentum. In effect, a Prime Minister's Department came to operate out of 10 Downing Street, staffed by unelected advisors, at times in apparent opposition to the departments of state. Its influence and role was most fully exposed to public scrutiny during the Hutton and Butler inquiries which arose out of the suicide of biological weapons expert Dr David Kelly and the failure to find Weapons of Mass Destruction (WMD) in post-war Iraq.[3] One consequence of this presidentialisation was effectively to downgrade the Cabinet as a decision-making body. Where the consent of particular ministers was required, this was sought in informal discussions away from the full Cabinet – Blair's so-called 'sofa diplomacy'. With regard to foreign and defence policies – areas that had bedevilled Labour from the time Blair stood as an unsuccessful candidate at the 1982 Beaconsfield by-election – Cabinet did not arrive at decisions as a result of discussion, it was informed of them. As one former Cabinet member recalled: 'At no stage over those first four years did we have a single Cabinet discussion about the principles, or conduct, of foreign policy. There was nothing about the justification or otherwise of going to war in any of our wars, nothing about the role of the United Nations, nothing about the special relationship with the US.'[4] As the constitutional expert Philip Norton has argued, the Cabinet 'is no longer a buckle that links government with parliament, no longer a body that collectively can make a difference. It was weakened under Thatcher but it has been rendered unconscious by Blair.'[5]

It was this bypassing of Cabinet government that International Development Secretary Clare Short highlighted in her resignation speech, telling the House of Commons that:

In the second term, the problem is centralisation of power into the hands of the Prime Minister and an increasingly small number of advisers who make decisions in private without proper discussion. It is increasingly clear that the Cabinet has become . . . a dignified part of the constitution, joining the Privy Council. There is no real collective, just diktats in favour of increasingly badly thought through policy initiatives that come from on high. The consequences of this are serious. Expertise in our system lies in departments. Those who dictate from the centre do not have full access to this expertise and they do not consult. This leads to bad policy . . . Thus we have the powers of a presidential-type system with the automatic majority of a parliamentary system.[6]

Blair's presidential position was further strengthened by the large parliamentary majorities secured in 1997 and 2001 and the absence of an effective Opposition. The Conservative Party rarely sought to create the kind of political space on key issues of war and global order that would have allowed it scope to criticise the government, and remained incapacitated on European questions.

Blair's presidential impulse also helps explain his increased interest in foreign policy by the time of his second government. Foreign policy was an area where his expertise and exposure was severely limited prior to 1997, and about which he had shown scant interest as a backbencher. However, it was here that he found he could act with a freedom that his and Chancellor Gordon Brown's caution had made impossible in domestic policy. Moreover, the 'special relationship' with the US clearly enhanced Blair's presidentialism. Journalist Alan Watkins observed at the time of the February 1998 'near-war' over Iraq how, 'Mr Clinton's attraction for Mr Blair is that it allows him to cavort on the international stage, now getting into aeroplanes, now getting out of them, appearing before us as a person of consequence and power.'[7] Peter Riddell has observed how, after 9/11, Blair transformed himself into Bush's 'Ambassador at Large', holding 54 meetings with various national leaders in the eight weeks following 9/11, involving 31 separate flights covering some 40,000 miles.[8] He won the gratitude of the US establishment, with the *New York Times* noting that Blair, 'often articulated the goals of the war against terrorism more eloquently than Mr Bush. He has not only been Washington's partner in facing the wider world, but on many occasions the world's ambassador to Washington. America should be grateful for both roles.'[9] At the same time, between the events of 9/11 and the end of September, Blair only convened one meeting of his full Cabinet.[10] By the time British forces were involved in a war in Afghanistan only one more had been held.

As with Afghanistan, so with Iraq, the decision to go to war was Blair's personal decision, taken in exactly the same manner as Bush took the decision on behalf of his administration. Reportedly, a week before the invasion of Iraq, Foreign Secretary Jack Straw – bullish in public but seemingly a more reluctant warrior behind closed doors – sent Blair a memo suggesting Britain back the imminent US action but not contribute troops to it.[11] From the same period, Bob Woodward recounts a March 2003 telephone call placed by a concerned President Bush to his embattled transatlantic ally in which he offered Blair the option of Britain participating in Iraq in some way short of sending troops. Blair's reported response was to tell Bush: 'I understand that . . . and that's good of you to say. I said, I'm with you . . . I'm there to the very end.'[12] Even this response was presidential – it is not a case here of his government, Cabinet, party, or even the British public being with the Bush administration. It is Blair personally.

However, this presidentialism merely created the space in which Blair could act independently of a variety of constraints. It does not of itself explain the alignment or interventionist impulse that arose out of it. To explain this requires us to consider three further factors.

II

Since 1945 the Labour Party has had something of a schizophrenic approach to the United States. On the one hand successive generations of frontbench politicians – Gaitskell, Crosland, Healey, Jenkins, Wilson, Williams, Hattersley, Owen et al – gravitated towards the US, mesmerised by the power of its example.[13] The lure of the US proved particularly powerful for Hugh Gaitskell, his biographer observing that Gaitskell's Atlanticist beliefs, 'were based on a deep sense of patriotism and a great affection for America and Americans; occasionally it is difficult to separate the two, but the patriotism *tended* to come first.'[14] On the other, US foreign policy was repeatedly at odds with the core values the wider party liked to believe lay at the root of its own foreign policy, while its conspicuous materialism and approach to social policy were at odds with values similarly held to be central to the party's purpose. As a result the party has traditionally accommodated a certain antipathy towards the US.

Nevertheless, by the time New Labour came to power in 1997, links with Bill Clinton's New Democrats were strong. Labour pollster Phillip Gould had advised candidate Clinton during the latter part of the 1992 presidential campaign, while post-1992 Clinton and his team provided something of a model for New Labour. Shortly after Clinton was elected, both Blair and Brown visited Washington to pick up tips on how his campaign team had persuaded middle-class voters to shift from the Republican Party by emphasising the importance of individual opportunity, community and mutual responsibility. David Halberstam has argued that Blair, 'was the first of a generation of international politicians who had learned their craft by studying Clinton and the deft way he handled modern media, choosing which issues he wanted to be associated with, and, of course, which he wanted to avoid'.[15] The most valuable lessons New Labour picked up from the Clinton team arguably related to campaigning rather than governing.[16] Still, the influence of Clinton's New Democrats on the New Labour government was clear. Just three weeks into it, journalist Larry Elliott was observing that: 'Almost every idea floated since the election – operational independence for the Bank of England, a beefed-up Securities and Investment Board, Welfare to Work, hit-squads in schools, an elected mayor for London – has its origins on the other side of the Atlantic.'[17] Not only did New Labour borrow from the Clinton team's ideas, it even borrowed from the name – the New Labour brand devised in imitation of Clinton's New Democrats.

Although the Blair government's initial foreign policy focus was on Europe, Blair was also at pains to emphasise the centrality of the US to British foreign policy, telling his audience at the 1997 Lord Mayor's banquet: 'When Britain and America work together on the international scene, there is little we can't achieve.'[18] Blair's support for unilateral US foreign policy actions, even where independent commentators saw in these a diversionary tactic away from the gathering clouds of impeachment, was partly rooted in this early master-student dynamic. However, it was also a consequence of other factors, such as the debt Blair owed Clinton after he intervened repeatedly to help secure the 1998 Good Friday Agreement in Northern Ireland, the moral certainty with which Blair acted in international affairs, and the ongoing bid to distance New Labour from the 'soft-on-defence' reputation acquired in the 1980s (both discussed further below).[19] Hence, Blair supported the August 1998 US cruise missile strike on the al-Shifa pharmaceutical plant in Khartoum and subsequently involved UK forces in the US-led aerial attack on Iraq following the withdrawal of the United Nations Special Commission (UNSCOM) inspection team. In relation to this latter attack, Downing Street deputy head of communications, Lance Price, noted in his diary that he, 'couldn't help feeling TB was relishing his first blooding as PM, sending the boys into action. Despite all the necessary stuff about taking action "with a heavy heart", I think he feels it is part of his coming of age as a leader.'[20] Already, one Cabinet member was explaining that, 'supporting the Americans is part of Tony's DNA'.[21]

However, the personal relationship between Blair and Clinton became strained over the Kosovo War, as Blair's evolving vision of an interventionist foreign policy that did not stop at state boundaries led to disagreement over the question of deploying ground troops. Blair's enthusiasm for such a deployment contrasted with the caution of the previous Major government, but as Halberstam has recorded:

> The White House was not entirely pleased by [Blair's] conversion and by the appearance of a major figure in the [NATO] alliance moving slightly ahead of the president. Though delighted to have Blair out front speaking for the war, the White House was not thrilled to have him and his people talking so openly about ground troops, which might cause fissures in the alliance and tended to make the prime minister look more assertive than the president. There was talk in private to reporters that Blair was grandstanding.[22]

The advent of a Republican administration whose foreign policy direction was largely determined by neo-conservative intellectuals around the President did not result in any change of approach on Blair's part. Never a 'tribal' politician in the manner of earlier Labour Party leaders, Blair made a concerted effort to follow the advice of the outgoing Clinton and make himself an equally invaluable ally to President Bush, a process that pre-dated the events of 9/11.

III

Blair's personal belief system is clearly important in explaining his commitment to the US over Iraq. There is no doubt that he is a conviction politician, in the mould of Margaret Thatcher, but with a burning moral certainty that, for some, invites comparisons with Gladstone. In February 2003, weeks before war with Iraq and against a backdrop of approximately one million anti-war demonstrators marching through London, Blair told the Scottish Labour Party conference: 'I do not seek unpopularity as a badge of honour. But sometimes it is the price of leadership. And it is the cost of conviction.'[23] As Lord Jenkins told the House of Lords:

> My view is that the Prime Minister, far from lacking conviction, has almost too much, particularly when dealing with the world beyond Britain. He is a little too Manichean for my perhaps now jaded taste, seeing matters in stark terms of good and evil, black and white, contending with each other, and with a consequent belief that if evil is cast down, good will inevitably follow.[24]

As Jenkins noted, Blair had a pronounced tendency towards portraying foreign policy as involving straightforward choices between 'good' and 'evil' and, at one remove from this, regularly drew from the well of Nazi and appeasement analogy, with scant regard for historical accuracy. Hence, in a major foreign policy speech in Chicago in 1999 he explained how: 'We have learned twice before in this century that appeasement does not work. If we let an evil dictator range unchallenged, we will have to spill infinitely more blood and treasure to stop him later', without pausing to reveal the identity of the second beneficiary of appeasement. During a further major foreign policy speech in Texas in 2002 he warned that ' . . . a brutal dictator, Slobodan Milosevic, was embarked upon a programme of ethnic cleansing of innocent people . . . the likes of which had not been seen since the Nazis'.[25]

His defence of these interventions has also thrown up instances where his moral certainty was misplaced. In April 1999, defending the intervention in Kosovo at a time when civilians had been killed by NATO bombing, Blair invoked a simple 'us' and 'them' dichotomy. The difference, he told the House of Commons, 'quite simply is this. Whenever there are civilian casualties as a result of allied bombs, they are by error. We regret them, and we take precautions to avoid them. The people whom the Serb paramilitaries are killing are killed deliberately.'[26] The reality was not so straightforward. The Foreign Affairs Committee identified a number of incidents during the war that raised ethical questions. One of these involved the question of high-altitude bombing, inherently less accurate than low-level bombing.[27] Rather than, as Blair suggested to Parliament, taking precautions to prevent civilian casualties, US forces adopted a high-altitude bombing approach, based on the calculation that the deaths of civilians on the ground was preferable to the risk of losing US aircraft and personnel as a result of bombing more accurately from a lower level.

Since assuming office Blair has generally avoided questions about his faith. However, it is clearly deeply held, something he shares with President Bush. However, while belief in God is a vote-winner in a US context, in a UK Prime Minister it is merely the stuff of *Whoops Apocalypse*-style black humour. Having given the order to begin Operation Iraqi Freedom to remove Saddam, Bush was able openly to admit that: 'Going into this period, I was praying for strength to do the Lord's will . . . I pray that I be as good a messenger of His Will as possible.'[28] (The former Palestinian Foreign Minister Nabil Shaath would subsequently claim Bush told him he had undertaken the war in Iraq in response to a command from God.[29]) In contrast, when Blair, in preparing his eve-of-war address to the nation, told his advisors, matter-of-factly, that he thought he would end the broadcast with the words 'God bless you', he induced minor panic. Still, in a subsequent front-page *Times* piece, Blair announced that he was ready to 'meet his Maker' and answer before God for 'those who have died or have been horribly maimed as a result of my decisions'.[30] Later still he told television interviewer Michael Parkinson that God would judge his decision to commit British troops to the invasion of Iraq.[31] Given this, it should come as no surprise that Blair framed his cause in terms of 'a new moral crusade'.[32] In the context of his track record of domestic caution, the moral certainty that Blair has consistently displayed over issues pertaining to war is striking.

IV

Alongside his beliefs, we need to consider Blair's emerging world view. The idea that Blair could be said to have any kind of world view may be considered surprising in view of his limited interest in foreign affairs prior to 1997, and the manner in which his pronouncements on foreign and defence policy immediately thereafter were more influenced by Gould's focus groups than ideological conviction.[33] An insight into this source of policy inspiration came in the summer of 2000, when spirited rummaging through Gould's dustbins recovered a number of memos written by Gould and Blair in response to focus group findings. These revealed Blair's belief that New Labour had still not fully ditched the legacy of the 1983 defence policy and his linked belief in the importance of demonstrating firmness on defence. In one memo Blair worried about:

> asylum and crime, where we are perceived as soft; and asserting the nation's interests where, because of the unpopularity of Europe, a constant barrage of small stories beginning to add up on defence and even issues like Zimbabwe, we are seen as insufficiently assertive . . . We are in fact, taking very tough measures on asylum and crime, Kosovo should have laid to rest any doubts about our strength in defence.[34]

Still, he worried about seeming 'out of touch' and warned Gould that 'we need to make the CSR [comprehensive spending review] work for defence. Big cuts and you can forget any hope of winning back ground on "standing up for Britain."'[35] Such revelations naturally raise the question of where beliefs ended and electoral calculations began.

Essentially, of course, New Labour was not an ideological entity. Rather, it was a generational phenomenon, the response of the young Labour parliamentary generation to the defeats of 1987 and, in particular, 1992. In a situation where the New Labour project would have been willing to cling to any ideological driftwood that helped carry it towards the political shore, the 'Third Way' baggage of Anthony Giddens floated by.[36] However, Blair's attachment to the Third Way proved transient. At the same time, the 'ethical foreign policy' announced by Blair's first Foreign Secretary, Robin Cook, was more a unilateral declaration of intent by Cook rather than a statement of core New Labour foreign policy values. Moreover, it was conducted in the face of stiff resistance from Downing Street – for example, with reference to Cook's attempts to pursue a more restrictive approach to arms exports.[37] Indeed, had the parliamentary arithmetic been different in May 1997, Cook may well not have been Foreign Secretary at all – Blair was willing to consider offering the post to Liberal Democrat leader Paddy Ashdown in return for assistance in forming a coalition government.

In terms of ideas, then, Blair's initial approach to foreign policy was essentially a blank sheet. However, unfolding events in Kosovo left a deep impression and led Blair to reflect in depth for the first time on questions of foreign policy, war and peace and, in particular, the question of humanitarian military intervention and its legitimacy. In the face of considerable public opposition to the NATO bombing of Belgrade a more identifiable Blair position on the politics of military intervention began to emerge. He also began to extract from the experience of Kosovo transferable principles that could act as a future guide.

Blair's April 1999 speech to the Chicago Economic Club represented his first extensive articulation of this emerging vision, the substance of it drafted for him by the academic Lawrence Freedman.[38] The context was important. The speech came at a time when Blair's muscular interventionism had begun to mark him out as more enthusiastic about the possible deployment of ground forces in Kosovo than Clinton. In it Blair set out a values-based foreign policy, based upon respect for human rights and international law but, crucially, one that carried with it the conviction that fighting for human rights – literally fighting – could involve violating the sovereignty of states. 'This is a just war', he explained with reference to Kosovo, 'based not on any territorial ambitions but on values.'[39]

In political and security terms, Blair spoke of 'the beginnings of a new doctrine of international community', the benefits of which were available to all who subscribed to the benefits of globalisation. However, he also highlighted the continued existence of states which stood apart from this community:

> Many of our problems have been caused by two dangerous and ruthless men – Saddam Hussein and Slobodan Milosevic. Both have been prepared to wage vicious campaigns against sections of their own

community . . . One of the reasons why it is now so important to win the conflict is to ensure that others do not make the same mistake in the future. That in itself will be a major step to ensuring that the next decade and the next century will not be as difficult as the past. If NATO fails in Kosovo, the next dictator to be threatened with military force may well not believe our resolve to carry the threat through.[40]

Notwithstanding the fact that Blair's vision of international community carried with it the right of the international community to intervene inside states, respect for international law figured prominently. Indicative of this, Blair outlined five considerations that should guide such interventions:

> First, are we sure of our case? War is an imperfect instrument for righting humanitarian distress; but armed force is sometimes the only means of dealing with dictators. Second, have we exhausted all diplomatic options? We should always give peace every chance, as we have in the case of Kosovo. Third, on the basis of a practical assessment of the situation, are there military operations we can sensibly and prudently undertake? Fourth, are we prepared for the long term? In the past we talked too much of exit strategies. But having made a commitment we cannot simply walk away once the fight is over; better to stay with moderate numbers of troops than return for repeat performances with large numbers. And finally, do we have national interests involved?[41]

This last point introduced a note of intellectual dissonance, the first indication of a potential tension between Blair's principles and the operation of states in the international system. It was a tension that was even more explicit by the time of Blair's April 2002 speech at the George Bush Presidential Library and Museum in Texas, against the back-drop of looming war in Iraq. Indeed, by this time contradictions between the globalisation/ inter-dependence view of the world central to Blair's vision and the neo-realist states' interests view were clearly evident.

For Giddens, conflicts between states were supposed to be a thing of the past, the post-Cold War liberal-democratic state was, he said, 'the state without enemies'.[42] The problem for Giddens and the Third Way idea was that the US kept defining new enemies – first as Clinton's National Security Advisor Anthony Lake's 'Backlash States' and, by the time Blair spoke in Texas, by Bush as the 'Axis of Evil'. Consequently, while still dipping into the vocabulary of the Third Way, states' interests came to assume a more prominent place in Blair's foreign policy vision. Alongside values, Blair now advocated 'an enlightened self-interest' that placed 'fighting for our values right at the heart of the policies necessary to protect our nations'.[43]

For Blair, there was no contradiction between interests and values.[44] Where the US fought to secure its interests it was also, by definition, fighting to preserve values universal to the West:

> We shouldn't be shy of giving our actions not just the force of self-interest but moral force. And in reality, at a certain point these forces merge. When we defend our countries as you did after 11 September, we aren't just defending territory. We are defending what our nations believe in: freedom, democracy, justice, tolerance and respect towards others. What makes America great is not its GDP alone or its military might. It is its freedom, its enterprise, its rejoicing in its different colours and cultures, the fact that someone of humble beginnings can aspire, work hard, succeed and be applauded for their success . . . Osama Bin Laden's philosophy is not just a security threat to us. It's an assault on our hearts and minds.[45]

Blair concluded by offering the US a guarantee of support over the coming war with Iraq that was unnecessary at the time and served to bind him to the Bush administration's plans with regard to Iraq:

> . . . we don't shirk our responsibility . . . when America is fighting for those values, then, however tough, we fight with her. No grandstanding, no offering implausible but impractical advice from the comfort of the touchline, no wishing away the hard not the easy choices on terrorism and WMD, or making peace in the Middle East, but working together, side by side . . . If the world makes the right choices now – at this time of destiny – we will get there. And Britain will be at America's side in doing it.[46]

V

The case of Iraq would not represent the first occasion on which a Labour Prime Minister faced criticism that he was committing British troops to a war without UN authorisation. In 1950 the Attlee government had to contend with criticism that its commitment of British troops in Korea was based on an irregular vote in the Security Council.[47] Then, the Cabinet agreed that Attlee should:

> argue that the action which the Western Powers were taking in South Korea was fully in accordance with the spirit of the United Nations

Charter . . . He would proceed to develop the argument that it was the duty of peace-loving nations to make the machinery of the United Nations work effectively, despite legal quibbles, and not to allow it to be frustrated by the abstentions of a single member; and that for this purpose they were entitled to take advantage of procedures which, though they might appear to conflict with the strict letter of the Charter, had been accepted as reasonable by member States.[48]

Hence, Blair's approach to the UN during the Iraq crisis was not without precedent. The Korean War also provides a parallel in terms of what Britain sought from close alignment with the US at a time of war. In the wake of that conflict, Sir Oliver Franks wrote that Britain's importance in the world lay 'in the effectiveness of our association with our friends', and that it was in this context alone that Britain could 'continue as a great power as within these Great Powers we take initiative, persuade our friends and lead'.[49] Then, as with Iraq, the US and UK governments sought different things from the alliance. Labour governments saw an opportunity to demonstrate Britain's continuing uniqueness as an ally able and willing to deploy force in support of what they chose to frame as shared goals, thereby helping actualise the vision of a 'special relationship' to which, for the reasons Franks articulated, they clung. In both Korea and Iraq, the British presence was important to the US in allowing it to 'internationalise' the conflict, as well as for its effect on US public opinion. While Britain thought that partnership would bring influence, it was to be disappointed in both cases.

In the immediate aftermath of the attacks of 9/11, Blair visited Washington, where he was made aware of a current within the Bush administration in favour of extending the 'war on terror' to Iraq. As Ambassador Christopher Meyer recalled: 'Rumours were already flying that Bush would use 9/11 as a pretext to attack Iraq. On the one hand, Blair came with a very strong message – don't get distracted; the priorities were al-Qaeda, Afghanistan, the Taliban. Bush said, "I agree with you, Tony. We must deal with this first. But when we have dealt with Afghanistan, we must come back to Iraq."'[50] On 30 January 2002 this determination was made explicit with Bush's identification of an 'Axis of Evil' signalling a new focus on Iraq.

In this context, a 7 March Cabinet meeting represented what Robin Cook described as 'the last meeting of the Cabinet at which a large number of ministers spoke up against the war',[51] with several (including David Blunkett, Patricia Hewitt and Cook himself) sounding a warning note. Cook recorded the occasion in his diary:

I am told, not that I have witnessed it, that in the old days Prime

Ministers would sum up the balance of view in the discussion. This would be simple in the present case as all contributions pointed in one direction. However, Tony does not regard the Cabinet as a place for decisions. Normally he avoids having discussions in Cabinet until decisions are taken and announced to it. Tony appeared totally unfazed that on this occasion the balance of discussion pointed strongly in the reverse direction of his intentions. Rather than attempt to sum up the discussion of this supreme body of collective government, he responded as if he was replying to a question and answer session from a party branch . . . 'I tell you that we must steer close to America. If we don't we will lose our influence to shape what they do.'[52]

This picture of Cabinet impotence is reinforced by Clare Short's recollection of subsequent Cabinet discussions on Iraq, wherein the Prime Minister:

> raised Iraq after the summer recess of 2002 at every cabinet meeting. He would start by saying a few words, inviting Jack Straw or Geoff Hoon to speak and then intervening repeatedly to inform the Cabinet of developments. Their advice was never sought. They were kept informed and most were willing to go along with the Prime Minister but there was no collective decision which was thrashed out in honest debate and to which the Cabinet then adhered.[53]

A day after the Cabinet meeting recorded by Cook, and marked by ministerial disquiet, the Cabinet Office Overseas and Defence Secretariat produced a 'Secret UK Eyes Only' options paper which warned that the Bush administration had 'lost confidence in containment and is now considering regime change', explaining that the 'success of Operation Enduring Freedom [in Afghanistan], distrust of UN sanctions and inspection regimes, and unfinished business from 1991 are all factors. Washington believes the legal basis for an attack on Iraq already exists.'[54] However, it also warned that, from a UK perspective, a 'legal justification for invasion would be needed' although none then existed given that regime change had no basis in international law. What was required was a strategy that would make a case for war, involving 'a staged approach, establishing military support, building up pressure on Saddam, and developing military plans. There is a lead time of about 6 months to a ground offensive.' UN Security Council backing was seen as key to the construction of a legal case for war. To this end, the other Permanent Five members 'would need to be convinced that Iraq was in breach of its obligations regarding WMD, and ballistic missiles. Such proof would need to be incontrovertible and of large-scale activity.

Current intelligence is insufficiently robust to meet this criterion.' British public opinion would also have to be prepared via 'a media campaign to warn of the dangers that Saddam poses'. Hence, it was known in March 2002 both that the justification for regime change had to lie in the threat posed by an active and deliverable Iraqi WMD programme and that the evidence for this was simply not there. It is no coincidence that from this point the useful role that a new weapons inspection regime could play became a theme. Either this would find something that justified war or Iraqi obstruction would itself justify war – a win-win situation. Whichever, the case for war was being assembled after the decision for war had been taken.

A week later, Blair's foreign policy adviser, David Manning, was in Washington meeting National Security Advisor Condoleezza Rice. He reported back to Blair on his conversation, and his assurance to Rice 'that you would not budge in your support for regime change but you had to manage a press, a Parliament and a public opinion that was very different than anything in the States'.[55] This message was reinforced days later by Ambassador Meyer who, in lunching with Paul Wolfowitz, stuck 'very closely to the script that you used with Condi Rice. We backed regime change, but the plan had to be clever and failure was not an option . . . I then went through the need to wrongfoot Saddam on the inspectors.'[56]

Hence, the Blair government's commitment to support a US-led war was emerging even prior to Blair's April 2002 visit to Bush's Texas ranch, despite the absence of firm proof that Iraq had or was developing WMD, let alone that it represented an imminent threat. This was a source of some concern within government, as Jack Straw's policy director warned:

> The truth is that what has changed is not the pace of Saddam Hussein's WMD programmes, but our tolerance of them post-11 September . . . even the best survey of Iraq's WMD programmes will not show much advance in recent years on the nuclear, missile or chemical weapons/biological weapons fronts: the programmes are extremely worrying but have not, as far as we know, been stepped up . . . To get public and Parliamentary support for military options we have to be convincing that the threat is so serious/imminent that it is worth sending our troops to die for.[57]

Straw himself summarised these concerns in a 25 March memo to Blair, advising that 'there is at present no majority inside the PLP for any military action against Iraq, (alongside a greater readiness in the PLP to surface their concerns)'. Here, again, Blair was warned that 'regime change per se is no justification for military action; it could form part of the method of any strategy, but not a goal. Of course, we may want credibly to assert that regime change is an essential part of the strategy by which we have to achieve our ends – that of the elimination of Iraq's WMD capacity: but the latter has to be the goal.'[58]

This, then, was the background to Blair's 5 – 7 April 2002 Texas visit, where a number of commentators locate his commitment to participate in a US-led war, even though he continued to insist in public that no decisions had yet been taken.[59] Lest there be any doubt about this, a 21 July 2002 Cabinet Office paper, *Iraq: Conditions for Military Action (A Note by Officials)* confirmed the commitment Blair made at Crawford, noting: 'When the Prime Minister discussed Iraq with President Bush at Crawford in April he said that the UK would support military action to bring about regime change, provided that certain conditions were met.' One of these, that 'the options for action to eliminate Iraq's WMD through the UN weapons inspectors had been exhausted', reflected governmental concern about the legality of the forthcoming war. As the paper warned: 'US views of international law vary from that of the UK and the international community. Regime change per se is not a proper basis for military action under international law. But regime change could result from action that is otherwise lawful.'[60]

As the leaked record of a Downing Street meeting attended by the Prime Minister, senior military and intelligence figures, the Foreign and Defence Secretaries and Attorney General shows, on 23 July 2002 the head of MI6 reported that in Washington 'military action was now seen as inevitable' and 'the intelligence and facts were being fixed around the policy'. Still voicing departmental concerns, Jack Straw warned that 'the case was thin. Saddam was not threatening his neighbours, and his WMD capability was less than that of Libya, North Korea or Iran.' Defence Secretary Geoff Hoon reported that the US had already begun 'spikes of activity' to pressurise the Iraqi regime and that 'the most likely timing in US minds for military action to begin was January, with the timeline beginning 30 days before the US Congressional elections'. For his part, the Attorney General provided yet another warning that regime change was not a legal basis for military action. The minutes of the meeting record Blair's response as being that 'it would make a big difference politically and legally if Saddam refused to allow in the UN inspectors. Regime change and WMD were linked in the sense that it was the regime that was producing the WMD . . . If the political context were right, people would support regime change.' The conclusion of the meeting was unequivocal: 'We should work on the assumption that the UK would take part in any military action . . . the Foreign Secretary would send the Prime Minister the background on the UN inspectors, and discreetly work up the ultimatum to Saddam.'[61] Hence, between March and July 2002, without full Cabinet knowledge, Blair utilised the space his presidential style created to make a commitment to the Bush administration consistent with his own notions of the legitimacy of humanitarian military intervention and the importance of the trans-Atlantic alliance and underpinned by a self-belief arising from both his own moral conviction and proven power to persuade the electorate in a domestic context.

By the time Blair flew to Camp David in early September 2002 to meet Bush, the British government was fully committed to the coming war. According to Woodward's account, Bush told Blair that he 'might have to send British troops. "I'm with you," the Prime Minister replied, looking Bush back in the eye, pledging flat out to commit British military forces if necessary, the critical promise Bush had been seeking.'[62] However, just days later International Development Secretary Clare Short's diary records: 'TB gave me assurances when I asked for Iraq to be discussed at Cabinet that no decision made and not imminent.'[63]

From this point on the Blair government pursued a policy of threat exaggeration,[64] through both speeches and the publication of three dossiers. The first of these was published in September 2002. The desperate effort to make the case for war led to the grateful but uncritical acceptance of any information that could make a positive contribution,[65] something captured well in Robin Cook's diary entry of 11 September 2002:

> [Blair] attaches great importance to the forthcoming dossier . . . He is particularly enthusiastic about a report they have that at a cabinet meeting Saddam has said that Iraq must get nuclear weapons to pose a threat to the West. Tony then added, 'Given the poor state of his conventional forces, it is not surprising that he wants to get his hands on nuclear weapons.' This is a curious aside. If Tony himself recognises that Saddam's conventional forces are much weaker than they were before, it is going to be difficult for him to be convincing that Saddam is now a greater threat to his region. And in any case there is no evidence that he has got any nuclear weapons with which to threaten us.[66]

In unveiling a second dossier, in December 2002, this time focused on human rights abuses in Iraq, but criticised by Amnesty International for being 'opportunistic and selective', Straw took the process of threat exaggeration too far, telling the BBC that Saddam 'probably' possessed nuclear weapons, a statement that required the Foreign Office to issue a correction.[67]

Did Blair believe that Iraq represented an imminent threat to its neighbours or the wider world on the eve of war, or did he become trapped by a commitment from which he could not easily disentangle himself? The precise answer is unknowable, but one scene that helps illuminate the question comes from Cook's diary entry for 5 March 2003, recording a meeting with Blair where the:

> most revealing exchange came when we talked about Saddam's arsenal. I told him, 'It's clear from the private briefing that I have had that Saddam has no weapons of mass destruction in a sense of weapons that could strike at strategic cities. But he probably does have several thousand battlefield chemical munitions. Do you never worry that he might use them against British troops?' 'Yes, but all the effort he has had to put into concealment makes it difficult for him to assemble them quickly for use.' There is logic to that response, but it is a logic that does not make a case for war but for a process of containment that prevents him from holding weapons in usable mode.[68]

When the Butler Report was published in July 2004 it concluded that the government's case, 'in the spring of 2002 that stronger action (although not necessarily military action) needed to be taken to enforce Iraqi disarmament was not based on any new development in the current intelligence picture on Iraq'. It found that 'there was no recent intelligence that would itself have given rise to a conclusion that Iraq was of more immediate concern than the activities of some other countries'.[69] Nevertheless, both in the Foreword to the September 2002 dossier and in his presentations to Parliament, the intelligence which his audience could not access for themselves was used by the Prime Minister to justify the urgent case for war. However, as Robin Cook argued, 'Downing Street did not worry that the intelligence was thin and inferential or that the sources were second-hand and unreliable, because intelligence did not play a big part in the real reason why we went to war.'[70]

VI

Tony Blair's decision to commit British forces to the US-led war to remove Saddam Hussein from power in Iraq was to divide the Labour Party and the British public more deeply than the Vietnam War with which it became unavoidably compared. In recognition of its divisiveness, the war and anarchic aftermath featured only fleetingly in the Labour Party's 2005 election manifesto, *Britain: Forward Not Back*. This did not touch on international issues – which had come to define Blair's time in office – until the seventh chapter, where it argued that: 'The best defence of our security at home is the spread of liberty and justice overseas.' On Iraq, it limited itself to explaining that:

> We mourn the loss of life of innocent civilians and coalition forces in the war in Iraq and the subsequent terrorism. But the butchery of Saddam is over and across Iraq eight million people risked their lives to vote earlier this year. Many people disagreed with the action we took in Iraq. We respect and understand their views. But we should all now unite to support the fledgling democracy in Iraq.[71]

During the campaign itself, those Labour MPs who had supported the war chose not to emphasise it, and those who had opposed it generally chose not to emphasise their opposition for fear that any discussion of Iraq could contribute to a protest vote that would unseat them.[72] There would be no Blair equivalent of Mrs Thatcher's triumphant visit to the Falkland Islands during the 1983 campaign to capitalise on a foreign policy triumph. While the Labour Party sought to draw a veil over the issue, the war exacted a toll at the polls, leaving the Labour Party in power, but with a majority reduced by almost 100 seats to 67.

Blair's commitment to the US left Britain more isolated in Europe than at any time since the late Thatcher era,[73] undermined the very foreign policy principles Blair himself had set out in major speeches in 1999 and 2002, set uncomfortable precedents in international law, overrode the interests of his party, acted as a spur to suicide bombings in London, and left Iraq in a state of anarchy, with those he spoke of liberating from Saddam's rule being slaughtered and maimed in a spiral of violence that by May 2006 had accounted for the lives of approximately 35–40,000 civilians.[74]

Ultimately, a relationship that began as a primary asset to New Labour was transformed into a grave liability. Initially a source of inspiration and strength, it became a source of weakness. Foreign Secretary Jack Straw proudly told an interviewer at the beginning of 2002 that: 'It has taken the foreign policy of the Prime Minister finally to lay the ghost of Suez.'[75] In reality, Blair's conduct of foreign policy came to be regularly compared with that of Eden, with no shortage of references to Chamberlain. The conduct of the British government in the run-up to the 2003 war with Iraq is going to be eagerly debated for generations to come. Whatever the outcome of those debates, it is clear that the question of Iraq will be central to all future assessments of Tony Blair's premiership, something he is obviously keen to avoid but cannot escape.

NOTES

Introduction

1 R. Vickers, *The Labour Party and the World, Volume I: The Evolution of Labour's Foreign Policy, 1900–51* (Manchester, 2003), pp. 16–19.

2 J. Gallagher and R. Robinson, 'The imperialism of free trade', *Economic History Review*, 2nd series, 6 (1953), pp. 1–15.

3 H. C. G. Matthew, *The Liberal Imperialists: The Ideas and Politics of a Post-Gladstonian Elite* (1973).

4 On this see A. Booth, 'The manufacturing failure hypothesis and the performance of British industry during the long boom', *Economic History Review*, 2nd series, 56 (2003), pp. 1–33; J. Tomlinson, 'The decline of the Empire and the economic "decline" of Britain', *Twentieth Century British History*, 14 (2003), pp. 201–21.

5 See H. Pelling (ed.), *The Labour Party Foundation Conference and Annual Conference Reports 1900–1905* (1967).

6 P. Poirier, *The Advent of the Labour Party* (1958), pp. 100–17.

7 M. Bevir, 'H. M. Hyndman: a re-reading and a re-assessment', *History of Political Thought*, 12 (1991), pp. 125–45.

8 D. Tanner, 'Ideological debate in Edwardian Labour politics: radicalism, revisionism and socialism', in A. J. Reid and E. F. Biagini (eds.), *Currents of Radicalism* (Cambridge, 1991), pp. 271–93; J. R. MacDonald, *Labour and the Empire* (1907).

9 J. Joli, *The Second International* (2nd edn., 1974), pp. 123–4.

10 N. Kirk, *Comrades and Cousins: Globalization, Workers and Labour Movements in Britain, the USA and Australia from the 1880s to 1914* (2003); C. Tsuzuki, *Tom Mann, 1856–1941: The Challenges of Labour* (Oxford, 1991), esp. pp. 124–40.

11 Kirk, *Comrades and Cousins*, pp. 149–218.

12 See e.g. T. Quelch, 'Black Labour', *The Call*, 25 January 1917.

13 J. Riddell (ed.), *Lenin's Struggle for a Revolutionary International, 1907–16: The Preparatory Years* (New York, 1984), pp. 33–6.

14 J. Horne, *Labour at War: France and Britain, 1914–1918* (Oxford, 1991).

15 C. Howard, 'MacDonald, Henderson, and the outbreak of war, 1914', *Historical Journal*, 20 (1977), pp. 871–91.

16 M. A. Hamilton, *Arthur Henderson* (1938), pp. 112, 118–19.

17 J. Turner, *British Politics and the Great War: Coalition and Conflict 1915–1918* (New Haven and London, 1992), pp. 133, 147, 151.

18 T. Jones, *Lloyd George* (1951), pp. 131–2.

19   C. A. Cline, *Recruits to Labour: The British Labour Party, 1914–31* (Syracuse, NY, 1963), esp. pp. 8–23, 68–99; D. Howell, *MacDonald's Party: Labour Identities and Crisis, 1922–31* (Oxford, 2002), pp. 311–12; R. A. Jones, *Arthur Ponsonby: The Politics of Life* (1989), p. 174.

20   J. M. Winter, 'Arthur Henderson, the Russian Revolution, and the reconstruction of the Labour Party', *Historical Journal*, 15 (1972), pp. 753–73; A. Henderson, *The Aims of Labour* (1917 and subsequent edns).

21   J. Price, *The International Labour Movement* (1945), pp. 31–2; C. Collette, *The International Faith: Labour's Attitudes to European Socialism, 1918–39* (Aldershot, 1998).

22   Z. Steiner, *The Lights that Failed: European International History, 1919–1933* (Oxford, 2005), pp. 67–70, 80, 99.

23   Ibid., pp. 380–2.

24   D. Carlton, *MacDonald versus Henderson: The Foreign Policy of the Second Labour Government* (1970), pp. 75–8, 94–9; H. Winkler, *Paths not Taken: British Labour and International Policy in the 1920s* (Chapel Hill, NC, 1994), esp. pp. 192–7; Steiner, *Lights that Failed*, pp. 755–63.

25   R. W. D. Boyce, *British Capitalism at the Crossroads, 1919–1932: A Study in Politics, Economics and International Relations* (Cambridge, 1987).

26   For more on this see A. Thorpe, *The British General Election of 1931* (Oxford, 1991), pp. 145, 252, 272; idem., 'The industrial meaning of "gradualism": the Labour Party and industry, 1918–31', *Journal of British Studies*, 35 (1996), pp. 84–113.

27   Labour Party, *Annual Report, 1933* (1933), pp. 185–91.

28   G. Lansbury, *Looking Backwards – and Forwards* (1935), p. 157; idem., *My England* (n.d. but 1934), pp. 190, 192.

29   H. Dalton, *The Fateful Years: Memoirs, 1931–1945* (1957), pp. 44–5.

30   Labour Party, *Annual Report, 1935* (1935), pp. 153–93.

31   M. I. Cole (ed.), *Twelve Studies in Soviet Russia* (1933).

32   B. Wootton, *Plan or No Plan* (1934), pp. 260, 301, 317.

33   See esp. S. and B. Webb, *Soviet Communism: A New Civilisation?* (1935).

34   See esp. W. Citrine, *I Search for Truth in Russia* (1936).

35   C. R. Attlee, *The Labour Party in Perspective* (1937), esp. pp. 17–20, 167; Labour Party, *New Zealand: Profess under Socialism* (1937); B. C. Malament, 'British Labour and Roosevelt's New Deal: the response of the left and the unions', *Journal of British Studies*, 17 (1978), pp. 136–67; S. Brooke, 'Atlantic crossing? American views of capitalism and British socialist thought, 1932–1962', *Twentieth Century British History*, 2 (1991), pp. 107–36.

36   See esp. E. F. M. Durbin, *The Politics of Democratic Socialism* (1940).

37   T. Buchanan, *The Spanish Civil War and the British Labour Movement* (Cambridge, 1991).

38   R. Griffiths, *Fellow Travellers of the Right: British Enthusiasts for Nazi Germany, 1933–39* (Oxford, 1983), pp. 312–13.

39   R. Toye, 'The Labour Party and the economics of rearmament, 1935–39', *Twentieth Century British History*, 12 (2001), pp. 303–26.

40   S. Brooke, *Labour's War: The Labour Party during the Second World War* (Oxford, 1992), pp. 34–5.

41   J. Barnes and D. Nicholson (eds.), *The Empire at Bay: The Leo Amery Diaries, 1929–1945* (1988), p. 570, entry for 2 September 1939.

42   See e.g. British Library of Political and Economic Science, Penistone DLP papers (microfilm), executive committee minutes 16 March 1940.

43   A. Thorpe, 'The membership of the Communist Party of Great Britain, 1920–1945', *Historical Journal*, 43 (2000), pp. 777–800.

44   See e.g. debate in Dulwich constituency Labour Party on a resolution from the Labour Pacifist Fellowship: Southwark Local Studies Library, Dulwich CLP papers, A390, meeting 24 September 1941.

45   Sir R. Vansittart, *Black Record: Germans Past and Present* (1941).

46   I. Tombs, 'The victory of socialist "Vansittartism": Labour and the German question, 1941–5', *Twentieth Century British History*, 7 (1996), pp. 287–309.

47   For more on this, see A. Thorpe, '"In a rather emotional state"? The Labour Party and British intervention in Greece, 1944–45', *English Historical Review*, 121 (2006), pp. 1075–1105.

48   M. I. Cole (ed.), *Beatrice Webb's Diaries 1924–1932* (1956), pp. 260, 273–5, entries for 28 December 1930 and 30 June 1931.

49   P. M. H. Bell, *John Bull and the Bear: British Public Opinion, Foreign Policy and the Soviet Union, 1941–1945* (1990), pp. 103, 179.

50   A. Bullock, *Ernest Bevin: Foreign Secretary, 1945–1951* (Oxford, 1985), pp. 239–45.

51   Labour Party, *A Pictorial History of the Labour Party, 1900–1975* (1975), pp. 42, 64.

52   J. Gallagher, *The Decline, Revival and Fall of the British Empire: The Ford Lectures and Other Essays* (Cambridge, 1982), pp. 144–5.

53   Bullock, *Ernest Bevin*, pp. 114–15, 243, 610.

54   Ibid., pp. 194–5.

55   K. O. Morgan, *Labour in Power, 1945–1951* (Oxford, 1984), p. 282.

56   See e.g. U. Jodah, 'The Hungarian Social Democrats and the British Labour Party, 1944–8', unpublished University of the West of England Ph.D. thesis, 2003.

57   P. Weiler, *British Labour and the Cold War* (Stanford, CA, 1988), esp. pp. 165–85.

58   D. Lilleker, *Against the Cold War: The History and Political Traditions of Pro-Sovietism in the British Labour Party* (2004).

59   For contrasting recent views, see J. L. Gaddis, *The Cold War* (2006); G. Roberts, *Stalin's Wars* (New Haven and London, 2006).

60   Morgan, *Labour in Power*, p. 237.

61   M. Jenkins, *Bevanism: Labour's High Tide* (Nottingham, 1979).

62   J. Darwin, *Britain and Decolonisation: The Retreat from Empire in the Post-War World* (1988), pp. 222–88.

63   See e.g. K. O. Morgan, *Callaghan: A Life* (Oxford, 1997), pp. 136–68; B. Castle, *Fighting all the Way* (1993), pp. 258–338.

64   B. Brivati, *Hugh Gaitskell* (1996), p. 414.

65   C. Ponting, *Breach of Promise: Labour in Power, 1964–1970* (1989), pp. 98–9.

66   J. Tomlinson, *The Labour Governments, 1964–70, Volume 3: Economic Policy* (Manchester, 2004), pp. 31–5.

67   H. Parr, *Britain's Policy Towards the European Community: Harold Wilson and Britain's World Role, 1964–1967* (2006); but see also J. Tomlinson, 'The Commonwealth, the balance of payments and the politics of international poverty: British aid policy 1958–71', *Contemporary European History*, 12 (2003), pp. 413–29.

68   J. W. Young, *The Labour Governments, 1964–70, Volume 2: International Policy* (Manchester, 2003), pp. 31–61, 115–41.

69   Ibid., p. 226.
70   See D. Butler and U. Kitzinger, *The 1975 Referendum* (1976).
71   Morgan, *Callaghan*, pp. 438–9, 589–91.
72   Personal recollection by the author.
73   D. Owen, *Time to Declare* (1992), pp. 380–2.
74   Labour Party, *New Hope for Britain: Labour's Manifesto, 1983* (1983), p. 35.
75   *The Times*, 3 October 1980.
76   M. Jones, *Michael Foot* (1994), pp. 484–5.
77   See e.g. A. Mitchell, *Four Years in the Death of the Labour Party* (1983).
78   M. Westlake, 'Neil Kinnock, 1983–92', in K. Jefferys (ed.), *Leading Labour: Labour Leaders from Keir Hardie to Tony Blair* (1999), p. 176; R. Heffernan and M. Marqusee, *Defeat from the Jaws of Victory: Inside Kinnock's Labour Party* (1992), pp. 233–60.
79   R. Holden, *The Making of New Labour's European Policy* (2002), pp. 21–93.
80   See e.g. R. Miliband, *Socialism for a Sceptical Age* (Cambridge, 1994).
81   P. Gould, *The Unfinished Revolution: How the Modernisers saved the Labour Party* (1998), pp. 161–2, 182–209.
82   Ibid., pp. 162–71.
83   J. Kampfner, *Robin Cook* (1998), pp. 133–4.
84   P. Hennessy, *The Prime Minister: The Office and its Holders since 1945* (rev. edn., 2001), pp. 506–7.
85   D. Hurd, *Memoirs* (2003), p. 476.
86   For a good overview of Labour's first years in office, see R. Little and M. Wickham-Jones (eds.), *New Labour's Foreign Policy: A New Moral Crusade?* (Manchester, 2000).
87   For the neocons, see esp. S. Halper and J. Clarke, *America Alone: The Neo-Conservatives and the Global Order* (Cambridge, 2004); for a recent example of neocon thinking, see D. Murray, *Neoconservatism: Why We Need It* (New York, 2006), esp. pp. 99–158.
88   P. Riddell, *Hug Them Close: Blair, Clinton, Bush and the 'Special Relationship'* (2004).
89   P. Norris and C. Wlezien 'Introduction: the third Blair victory: how and why?', *Parliamentary Affairs*, 58 (2005), pp. 669–70.

Chapter 1

1   I wish to thank Professor Keith Laybourn, Professor Kenneth O. Morgan, Dr Janet Shepherd and Professor Chris Wrigley and the editors, Dr Paul Corthorn and Dr Jonathan Davis, for their comments on an early draft of this chapter. I am grateful for permission of HM Queen Elizabeth II to quote from material in The Royal Archives and similarly to the copyright holders for the following collections: Viscount Haldane, Sir Maurice Hankey, James Ramsay MacDonald, E. D. Morel, Lord Ponsonby and J. H. Thomas Papers.
2   For recent surveys of Labour's international policy, see H. R. Winkler, *Britain Seeks a Foreign Policy 1900–1940* (New Brunswick, 2005) and his *Paths Not Taken: British Labour and International Policy in the 1920s* (Chapel Hill, 1994); R. Vickers, *The Labour Party and the World: Volume 1 The evolution of Labour's foreign policy, 1900–51* (Manchester, 2003). See also R. W. Lyman, *The First Labour Government, 1924* (1957); J. Shepherd and K. Laybourn, *Britain's First Labour Government* (Basingstoke, 2006).

3   H. Nicholson, *King George V: His Life and Reign* (1984), p. 384.
4   For MacDonald's background, see D. Marquand, *Ramsay MacDonald* (1977), pp. 4–10. For Curzon, see D. Gilmour, *Curzon* (London and Basingstoke, 1995).
5   *Labour Party Annual Conference Report*, 1958, quoted in Vickers, *The Labour Party and the World*, p. 3.
6   This was a direct reference to the Bolshevik regime responsible for the assassination in 1918 of George V's cousins, the Russian Tsar and his family. MacDonald Diary, 22 January 1924, The National Archives (from here TNA), 30/69/1753.
7   R. Rhodes James (ed.), *Winston S. Churchill: His Complete Speeches 1897–1963, Vol. III: 1914–1922* (New York and London, 1974), p. 2921.
8   The radical journalist H. W. Massingham reported on the Labour rally in *Nation*, 6 February 1924 (emphasis added).
9   For MacDonald's opening parliamentary speech along these lines, see *Parliamentary Debates*, 5th series, 12 February 1924, vol. 169, cols. 749–50, 768, 771–2.
10 MacDonald Diary, 10 December 1923.
11 H. Wilson, *A Prime Minister on Prime Ministers* (1977), p. 198.
12 Winkler, *British Labour Seeks a Foreign Policy, passim*.
13 N. Angell, *After All: The Autobiography of Norman Angell* (1951), p. 239.
14 Ibid.
15 For a reappraisal of MacDonald's political outlook, see D. Tanner, '(James) Ramsay MacDonald' in R. Eccleshall and G. Walker (eds.) *Biographical Dictionary of British Prime Ministers* (1998), pp. 218–88.
16 For an illuminating portrait of Ramsay MacDonald, see K. O. Morgan, *Labour People: Leaders and Lieutenants, Hardie to Kinnock* (Oxford, 1987), pp. 39–53.
17 *Spectator*, 6 December 1924.
18 Marquand, *Ramsay MacDonald*, pp. 50–3, 131–5. For Ramsay MacDonald's memoir of his wife, see J. R. MacDonald, *Margaret Ethel MacDonald* (1913), *passim*.
19 Included in this grouping: C. R. Buxton, Noel Buxton, Ramsay MacDonald (politicians), W. N. Gillies (later Head of Labour's International Department), H. N. Brailsford, Norman Angell, Leonard Woolf (journalists and authors), and Tom Shaw and Will Thorne (trade unionists and MPs). W. P. Maddox, *Foreign Relations in British Labour Politics* (Cambridge Mass., 1934), pp. 70–4.
20 G. Glasgow, *MacDonald as Diplomatist: The Foreign Policy of the First Labour Government in Great Britain* (1924), pp. 31–3.
21 C. R. Attlee, *The Labour Party in Perspective* (1937), ch. 5.
22 E. Windrich, *British Labour's Foreign Policy* (Stanford California, 1952), esp. chs. 1, 5.
23 M. R. Gordon, *Conflict and Consensus in Labour's Foreign Policy 1914–1965* (Stanford California, 1969), chs. 1–2.
24 K. E. Millar, *Socialism and Foreign Policy: Theory and Practice in Britain to 1931* (The Hague, 1967), chs. 1, 4.
25 S. Howe, 'Labour and international affairs' in D. Tanner et al (eds.), *Labour's First Century* (Cambridge, 2000), ch. 4. See also S. Berger, 'Labour in comparative perspective', ch. 10 in the same volume.
26 Vickers, *The Labour Party and the World*, pp. 5, 193.

27   Winkler, *British Labour Seeks a Foreign Policy*, ch. 4.
28   Marquand, *Ramsay MacDonald*, pp. 182–3, 197–9, 218–20, 248–54, 252–5, 257–60.
29   For the Union of Democratic Control, see M. Schwarz, *The Union of Democratic Control in British Politics in the First World War* (Oxford, 1971); S. Harris, *Out of Control: British Foreign Policy and the Union of Democratic Control 1914–1918* (Hull, 1996); A. J. P. Taylor, *The Troublemakers. Dissent over Foreign Policy 1792–1939* (1969), chs. 5–6.
30   C. R. Attlee, *As It Happened* (1954), p. 60. (emphasis added).
31   R. A. Jones, *Arthur Ponsonby: The Politics of Life* (Bromley, 1989), pp. 98–100.
32   Ponsonby to MacDonald, 11 December 1923, MacDonald Papers, 30/60/196.
33   MacDonald to Thomas, 19 December 1923, Kent Record Office, J. H. Thomas Papers, Ulb23 C93. See also G. Blaxland, *J. H. Thomas: A Life For Unity* (1964), pp. 166–7.
34   D. Howell, *MacDonald's Party* (Oxford, 2002), p. 9; Blaxland, *Thomas*, ch. 18.
35   MacDonald to Thomas, 19 December 1923, Thomas Papers, Ulb23 C93.
36   For Sydney Olivier, see F. Lee, *Fabianism and Colonialism: The Life and Political Thought of Lord Sydney Olivier* (1988), esp. ch. 5.
37   S. Webb, 'The First Labour Government', *Political Quarterly*, 32, 1961, p. 21.
38   Ibid., pp. 18–20.
39   MacDonald Diary, 3 February 1924.
40   A. Willert, *Washington and Other Memories*, (Boston, 1972), p. 166.
41   Hankey Diary, 11 October 1924, Churchill College, Cambridge, Sir Maurice Hankey Papers. See also, J. F. Naylor, *A Man and an Institution: Sir Maurice Hankey, the Cabinet Secretariat and the custody of Cabinet secrecy* (Cambridge, 1984), pp. 133–5.
42   MacDonald Diary, 3 February 1924. (emphasis added)
43   Vickers, *The Labour Party and the World*, p. 38.
44   Ibid., pp. 34–5.
45   R. E. Dowse, 'The Independent Labour Party and Foreign Politics 1918–1923', *International Review of Social History*, 7, 1962, pp. 45–6.
46   Shepherd and Laybourn, *Britain's First Labour Government*, pp. 34–5.
47   MacDonald Diary, 21 January 1924.
48   F. W. Pethick Lawrence, 'The True Significance of the Election', *Foreign Affairs*, January 1924.
49   E. D. Morel, 'First Steps Towards Democratic Control of Foreign Policy', *Foreign Affairs*, May 1924.
50   C. A. Cline, 'E. D. Morel and the Crusade Against the Foreign Office', *Journal of Modern History*, 39, 2 (1967), pp. 126–37.
51   A. Ponsonby, *Brief Glimpses: E. D. Morel.* (n.d.), Shulbrede Priory, Lord Ponsonby Papers. See also Morel to Parmoor, 2 February 1924, British Library of Political and Economic Science, E. D. Morel Papers, F2 1/12; Ponsonby to Morel, 23 May 1924, Morel Papers, F8/123. For Morel's lobbying for parliamentary control of foreign policy, including using correspondence from Dominion MPs, see *Foreign Affairs*, February, March and May 1924.
52   C. Sylvest, 'A commanding group'? Labour's Advisory Committee on International Questions 1918–1931' in this volume.

53 F. M. Leventhal, *The Last Dissenter: H. N. Brailsford* (Oxford, 1985), pp. 182–6.
54 For a recent study of these events, see E. Y. O'Riordan, *Britain and the Ruhr Crisis* (Basingstoke, 2001).
55 MacDonald Diary, 3 February 1924.
56 TNA, Cabinet 23/47 (8) 24, 28 January 1924.
57 D'Abernon to MacDonald, 11 February, 4 March 1924, British Library, Lord D'Abernon Papers, Add Ms 48926 ff. 9–11; 13–14.
58 *The Times*, 3 March 1924.
59 MacDonald Diary, 10 April 1924.
60 Marquand, *Ramsay MacDonald*, pp. 334–9.
61 TNA, Cabinet 23/47 (26)(24), 10 April 1924.
62 *Proceedings of the London Reparation Conference July and August 1924*, Cmd 2270, Pt I, pp. 7–9 in *Parliamentary Papers*, 1924, vol. XXVII.
63 Ibid., pp. 23–5.
64 MacDonald Diary, 8 August 1924.
65 A. Hutt, *The Post-War History of the British Working Class* (1937), p. 89.
66 *Proceedings of the London Reparations Conference*, vol. 2, pp. 7–8.
67 T. Jones, *Whitehall Diary*, vol. 1, (Oxford, 1968), 20 March 1924 entry, p. 273.
68 Ibid., 9 April 1924, pp. 276–7.
69 Hankey to Smuts, 1 April 1924, Hankey Papers, 4/16.
70 Robert Cecil to Lady Cavendish, 18 February 1924, British Library, Sir Robert Cecil Papers, Add Ms. 51164. f. 4.
71 Robert Cecil to Gertrude Bell, 22 February 1924, Cecil Papers, f. 9.
72 Parliamentary Labour Party (PLP), *Minutes*, 4 June 1924.
73 For more on these backbench revolts, see R. E. Dowse, 'The Left Wing Opposition during the first two Labour governments', *Parliamentary Affairs*, 16, 1, winter 1960–1.
74 See J. Neidpath, *The Singapore Naval Base and the Defence of Britain's Eastern Empire 1919–1941* (Oxford, 1981); also Lyman, *First Labour Government 1924*, pp. 211–13.
75 Prime Minister's Private Office Papers, 1, 37, quoted in Howell, *MacDonald's Party*, pp. 144, 144–5.
76 Marquand, *Ramsay MacDonald*, p. 339.
77 League of Nations, *Official Journal, Records of the Fifth Assembly, Text of Debates* (Geneva, 1924), pp. 41–5.
78 Attlee, *Labour in Perspective*, p. 207.
79 Mercator's map projection – which navigators favoured in plotting the quickest route across an ocean – grossly distorted landmasses towards both poles. Therefore, some countries in the British Empire, such as Canada and Australia, appeared more extensive on these maps.
80 D. Sandbrook, *Never Had It So Good: A History of Britain From Suez to the Beatles* (2005), pp. 261–2.
81 For Labour Party attitudes to Empire, see S. Howe, *Anti-Colonialism in British Politics* (Oxford, 1993), pp. 44–52.
82 J. H. Thomas, 'Labour and the Empire', *World Today*, May 1924, pp. 487–9.
83 K. O. Morgan, *Keir Hardie: radical and socialist* (1975), ch. 9; J. R. MacDonald, *The Awakening of India* (1910), p. 187, quoted in Marquand, *Ramsay MacDonald*, p. 118.

84   D. Judd, *The Lion and the Tiger: The Rise and Fall of the British Raj* (Oxford, 2004), ch. 8.

85   Lee, *Fabianism and Colonialism*, p. 139.

86   J. L Cox, 'A Splendid Training Ground: the Importance to the Royal Air Force of its Role in Iraq 1919–32', *Journal of Imperial and Commonwealth History*, 13, 2 (1985), pp. 157–84.

87   Labour History Archive and Study Centre, Manchester, Labour Party Archives, LP/DH/24/6; *Daily Herald*, 13, 14 August 1924.

88   B. Wasserstein, *Herbert Samuel: A Political Life* (Oxford, 1992), ch. 9.

89   For these British Labour visits, see J. Davis, 'Left Out in the Cold: British Labour Witnesses the Russian Revolution', *Revolutionary Russia*, 18, 1 (2005), pp. 71–87.

90   Hutt, *The Post-war History of the British Working Class*, pp. 90–1.

91   See, for example, Ponsonby's diary entries: 'J.R.M . . . [is] the outstanding figure in both the House and outside [and] is receiving great praise' (7 April 1924) compared to ' . . . how difficult it is to get into anything like close touch with J.R.M. I hear complaints all round from Ministers . . . ' (25 August 1924) Ponsonby Diary, Ponsonby Papers (Shulbrede).

92   TNA, Cabinet 23/47 (44) (24), 30 July 1924.

93   Article 12 of the Anglo-Irish Treaty of 1921 had established a three-man boundary commission to settle the border between the Irish Free State and the six counties of Northern Ireland, but the Ulster government had refused to nominate a representative to serve on the commission. At MacDonald's behest, Baldwin tried unsuccessfully in 1924 to mediate with Sir James Craig, the Ulster premier. After the summer recess, the Speaker recalled Parliament early to pass a short bill at Westminster with all-party support to appoint the third commissioner.

94   *Manchester Guardian*, 3 September 1924.

95   *The Times*, 22 September 1924.

96   MacDonald Diary, 26 September 1924.

97   *The Times*, 29 September 1924.

98   Ponsonby to MacDonald, 14 September 1924, MacDonald Papers, 30/69/1264.

99   Lyman, *The First Labour Government*, 1924, p. 164.

100 AC5/1/334, Chamberlain to Ida, 5 October 1924 in R. C. Self (ed.), *The Austen Chamberlain Diary Letters: The Correspondence of Sir Austen Chamberlain with his sisters Hilda and Ida, 1916–1937* (Cambridge, 1995).

101 For the Zinoviev Letter, see *A Most Extraordinary and Mysterious Business – the Zinoviev Letter of 1924* (Foreign and Commonwealth Office official document Historians, LRD No. 14, 1999. Available online at www.fco.gov.uk). For British intelligence and the Labour Party, see also C. Andrew, *Secret Service: The Making of the British Intelligence Community* (1992), ch. 10.

Chapter 2

1   I would like to thank Paul Corthorn and Jonathan Davis for asking me to contribute to this project. Also, I would like to thank Duncan Bell, Eugenio Biagini, Paul Corthorn, Charles Jones and Zaheer Kazmi for comments on earlier versions of this chapter.

2   *Labour and the New Social Order* (1918), p. 23 as quoted in J. Harris, 'Labour's

Social and Political Thought', in D. Tanner, P. Thane, and N. Tiratsoo (eds.), *Labour's First Century* (Cambridge, 2000), pp. 8–45, at p. 8.

3   L. Woolf, *Beginning Again. An Autobiography of the Years 1911–1918* (1964), p. 227; L. Woolf, *Downhill All the Way. An Autobiography of the Years 1919–1939* (1967), p. 238.

4   D. Mitrany, *The Functional Theory of Politics* (1975), p. 8.

5   A. J. P. Taylor, *The Trouble Makers. Dissent over Foreign Policy, 1792–1939* (1957), p. 154.

6   W. P. Maddox, *Foreign Relations in British Labour Politics. A Study of the Formation of Party Attitudes on Foreign Affairs, and the Application of Political Pressure Designed to Influence Government Policy, 1900–1924* (Cambridge, MA, 1934), pp. 88–91, 103, 239.

7   See e.g. S. Davis, *The British Labour Party and British Foreign Policy 1933–39* (Ph.D., University of London/LSE, 1952), pp. xliv–xlv.

8   See for example D. S. Birn, 'The League of Nations Union and Collective Security', *Journal of Contemporary History*, 9, 1 (1974), pp. 131–59; M. Ceadel, *Semi-Detached Idealists. The British Peace Movement and International Relations, 1854–1945* (Oxford, 2000); P. Laity, *The British Peace Movement, 1870–1914* (Oxford, 2001); M. Swartz, *The Union of Democratic Control in British Politics During the First World War* (Oxford, 1971).

9   J. R. MacDonald, *Labour and the Empire* (1907), p. 108. T. Blair, 'The Third Way', speech given at the French National Assembly, Paris, 24 March 1998.

10 S. Howe, 'Labour and International Affairs', in Tanner et al, *Labour's First Century*, pp. 119–50, at p. 119.

11 See R. Vickers, *The Evolution of Labour's Foreign Policy 1900–51* (Manchester, 2003). See also Davis, *The British Labour Party*; M. R. Gordon, *Conflict and Consensus in Labour's Foreign Policy, 1914–1965* (Stanford, CA, 1969); J. F. Naylor, *Labour's International Policy. The Labour Party in the 1930s* (1969); G. W. Shepherd, *The Theory and Practice of Internationalism in the British Labour Party with Special Reference to the Interwar Period* (Ph.D., University of London, 1951).

12 H. R. Winkler, 'The Emergence of a Labor Foreign Policy in Great Britain 1918–1929', *The Journal of Modern History*, vol. 28, no. 3 (1956), pp. 247–58; H. R. Winkler, *Paths Not Taken: British Labour and International Policy in the 1920s* (Chapel Hill, NC, 1994); and, most recently, H. R. Winkler, *British Labour Seeks a Foreign Policy, 1900–1940* (2005). My own study of the committee supports this interpretation. See C. Sylvest, 'Interwar Internationalism, the British Labour Party and the Historiography of International Relations', *International Studies Quarterly*, 48, 2 (2004), pp. 409–32. See also D. Carlton, *MacDonald Versus Henderson. The Foreign Policy of the Second Labour Government* (1970); K. E. Miller, *Socialism and Foreign Policy. Theory and Practice in Britain to 1931* (The Hague, 1968); A. Wolfers, *Britain and France between Two Wars. Conflicting Strategies of Peace from Versailles to World War II* (New York, 1962 [1940]).

13 See Vickers, *The Evolution of Labour's Foreign Policy*. Vickers refers to Winkler's 1956 article, but the 1994 book is not mentioned in this otherwise valuable study.

14 I use the term ideology in a rather loose sense to encompass both a language of politics based on discursive conventions and, more specifically, as a system of political thinking, 'loose or rigid, deliberate or unintended through which

individuals and groups construct an understanding of the political world they, or those who preoccupy their thoughts, inhabit, and then act on that understanding'. M. Freeden, *Ideologies and Political Theory. A Conceptual Approach* (Oxford, 1996), p. 3.

15   For a discussion of the importance of international questions for the progressive tradition in British politics, see D. Blaazer, *The Popular Front and the Progressive Tradition. Socialists, Liberals, and the Quest for Unity, 1884–1939* (Cambridge, 1992).

16   See C. Sylvest, 'Continuity and Change in British Liberal Internationalism, c. 1900–1930', *Review of International Studies*, 31, 2 (2005), pp. 263–83; J. Bartelson, 'The Trial of Judgment: A Note on Kant and the Paradoxes of Internationalism', *International Studies Quarterly*, 39, 2 (1995), pp. 255–79. See also H. Suganami, *The Domestic Analogy and World Order Proposals* (Cambridge, 1989).

17   See H. Perkin, *The Rise of Professional Society. England since 1880* (1990).

18   J. R. Vincent, *The Formation of the Liberal Party, 1857–1868* (1966), p. 257.

19   Some of these themes are addressed in R. J. Harrison, *The Life and Times of Sidney and Beatrice Webb, 1858–1905. The Formative Years* (2000).

20   For Labour's national turn, see P. Ward, *Red Flag and Union Jack. Englishness, Patriotism and the British Left 1881–1924* (Woodbridge, 1998).

21   G. R. Searle, *A New England? Peace and War 1886–1918* (Oxford, 2004), p. 828.

22   R. McKibbin, *The Evolution of the Labour Party 1910–1924* (Oxford, 1983), p. 214.

23   *Labour Party Conference Report* (London: Labour Party, 1917), p. 141.

24   The first chair in the subject, which appropriately took its name from the American President Woodrow Wilson, was set up in 1919 at the University of Wales, Aberystwyth. The chair was first occupied by the internationalist Alfred Zimmern (1879–1957), unsuccessful Labour candidate in the 1924 general election. Zimmern attended one meeting of the ACIQ in 1919.

25   See Ceadel, *Semi-Detached Idealists*; Swartz, *The Union of Democratic Control*; H. R. Winkler, 'The Development of the League of Nations Idea in Great Britain, 1914–1919', *The Journal of Modern History*, 20, 2 (1948), pp. 95–112.

26   There were many more, though. For information and analysis of war-time writings on international politics, see Sylvest, 'Continuity and Change'; M. Ceadel, 'Supranationalism in the British Peace Movement During the Early Twentieth Century', in A. Bosco (ed.), *The Federal Idea* (1991), pp. 169–91.

27   This was G. Lowes Dickinson at King's College, Cambridge, but his appointment was not specifically related to international politics.

28   In Winkler's account, the treatment of many of these individuals, who were influential in helping Henderson turn around opinion in the party, is relatively sketchy. In IR, there is now a rather substantial literature on these intellectuals. See, for example, D. Long and P. Wilson, *Thinkers of the Twenty Years' Crisis. Inter-War Idealism Reassessed* (Oxford, 1995); J. D. B. Miller, *Norman Angell and the Futility of War. Peace and the Public Mind* (1986); P. Wilson, *The International Theory of Leonard Woolf: A Study in Twentieth Century Idealism* (2003). For further references, see Sylvest, 'Interwar Internationalism'.

29   See, for example, Laity, *The British Peace Movement, 1870–1914*; D. J. Newton, *British Labour, European Socialism and the Struggle for Peace, 1889–1914* (Oxford, 1985).

30 A. Thorpe, *A History of the British Labour Party* (Basingstoke, 1997), p. 42. See also Winkler, *British Labour Seeks a Foreign Policy*, ch. 1.

31 The best-known pre-war text to originate from within the Labour movement was The Fabian Society, *Fabianism and the Empire* (1900), which was edited by G. B. Shaw. For an interpretation which, to my mind, considerably overrates the importance of this tract *vis a vis* war-time writings, see B. Porter, 'Fabians, Imperialists and the International Order', in B. Pimlott (ed.), *Fabian Essays in Socialist Thought* (1984), pp. 54–67.

32 There exists a number of different lists of members, but most of them rely on the memory of participants. See e.g. Mitrany, *The Functional Theory of Politics*, p. 49; Winkler, *Paths Not Taken*, p. 202; Maddox, *Foreign Relations*, p. 100. The information in the table above has been drawn from the minutes of the ACIQ (Labour History and Archive Centre, Manchester).

33 From 1926 one would also have to include Will Arnold-Forster in this group, another supporter of Henderson and Dalton. See W. Arnold-Forster, 'Labour's Foreign Policy,' *Foreign Affairs*, vol. 11 (1929), pp. 127–30.

34 Henderson to Woolf, 22 April 1918, quoted in D. Wilson, *Leonard Woolf. A Political Biography* (1978), p. 127 (my italics).

35 ACIQ, 'Letter to the Executive Committee', no. 149a, July 1920, p. 1. As the letter concerns the future of the committee, it was probably written by Leonard Woolf, the secretary of ACIQ.

36 Woolf, *Beginning Again*, p. 227.

37 On Cole, see M. Cole, *The Life of G. D. H. Cole* (1971).

38 McKibbin, *Evolution of the Labour Party*, p. 221. The occasion was the unemployment insurance bill and its provisions for the agricultural labourers.

39 Mitrany, *The Functional Theory of Politics*, pp. 8–9. See also John Shepherd's excellent analysis (in this volume) of the various influences in the making of foreign and imperial policy during the time of the first Labour government.

40 Mitrany, *The Functional Theory of Politics*, pp. 8–9. Mitrany remained a member until 1931, when 'after the split with Ramsay MacDonald the Executive decided that only Party Members should sit on Advisory Committees. So I simply dropped out' (p. 9).

41 A. Greenwood, 'The Nature of Nationality', *The Political Quarterly*, February 1915, pp. 82–100, at pp. 96–7.

42 Although he was secretary to Labour's advisory committees during most of the 1920s and from 1927 head of Labour's research department, Greenwood seems only to have been directly associated with the ACIQ in 1922. After having lost the leadership election in 1935, Greenwood became – almost by default – deputy leader of the party. See R. C. Whiting, 'Greenwood, Arthur ', *Oxford Dictionary of National Biography* (Oxford, 2004) [http://www.oxforddnb.com/view/article/33543, accessed 14 April 2005].

43 This ethical internationalism had strong ties with the overarching 'ethical socialism' recently identified by Howell. See D. Howell, *MacDonald's Party: Labour Identities and Crisis, 1922–1931* (Oxford, 2002), esp. p. 232.

44 ACIQ, 'Letter to the Executive Committee', no. 149a, July 1920, p. 1.

45 Howell, *MacDonald's Party*.

46 For a fuller discussion, see Sylvest, 'Interwar Internationalism'. From this sketch of identities, I have left out one that especially until the mid-1920s continued to lurk in the background, and which resurfaced with increased intensity after the

formation of the National government in 1931. This was a radical (socialist) internationalist identity, often, but not exclusively, emerging from the process of radicalisation that the ILP was undergoing. The most persistent exponent of this position was Brailsford, who was a member of the ACIQ in the first five years after the war. In the mid-1920s his critique was voiced in the pages of the *New Leader*. See also H. N. Brailsford, *A League of Nations* (1917); and H. N. Brailsford, *Olives of Endless Age* (1928). For excellent discussions, see P. Corthorn, 'The Labour Party and the League of Nations: The Socialist League's Role in the Sanctions Crisis of 1935', *Twentieth Century British History*, 13, 1 (2002), pp. 62–85; Winkler, *British Labour Seeks a Foreign Policy, passim*.

47   J. R. MacDonald, 'Continuity in Foreign Policy', *Spectator*, 133 (1924), pp. 872–3, at p. 873. On Morel, see A. Hochschild, *King Leopold's Ghost. A Story of Greed, Terror, and Heroism in Colonial Africa.* (1998); S. Spear, 'Pacifist Radicalism in the Post-War British Labour Party: The Case of E.D. Morel', *International Review of Social History*, 23 (1978), pp. 224–41. This position was subsequently ridiculed by the pragmatic internationalist intellectuals. For example, in retrospect Angell doubted whether MacDonald 'had worked out in his mind a foreign policy which differed from the somewhat naive optimism of the old Liberal who was satisfied with political laissez-faire in the international field, sustained by moving rhetoric about the wickedness of armaments, the balance of power, secret diplomacy and so forth'. N. Angell, *After All. The Autobiography of Norman Angell* (1951), p. 239. Woolf also thought little of MacDonald. See Woolf, *Beginning Again*, esp. pp. 217–21. There seems to be some truth in these reflections, but as always when encountering judgements on MacDonald post-1931 we should not attribute them too much significance.

48   ACIQ, 'Sanctions in the Covenant and the Protocol', no. 358, by C. R. Buxton, March 1927, p. 1.

49   Woolf, *Downhill All the Way*, pp. 243–4.

50   ACIQ, 'A Labour Policy on Sanctions', no. 366, by David Mitrany, 1927, p. 1.

51   N. Angell, *The Fruits of Victory. A Sequel to the Great Illusion* (1921), p. 185.

52   ACIQ, 'Draft Report for the International Socialist Conference. The League of Nations and Disarmament', no. 251, by L. S. Woolf, 1922, p. 3.

53   ACIQ, 'Labour and the Proposed Alliance. Interview with Mr Arthur Henderson', no. 114, 1919, p. 1. See also A. Henderson, 'War against War', *Labour Magazine*, 1 (1923), pp. 392–3.

54   Howell, *MacDonald's Party*, p. 12.

55   See Carlton, *MacDonald Versus Henderson*; Winkler, *Paths Not Taken*; Winkler, *British Labour Seeks a Foreign Policy.*

56   ACIQ, minutes, 20 July 1927.

57   ACIQ, Untitled memorandum [decision to set up the ACIQ], no. 2, 1918, p. 1.

58   ACIQ, 'Reform of the Foreign Services', no. 10, by G. Young, July 1918, p. 1.

59   Sylvest, 'Interwar Internationalism'; Winkler, *Paths Not Taken.*

60   In making this distinction I was inspired by Kenneth Waltz's distinction between the immediate and underlying causes of wars. See K. Waltz, *Man, the State and War. A Theoretical Analysis* (New York, 1959).

61   Sylvest, 'Interwar Internationalism'.

62   R. Cook, 'British Foreign Policy', speech at the launch of the Foreign Office Mission Statement, Locarno Suite, FCO, 12 May 1997. See also M. Wickham-

Jones and R. Little, *New Labour's Foreign Policy. A New Moral Crusade?* (Manchester, 2000).

63   For discussions of Blair's foreign policy, see J. Kampfner, *Blair's Wars* (2004); C. Hill, 'Putting the World to Rights: Tony Blair's Foreign Policy Mission', in A. Seldon and D. Kavanagh (eds.), *The Blair Effect, 2001–5* (Cambridge, 2005), pp. 384–409.

Chapter 3

1   See S. Berger, '"Organising Talent and Disciplined Steadiness": the German SPD as a model for the British Labour Party in the 1920s', *Contemporary European History*, 5, 2 (1996), pp. 171–90.

2   For more on Labour's political thought see J. Harris, 'Labour's political and social thought' in D. Tanner et al (eds.), *Labour's First Century* (Cambridge, 2000), ch. 1, and G. Foote, *The Labour Party's Political Thought. A History* (1997). For more on Labour's political thought and the USSR, see J. Davis, 'Altered Images: The Labour Party and the Soviet Union in the 1930s' (Ph.D. thesis, De Montfort University, Leicester, 2002). For Labour and the Soviet Union see K. Morgan, *Labour Legends and Russian Gold* (2006), A. Williams, *Labour and Russia: The attitude of the Labour Party to the USSR, 1924–1934* (Manchester, 1989) and B. Jones, *The Russia Complex. The British Labour Party and the Soviet Union*, (Manchester, 1977).

3   See J. Davis, 'Left out in the Cold: British Labour witnesses the Russian Revolution', *Revolutionary Russia*, 18, 1 (2005), pp. 71–87.

4   Labour Party, *Unity – True or Sham?* (1939), p. 7.

5   For more on Moscow and the CPGB, see A. Thorpe, *The British Communist Party and Moscow 1920–1943* (Manchester, 2000).

6   *Daily Herald*, 2 June 1917.

7   See *What Happened at Leeds* – Report published by the Council of Workers and Soldiers' Delegates (1917).

8   *Labour Leader*, 10 May 1917.

9   *Labour Leader*, 7 June 1917.

10   Jones, *The Russia Complex*, p. 1.

11   Ibid., p. 4.

12   Cited in ibid.

13   T. Cliff and D. Gluckstein, *The Labour Party – a Marxist History* (1988), p. 72.

14   Foote, *The Labour Party's Political Thought*, p. 71.

15   S. Fielding, *The Labour Party, continuity and change in the making of 'New' Labour* (Basingstoke, 2003), p. 62.

16   For more on changes to the Labour Party in this period, see A. Thorpe, *A History of the British Labour Party* (Houndmills, 2001), ch. 2 and J. M. Winter, 'Arthur Henderson, the Russian Revolution, and the Reconstruction of the Labour Party', *Historical Journal*, 15, 4 (1972), pp. 753–73.

17   Davis, 'Left out in the Cold', pp. 82–3.

18   MacDonald Papers, The National Archives (from here TNA), 30/69/104.

19   *Dokumenti vneshney politiki SSSR*, vol. VII, (from here *Dok. vne. pol.*), (Moscow, 1963), p. 66.

20   *Manchester Guardian*, 4 February, 1924. For more on the Soviet response to negotiations with the Labour government, see *Dok. vne. pol.*, vol. VII, *passim* and J. Degras (ed.) *Soviet Documents on Foreign Policy*, vol. I, 1917–1924 (1951), *passim*.

21	For a full discussion of Labour's ideas on planning, see R. Toye, *The Labour Party and the Planned Economy* (Woodbridge, 2003).

22	*The Official Report of the British Trade Union Delegation to Russia in November and December 1924*, (1925), p. 59.

23	For details of what was happening in the Soviet Union between the wars, see C. Read, *The Making and Breaking of the Soviet* System (Houndmills, 2001), chs. 2–6, G. Hosking, *A History of the Soviet Union, 1917–1991* (1992), chs. 2–8. For ideological developments, M. Sandle, *A Short History of Soviet Socialism* (1999), chs. 2–6.

24	Labour Party, *Labour and the Nation* (1928), p. 49.

25	*New Leader*, 21 June, 1929.

26	*Daily Herald*, 3 April, 1929.

27	Ibid.

28	See *Pravda*, March and April 1929, among other articles – *Priezd delegatsii angliyskikh promishlennikov v moskvu*; *Anglo-sovetskie otnosheniya*; *Zayavlenie makdonal'da ob anglo-sovetskikh otnosheniyakh*; *Angliyskie otkliki na zayavlenie tov. Pyatikova.*

29	*Pravda*, 10 April 1929.

30	*Daily Herald*, 9 April, 1929

31	Ibid.

32	Cited in F. M. Leventhal, *Arthur Henderson* (Manchester, 1989), pp. 155–6.

33	Henderson Papers, TNA, FO 800/280.

34	For details of Labour-Soviet negotiations in this period see *Dok. vne. pol.*, vols. XII–XIV, *passim* and J. Degras (ed.) *Soviet Documents on Foreign Policy*, vol. II, 1925–1932, *passim.*

35	Williams, *Labour and Russia*, p. 128.

36	For examples of both see *Daily Herald*, 17 February 1930 and *New Statesman and Nation*, 21 March 1931.

37	TNA, FO 418/73.

38	Williams, *Labour and Russia*, p. 108.

39	A. Thorpe, *Britain in the 1930s* (Oxford, 1992), p. 26.

40	Ibid., p. 27.

41	Ibid., p. 23.

42	W. Citrine, *I Search for Truth in Russia* (1936), p. 131.

43	B. Pimlott, *Hugh Dalton* (1985), p. 209.

44	*New Clarion*, 2 June 1932.

45	H. Dalton, 'A General View of the Soviet Economy *with Special Reference to Planning*' in M. I. Cole (ed.), *Twelve Studies of Soviet Russia* (1933), p. 15.

46	H. Dalton, *The Fateful Years: Memoirs, 1931 1945* (1957), p. 26.

47	Dalton, 'Soviet Economy', pp. 33–4.

48	Dalton, *Fateful Years*, p. 29.

49	Dalton, 'Soviet Economy', p. 16.

50	Ibid.

51	Ibid.

52	Ibid., p. 19.

53	Certain individual members, including Attlee and Greenwood, were part of Churchill's War Cabinet.

54	Pimlott, *Hugh Dalton*, p. 211.

55	Cited in ibid.

56 Labour Party, *For Socialism and Peace: the Labour Party's Programme of Action* (1934), p. 6.
57 Ibid., p. 21.
58 For details of Labour and both the USA and Sweden, see B. C. Malament, 'British Labour and Roosevelt's New Deal: The response of the Left and the Unions', *Journal of British Studies*, 17, 2 (1978), pp. 136–67, and S. Berger, 'Labour in comparative perspective' in Tanner et al (eds.), *Labour's First Century*, ch. 10.
59 H. Dalton, *Practical Socialism for Britain* (1935), p. 247.
60 Ibid., p. 249.
61 *New Statesman and Nation*, 23 May 1936.
62 G. D. H. Cole, *Socialism and Fascism 1931–1939* (1961), p. 85.
63 Thorpe, *A History of the British Labour Party*, p. 87.
64 New Fabian Research Bureau, *Why the USSR Joined the League* (1935), p. 3.
65 Ibid.
66 For more on Labour's international policy, see J. Naylor, *Labour's International Policy: the Labour Party in the 1930s* (1969); S. Howe, 'Labour and international affairs' in Tanner et al (eds.), *Labour's First Century*, ch. 4, and R. Vickers, *The Labour Party and the World: 1900–1951* (Manchester, 2003).
67 Labour Party, *Labour's Foreign Policy* (1933), p. 4.
68 Ibid., p. 2.
69 Russian State Archive of Socio-Political History (from here RGASPI), 495/100/881.
70 *New Leader*, 7 April 1933.
71 RGASPI, 495/100/1001.
72 RGASPI, 495/100/881.
73 Ibid.
74 Labour Party, *The Labour Party and the so-called 'Unity Campaign'* (1937), p. 1.
75 National Joint Council, *Communist and Other Organisations* (1933).
76 *New Clarion*, 16 September 1933.
77 Labour Party, *The Communist Solar System: The Communist International* (1933), p. 2.
78 Labour Party, *The 'Popular Front' Campaign: Declaration by the National Executive Committee* (1939), p. 1.
79 National Joint Council, *Democracy versus Dictatorship* (1933).
80 H. Pelling, *Trade Unionism* (Harmondsworth, 1987), p. 188.
81 Labour Party, *Unity - True or Sham?* (1939), p. 5.
82 Labour Party, *Socialism or Surrender? Labour Rejects the 'Popular Front'* (1939), p. 4.
83 Ibid., p. 3.
84 *New Statesman and Society*, 13 June 1936. Cole did later become a supporter of popular front activity, writing *A People's Front* in 1937.
85 *Manchester Guardian*, 26 March 1917.
86 Cited in Jones, *The Russia Complex*, p. 27.
87 Cited in M. Jones, *Michael Foot* (1994), p. 55.
88 C. Attlee, *The Labour Party in Perspective* (1937), p. 116.
89 Cited in Jones, *The Russia Complex*, p. 27.
90 M. Muggeridge, *The Thirties* (1967), p. 226.
91 Citrine, *I Search for Truth*, p. 256.
92 *Daily Herald*, 9 July 1937.

93   *The Times*, 22 October 1924.

94   Attlee, *The Labour Party in Perspective*, p. 274.

Chapter 4

1   I am grateful to Casper Sylvest for useful comments on an earlier draft of this chapter.

2   T. D. Burridge, *British Labour and Hitler's War* (1976), ch. 1.

3   Ibid., pp. 45–7.

4   S. Brooke, *Labour's War: The Labour Party During the Second World War* (1992), pp. 270–5.

5   Burridge, *British Labour*, pp. 41–7. Ibid., p. 16 is explicit about the reason for this emphasis: 'No international question was as significant or acute as that of Germany's future.'

6   For discussion of the notoriously loose concept of internationalism, see R. Vickers, *The Labour Party and the World: The Evolution of Labour's Foreign Policy 1900–51, volume 1* (2004), pp. 5–9; C. Slyest, 'Interwar Internationalism, the British Labour Party, and the Historiography of International Relations', *International Studies Quarterly*, 48 (2004), pp. 409–32; R. M. Douglas, *The Labour Party, Nationalism and Internationalism* (2004), pp. 5–10.

7   Vickers, *Labour Party and the World*.

8   Douglas, *Labour Party and Internationalism*, chs. 2 and 3.

9   P. Corthorn, 'Labour, the Left and the Stalinist Purges of the late 1930s', *Historical Journal*, 48, 1 (2005), pp. 179–207.

10   Vickers, *Labour Party and the World*, pp. 6–7, emphasises this strand of Labour's internationalism.

11   B. Jones, *The Russia Complex* (1977), ch. 3. Burridge, *British Labour*, pp. 26–30, 37–40, also stresses differences in the range of Labour responses to Soviet policy at this time.

12   Dalton diary, 15 March 1940, in B. Pimlott (ed.), *The Political Diary of Hugh Dalton, 1918–1940, 1945–1960* (1986), p. 323.

13   Editorial, *Daily Herald*, 23 August 1939.

14   Francis Williams, 'This is the hour', *Daily Herald*, 25 August 1939.

15   W. Citrine, *Men and Work* (1964), p. 372.

16   B. Castle, *Fighting All the Way* (1993), p. 102.

17   K. Martin, *Harold Laski: a biographical memoir* (1953), p. 123.

18   For discussion of the twists and turns in this process see H. Winkler, *Paths Not Taken: British Labour and International Policy in the 1920s* (1994).

19   A. J. Williams, *The Labour Party and Russia 1924–34* (Manchester, 1989), pp. 234–5.

20   P. Corthorn, 'The Labour Party and the League of Nations: The Socialist League's Role in the Sanctions Crisis of 1935', *Twentieth Century British History*, 13, 1 (2002), pp. 62–85.

21   L. G. Shaw, *The British Political Elite and the Soviet Union 1937–39* (2003), pp. 77, 80.

22   Dalton diary, 3 May 1939, in Pimlott (ed.), *Political Diary*, p. 263.

23   NEC Report, *Labour Party Annual Conference Report*, 1940 [hereafter *LPACR*, year], p. 6.

24   P. Corthorn, *In the Shadow of the Dictators: The British Left in the 1930s* (2006), pp. 191–2, 197–8, 204, 206.

25 *Tribune*, 25 August 1939.
26 Jones, *Russia Complex*, p. 45.
27 Castle, *Fighting All the Way*, p. 102.
28 *Daily Herald*, 28 August 1939.
29 Editorial, *Daily Herald*, 28 August 1939.
30 Dalton diary, 15 September 1939, in Pimlott (ed.), *Political Diary*, pp. 300–1.
31 Brailsford, 'Meaning of Stalin's Move', *Reynolds News*, 27 August 1939, Labour History Archive and Study Centre (LHASC), Manchester, H. N. Brailsford papers, HNB/25/20.
32 Quotation from TUC General Council Declaration, NEC Report, *LPACR*, 1940, p. 11. For the NEC manifesto see *Daily Herald*, 2 September 1939.
33 Laski to editor, *New Statesman*, 26 August 1939.
34 Brailsford, 'The Moves that led to War', *Reynolds News*, 3 September 1939, Brailsford papers, HNB/31/12.
35 Laski to Franklin Delano Roosevelt, 4 September 1939, in Martin, *Laski*, p. 140.
36 Brailsford, 'Our Way with Neutrals', *New Statesman*, 16 September 1939.
37 Brailsford, 'We Must Plan for Peace Now', *Reynolds News*, 17 September 1939, Brailsford papers, HNB/25/22.
38 Martin, 'The War and the NS and N', *New Statesman*, 9 September 1939.
39 Laski to editor, *New Statesman*, 26 August 1939.
40 Brailsford, 'We Must Plan for Peace Now', *Reynolds News*, 17 September 1939, Brailsford papers, HNB/25/22.
41 Laski to editor, *New Statesman*, 26 August 1939.
42 Brailsford, 'We Must Plan for Peace Now', *Reynolds News*, 17 September 1939, Brailsford papers, HNB/25/22.
43 Ibid.
44 Martin, 'The War and the NS and N', *New Statesman*, 9 September 1939.
45 A. Henderson, *Labour's Foreign Policy* (1933), pp. 19–22.
46 'War and Peace', *LPACR*, 1934, Appendix II, pp. 242–5.
47 Corthorn, 'Labour Party and League of Nations'.
48 Gordon Walker diary, 8 September 1939, in R. Pearce (ed.), *Patrick Gordon Walker: Political Diaries 1932–71* (1991), p. 97.
49 Brailsford, 'We Must Plan for Peace Now', *Reynolds News*, 17 September 1939, Brailsford papers, HNB/25/22.
50 Brailsford, 'Our Way with Neutrals', *New Statesman*, 16 September 1939.
51 Ibid.
52 Laski to Franklin Delano Roosevelt, 4 September 1939, in Martin, *Laski*, p. 140.
53 *Daily Herald*, 18 September 1939.
54 Editorial, *Daily Herald*, 18 September 1939.
55 *Daily Worker*, 19 September 1939, LHASC, Manchester, Rajani Palme Dutt papers, CP/IND/DUTT/31/07. Labour Party leadership's attitude to Soviet Union attacked in CC statement, *Daily Worker*, 23 September 1939, Dutt papers, CP/IND/Dutt/31/07.
56 CP Central Committee, 24 September 1939, LHASC, Manchester, Harry Pollitt papers, CP/IND/POLL/2/7.
57 Cripps diary, 4 October 1939, Bodleian Library, Oxford, Sir Stafford Cripps papers (not catalogued at time of use).
58 Gordon Walker diary, 17 September 1939, in Pearce (ed.), *Gordon Walker Diaries*, p. 98.

59   *Tribune*, 24 September 1939.
60   *Tribune*, 6 October 1939. C. P. Trevelyan was another on the Labour left who wanted serious consideration given to the Nazi-Soviet proposal to discuss peace terms: Charles Treveylan to editor, *New Statesman*, 7 October 1939.
61   Dalton diary, 18 September 1939, in Pimlott (ed.), *Political Diary*, p. 301.
62   Ibid., p. 303.
63   Dalton diary, 25 September 1939, in Pimlott (ed.), *Political Diary*, p. 305.
64   NEC minutes, 25 October 1939.
65   *Daily Herald*, 7 September 1939.
66   NEC minutes, 25 October 1939.
67   NEC International Sub-committee minutes, 7 November 1939.
68   Ibid.
69   Ibid., 18 December 1939.
70   Brailsford, 'Why Britain Must Fight it Out', *Reynolds News*, 15 October 1939, Brailsford papers, HNB/31/15.
71   Brailsford, 'Peace Plan for Europe', *Reynolds News*, 8 October 1939, Brailsford papers, HNB/31/14.
72   Williams, 'What are we Fighting for?', *Daily Herald*, 29 September 1939.
73   Williams, 'What kind of War is this?', *Daily Herald*, 13 October 1939.
74   'Let the People Speak: Lord Ponsonby versus Philip Noel Baker, *Daily Herald*, 8 November 1939.
75   Charles Treveylan to editor, *New Statesman*, 7 October 1939.
76   *Daily Herald*, 11 October 1939, reporting Attlee's broadcast on 'Labour and the War' on 10 October 1939.
77   Attlee, 'Labour's Peace Aims', *Daily Herald*, 9 November 1939.
78   C. R. Attlee, *An International Police Force* (1934).
79   The fullest account is R. Toye, *The Labour Party and the Planned Economy* (2003).
80   Attlee, 'Labour's Peace Aims', *Daily Herald*, 9 November 1939.
81   Ibid.
82   Brailsford, 'Peace Plan for Europe', *Reynolds News*, 8 October 1939, Brailsford papers, HNB/31/14. Earlier Brailsford had expressed his desire 'to make an end of the sordid privileges of imperialism': Brailsford, 'The Moves that led to War', *Reynolds News*, 3 September 1939, Brailsford papers, HNB/31/12.
83   *Daily Herald*, 11 October 1939.
84   Brailsford, 'Peace Plan for Europe', *Reynolds News*, 8 October 1939, Brailsford papers, HNB/31/14.
85   Brailsford, 'Truth Behind Propaganda', *Reynolds News*, 5 November 1939, Brailsford papers, HNB/31/5.
86   Cole, 'The Essentials of Federation', draft for OULC Bulletin, 13 November 1939, Nuffield College, Oxford, G. D. H. Cole papers, GDHC/A1/71/2/1–3; Oxford University Labour Club Bulletin, 22 November 1939, Cole papers, GDHC/D2/6/5/1–6.
87   Cole, 'The Essentials of Federation', draft for OULC Bulletin, 13 November 1939, Cole papers, GDHC/A1/71/2/1–3; Oxford University Labour Club Bulletin, 22 November 1939, Cole papers, GDHC/D2/6/5/1–6. Cole repeated his argument about US reluctance to be involved in a federation: Cole, 'British War Aims', draft for NY Nation, n.d., Cole papers, GDHC/A1/71/4/1–9.
88   Editorial, *Daily Herald*, 30 November 1939.

89   Ibid., 1 December 1939, emphasis in original.
90   Greenwood, 'No Excuse for Russia', *Daily Herald*, 4 December 1939.
91   Editorial, *New Statesman*, 2 December 1939.
92   Brailsford, 'Why Stalin Struck', *Reynolds News*, 3 December 1939, Brailsford papers, HNB/31/18.
93   Ibid.
94   Williams, 'To Help Finland We must Beat Hitler First', *Daily Herald*, 15 December 1939.
95   Editorial, *Daily Herald*, 1 December 1939.
96   Cole, 'British War Aims', draft for NY Nation, n.d., Cole papers, GDHC/A1/71/4/1–9.
97   G. D. H. Cole, *Socialism and Fascism 1931–39* (1960), pp. 27–30.
98   Corthorn, *In the Shadow of the Dictators*, pp. 175–8.
99   Laski to Frankfurter, 7 December 1939, quoted in Martin, Laski, p. 139.
100 D. Jay, *Change and Fortune* (1980), pp. 72–3.
101 E. F. M. Durbin, *The Politics of Democratic Socialism: an essay on social policy* (1940), p. 25.
102 Laski to editor, *New Statesman*, 9 March 1940. Durbin subsequently replied that the issue of torture was 'a minor point' given 'the use of both regimes of other instruments of terror, imprisonment without trial, exile and mass executions': E. F. M. Durbin to editor, *New Statesman*, 23 March 1940.
103 Appendix III, NEC minutes, 20 March 1940.
104 NEC Report, *LPACR*, 1940, p. 13.
105 Greenwood, 'No Excuse for Russia', *Daily Herald*, 4 December 1939.
106 NEC Report, *LPACR*, 1940, p. 13.
107 Williams, 'To Help Finland We must Beat Hitler First', *Daily Herald*, 15 December 1939.
108 Editorial, *Daily Herald*, 14 December 1939.
109 B. Donoughue and G. W. Jones, *Herbert Morrison: Portrait of a Politician* (1973), p. 249.
110 H. Morrison, *What are We Fighting For?* (1939), Bodleian Library, Oxford, Clement Attlee papers, Ms. Attlee dep. 1, pp. 7–8.
111 NEC minutes, 20 December 1939.
112 NEC report, *LPACR*, 1940, p. 13.
113 Ibid., p. 14.
114 NEC International Sub-committee minutes, 19 January 1940.
115 Martin, *Laski*, p. 139.
116 NEC International Sub-committee minutes, 19 January 1940.
117 Attlee address at Fabian Society, 17 January 1940, Attlee papers, Ms. Attlee. Dep. 1.
118 Crosland to editor, *Oxford University Labour Club Bulletin*, 13 February 1940, Cole papers, GDHC/D2/6/8/1–6.
119 Draft of Attlee speech at a Labour Party conference at Blackburn, January 1940. Enclosed in Private Secretary to W. W. Henderson of Transport House, 11 January 1940, Attlee papers, Ms. Attlee. Dep. 1.
120 Attlee address at Fabian Society, 17 January 1940, Attlee papers, Ms. Attlee. Dep. 1.
121 Attlee speech on 'War and the Moral Issue', 3 February 1940, Attlee papers, Ms. Attlee. Dep. 1.

122 Dalton diary, 'Middle of February' 1940, in Pimlott (ed.), *Political Diary*, p. 318.
123 Labour Party, *Labour, the War, and the Peace* (1940), pp. 3, 7.
124 NEC report, *LPACR*, 1940, p. 14.
125 Tom Buchanan has shown that Bevin and Citrine were concerned that more extensive involvement in Spain would have divided the Labour movement in an extremely factious dispute. In particular, he has emphasised their concern not to alienate Catholic members of the Labour movement by openly supporting the anti-Catholic Republican side: T. Buchanan, *The Spanish Civil War and the British Labour Movement* (Cambridge, 1991).
126 NEC report, *LPACR*, 1940, p. 14.
127 Dalton diary, 15 March 1939, in Pimlott (ed.), *Political Diary*, pp. 322–3.
128 NEC minutes, 20 March 1940.
129 Richard Acland, H. N. Brailsford, J. B. S. Haldane, Hewlett Johnson, P. Chalmers Mitchell, Listowel, G. Bernard Shaw, Sybil Thorndike, Charles Trevelyan, S. and B. Webb to editor, *New Statesman*, 9 March 1940.
130 Martin, *Laski*, p. 138.
131 'Memorandum on the constitutional position of those members of the Labour Party who give their support to Russian aggression in Finland', NEC minutes, 20 March 1940.
132 Corthorn, *In the Shadow of the Dictators*, pp. 32–3.
133 *LPACR*, 1934, pp. 152–8, for Henderson's speech. Speaking in support of *War and Peace* at the TUC annual meeting in September 1934, Critine also emphasised the involvement of the Soviet Union in the League of Nations: *Trades Union Congress Annual Report*, 1934, pp. 334–8.
134 NEC minutes, 20 March 1940.
135 Morrison speaking in October 1937: *LPACR*, 1937, p. 164.
136 Bevin to Cole, 27 January 1937, Modern Records Centre, University of Warwick, TUC archive, MSS.126/TG/2000, box 9, dep. 5/5/00.
137 See Corthorn, *In the Shadow of the Dictators*, chs 6–7.
138 NEC minutes, 27 September 1939.
139 Ibid., 20 December 1939.
140 Draft of Attlee speech at a Labour Party conference at Blackburn, January 1940. Enclosed in Private Secretary to W. W. Henderson of Transport House, 11 January 1940, Attlee papers, Ms. Attlee. Dep. 1. See *Daily Herald*, 15 January 1940 reporting his speech given on the 13th.
141 NEC minutes, 17 April 1940.
142 Cripps diary, 20 May 1940, Cripps papers.
143 This is not to underestimate the extent to which 'Labour retained a distinctive programme' during the war. Brooke, *Labour's War*, p. 10.
144 Durbin, *Politics of Democratic Socialism*, p. 329.
145 Martin, *Laski*, p. 142.
146 *LPACR*, 1940, p. 161. The resolution was passed by 1,739,000 to 727,000.
147 *LPACR*, 1940, pp. 164–5.
148 Jones, *Russia Complex*, pp. 59–60.
149 Douglas, *Labour Party and Internationalism*, chs. 2 and 3.
150 Draft of the Lord Privy Seal's Broadcast, n.d. but c. 22 June 1941, Attlee papers, Ms. Attlee. dep. 3.
151 NCL, 'The Russo-German War', 25 June 1941, Appendix II, NEC minutes, 25 June 1941.

152 'The British Labour Movement, the War and the Communist Party', 31 July 1941, Attlee papers, Ms. Attlee. dep. 3.

153 Draft of the Lord Privy Seal's Broadcast, n.d. but c. 22 June 1941, Attlee papers, Ms. Attlee. dep. 3.

154 Editorial, *Daily Herald*, 26 June 1941.

155 'The British Labour Movement, the War and the Communist Party', 31 July 1941, Attlee papers, Ms. Attlee. dep. 3.

156 Laski, 'Towards Friendship with the Soviet Union', *New Statesman*, 5 July 1941.

157 G. D. H. Cole, *Europe, Russia and the Future* (1941), p. 31.

158 This is presumably why Douglas attributed little significance to the opening months of the war. Douglas, *Labour Party and Internationalism*, p. 60, states: 'In the nine months following the outbreak of the Second World War, party spokesmen offered little to the debate on the breakdown of the international system.'

159 Cole, *Europe, Russia and the Future*, p. 33.

Chapter 5

1 *Labour Party Annual Conference Report*, (1939), [henceforward *LPACR*, year], p. 243.

2 Ibid., p. 250

3 Ibid., pp. 243–5.

4 A. Bullock, *Ernest Bevin: Trade Union Leader, 1881–1940* (1960), pp. 622–34.

5 D. K. Fieldhouse, 'The Labour Governments and the Empire Commonwealth' in R. Ovendale (ed.), *The Foreign Policy of the British Labour Governments, 1945–51* (Leicester, 1984), p. 95.

6 Sir Orme Sargent, 'Stocktaking After VE Day', The National Archives (TNA), FO371/50912.

7 Quoted in J. Kent, 'The British Empire and the Origins of the Cold War', in A. Deighton (ed.), *Britain and the First Cold War* (1990), p. 171.

8 TNA, FO371, 50920: Memorandum from Secretary of State for Foreign Affairs (Ernest Bevin), 4 October 1945.

9 TNA, FO371/57170: Italian Colonies and UNO Collective Trusteeship, January 1946; memorandum from J. G. Ward, 6 February 1946.

10 TNA, FO371/49069: Letter from South African High Commissioner, 26 January 1946; Bevin to Attlee, 9 February 1946.

11 B. Pimlott (ed.), *The Political Diary of Hugh Dalton 1918–1940, 1945–1960* (1986), pp. 368–9.

12 TNA, FO371/57171: Telegram from General Paget, 8 February 1946.

13 TNA, FO371/57278: Proceedings of the Second Plenary Conference of the Council of Ministers, Paris 25 April–16 May 1946, p. 103; CAB 128, volume 12, 5 February 1948.

14 G. Balfour-Paul, *The End of Empire in the Middle East* (Cambridge, 1991), pp. 9 and 14.

15 G. Kolko and J. Kolko, *The Limits of Power* (New York, 1972), p. 312.

16 Quoted in M. Walker, *The Cold War* (1993), p. 42.

17 The story of Attlee's resistance is told by R. Smith and J. Zametica, 'The Cold Warrior: Clement Attlee Reconsidered, 1945–7', *International Affairs*, 61, 2 (1985), pp. 237–52.

18 R. H. S. Crossman et al, *Keep Left* (*New Statesman* pamphlet, May 1947).

19   An amendment and an Early Day Motion supporting this idea were put before the House in 1946 and 1947 respectively, gaining the support of 72 MPs. Another Early Day Motion in favour of European political integration was supported by 100 MPs in March 1948 and the party's annual congress adopted a federalist resolution in the same year.

20   TNA, FO371/67673: Record of Conversation between the Secretary of State and M. Ramadier, 22 September 1947.

21   TNA, FO371/67673: Record of Foreign Office meeting, 8 October 1947.

22   TNA, FO371/67673: Anglo-French Co-operation: Meeting of Bevin, Oliver Harvey, Edmund Hall-Patch, and Esler Dening, 26 September 1947.

23   TNA, FO371/168: Memorandum on European Recovery Programme, prepared for the Cabinet Economic Policy Committee, 23 December 1947.

24   Quoted in M. J. Hogan, *The Marshall Plan: America, Britain and the Reconstruction of Western Europe, 1947–52* (Cambridge, 1987), pp. 46–9.

25   Quoted in B. Pimlott, *H. Dalton* (1985) p. 577.

26   TNA, FO371/62740: Cabinet Economic Policy Committee, 7 November 1947.

27   Some historians persist in the error of depicting Labour as 'ragged-trousered philanthropists' in colonial matters, focusing on the comic wrong-headedness of the groundnuts scheme and the apparent generosity of the Colonial Development and Welfare Act as amended in 1945, to the exclusion of the main business. For these typical errors see K. O. Morgan, *Labour in Power, 1945–51* (Oxford, 1984), pp. 201, 230 and F. S. Northedge, *Descent From Power: British Foreign Policy, 1945–73* (1974), p. 221. For the main business see Fieldhouse, 'Labour Governments and the Empire Commonwealth', and D. A. Low and A. Smith (eds.), *Oxford History of East Africa,* volume three (Oxford, 1976).

28   J. Tomlinson, 'The Attlee Governments and the Balance of Payments, *Twentieth Century British History*, 2, 1 (1991), pp. 61–3.

29   TNA, FO371/5666: Minute to Attlee from Bevin, 8 July 1947 and Creech Jones to Bevin, 12 August 1947.

30   TNA, FO371/5132, documents UE 11531 and UE 12502.

31   TNA, CAB 128, volume 12, 8 January 1948.

32   TNA, CAB 129/37, CP(49)208, 'European Policy', memo from Bevin, 18 October 1949.

33   Ibid.

34   F. Hutchins, 'India Leaves Britain' in T. Smith (ed.), *The End of European Empire: Decolonisation after World War Two* (1975), p. 35.

35   Quoted in B. R. Tomlinson, *The Political Economy of the Raj* (1979), p. 142.

36   A. Bullock, *Ernest Bevin: Foreign Secretary* (1983), pp. 359–61.

37   W. R. Louis, *The British Empire in the Middle East*, (Oxford, 1984) p. viii.

38   Ibid., pp. 32–3.

39   See J. Callaghan, *Socialism in Britain* (Oxford, 1990), pp. 147–61.

Chapter 6

1   The research for this chapter was undertaken as part of the author's MA thesis, 'The Labour Party and Rearmament, 1950–55' (University of Leeds, 2004). I am grateful to my supervisors, Dr. Owen A. Hartley and Professor Richard Whiting, as well as the editors, for their comments on an earlier version of this chapter.

2   M. Foot, *Aneurin Bevan: A Biography, volume two, 1945–1960* (1973); P. M. Williams, *Hugh Gaitskell: A Political Biography* (1979).

3   The chief biographies of the key figures provide excellent examinations of the issue. For more specific work on Korea and Labour, see P. Lowe, *Containing the Cold War in East Asia: British Policies towards Japan, China and Korea, 1948–53* (Manchester, 1997). The diaries of Gaitskell, Crossman and Dalton also give accounts of the subject.

4   The primary work that has been carried out on West Germany and the party is R. G. Hughes, "'We are not seeking strength for its own sake'": The British Labour Party, West Germany and the Cold War, 1951–64', *Cold War History*, 3, 1 (2002), pp. 67–94. See also S. Dockrill, *Britain's Policy for West German Rearmament, 1950–55* (Cambridge, 1991), and S. Mawby, *Containing Germany: Britain and the Arming of the Federal Republic* (1999).

5   B. Pimlott (ed.), *The Political Diary of Hugh Dalton, 1918–40, 1945–60* (1986) (hereafter Dalton Diary), entry for 'End of 1948', pp. 445–6.

6   The Daltonian group consisted of Dalton, A.V. Alexander, James Callaghan, James Chuter Ede, Jim Griffiths, Hector McNeil, Alf Robens, John Strachey and Kenneth Younger.

7   Ben Pimlott's *Hugh Dalton* biography (1985) seems to be the only partial exception to this thus far. Dalton's anti-German rearmament activities are discussed sporadically between pp. 608–19. The Gaitskellites were Gaitskell, Arthur Allen, Aiden Crawley, Anthony Crosland, John Edwards, Denis Healey, Douglas Jay, Roy Jenkins, Frank Pakenham, and Woodrow Wyatt. The Morrisonians consisted of Morrison, Arthur Bottomley, George Brown, Patrick Gordon Walker, Sir Hartley Shawcross, Christopher Mayhew, Emmanuel Shinwell, Richard Stokes, George Strauss, and Tom Williams.

8   National Museum of Labour History, Labour Party Archive (LPA), NEC International Sub-committee, 'Foreign Policy Aims', 1951 (all cited Labour Party records are located at the LPA).

9   Dockrill, *Britain's Policy for West German Rearmament*; Mawby, *Containing Germany*.

10 See Cabinet, PLP and NEC minutes for mid-late September 1950.

11 The National Archives (TNA), PREM 8/1429 part 1, Eliot brief for Defence Committee meeting of 25 November 1950 (all cited government papers are located at TNA).

12 Dalton Diary, 20 December 1950, p. 495.

13 Ibid.

14 CM(51)12, CAB 128/19 (8 February 1951); Dalton Diary, entry for 'Mid-February 1951', pp. 503–5.

15 Dalton Diary, entry for 'Mid-February 1951', pp. 503–5; CM(51)12, CAB 128/19 (8 February 1951).

16 Dalton Diary, entry for 'Mid-February 1951', pp. 503–5.

17 *1950 Labour Party Annual Conference Report* (hereafter *LPACR*), pp. 130–42.

18 Dalton Diary, 9 February 1951, p. 501, and entry for 'Mid-February 1951', pp. 503–5.

19 *House of Commons Debates, Fifth Series* (hereafter *Hansard*), 12 February 1951, vol. 484, cols. 65–7.

20 DO(51)89, CAB 131/11 (24 July 1951).

21 Foot, *Bevan*, p. 305.

22   CM(50)63, CAB 128/18 (9 October 1950); CM(50)86, CAB 128/18 (14 December 1950).
23   PREM 8/1429, part 1, Dalton to Attlee (10 July 1951); Foot, *Bevan*, p. 425.
24   Foot, *Bevan*, p. 425; British Library of Political and Economic Science, Hugh Dalton Diaries (unpublished), part 1, volume 41, entry for 'August 1951'; Mawby, *Containing Germany*, p. 67.
25   DO(51)89, CAB131/11 (24 July 1951).
26   DO(51)89, CAB 131/10 (24 July 1951); CM(51)56, CAB 128/20 (30 July 1951); PREM 8/1429, part 2, Dalton to Attlee, 31 July 1951; CM(51)58, CAB 128/20 4 September 1951; Dalton Diary, 4 September 1951, pp. 552–3. In the Cabinet split, Dalton had the open support of A. V. Alexander, Ede, Griffiths, Hector McNeil, Robens and Strachey, and the clear sympathy of the Prime Minister.
27   Dalton Diary, 4 September 1951, pp. 552–3.
28   Ibid.
29   Dalton Diary, 2 May 1952, p. 586, 11 June 1952, p. 589, and 24 July 1952, p. 594.
30   Dalton Diary, 4 September 1951, pp. 552–3; CM(51)58, CAB 128/20 (4 September 1951).
31   CM(51)58, CAB 128/20 (4 September 1951).
32   Mawby, *Containing Germany*, p. 71.
33   Dalton Diary, 13 October 1951, pp. 560–1.
34   Ibid.
35   At the 1951 Conference, Dalton won 545,000 votes, compared to the 654,000 that he attracted in 1950 – *1950 LPACR*, p. 97, and *1951 LPACR*, p. 98.
36   Dalton Diary, 13 October 1951, pp. 560–1. Dalton recorded that the Bevanites had discouraged CLPs from voting for him.
37   Dalton Diary, 14 December 1951, p. 575; J. Morgan (ed.), *The Backbench Diaries of Richard Crossman* (1981) (hereafter Crossman Diary), 19 December 1951, pp. 56–7.
38   Crossman Diary, 19 December 1951, pp. 56–7.
39   NEC minutes, 30 April 1952; Dalton Diary, 2 May 1952, pp. 585–6.
40   LPA, Meeting of Dalton, Healey and Morrison, Foreign Office, (12 April 1951); International Sub-Committee, Labour-SPD-SIFO meeting, 27 April 1952; International Sub-Committee, S. Rose report on SPD Congress, Dortmund, 24–28 September 1952. Adenauer himself said that 'our chief reason for wanting to enter the European Army is to be able to recover our Eastern territories' – Adenauer speech in Hanover, December 1951, cited in A. Bevan, B. Castle, R. Crossman, T. Driberg, I. Mikardo, and H. Wilson, *It Need Not Happen: The Alternative to German Rearmament* (1954).
41   NEC minutes, 30 April 1952.
42   Dalton Diary, 2 May 1952, pp. 585–6.
43   NEC minutes, 30 April 1952, and NEC statement on German rearmament, 30 April 1952.
44   Crossman Diary, 1 May 1952, p. 103; NEC minutes, 30 April 1952.
45   Dalton Diary, 2 May 1952, p. 585.
46   Dalton Diary, 14 May 1952, pp. 587–8.
47   Pimlott, *Dalton*, p. 610.
48   Crossman Diary, 1 May 1952, pp. 102–3.

49 Crossman Diary, 1 May 1952, p. 103. Crossman recorded that the opposition of Morrison and Shinwell to the statement was so explosive that they 'blew off their heads'; Dalton Diary, 2 May 1952, p. 586; PLP Executive Committee minutes, 30 April 1952.
50 Crossman Diary, 1 May 1952, p. 103.
51 PLP minutes, 6 May 1952; Crossman Diary, 6 May 1952, p. 104.
52 *Hansard*, 14 May 1952, v. 500, cols. 1473–80; Crossman Diary, 20 May 1952, pp. 106–7.
53 *Hansard*, 14 May 1952, v. 500, cols. 1511–23.
54 Crossman Diary, 20 May 1952, p. 107; *Tribune*, 22 May 1952 and PLP minutes.
55 Dalton Diary, 27 May 1952, p. 588.
56 Dalton Diary, 11 June 1952, p. 589.
57 Dalton Diary, 27 May 1952, p. 588.
58 Dalton Diary, 11 June 1952, p. 589, 26 June 1952, p. 590 and 30 June 1952, p. 591.
59 Dalton Diary, 30 June 1952, p. 591.
60 Dalton Diary, 17 July 1952, p. 593.
61 PLP Executive Committee minutes, 24 July 1952; Dalton Diary, 24 July 1952 pp. 594–5; Crossman Diary, 24 July 1952, p. 127.
62 Crossman Diary, 24 July 1952, p. 127.
63 PLP minutes, 24 July 1952.
64 Ibid. See also Dalton Diary, 24 July 1952, p. 595. Bevan's diatribe apparently saw him call Brown a 'bastard' and a 'pimp' during the meeting.
65 Dalton Diary, 24 July 1952, p. 595.
66 Dalton Diary, 4 August 1952, p. 597.
67 PLP Executive Committee minutes, 28 July 1952; Crossman Diary, 1 August 1952, pp. 128–9; Dalton Diary, 29 July 1952, p. 596.
68 PLP Executive Committee minutes, 28 July 1952 and PLP minutes, 29 July 1952.
69 PLP minutes, 29 July 1952; Crossman Diary, 1 August 1952, p. 129.
70 Crossman Diary, 1 August 1952, p. 129; PLP minutes, 29 July 1952. See also Dalton Diary, 29 July 1952, p. 596.
71 Dalton Diary, 29 July 1952, p. 596.
72 One again, most previous work has adopted this view. See, for example, Campbell, *Bevan*.
73 *1952 LPACR*, p. 87.
74 Ibid. See also NEC minutes, 15 September 1953.
75 NEC minutes, 15 September 1953; Crossman Diary, 16 September 1953, pp. 263–5.
76 *Tribune*, 11 September 1953.
77 NEC minutes, 15 September 1953; Crossman Diary, 16 September, pp. 264–5.
78 *1953 LPACR*, p. 151.
79 Ibid.
80 Ibid.
81 Ibid., p. 164.
82 Crossman Diary, 3 March 1954, p. 291.
83 LPA, Hugh Dalton Press Cuttings file, Dalton in the *Manchester Guardian*, 16 January 1954.
84 Ibid. See also PLP Executive Committee minutes, 16 February 1954.

85   PLP Executive Committee minutes, 16 February 1954; Crossman Diary, 3 March 1954.

86   PLP Executive Committee minutes, 16 February 1954.

87   Crossman Diary, 3 March 1954, pp. 290–1; NEC International Sub-Committee minutes, 16 February 1954.

88   NEC International Sub-Committee minutes, 16 February 1954; PLP minutes, 23 February 1954.

89   PLP minutes, 23 February 1954; Crossman Diary, 3 March 1954, p. 292.

90   PLP minutes, 23 February 1954; Crossman Diary, 3 March 1954, p. 292; B. Donoghue and G. W. Jones, *Herbert Morrison: Portrait of a Politician* (1973), p. 530.

91   NEC minutes, 24 February 1954; Crossman Diary, 3 March 1954, pp. 292–3. Cooper was Chairman of the National Union of General and Municipal Workers, and Gooch was President of the National Union of Agricultural Workers.

92   Crossman Diary, 3 March 1954, pp. 292–3; NEC minutes, 24 February 1954.

93   Bevan et al, *It Need Not Happen*.

94   Ibid.

95   Ibid.

96   He did take a rather more positive view of German Jews, however.

97   NEC International Sub-Committee minutes, 21 September 1954; NEC minutes, 22 September 1954.

98   *1954 LPACR*, pp. 92–4.

99   See debate, *1954 LPACR*, pp. 92–108. The Conference did witness many speeches by those supportive of the resolution, most notably Morrison, George Brown, Deakin and Healey.

100 The result was 3,270,000 for the Executive, 3,022,000 against – *1954 LPACR*, p. 108. Even this was only secured when Attlee persuaded the Woodworker's Union to change its vote.

101 Dalton Diary, 14 November 1954, pp. 635–40. Callaghan intimated that he would resign with Dalton if necessary.

102 Dalton Diary, entry for '5 to 8 November', p. 635.

103 Ibid.

104 Dalton Diary, 14 November 1954, pp. 635–40.

105 Ibid.

106 Ibid.

107 Ibid; PLP Executive Committee minutes, 9 November 1954.

108 PLP Executive Committee minutes, 9 November 1954; Dalton Diary, 14 November, p. 638.

109 Dalton Diary, 14 November, p. 638; PLP Executive Committee minutes, 9 November 1954.

110 Dalton Diary, 14 November 1954, pp. 638–9.

111 Ibid; PLP Executive Committee minutes, 9 November 1954.

112 PLP Executive Committee minutes, 9 November 1954; Dalton Diary, 14 November 1954, pp. 638–9.

113 PLP minutes, 10 and 11 November 1954; Dalton Diary, 14 November 1954, p. 639; Crossman Diary, 11 November 1954, pp. 362–3.

114 Dalton Diary, 14 November 1954, pp. 639–40.

115 Ibid; Crossman Diary, 22 November 1954, pp. 365–9.

116 Dalton Diary, entry for 'Christmas 1954', p. 641.
117 Lord Callaghan, in correspondence with the author.
118 Indeed, the official biography, K. O. Morgan, *Callaghan: A Life* (Oxford, 1997), omits any reference to his Daltonian activities.
119 Lord Callaghan, in correspondence with the author.

Chapter 7

1 *Trades Union Congress Annual Report*, 1961, pp. 313–14.
2 L. Black, *The Political Culture of the Left in Affluent Britain, 1951–64* (Basingstoke, 2003), pp. 189–90. Related arguments are advanced in, for example, N. Tiratsoo, 'Popular politics, affluence and the Labour Party in the 1950s', in A. Gorst, L. Johnman and W. Scott Lucas (eds.), *Contemporary British History 1931–61: Politics and the Limits of Policy* (1991), pp. 44–61; and I. Zweiniger-Bargielowska, *Austerity in Britain: Rationing, Controls and Consumption, 1939–1955* (Oxford, 2000).
3 S. Schwarzkopf, 'They do it with Mirrors: Advertising and British Cold War Consumer Politics', *Contemporary British History*, 19, 2 (2005), pp. 133–50 at p. 134.
4 This is not, of course, to say that the relationship between these issues has gone entirely unidentified, or that no-one has ever said anything worthwhile about it. Ben Pimlott's analysis of Wilson's 1963 conference speech is one example of insightful analysis: *Harold Wilson* (1992), pp. 302–5.
5 Some preliminary suggestions were made in R. Toye, 'The forgotten revisionist: Douglas Jay and Britain's transition to affluence, 1951–64', in L. Black and H. Pemberton (eds.), *An Affluent Society? Britain's Post-War 'Golden Age' Revisited* (Aldershot, 2004), pp. 53–67, and in a paper given at the 'Labour and the Wider World' conference, Anglia Ruskin University, in July 2004. Key aspects of the discourse are explored in depth in N. Lawton, 'The Cold War and the Labour Party: Political Thought and Policy c. 1959 to the 1964 General Election', unpublished M. Phil thesis, University of Cambridge, 2005, on which this chapter draws in part.
6 Balogh also pressed his ideas on Gaitskell, and although it is doubtful he can be counted as a major direct influence on him, there were some similarities in the two men's views on the EEC, as will be seen below. See the correspondence in the Hugh Gaitskell Papers, University College, London, C 281.
7 Quoted in D. Acheson, *Present At The Creation: My Years in the State Department* (New York, 1969), p. 222.
8 A. L. Hamby, *Man of the People: A Life of Harry S. Truman* (Oxford, 1995), p. 509.
9 *Hansard, House of Commons*, 5th series, vol. 474, 19 April 1950, col. 203.
10 Ibid., 21 April 1950, col. 517.
11 H. Wilson, *The War on World Poverty: An Appeal to the Conscience of Mankind* (1953), p. 10.
12 *Hansard, House of Commons*, 5th series, vol. 486, 10 April 1951, col. 867.
13 Ibid., vol. 487, 23 April 1951, cols. 37–9.
14 This was a consequence of the power struggle that followed Stalin's death. Khrushchev, who was General Secretary by 1953, and Soviet Prime Minister Georgy Malenkov, both spoke about more 'peaceful' relations with the West.
15 See J. Toye and R. Toye, *The UN and Global Political Economy* (Bloomington, Indiana, 2004), pp. 163–5; and A. Z. Rubinstein, *The Soviets in International*

Organizations: Changing Policy Toward Developing Countries, 1953–1963 (Princeton, New Jersey, 1964).

16   S. E. Reid, 'The Khrushchev Kitchen: Domesticating the Scientific-Technological Revolution', *Journal of Contemporary History*, 40, 2 (2005), pp. 289–316; C. Matthews, *Kennedy & Nixon: The Rivalry That Shaped Postwar America* (New York, 1996), p. 125.

17   'Extract from speech to be given by The Rt. Hon. Harold Wilson, M.P., at Prescot, Lancashire, on Sunday evening, 18th October, 1953', Bodleian Library, Oxford, Harold Wilson Papers, MS Wilson c.1111 ff. 149–50. Wilson also stressed, in a pamphlet on 'social enterprise' published the following month, the need for Britain to 'assume the moral leadership of the world': *Social Ownership in Britain's Fight for Independence*, Co-operative Co-partnership Propaganda Committee, n.p., 28 November 1953, p. 14 , copy in MS Wilson c. 1111, ff. 211–220.

18   It is worth noting, though, that earlier in 1953 he had counselled against treating the promotion of economic development as a 'gimmick' in the Cold War. He argued that 'the war on world poverty will be a limited campaign unless we can persuade the Soviet people to march with us – as co-belligerents if not as allies'. Wilson, *War*, pp. 24–5.

19   Pimlott, *Harold Wilson*, p. 198.

20   T. Balogh, 'The Political Economy of the Cold War', in T. E. M. McKitterick and K. Younger (eds.), *Fabian International Essays* (1957), pp. 41–77 at p. 46.

21   See P. R. Gregory, and R. C. Stuart, *Russian and Soviet Economic Performance and Structure*, Sixth Edition, (Reading, Mass., 1997), pp. 225–7. We are grateful to Nick Baron for this reference.

22   R. H. S. Crossman, 'The Spectre of Revisionism: A reply to Crosland', *Encounter*, 14, 4 (April 1960).

23   J. Tomlinson, *The Labour Governments 1964–70, Vol. 3: Economic Policy* (Manchester, 2004), p. 71.

24   Toye, 'The Forgotten Revisionist', p. 58.

25   R. Winstone, (ed.), *Tony Benn: Years of Hope: Diaries, Letters and Papers 1940–1962* (1994), p. 351 (entry for 21 October 1960). Interestingly, Crossman noted 'Tony Benn is obviously in much the same mind as I was after my visit to Russia-China. Never much interested in public ownership before, he at last sees the point of it and he is now discussing quite openly how to get rid of Hugh': J. Morgan, (ed.), *The Backbench Diaries of Richard Crossman* (1981), p. 874 (entry for 20 September 1960).

26   *Hansard, House of Commons*, 5th Series, vol. 493, col. 348, 8 November 1951.

27   F. W. S. Craig, (ed.), *British General Election Manifestos 1918–1966* (Chichester, 1970), pp. 177, 180.

28   Balogh, 'Political Economy', p. 76.

29   C. A. R. Crosland, *The Future of Socialism* (1956), pp. 381–4.

30   K. Jefferys, *Anthony Crosland: A New Biography* (1999), p. 63.

31   H. Gaitskell, 'Economic Challenge to Freedom', 12–17 September 1955 (contribution to Milan Conference on 'The Future for Freedom'), Gaitskell papers, D11.1.

32   H. Gaitskell, *The Challenge of Coexistence* (1957), pp. 67, 73, 78–9.

33   Craig, *Manifestos*, pp. 197, 205–6.

34   J. Tomlinson, 'Inventing "decline": the falling behind of the British economy in the postwar years', *Economic History Review*, 49, 4 (1996), pp. 731–57.

35   H. Pemberton, 'Affluence, Relative Decline and the Treasury', in Black and Pemberton (eds.), *An Affluent Society?*, pp. 107–27 at p. 113.

36   See his comments in the preface to the 1962 Pelican edition of J. K. Galbraith, *The Affluent Society* (Harmondsworth, 1962), p. 10. See also R. Parker, *John Kenneth Galbraith: His Life, His Politics, His Economics*, (New York, 2005), ch. 14. It should be noted, though, that Galbraith thought that rapid Soviet growth was a function of the 'demonstrative effect' of the USA, and hence it would slow down as it approached parity. J. K. Galbraith, *The Liberal Hour* (1960), p. 22.

37   C. A. R. Crosland, *The Conservative Enemy: A Programme of Reform for the 1960s* (1962), p. 103.

38   Crossman's favourable verdict is recorded on the back of the 1962 Pelican edition of the book.

39   T. Balogh, 'On from Keynes', *New Statesman*, 4 October 1958.

40   M. Shanks, *The Stagnant Society* (Harmondsworth, 1961), pp. 16–17.

41   *Labour Party Annual Conference Report* (henceforward *LPACR*), 1959, p. 153.

42   Quoted in B. Brivati, 'Internationalism', in R. Plant, M. Beech and K. Hickson (eds.), *The Struggle for Labour's Soul: Understanding Labour's political thought since 1945* (2004), pp. 229–44 at p. 238.

43   C. A. R. Crosland, 'The Future of the Left', *Encounter*, 14, 3 (March 1960).

44   Crossman, 'Spectre of Revisionism'. Crossman noted elsewhere that he owed a debt to Balogh's ideas: R. H. S. Crossman, *Labour in the Affluent Society* (1960), p. 17 n.

45   Crossman, *Labour in the Affluent Society*, pp. 1–9. As an argument in support of retaining Clause IV, he suggested that when the crisis came, Labour without the Clause would haemorrhage support to the Communist Party of Great Britain. This was, perhaps, a trifle implausible.

46   R. H. S. Crossman, 'Secret Decisions' (review of C. P. Snow, *Science and Government*), *Encounter*, June 1961.

47   Balogh, 'Political Economy' pp. 43–4.

48   Crosland, *Conservative Enemy*, p. 129.

49   Morgan, *Backbench Diaries*, p. 839 (entry for 3 May 1960).

50   See R. Toye, The *Labour Party and the Planned Economy, 1931–1951* (2003), pp. 36–8.

51   Schwarzkopf, 'They do it with Mirrors', pp. 135–6.

52   Crossman, *Labour in the Affluent Society*, p. 9.

53   This seems very clear, as the 'Cold War-affluence' discourse was heightened at times of internal party wrangling (e.g. 1951 and 1959), but became rather subdued as Labour's programme settled (e.g. 1963–4).

54   S. Fielding, '"White Heat" and white collars: the evolution of "Wilsonism"', in R. Coopey, S. Fielding, and N. Tiratsoo (eds.), *The Wilson Governments, 1964–70* (1993), p. 38.

55   Crossman and Wilson certainly were involved. See N. J. Vig, *Science and Technology in British Politics* (1968), p. 82, and Morgan, *Backbench Diaries*, pp. 868, 954.

56   Fielding, '"White Heat"', p. 38.

57   Labour Party, *Labour in the Sixties* (1960), p. 7, emphasis added.

58   Ibid., pp. 7–8.

59   Ibid., p. 17.

60   R. Clements, 'Death Knell of Revisionism?', *Tribune*, 12 August 1960. See also I. Mikardo, 'Why does Morgan's Testament frighten the leadership?', *Tribune*, 23 September 1960.

61   I. Favretto, 'Wilsonism Reconsidered: Labour Party Revisionism 1952–64', *Contemporary British History*, 14, 4 (2000), pp. 54–80 at p. 57. Like Favretto, Tomlinson correctly emphasises the growing importance of the concept of planning during the very early 1960s: *Labour Governments Vol. 3*, p. 73. See also Pimlott, *Harold Wilson*, p. 272.

62   Wilson was elected chairman on 7 November 1960. At the next NEC meeting, on 23 November, it was noted that the policy papers that were to follow *Labour in the Sixties* should now be produced. NEC Minutes, 7 & 23 November 1960), Labour Party Archive, Labour History Archive and Study Centre, Manchester. For the document's authorship, in which Crossman and Wilson seem again to have played major parts, with Gaitskell proposing amendments, see N. Ellison, *Egalitarian Thought and Labour Politics* (1994), p. 63; P. Ziegler, *Wilson: The Authorised Life of Lord Wilson of Rievaulx* (1993), p. 112; A. Howard, *Richard Crossman: The Pursuit of Power* (1990), p. 239; Morgan, *Backbench Diaries*, pp. 952–4 (entry for 28 June 1961).

63   *Signposts*, p. 7.

64   Labour Party, *Science and the Future of Britain* (1961), pp. 8, 20. See also H. Wilson, 'A Four Year Plan for Britain', *New Statesman*, 24 March 1961, pp. 462–8.

65   Elements of this view had been in circulation for some time. Consider, for example, Denis Healey's assertion that 'the European economies are largely competitive rather than complementary . . . In too many fields the European countries have soft high cost economies.' This was in his essay 'Beyond Power Politics', in McKitterick and Younger, *Fabian International Essays*, pp. 195–219 at p. 207.

66   See, for example, T. Balogh, 'The Alternative to the Common Market', 3 December 1962, Common Market Alternatives Committee (November–December 1962), Labour Party Archives, Labour History Archive and Study Centre, Manchester.

67   'Attlee on the Common Market', *Tribune*, 11 August 1961.

68   *Hansard, House of Commons*, 5th Series, vol. 645, 3 August 1961, cols. 1664, 1669.

69   Labour Party, *Africa Today* (1960), p. 23.

70   P. Ignotus, 'Lessons from Britain', *Socialist Commentary*, January 1964.

71   *LPACR*, 1962, p. 161.

72   B. Brivati, *Hugh Gaitskell* (1996), p. 414.

73   For the latter, see Tomlinson, *Labour Governments 1964–70*, p. 23.

74   *LPACR*, 1963, pp. 135, 137, 140–1.

75   H. Wilson, *The New Britain: – Labour's Plan: Selected Speeches* (Harmondsworth, 1964), p. 42.

76   Broadcast of 12 October 1964, Master File of Speeches, Secretary's Papers, 1964 General Election Boxes, Miscellaneous Correspondence, Labour Party Archives.

77   A. Howard and R. West, *The Making of the Prime Minister* (1965), p. 121.

78   Wilson, *New Britain*, p. 97.

79   H. Wilson, *The Relevance of British Socialism* (1964), p. 109. This success in

tackling domestic Communism, he believed, had been a consequence of the Attlee government's social and economic reforms, and he thought that this lesson should be applied internationally. In other words, this was a way in which Britain had demonstrated international moral leadership. The point was similar to that made by Bevan in his 1951 resignation statement.

80   Fielding, '"White Heat"', p. 43.

81   D. Butler and A. King, *The British General Election of 1964* (1965), p. 70; Howard and West, *Making of the Prime Minister*, p. 128; D. Butler and D. Stokes, *Political Change in Britain: Forces Shaping Electoral Choice* (1969), p. 483.

82   Howard and West, *Making of the Prime Minister*, p. 123.

83   T. Benn, *Out of the Wilderness: Diaries 1963–67* (1987), pp. 92–3, 99 (entries for 6 February and 18 March 1964). Wilson had previously told Patrick Gordon Walker: 'We could not win elections here [on foreign affairs], but could lose them.' R. Pearce, (ed.), *Patrick Gordon Walker: Political Diaries 1932–71* (1991), p. 278 (entry for 20 February 1963).

84   Butler and King, *General Election*, p. 129.

85   'Private and Confidential: General Election 1964. Final Report by the General Secretary', and 'Questionnaire to Parliamentary candidates', Secretary's Papers, 1964 General Election Boxes, Miscellaneous Correspondence, Labour Party Archives.

86   Butler and King, *General Election*, p. 132.

87   'Seize Chances To Expand Production, Mr. Wilson tells the T.U.C. Delegates', *The Times*, 8 September 1964.

88   G. Cunningham, 'Background Paper: The Commonwealth', 16 September 1964, Secretary's Papers, 1964 General Election Boxes, Miscellaneous Correspondence, Labour Party Archives; Tomlinson, *Labour Governments*, pp. 23–4.

89   Tomlinson, 'Inventing decline', p. 734.

90   Wilson, *Relevance*, pp. 42–3.

91   See D. Seers and P. Streeten, 'Overseas development policies', in W. Beckerman (ed.), *The Labour Government's Economic Record: 1964–70* (1972), pp. 118–56.

92   *LPACR*, 1963, p. 139.

Chapter 8

1   I would like to thank the participants at the 'Labour and the Wider World' conference, held in Cambridge in July 2004 for commenting on an earlier version of this chapter. I would also like to thank Dr Alan Sked of the London School of Economics for the opportunity to present the paper at the Departmental Research Seminar, International History Department, at LSE in February 2006. Finally, I wish to thank Dr Alastair Reid of Girton College, Cambridge for his comments.

2   B. Pimlott, *Harold Wilson* (1992), p. 59.

3   Ibid., p. 513; A. Marwick, *The Sixties: Cultural Revolution in Britain, France, Italy and the United States, c.1958–c.1974* (Oxford, 1998), p. 555.

4   See Marwick, *The Sixties*, for the most comprehensive survey of student life in 1960s' Britain. Information on British students travelling to Paris in May 1968 was supplied by my former colleague at Queen's University Belfast, Mr Peter Blair (a student at LSE at the time).

5   Marwick, *The Sixties*, p. 555; K. Morgan, *The People's Peace: British History since 1945* (2nd edition, Oxford, 1999), pp. 240–1.

6   There is a huge secondary literature on '1968', but for background see W. J. Rorabaugh, *Berkeley at War: the 1960s* (Oxford, 1989); Marwick, *The Sixties*,

258   THE BRITISH LABOUR PARTY AND THE WIDER WORLD

ch. 12; C. Fink et al (eds.), *1968: the World Transformed* (Cambridge, 1998); and
R. Fraser, *1968: a Student Generation in Revolt* (New York, 1988).

7   Cited in A. Morgan, *Harold Wilson* (1992), pp. 336–7.

8   Benn's involvement in the Bristol University students' 'sit-in' is mentioned in
Morgan, *Wilson*, p. 337; Wilson quotation cited in S. Fielding, *Labour and
Cultural Change* (Manchester, 2003), p. 228 n. 52.

9   Morgan, *Wilson*, p. 336.

10 T. Ali, *Street Fighting Years: an Autobiography of the Sixties* (1987), pp. 227–8.

11 Morgan, *People's Peace*, p. 297.

12 This was the most commonly-used nickname he was given in the British press
of the period. Even the broadsheets adopted the term. See, for example, *Daily
Telegraph*, 15 June 1968, p. 13; *The Observer*, 12 May 1968, p. 1. See also *Daily
Mail*, 13 June 1968, p. 1. *The London Evening Standard* ran a cartoon of Cohn-
Bendit, known in France as 'Danny le Rouge', mistaken by a BBC television
producer for Danny La Rue, a popular television drag artiste at the time. See
Evening Standard, 13 June 1968, p. 6.

13 Marwick's immensely rich and learned survey, *The Sixties*, entirely overlooks
Cohn-Bendit's visit to Britain in June 1968, as do Kenneth Morgan in *The
People's Peace* and Steven Fielding in *Labour and Cultural Change*. None of the
Wilson biographers mention it either. Fielding is the only other historian, it
appears, who has examined the Labour government's files on the student
protests. For his rather brief, but cogent, discussion of student protests in
Britain see Fielding, *Labour and Cultural Change*, pp. 177–80.

14 Callaghan was severely criticised in the Commons debate on Cohn-Bendit for
extending his 24-hour visa (see below), and told Parliament he had warmed to
the young Frenchman after meeting him. But later in the year, in October,
when Cohn-Bendit applied to visit Britain again Callaghan refused to allow
him back into the country. The proposed visit just happened to coincide with
a large anti-Vietnam demonstration through London and Callaghan felt it was
not safe to allow Cohn-Bendit to join this protest. See J. Callaghan, *Time and
Chance* (1987), p. 259.

15 It is very clear from government records that Special Branch monitored student
protest in Britain during the late sixties, but exactly how, where, when and
with what results are not easy to determine. It was claimed in the press that
Special Branch officers accompanied Daniel Cohn-Bendit to the BBC television
studios during his visit to Britain; see *Daily Mail*, 13 June 1968, p. 1. There
are also in existence Special Branch reports on 'student militancy' covering
these years; but, frustratingly, they have been 'Temporarily retained by the
Department (i.e. The Home Office)'. See National Archives, Kew, HO 325/12/
(hereafter HO etc.). Several foreign students studying in London claimed that
Special Branch tried to recruit them to spy on radical students at British
universities. See *Daily Express*, 19 June 1968, p. 9.

16 R. Dahrendorf, *LSE: A History of the London School of Economics and Political
Science, 1895–1995* (Oxford, 1995), p. 456.

17 C. Crouch, *The Student Revolt* (1970), p. 109.

18 Morgan summarises the impact of student protest in Britain in 1968 thus in
The People's Peace, pp. 354–5: 'The student revolts of the 1968 period had been
transient affairs, with only a limited impact beyond the narrow, cloistered
confines of the universities.'

19   D. Rossinow, *The Politics of Authenticity: Liberalism, Christianity and the New Left in America* (New York, 1998).

20   Ibid. This immensely scholarly book deals in detail with the travels American students undertook to preach social revolution (mostly across America); but he does not deal at all with the large numbers of American students who travelled to Britain and Europe to study and therefore with the cultural networks between British and American campuses.

21   Dahrendorf, *LSE*, p. 456.

22   The programme was discussed in all the leading national newspapers – *The Times*, *The Guardian*, *The Daily Telegraph*, *The Daily Mail*, *The Daily Express* and *The Daily Mirror*, to name all of those consulted.

23   See *The Sunday Times*, 26 May 1968, pp. 1, 7, for the background to the Paris students' revolt, which includes details of Cohn-Bendit's confrontation with the French Minister for Youth, Francois Missoffe (who had written a book on French youth) during the minister's visit to Nanterre. As the minister stepped from his car, Cohn-Bendit addressed him thus: 'M. Missoffe, I have read your book. I don't altogether agree with you on some points.' He went on: 'There is nothing in it, from beginning to end, about the sexual problems of French youth.' The minister tried a put-down: 'I remember when I was young. In my day . . . it was better to go to the swimming pool to solve these problems.' Events quickly overtook the minister, however, who was eventually forced to resign, while Cohn-Bendit became the spokesman for the entire Paris student body of over 30,000 students.

24   *The Sunday Times*, 26 May 1968, pp. 7–8; *The Observer*, 12 May 1968, p. 1; *The Observer*, 19 May 1968, p. 2.

25   Two of *The Observer*'s reporters, Patrick Seale and Maureen McConville, heard Cohn-Bendit give speeches in Paris during May 1968 and praised him highly as 'a born leader, a mob orator of real talent'. *The Observer*, 19 May 1968, p. 2. Dr Robert Boyce of the Department of International History at LSE, who also heard Cohn-Bendit speak in Paris during May 1968, confirmed that he was a gifted speaker and a real intellectual. (Information from Dr Robert Boyce, February 2006). For Cohn-Bendit's fluent command of several languages see *The Times*, 29 May 1968, p. 1. For his peripatetic existence during May 1968 see *Daily Telegraph*, 25 May 1968, p. 22. For Cohn-Bendit's speech at the Odeon cinema in Paris see *Daily Telegraph*, 27 May 1968, p. 10.

26   The following details are taken from an analysis of the British newspaper coverage of the student protests during May and June 1968. The newspapers consulted were: *The Times*, *The Guardian*, *The Daily Telegraph*, *The Daily Mail*, *The Daily Express*, *The Daily Mirror*, *The Sunday Times*, *The Sunday Telegraph* and *The London Evening Standard*.

27   The event took place on 17 June 1968.

28   Around 100 students at Bristol launched the 'Free University', out of a student population of 2000 – a tiny proportion (5% of the total). See *The Times*, 11 June 1968, p. 10.

29   The Free University movement in Cambridge, Simon Hoggart's role and his father, Richard Hoggart's, reactions to student protest movements of the late 1960s are discussed at greater length in D. Fowler, 'From Juke Box Boys to Revolting Students: Richard Hoggart and the Study of British Youth Culture', *International Journal of Cultural Studies*, 10, 1 (2007), pp. 73–84.

30   There is a good discussion of the Cambridge protest in *The Times*, 7 June 1968, p. 3.

31   *The Times*, 12 June 1968, p. 11 (Elton); *The Times*, 10 June 1968, p. 9 (Frend); *The Times*, 13 June 1968, p. 11 (response from a Fellow of Darwin College, Cambridge); *The Times*, 12 June 1968, p. 11 (response from an Oxford don at Hertford College, Oxford).

32   See *The Times*, 12 June 1968, p. 11, for the following details.

33   The concept of 'student power' was widely publicised in Britain with the publication of a collection of essays by radical students in 1969. See A. Cockburn and R. Blackburn (eds.), *Student Power: Problems, Diagnosis, Action* (1969).

34   *The Times*, 7 June 1968, p. 3; *The Times*, 10 June 1968, p. 9.

35   *The Times*, 3 June 1968, p. 7. In his letter to *The Times*, Rowthorn described the Cambridge students' demands as 'student power'; a full year before the publication of the Penguin volume *Student Power*. For Lord Ashby's views of Cambridge students see *The Times*, 30 May 1968, p. 2.

36   *The Times*, 12 June 1968, p. 1.

37   Ibid. See also *Daily Telegraph*, 25 May 1968, p. 22; *Daily Telegraph*, 30 May 1968, p. 27.

38   *The Times*, 13 June 1968, p. 1.

39   Callaghan, *Time and Chance*.

40   *The Times*, 13 June 1968, p. 10.

41   *The Daily Mail* reported that 'in private Mr Callaghan, Home Secretary, is seething'; the reason being that the BBC had not told him about the visit. See *Daily Mail*, 14 June 1968, p. 2.

42   *The Times*, 28 May 1968, p. 1.

43   Ibid.

44   All the broadsheets carried profiles of Cohn-Bendit during May and June 1968, but see especially the series of articles in *The Times* by Richard Davey, published in late May 1968.

45   The idea for the 'Students in Revolt' programme seems to have been dreamed up by its colourful and 'with-it' producer Anthony Smith, who, as well as being a BBC producer, was also a balloonist and a zoologist. On the day of the broadcast, it was noticed that he wore an exotic shirt. See *The Guardian*, 13 June 1968, p. 20. For biographical details see *The Times*, 13 June 1968, p. 10. For Smith's own account of the experience see *The Listener*, 20 June 1968, pp. 806–7.

46   See *The Times*, 29 May 1968, p. 1; *The Times*, 12 June 1968, p. 1; *The Times*, 13 June 1968, p. 1.

47   Throughout, *The Times'* coverage of Cohn-Bendit was portentous; hinting at the fact that he might be a very dangerous subversive indeed. For example, it reported his comment to an English reporter: 'The Wilson Government is not doing too well in England, is it? Perhaps you will have a revolutionary movement there . . . very soon.': *The Times*, 29 May 1968, p. 1. The paper's sinister use of the phrase 'Herr Cohn-Bendit' to scare its readers has been noted above. Some of its readers did not like this criminalising of Cohn-Bendit, and among these was the Oxford Philosophy don Iris Murdoch: 'Sir', she wrote in to the paper, 'Danny Cohn-Bendit is not a criminal, and what he has to say, whether we agree with it or not, is interesting and important.' Iris Murdoch, letter, *The Times*, 18 June 1968, p. 9. Interestingly, it was *The Daily Telegraph*

that revealed Cohn-Bendit to be the son of a German Jew. See *Daily Telegraph*, 25 May 1968, p. 22. *The Times* neglected to mention that, though holding a German passport, he had spent most of his life in France and the fact that his father was a German Jew. See *The Times*, 29 May 1968, p. 1.

48 *The Times*, 12 June 1968, p. 1.

49 Ibid. See also *Daily Telegraph*, 12 June 1968, p. 1; *The Guardian*, 12 June 1968, p. 1.

50 For Davy's detailed description of the party see *The Times*, 13 June 1968, p. 10. For the guests see *The Guardian*, 13 June 1968, p. 10.

51 *The Times*, 13 June 1968, p. 10.

52 Ibid.

53 Ibid.

54 Ibid.

55 Ibid. See also *The Guardian*, 13 June 1968, p. 20.

56 *The Times*, 13 June 1968, p. 10.

57 Ibid. During the trip to Highgate Cemetery Cohn-Bendit and his fellow students were accidentally locked in the cemetery – not with any malicious intent it seems. See *The Guardian*, 13 June 1968, p. 20.

58 *Evening Standard*, 13 June 1968, p. 1.

59 See note 22 above.

60 Until the Special Branch and Home Office papers on Cohn-Bendit's visit are released, we will not know the precise facts. The pressure to allow him to stay was exerted on the Home Office by Anthony Smith of the BBC; the National Council for Civil Liberties was also involved in the discussions with the Home Office, along with two senior Labour MPs Lord Brockway and Eric Lubbock. Smith conducted his part of the discussions by 'phone; Dr Zander of LSE attended the Home Office in person on behalf of Cohn-Bendit. Callaghan, the Home Secretary, made the final decision just before Cohn-Bendit's visa was about to expire. See *Evening Standard*, 13 June 1968, p. 1.

61 *The Times*, 14 June 1968, p. 7.

62 *The Times*, 13 June 1968, p. 10, on the participants and their countries. For comments on the student discussion see *Daily Telegraph*, 14 June 1968, p. 36; *The Guardian*, 14 June 1968, p. 10. Apparently, the BBC's Chairman of Governors had a meeting with the BBC's Director General Sir Hugh Greene about Cohn-Bendit on 13 June, before the programme was shown. Greene had watched the programme himself and 'approved it'. The BBC then issued a statement to the press defending their decision to show it. See *Daily Mail*, 14 June 1968, p. 1.

63 *Daily Telegraph*, 24 June 1968, p. 15.

64 *The Guardian*, 14 June 1968, p. 10.

65 Ibid.

66 Tariq Ali was not technically a student at all in 1968, but a journalist. Another of the 'students' who appeared on the programme had a Ph.D., Dr Krippendorf of Germany. For one television critic, the Japanese student also looked mature beyond his years: 'If still a student Mr Ishii from Japan must, to judge from appearances, have started his academic career in the reign of the Emperor Meiji.' See *The Listener*, 20 June 1968, p. 814.

67 See *The Times*, 20 June 1968, pp. 3, 8, for a summary of the House of Lords' debate (which took place on 19 June from 2.30pm to 10.20pm).

68   Reported in *The Times*, 14 June 1968, p. 6.

69   Ibid.

70   *House of Commons Debates*, Fifth Series, vol. 766, session 1967–8, June 1968, cols. 438–9.

71   *House of Lords Debates*, Fifth Series, vol. 293, session 1967–8, June 1968, cols. 215–28; *House of Commons Debates*, Fifth Series, vol. 766, session 1967–8, June 1968, cols. 104–5.

72   *The Guardian*, 15 June 1968, p. 3.

73   Ibid., 13 June 1968, p. 1.

74   *The Times*, 13 June 1968, p. 1

75   Reported ibid.

76   *The Times*, 14 June 1968, p. 1; *Daily Telegraph*, 15 June 1968, p. 13.

77   *Daily Telegraph*, 15 June 1968, p. 13.

78   Ibid. See also *Daily Telegraph*, 17 June 1968, p. 13.

79   *The Times*, 14 June 1968, p. 6.

80   Ibid.

81   Ibid.

82   *The Times*, 13 June 1968, p. 10.

83   Editorial, *Daily Telegraph*, 13 June 1968, p. 18.

84   See below for an assessment of Marcuse's impact on British students of the late 1960s.

85   CAB151/67, Notes on 'Youth', Office of the Minister without Portfolio, 3 February 1970.

86   CAB151/67, Extract from *House of Commons Debates*, 21 November 1968, cols. 1526–7.

87   CAB151/66, Extract from *House of Commons Debates*, 10 February 1969, cols. 856–7.

88   The best discussion of the LSE 'Troubles', 1967–1969, is in H. Kidd, *The Trouble at LSE, 1966–1967* (Oxford, 1969), *passim* and Dahrendorf, *LSE*.

89   Short's speech on LSE students, delivered on 29 January 1969 in the House of Commons, was a provocative account of the subversive influence of foreign students in British universities of the period. It is mentioned in Fielding, *Labour and Cultural Change*, pp. 179–80. Short was pointing the finger, largely, at the American students studying at LSE. The Home Office, meanwhile, was investigating whether they could expel foreign students involved in the LSE dispute from Britain: 'we will examine individually those aliens against whom the LSE have obtained an injunction in the High Court'. See HO325/126, Note on Students at LSE, 31 January 1969. Not all of these 'aliens' who had been banned from LSE were Americans; indeed not even a majority were. Thirteen students were banned from using LSE after the 'Gates' incident. Of these, six were British students, three were Americans, two were South Africans, one was an Australian and one was Italian. HO325/126, Notes on Student Leaders in 1968–1969, n.d. 1969? Altogether, 35 students at LSE were arrested in January 1969 over the 'Gates' incident and the government's statistics make clear that only three were American. The vast majority were British. See HO325/126, Metropolitan Police to Home Office, 21 March 1969. In effect, therefore, Edward Short was not only exaggerating the disruptive role of American and 'alien' students at LSE, but seriously distorting it.

90   The Prime Minister seems to have abolished the post of Minister of Youth in

November 1969. See CAB151/67, R. Jardine to 'Minister without Portfolio', 3 November 1969.

91 CAB151/67, extract from *Birmingham Post* (n.d., October 1968?); Judith Hart to Birmingham Settlement, 23 October 1968.

92 CAB151/67, Judith Hart to Birmingham Settlement, 23 October 1968.

93 The following quotations are from newspaper extracts, all presumably November 1968, in CAB151/67.

94 Ibid.

95 *The Daily Express and Star*, 7 November 1968.

96 CAB151/67, newspaper extracts, November 1968.

97 Much of the material is in the following files: CAB151/66; CAB151/67; FCO68/128; HO325/46; HO325/126; HO325/128; HO325/129; CO1045/858.

98 CAB151/67, Office of the Minister without Portfolio, Notes on Youth, 3 February 1970.

99 The statistics on student numbers are in CAB151/67. Senior civil servants' reflections on the scale and nature of student protest in Britain are dispersed across the files cited in note 97. Separate files were kept on student protest in Northern Ireland; and in the Republic of Ireland. See HO325/48, HO221/146, CJ3/30, CJ3/41, CJ4/33 on Northern Ireland; FCO33/1198 on the Republic of Ireland.

100 On the Northern Irish political situation in 1969 see the brilliant discussion in J. J. Lee, *Ireland, 1912–1985: Politics and Society* (Cambridge, 1989), ch. 6.

101 See CAB151/66, Student Protest in 1968, typed report, October 1968, pp. 1–3, for the government figures.

102 CAB151/66, Student Protest in 1968, p. 3.

103 Ibid., pp. 3–5; Dahrendorf, *LSE, passim*.

104 On Marshall Bloom see Kidd, *Trouble at LSE, passim*, but especially pp. 121–2. Bloom, a graduate of Amherst College in the United States, was a graduate student at LSE and had been an active member of the 'New Left' in the United States before moving to Britain. On returning to the United States in 1969, he committed suicide. This is not mentioned in Crouch, *Student Revolt*, but discussed in T. Gitlin, *The Sixties: Years of Hope, Days of Rage* (New York, 1993).

105 The comment was made on Radio 4 during Cohn-Bendit's visit to Britain in June 1968. It is mentioned in *The Times*, 17 June 1968 and in Fielding, *Labour and Cultural Change*, p. 179 n. 87.

106 See note 104 above.

107 The author is currently undertaking further research on the cultural networks of British students and foreign students studying in Britain during the late 1960s.

108 CAB151/66, Student Protest in 1968, pp. 3–5.

109 See note 107 above.

110 FCO68/128, The Pattern of Unrest: Youth in Revolt, An International Report, 1969, p. 3.

111 CAB151/66, Extract from *Evening Standard*, 8 May 1968, cited in Student Protest in 1968, p. 5.

112 Ibid., pp. 5–6.

113 Ibid., p. 6.

114 Ibid., p. 10.

115 Ibid.

116 Ibid., pp. 10–11.

117   Ibid., p. 11.
118   CAB151/66, Student Protest in 1968–1969, February 1969, pp. 12–13.
119   Ibid.
120   CAB151/66, Note by R. Jardine, Student Protest, 10 April 1969; Student
      Protest in 1968, p. 4; FCO68/128, Student Protest, 1968–1969, September
      1969, p. 4.
121   CAB151/66, R. Jardine to Mr Isserlis, Student Protest, 10 April 1969.
122   Ibid. See also FCO68/128, Student Protest, 1968–1969, p. 4.
123   Crouch, *Student Revolt*, ch. 6.
124   CAB151/66, University Students, April 1969; A.R. Isserlis to Paymaster
      General, 2 June 1969.
125   CAB151/66, A. R. Isserlis to Paymaster General, 17 April 1969.
126   FCO68/128, R. Jardine, Paymaster General's Office to the FCO, 15 September
      1969.
127   Ibid.
128   On the Labour Cabinet's discussions of youth votes see PREM13/2076; on
      Harold Wilson's response to the closure of LSE see PREM13/2787. It was only
      a short comment to his Education Secretary, Edward Short.
129   HO325/128 Prime Minister's Meeting with Vice Chancellors of Universities,
      15 April 1970.
130   FCO68/128 Parliamentary Conference, Trinidad and Tobago, 1969: Youth in
      Revolt.

Chapter 9

1   I would like to thank Hugo Frey and Paul Corthorn for their helpful comments
     and advice during the writing of this chapter.
2   J. Kampfner, *Blair's Wars* (2003), p. 61.
3   R. Cook, 'British Foreign Policy', 12 May 1997. *http://www.guardian.co.uk/print/
     0,3858,3811385–103547,00.html*
4   There are various works that examine the relationship between the British left
     and foreign policy. Some examples to consider are: D. Childs, 'The Cold War and
     the 'British Road', 1946–53', *Journal of Contemporary History*, 23 (1988)
     pp. 551–72; and P. Stansky (ed.), *The Left and War: The British Labour Party and
     World War I* (New York, 1969). For a European-wide analysis of left-of-centre
     political parties in the years since 1989, the following edited collection is useful,
     D. Sassoon (ed.), *Looking Left: European Socialism after the Cold War* (1997).
5   There is a wide variety of literature that deals with the history and development
     of the Labour Party. Selected examples include: A. J. Davies, *To Build a New
     Jerusalem* (1992); G. Foote, *The Labour Party's Political Thought: A History*
     (1997); K. Jefferys, *The Labour Party since 1945* (Basingstoke, 1993); E. Shaw,
     The Labour Party since 1945 (Oxford, 1996); and A. Thorpe, *A History of the
     British Labour Party* (Basingstoke, 1997).
6   Selected titles that study that Labour Party's response to specific foreign-policy
     issues and events include: J. F. Naylor, *Labour's International Policy: The Labour
     Party in the 1930s* (1969); J. Saville, *The Politics of Continuity: British Foreign
     Policy and the Labour Government 1945–46* (1993); and H. R. Winkler, *Paths Not
     Taken: British Labour and International Policy in the 1920s* (Chapel Hill, 1994).
7   The following titles examine the relationship between Labour's foreign policy
     and the principles that define a left-wing foreign policy: M. R. Gordon, *Conflict*

and Consensus in Labour's Foreign Policy 1914–1965 (Stanford, 1969); E. J. Meehan, *The British Left Wing and Foreign Policy: A Study of the Influence of Ideology* (New Brunswick, 1960); K. E. Miller, *Socialism and Foreign Policy: Theory and Practice in Britain to 1931* (The Hague, 1967).

8   The following edited collection provides a wide-ranging analysis of New Labour's foreign policy: R. Little and M. Wickham-Jones (eds.), *New Labour's Foreign Policy: A new moral crusade?* (Manchester, 2000).

9   For part of the period studied here, the *New Statesman* was known as the *New Statesman & Society*. However, for the purpose of this chapter it will be referred to throughout by its more familiar name, that is, the *New Statesman*.

10   These publications do not, of course, represent the left-wing press in its entirety.

11   Editors of *The Observer* 1991–2000: Donald Trelford (1975–1993); Jonathan Fenby (1993–1995); Andrew Jaspan (1995–1996); Will Hutton (1996–1998); and Roger Alton (1998–present day). Editors of *New Statesman* 1991–2000: Steve Platt (1991–1996); Ian Hargreaves (1996–1998); and Peter Wilby (1998–2005).

12   T. Blair, 'The doctrine of the international community' speech, Economic Club of Chicago, USA, 22 April 1999. *http://www.globalpolicy.org/globaliz/politics/blair.htm*; R. Cook, 'British Foreign Policy', 12 May 1997. *http://www.guardian.co.uk/print/0,3858,3811385–103547,00.html*

13   Brendan Simms gives a detailed assessment of British policy in the Balkans in *Unfinest Hour: Britain and the Destruction of Bosnia* (2001). For an analysis of the media coverage of the conflict in the Balkans see J. Gow, R. Paterson and A. Preston (eds.), *Bosnia by Television* (1996). Also, see J. Sanders Pearson, 'British press reactions to the on-set of war in ex-Yugoslavia', (Ph.D. dissertation, University of Cambridge, 2001).

14   After all, the much heralded 'foreign policy with an ethical dimension' was a key tenet of the party's approach to international relations following its successful election in 1997.

15   Anthony Seldon provides a detailed study of the events surrounding the NATO intervention against Serbia, and Blair's role in that policy, in his biography of the Prime Minister: A. Seldon, *Blair* (2005). Also, see Kampfner, *Blair's Wars*.

16   For the terms of this short exercise I will offer an impressionistic but comprehensive review of the editorials. I will not, on this occasion, develop a systematic media/socio-linguistic analysis. Instead, I take my lead broadly from the field of contemporary history. For example, see T. Garton Ash, *History of the Present: Essays, Sketches and Despatches from Europe in the 1990s* (1999).

17   Editorial, 'Balkan brink', *New Statesman & Society*, 9 August 1991, p. 5.

18   Editorial, 'Our dilemma in the Balkans', *The Observer*, 22 September 1991, p. 22.

19   Editorial, 'Balkan agony', *The Observer*, 9 February 1992, p. 24.

20   Editorial, 'Serbia must be stopped', *The Observer*, 17 May 1992, p. 20.

21   Editorial, 'Bosnian betrayal', *New Statesman & Society*, 17 July 1992, pp. 5–6.

22   Editorial, 'Give Serbs a taste of their own medicine', *The Observer*, 9 August 1992, p. 18.

23   Editorial, 'Time for the stick', *New Statesman & Society*, 23 April 1993, pp. 5–6.

24   Editorial, 'The "wimp that roared"', *New Statesman & Society*, 2 July 1993, p. 5.

25   Editorial, 'The Save Bosnia Appeal', *New Statesman & Society*, 3 September 1993, p. 5.

26   Editorial, 'Sarajevo needs relief not revenge', *The Observer*, 6 February 1994, p. 22.

27   Editorial, 'Vote for Bosnia', *New Statesman & Society*, 20 May 1994, p. 5.
28   Editorial, 'No time to give up on Bosnia', *The Observer*, 31 July 1994, p. 22.
29   Editorial, 'Stand up to the Serb bully', *The Observer*, 16 July 1995, p. 24.
30   Editorial, 'An unjust peace', *New Statesman & Society*, 1 December 1995, p. 5.
31   Editorial, 'Missing in action', *New Statesman & Society*, 4 September 1992, p. 5.
32   Michael Meacher, 'Last chance to tip the balance', *New Statesman & Society*, 20 November 1992, p. 12.
33   Editorial, 'Lessons of 1938', *New Statesman & Society*, 20 November 1992, pp. 5–6. At this time, the Shadow Foreign Secretary was Jack Cunningham.
34   Ibid.
35   Editorial, 'A pusillanimous response', *New Statesman & Society*, 22 April 1994, p. 4.
36   Operation Desert Fox against Iraq in December 1998 lasted for just three days.
37   There are plenty of references to the earlier conflict in Hansard. The following are just a few examples: Robin Cook, *Kosovo* (Official Report, Hansard, 10 March 1998) vol. 308, columns 320–1; Robin Cook, *Kosovo* (Official Report, Hansard, 19 October 1998) vol. 317, column 956; Mike Gapes (Ilford, South) and Robin Cook, *Oral Answers, Foreign Affairs, Kosovo* (Official Report, Hansard, 16 February 1999) vol. 325, columns 721–2).
38   Robin Cook, 'British Foreign Policy', 12 May 1997. *http://www.guardian.co.uk/print/0,3858,3811385–103547,00.html*
39   Selected work that explores the theme of foreign policy with an 'ethical dimension' includes: T. Dunne and N. J. Wheeler, 'Blair's Britain: a force for good in the world' in K. E. Smith and M. Light (eds.), *Ethics and Foreign Policy* (Cambridge, 2001); D. MacShane, 'New Labour, New Foreign Policy? A Labour Perspective', *Oxford International Review*, 9, 1 (Winter 1998–9) pp. 22–30; N. J. Wheeler and T. Dunne, 'Good international citizenship: a third way for British foreign policy', *International Affairs*, 74, 4 (1998) pp. 847–70; and M. Wickham-Jones, 'Labour's trajectory in foreign affairs: the moral crusade of a pivotal power?' and R. Vickers, 'Labour's search for a Third Way in foreign policy', both in Little and Wickham-Jones (eds.), *New Labour's Foreign Policy*.
40   R. Cook, 'British Foreign Policy', 12 May 1997. *http://www.guardian.co.uk/print/0,3858,3811385–103547,00.html*
41   Ibid.
42   Little and Wickham-Jones (eds.), *New Labour's Foreign Policy*, provides a far-reaching selection of studies concentrating on different elements of Labour's foreign policy.
43   Gordon, *Conflict and Consensus,* pp. 38–43.
44   T. Blair, 'The doctrine of the international community' speech, Economic Club of Chicago, USA, 22 April 1999. *http://www.globalpolicy.org/globaliz/politics/blair.htm*
45   Ibid.
46   Editorial, 'Give Serbs a taste of their own medicine', *The Observer*, 9 August 1992, p. 18, and Editorial, 'The Save Bosnia Appeal', *New Statesman & Society*, 3 September 1993, p. 5.
47   See, in particular, Editorial, 'Lessons of 1938', *New Statesman & Society*, 20 November 1992, pp. 5–6; Editorial, 'Appeasement 1993', *New Statesman & Society*, 28 May 1993, p. 5; Editorial, 'A pusillanimous response', *New Statesman & Society*, 22 April 1994, p. 4; and Editorial, 'Bosnia is a test of will', *The Observer*, 15 August 1993, p. 16.

48 Tony Blair, 'The doctrine of the international community' speech, Economic Club of Chicago, USA, 22 April 1999. *http://www.globalpolicy.org/globaliz/politics/blair.htm*

49 Interestingly, even Clare Short, who later spoke out against the war in Iraq, supported the NATO action. Indeed, at this time the Cabinet was united. See Kampfner, *Blair's Wars*, p. 47, for an analysis of the role played by Clare Short during the NATO campaign.

50 R. Cook, *Kosovo* (Official Report, Hansard, 10 March 1998) vol. 308, column 317.

51 Ibid.

52 The Contact Group comprised Great Britain, the USA, Russian Federation, France, Germany and Italy.

53 R. Cook, *Kosovo* (Official Report, Hansard, 10 March 1998) vol. 308, column 322.

54 Britain and France presented the Security Council with resolution 1199 in September 1998. It demanded that Milosevic cease fire, withdraw Serbian troops, allow the safe return of refugees, and begin negotiations on the political future of Kosovo. Richard Holbrooke was then sent to Belgrade by the Contact Group with the aim of getting an agreement to the Security Council resolution. See R. Cook, *Kosovo* (Official Report, Hansard, 19 October 1998) vol. 317, column 953.

55 R. Cook, *Kosovo* (Official Report, Hansard, 19 October 1998) vol. 317, column 953.

56 Ibid., columns 954–5.

57 R. Cook, *Foreign Affairs and Defence* (Official Report, Hansard, 27 November 1998) vol. 321, column 440.

58 George Robertson, *Foreign Affairs and Defence* (Official Report, Hansard, 27 November 1998) vol. 321, columns 508–9.

59 At Racak, more than 40 civilians of all ages were found shot in the head or neck. International observers said that none of the victims were wearing uniforms and that there was no evidence of fighting, clearly refuting Serbian claims of thwarting a terrorist operation.

60 R. Cook, *Kosovo* (Official Report, Hansard, 18 January 1999) vol. 323, columns 566–7.

61 Ibid., column 569.

62 Donald Anderson (Swansea, East), *Kosovo* (Official Report, Hansard, 18 January 1999) vol. 323, column 569.

63 Robin Cook, *Kosovo* (Official Report, Hansard, 18 January 1999) vol. 323, column 570.

64 Ibid., column 576.

65 *Kosovo* (Official Report, Hansard, 23 March 1999) vol. 328, columns 161–74.

66 Ibid. See Donald Anderson, column 166, Bruce George (Walsall, South), columns 166–7, Clive Soley (Ealing, Acton and Shepherd's Bush), columns 167–8, and David Winnick (Walsall, North), column 171–2.

67 Tony Benn (Chesterfield), *Kosovo* (Official Report, Hansard, 19 October 1998) vol. 317, columns 957–8.

68 See Tony Benn in *Kosovo* (Official Report, Hansard, 18 January 1999) vol. 323, column 571; *Kosovo* (Official Report, Hansard, 11 February 1999) vol. 325, column 568; *Kosovo* (Official Report, Hansard, 24 February 1999) vol. 326, columns 409–10; and *Kosovo* (Official Report, Hansard, 23 March 1999) vol. 328, columns 168–9.

69   Examples of Tam Dalyell's (Linlithgow and Falkirk East) interventions on
      Kosovo can be found in the following places: *Cardiff European Council* (Official
      Report, Hansard, 11 June 1998) vol. 313, columns 1273, 1282; and *Kosovo*
      (Official Report, Hansard, 24 February 1999) vol. 326, column 412.

70   There is obviously not the opportunity here to examine in depth the views of
      both *The Observer* and *New Statesman* with regard to the NATO action against
      Serbia. Analysis of both publications and their respective views on the
      situation could fill a chapter in its own right. However, broadly speaking,
      The Observer argued that the nature of intervention that had been undertaken
      was too little, too late. In contrast, the *New Statesman* despaired at the way
      that war had begun due to a point of principle with issues of practicality
      being put to one side (see Editorial, 'Think, before it's too late', *New
      Statesman*, 26 April 1999, p. 4). Essentially, the editorials offered a critique
      as to what was happening in the region but with differing ideas on how the
      situation could be improved.

Chapter 10

1   B. Woodward, *Plan of Attack* (2004), pp. 346–7. Similarly, there was no
     enthusiasm for having Bush visit London for fear of massive anti-war
     demonstrations. Ibid., p. 357.

2   R. McKibbin, 'Why Did He Risk It?' *London Review of Books*, 3 April 2003.
     http://www.lrb.co.uk/v25/n07/mcki01_.html

3   Lord Hutton, *Report of the Inquiry into the Circumstances Surrounding the Death of
     Dr David Kelly CMG* (HC 247, London, TSO, 2004); Lord Butler, *Review of
     Intelligence on Weapons of Mass Destruction: Report of a Committee of Privy Councillors*
     (HC 898, London, TSO, 2004), henceforward Butler Report.

4   J. Kampfner, *Blair's Wars* (2003), p. 14.

5   P. Norton, 'The Presidentialization of British Politics', *Government and
     Opposition*, Spring 2003, p. 277.

6   For the full statement, see C. Short, *An Honourable Deception? New Labour, Iraq,
     and the Misuse of Power* (2004), pp. 216–22.

7   Cited in J. Dumbrell, *A Special Relationship: Anglo-American Relations in the Cold
     War and After* (Basingstoke, 2001), p. 121.

8   P. Riddell, *Hug Them Close: Blair, Clinton, Bush and the 'Special Relationship'*
     (2003), p.161.

9   Kampfner, *Blair's Wars*, p.137.

10   Ibid., p.121.

11   J. Naughtie, *The Accidental American: Tony Blair and the Presidency* (Basingstoke,
     2004), p. 210.

12   Woodward, *Plan of Attack*, p. 338.

13   See S. Fielding, '"But Westward, Look, The Land is Bright": Labour's
     Revisionists and the Imagining of America, c. 1945–64', in J. Hollowell (ed.)
     Twentieth-Century Anglo-American Relations (Basingstoke, 2001), pp. 87–103.

14   B. Brivati, *Hugh Gaitskell* (1996), p. 99. My emphasis.

15   D. Halberstam, *War in a Time of Peace: Bush, Clinton and the Generals* (2003), p. 461.

16   Riddell recalls an interview with Blair shortly before the 1997 general election
     in which he 'suggested that Clinton had not achieved much during more than
     four years in office, Blair snapped back: "Well, he got re-elected, didn't he?"'
     Riddell, *Hug Them Close*, p. 69.

17 Cited in Dumbrell, *A Special Relationship*, p. 120.

18 Speech by the Prime Minister Tony Blair at the Lord Mayor's Banquet, 10 November 1997. http://www.number-10.gov.uk/output/Page1070.asp He also offered his view that: 'We cannot in these post-Empire days be a super-power in a military sense. But we can make the British presence in the world felt. With our historic alliances, we can be pivotal. We can be powerful in our influence – a nation to whom others listen. Why? Because we run Britain well and are successful ourselves. Because we have the right strategic alliances the world over. And because we are engaged, open and intelligent in how we use them.'

19 An early example of this occurred when, as Opposition leader, Blair mandated Shadow Cabinet support of the September 1996 Anglo-US air strikes against Iraq. Kampfner, *Blair's Wars*, pp. 20–1.

20 M. Kite, 'Tony Blair "Relished" Sending British Soldiers Off to War', *Daily Telegraph*, 18 September 2005. http://www.telegraph.co.uk/news/main.jhtml?xml=/news/2005/09/18/nblur18.xml In the published version, this entry was altered to: 'I couldn't help feeling TB had mixed emotions about sending the boys into action.' L. Price, *The Spin Doctor's Diary: Inside Number 10 with New Labour* (2005), p. 62.

21 Kampfner, *Blair's Wars*, p. 33.

22 Halberstam, *War in a Time of Peace*, p. 462.

23 Cited in Naughtie, *The Accidental American*, p. 150.

24 Quoted in Riddell, *Hug Them Close*, p. 8.

25 Speech by Tony Blair, Prime Minister United Kingdom at the George Bush Presidential Library and Museum, College Station, Texas, 7 April 2002. http://www.number-10.gov.uk/output/Page1712.asp

26 Cited in D. Runciman, 'The Politics of Good Intentions', *London Review of Books*, 8 May 2003, p. 8.

27 Foreign Affairs Committee, *Kosovo* (Fouth Report, Session 1999–2000, HC-I), paras. 145–8.

28 Woodward, *Plan of Attack*, p. 379.

29 According to Shaath, Bush confided in him: 'I am driven with a mission from God. God would tell me, "George go and fight these terrorists in Afghanistan". And I did. And then God would tell me "George, go and end the tyranny in Iraq." And I did.' E. MacAskill, 'George Bush: "God Told Me to End the Tyranny in Iraq"', *The Guardian*, 7 October 2005.

30 C. Brown, 'Campbell Interrupted Blair as he Spoke of his Faith: "We Don't Do God"', *Daily Telegraph*, 4 May 2003.

31 M. White, 'God Will Judge Me, PM Tells Parkinson', *The Guardian*, 4 March 2006.

32 Kampfner, *Blair's Wars*, p. 60.

33 A number of biographers and commentators have highlighted this absence of ideology or even detailed political knowledge. For example, Riddell talks of Blair as being, 'more of an instinctive than an intellectual politician', who 'prefers the big picture. He is not a pointillist. He does not have a vast storehouse of political or policy knowledge.' Riddell, *Hug Them Close*, pp. 4–5. See also A. Seldon, *Blair* (2005), pp. 147–8. For his part, John Kampfner titled the first chapter of *Blair's Wars*, 'Travelling Light'.

34 P. Wintour, 'What the Memo Tells us About Tony Blair's Style of Leadership', *The Guardian*, 18 July 2000.

35   Ibid.
36   A. Giddens, *The Third Way: Renewal of Social Democracy* (Cambridge, 1998). See also A. Callinicos, *Against the Third Way* (Cambridge, 2001).
37   M. Phythian, *The Politics of British Arms Sales Since 1964* (Manchester, 2000), pp. 287–307. See also J. Kampfner, *Robin Cook* (1998), esp. ch. 11.
38   As one of Blair's biographers describes the background: 'Blair decided he would use the peg of a major speech on 22 April . . . to articulate thoughts that had been forming in his mind over the previous year on the justifications for military action. He had never in his life before seriously addressed himself to the philosophy of foreign and defence policy, in contrast to his frequent musings on domestic policy, and his thoughts were inchoate.' Seldon, *Blair*, p. 398. Indicative of his presidential style, the Foreign Office knew nothing about this major statement of British foreign policy. Kampfner, *Blair's Wars*, p. 53.
39   'Doctrine of the International Community', Remarks by British PM Tony Blair, Economic Club of Chicago, 22 April 1999. http://www.number-10.gov.uk/output/Page1297.asp
40   Ibid.
41   Ibid.
42   Giddens, *The Third Way*, p. 70.
43   http://www.number-10.gov.uk/output/Page1712.asp
44   In his Chicago speech, Blair explained that: 'At the end of this century the US has emerged as by far the strongest state. It has no dreams of world conquest and is not seeking colonies . . . America's allies are always both relieved and gratified by its continuing readiness to shoulder burdens and responsibilities that come with its sole superpower status.' http://www.number-10.gov.uk/output/Page1297.asp
45   http://www.number-10.gov.uk/output/Page1712.asp
46   Ibid.
47   Article 27 of the Charter stated that Security Council decisions on all but procedural matters required the agreement of all permanent members. When the vote on action in relation to Korea was taken on 27 June 1950, the Soviet representative had been absent, hence the resolution was passed, but without the agreement of one permanent member. Article 51 of the Charter allowed for individual or collective self-defence against aggression committed against members, but South Korea was not a member of the UN at this time. See, Conclusions of the Cabinet meeting held on 4 July 1950, in Yasamee & Hamilton (eds.), *Documents on British Policy Overseas, Series II: Volume IV, Korea June 1950 – April 1951* (1991), pp. 27–8.
48   Ibid., p. 28.
49   O. Franks, *Britain and the Tide of World Affairs* (Oxford, 1955), p. 12.
50   B. Burrough, E. Peretz, D. Rose and D. Wise, 'The Path to War', *Vanity Fair*, May 2004, p. 110
51   R. Cook, *The Point of Departure* (2003), p. 116.
52   Ibid., pp. 115–16.
53   C. Short, 'There Was Never an Honest Debate in Cabinet', *The Independent*, 19 July 2004. See also Short, *An Honourable Deception?* pp. 150–1. On Cabinet government during this period, the 2004 Butler report concluded: 'Without papers circulated in advance, it remains possible but is obviously much more difficult for members of the Cabinet outside the small circle directly involved to

bring their political judgement and experience to bear on the major decisions for which the Cabinet as a whole must carry responsibility. The absence of papers on the Cabinet agenda so that ministers could obtain briefings in advance from the Cabinet Office, their own departments or from the intelligence agencies, plainly reduced their ability to prepare properly for such discussions, while the changes to key posts at the head of the Cabinet Secretariat lessened the support of the machinery of government for the collective responsibility of Cabinet in the vital matter of war and peace.' Butler Report, pp. 147–8.

54 The minutes of meetings and memoranda quoted here and below are contained in documents leaked to journalist Michael Smith and originally published in September 2004 and May 2005. They are available on the internet in full at http://www.downingstreetmemo.com/memos.html

55 Ibid.

56 Ibid.

57 Ibid.

58 Ibid.

59 See, for example, Kampfner, *Blair's Wars*, p. 168: 'Crawford was a turning point for Blair. That weekend he and [foreign policy advisor David] Manning concluded that nothing would stand in the way of Bush and his mission. The question was not *if* there would be war, but on what terms it would be fought. They told the President that . . . Britain would support him come what may.'

60 http://www.downingstreetmemo.com/memos.html

61 Ibid.

62 Woodward, *Plan of Attack*, p. 178.

63 Burrough et al, 'The Path to War', p. 172.

64 See A. Doig and M. Phythian, 'The National Interest and Politics of Threat Exaggeration: The Blair Government's Case for War Against Iraq', *The Political Quarterly*, 76, 3 (July–September 2005), pp. 368–76

65 See M. Phythian, 'Hutton and Scott: A Tale of Two Inquiries', *Parliamentary Affairs*, 58, 1 (January 2005), pp. 124–37.

66 Cook, *The Point of Departure*, p. 203.

67 According to Straw: 'He's got these weapons of mass destruction, chemical, biological and, probably, nuclear weapons which he has used in the past against his own people as well as his neighbours and could almost certainly use again in the future.' See E. MacAskill and N. Watt, 'Anger Over Straw's Dossier on Iraqi Human Rights', *The Guardian*, 3 December 2002.

68 Cook, *The Point of Departure*, pp. 309–10.

69 Butler Report, p. 105, para. 427.

70 R. Cook, 'The Die Was Cast: The Dossiers Were Irrelevant', *The Independent on Sunday*, 18 July 2004.

71 http://a4.g.akamai.net/7/4/15010/1/labourparty1.download.akamai.com/15010/manifesto_13042005_a3/flash/manifesto_2005.swf

72 J. Freedland, 'War: The Great Unknown Among Election Issues'; A. Gillan, S. Morris and H. Carter, 'Why Rake Up the War?', *The Guardian*, 18 April 2005.

73 For some commentators, thereby eliminating the only policy that distinguished Blairism from Thatcherism. See J. Gray, 'Blair's Project in Retrospect', *International Affairs*, 80, 1 (January 2004), pp. 39–48.

74 http://www.iraqbodycount.net/database/ Some estimates were far higher, most

notably that published in the medical journal *The Lancet* in October 2004 which estimated the death toll at approximately 100,000. L. Roberts, R. Lafta, R. Garfield, J. Khudhairi and G. Burnham, 'Mortality Before and After the 2003 Invasion of Iraq: Cluster Sample Survey', *The Lancet*, 364, 9448 (2004), pp. 1857–64.

75   Quoted in Riddell, *Hug Them Close*, p. 145.

INDEX